ST. MICHAEL'S R.C. SCHOOL

Presented to

JOSEPH   CHRISTOFI

FOR ATTAINMNET

DECEMBER 1980

P.A.NEWSAM
Education Officer
Inner London Education Authority

Published 1980 by
The Hamlyn Publishing Group Limited
London · New York · Sydney · Toronto
Astronaut House, Feltham, England
© Text copyright 1973 Arnoldo Mondadori Editore, Milano
© Text this edition copyright 1974, 1980 The Hamlyn Publishing Group Limited
© Illustrations copyright 1974, 1980 The Hamlyn Publishing Group Limited.

ISBN 0 600 34621 8

Printed in Czechoslovakia

The material in this book appeared originally in the following
titles: The Hamlyn Book of How, The Hamlyn Book of Why,
The Hamlyn Book of When, and The Hamlyn Book of Where.

This edition produced exclusively for W. H. Smith Ltd.
by The Hamlyn Publishing Group Limited
London · New York · Sydney · Toronto
51156

TELL ME THE ANSWER

THE

ANSWER

Written by Andrea Bonanni, Pinuccia Bracco,
Glauco Pretto and Giuseppe Zanini.
Adapted by Christine Casley

This edition produced exclusively for
 WHSMITH
by The Hamlyn Publishing Group Limited
London . New York . Sydney . Toronto

INTRODUCTION

This book has been designed to answer some of the many *How?* *When?* *Why?* and *Where?* questions frequently raised by children. A wide variety of interesting and unusual facts have been carefully selected to cover many different areas of knowledge, ranging from geography and natural history to science and the arts.

The layout of the text, simple vocabulary and colourful illustrations make the book both easy and enjoyable to read. Every child will find some new item of information which will make him, or her, want to read on and discover more about the subject.

In planning the book, the intention was not to compile a complete encyclopedia, but to present, in an easy to follow form, the answers to some questions, whilst encouraging the reader to ask more questions, opening up wider horizons and leading to further study of specific subjects.

CONTENTS

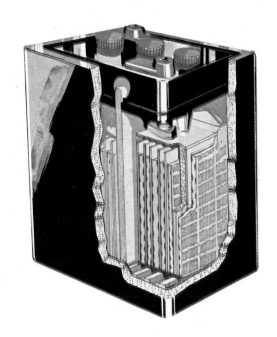

THE HOW OF PLANTS

Dionaea muscipula

Pinguicola

Nephentes alba marginata

Sarracenia

Byblis gigantea

How Linnaeus classified plants

As botanists gradually came to know more and more new plants after each great voyage of discovery, the need grew for a system in which all these plants could be put neatly into various groups. When we think of how many plants there are and how different they are from one another, we can see just how difficult it must have been to devise a way of classifying them.

The first scientist to carry out this great task was Carolus Linnaeus (1707–78), a Swedish naturalist. Linnaeus grouped plants according to their flowers and the number and type of stamens and pistils on these flowers.

Today, Linnaeus's classification has been replaced by newer and more accurate systems, but the achievement of Linnaeus remains great because he gave each plant two Latin names. The first name indicated the genus, or family, of the plant, and the second name gave the species, or particular member, of the family.

Linnaeus's system of naming plants is still used throughout the world today and at the major international botany congresses that are held every four years.

How the *Drosera* catches insects

Droseros is the Greek word for 'dewy' and the first thing that one notices about the *Drosera*, or sundew plant, is the sticky stem covered in soft, downy hair and scattered with glistening little bubbles that look like dewdrops. When insects see these 'dew-drops' they land on the plant for a drink. As soon as they touch the stem, the insects become stuck and the plant's downy hair curls round them like tentacles. The *Drosera* produces a liquid which breaks down the captured insects into food which the plant then absorbs.

The *Drosera* is, therefore, a carnivorous plant. It grows wild in damp places in Europe and North America and is about 20 centimetres high. One variety which occurs in Australia and South Africa reaches a height of one metre.

How the bladderwort catches its victims

Early in the summer pretty little bunches of golden-yellow flowers about a centimetre across appear floating on the water of ponds and ditches. This is the bladderwort, or *Utricularia*, a plant that keeps most of its body under water and looks very innocent. However underneath its leaves the *Utricularia* has lots of little bladders which turn into deadly traps should any unwary insect go too near them.

These bladders have a small opening surrounded by short hairs. When an insect explores the opening the plant swallows the insect and closes the opening with a special little lid. The plant then digests the captured animal through millions of microscopic tubes in its tissue.

This plant grows all over the world, on land as well as on the water, but the bulk of the species are found in tropical regions and only about four occur in Europe.

How pollen is made

All the higher forms of plant life reproduce themselves from seeds. These seeds are produced inside the flower of the plant after it has been fertilized. The stamens and the anthers are extremely important parts of the flower because they produce the pollen. Pollen is the very fine, yellow dust that comes away on the fingers whenever we touch the inside of a flower. These tiny yellow grains are one of the most precious substances in nature because they contain the secret of plant life.

It is pollen which fertilizes the ovary and sets off the process that finally produces the seeds. When pollen is examined under a microscope the minute specks of dust are enlarged and we can see the many different shapes of the individual grains which vary according to the plant of origin. Some pollen grains are oval, others are cylindrical and others are round. There are also pointed grains, some which are crescent-shaped and others with prickles on them.

The grains are smaller and flatter if the pollen comes from plants which are pollinated by the wind. This shape helps them to fly through the air. If the pollen is meant to be carried to other flowers by insects then the grains are larger and stickier.

How the *Nepenthe* of the tropical forests feeds itself

There are some seventy different varieties of *Nepenthe*, most of which grow in the tropical forests of Africa. These are rather strange plants which have clever traps

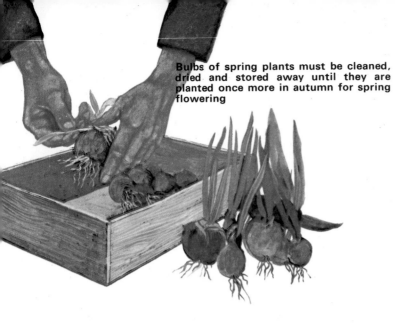

Bulbs of spring plants must be cleaned, dried and stored away until they are planted once more in autumn for spring flowering

How some plants can flower in the snow

One of the plants that flowers when the snow is still lying on the ground is the snowdrop.

The reason why this pretty little white flower can appear so early in the year, despite the cold weather, is the bulb from which it grows.

This bulb lies under the ground

to catch insects and other small creatures who are unwary enough to venture close to them.

The *Nepenthe* is a climbing plant which produces flowers in bunches. The plant's insect-traps are located at the tip of the leaves. These traps are an extension of the main vein of the leaf and look like stems with a small bladder on the end. This bladder is known as the ascidium and insects are attracted by its colour and its sugary contents. The insects go inside the ascidium but they cannot get out again because of hundreds of little stiff, downward-pointing hairs. Below these is a highly polished area, without hairs, which is like a greased slide. The more the insect struggles, the farther down it slips until it drowns in an evil-smelling liquid.

Galanthus nivelis or snowdrop

Winter aconite

Spring crocuses should be planted to produce patches of colour

and out of reach of the frost. It uses whatever warmth is left in the soil and when the air becomes warmer outside it sends out green leafy shoots.

The snowdrop is about 10 to 20 centimetres high. The petals that form the corolla have a small green spot at the end.

Snowdrops are common in meadows, along the banks of streams and in woods and forests.

How plants protect themselves from frost

Some plants are killed by the frost when winter arrives but the seeds they dropped on the ground in the autumn ensure that new plants grow to replace them in the spring.

Other plants spread out their leaves and flatten them against the ground in order to obtain whatever warmth is left in the soil. The violet is a plant that does this.

Myrtle and heather allow their upper plant to wither and die, but the lower part of the stem stays alive and produces buds when the growing season comes.

Many other plants escape from the cold weather by hiding under the soil. These plants are tubers, bulbs and roots which have stored up all the food they need. When the warm weather returns they are ready to push out green leaves and new buds.

Sometimes mechanical means are used to protect plants from frost. In regions where citrus fruits are grown oil heaters, called smudge pots, are placed in the groves and huge fans are also used to keep the air moving and prevent the cold air from settling on the fruit trees.

How conifers are protected from the frost

Not all trees shed their leaves in winter. Some have special defences which enable them to stand up to snow and ice. These trees are known as evergreens. One of the most common examples is the fir tree, better known as the Christmas tree.

Fir trees look extremely pretty when they are covered in snow, but the snow does not remain on them for long. The branches of the fir tree are made to bend under a weight and when the snow becomes too heavy the branch sags downwards and the snow slides off. This is how the fir tree protects itself against the weight of snow that falls in the mountains and which would otherwise crush the tree.

Conifers are so well protected from the rigours of winter that they can wear their beautiful green foliage when the weather is bitterly cold. The leaves of conifers are as thin as needles and covered in a special substance which protects them from the frost. This substance also prevents excessive evaporation of the moisture from the leaf which would cause the leaf to wither and drop off.

When the branch of a conifer is broken the wound is soon covered with a waterproof resin which heals the scar. This resin, which has an aromatic smell, is produced in large quantities by conifers.

Leaving aside food plants, conifers include some of our most useful plants. More than three-quarters of commercial timber is obtained from them and a large amount of coniferous wood is used as pulp in the manufacture of paper.

Gladiolus bulb

Iris root or rhizome

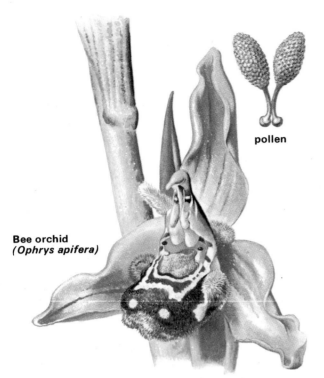

pollen

Bee orchid
(*Ophrys apifera*)

Sage
(*Salvia patens*)

How a flower is made

A flower consists, first of all, of a pedicle, or stem, that joins it to the plant. The stem broadens out into a hollow cup known as the receptacle. This is surrounded by green sepals which form the calyx. The flower's petals grow from the calyx in all kinds of shapes and colours.

At the centre of the flower there is a part that resembles a long-necked bottle. This is the pistil. The top of the pistil is called the stigma, the neck is called the style and the bottom, which is wider than the rest, is the ovary. Inside the ovary lie several tiny grains called ovules. Each one of these grains will become a seed. The ovary around the seeds will grow larger and turn into a fruit. The pistil is surrounded by several thread-like filaments, the stamens. At the top of each stamen there is a bag-like structure called the anther which contains the pollen.

How cross-pollination of plants takes place

Everything inside a flower is arranged to make pollination possible. This operation involves the transfer of pollen from the anthers of the stamens to the pistil.

It is very rare, however, that the pollen produced by one flower is used to fertilize the pistil in the same flower. Instead, flowers are designed to obtain pollen from other plants and their flowers. This enables better seeds and fruits to be produced and is known as cross-pollination. Its usefulness was demonstrated by the great naturalist, Charles Darwin, in 1859.

Cross-pollinating flowers occasionally have their pollen waiting on the stamens before the pistil is ready to take it; or the pistil may be ready but the stamens have produced no pollen. Some plants produce flowers with stamens only (male flowers) while others produce flowers with only pistils (female flowers). These plants are pollinated with the help of the wind which blows the pollen grains through the air.

Such plants produce huge amounts of pollen because much of it is lost in the air and only a small quantity finally reaches its proper destination.

How plants attract insects for pollination

Some plants entrust their pollen to the winds. Others use water as a carrier and still others simply pollinate themselves. However in most cases the vital task of pollination is carried out by insects.

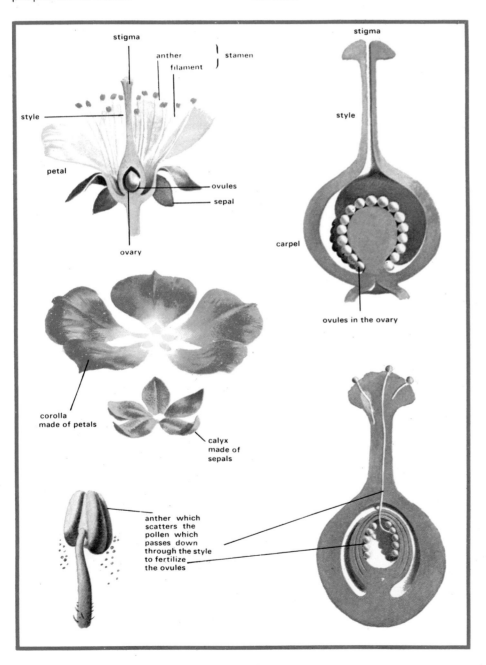

stigma

anther } stamen
filament

style

petal

ovules
sepal

ovary

stigma

style

carpel

ovules in the ovary

corolla
made of petals

calyx
made of
sepals

anther which
scatters the
pollen which
passes down
through the style
to fertilize
the ovules

To attract insects plants produce flowers that have beautiful scents and colours. The shape of the flower's corolla, the part with the petals, is designed to let pollinating insects in but to keep out other unwelcome creatures.

Sometimes the pollinating mechanism inside a flower is amazingly complex. An example is the sage flower: when a bee is attracted by the scent or the nectar, it stands on the lowest petal to enter the flower. As it does so, the bee presses on a kind of lever which makes the flower's stamens come down and touch the hairy back of the bee, covering

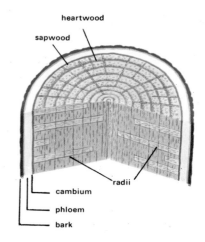

Diagram of a tree trunk showing the xylomatic, or woody, mass and the annual rings

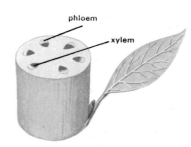

Cross-section of a stem showing the vessel structure at the rim

it with pollen. The bee then enters another flower and the whole operation is repeated.

The sage is one of those plants that lets its stamens ripen before its pistil. So when the bee lands on a flower where the stamens and the anthers have withered away, there is a pistil waiting to pick up the pollen from the bee's back to fertilize itself.

Cross-section of a root showing the central vascular tissue which supports the plant

How plants absorb water

Every plant has to feed itself in order to carry out its vital functions. Usually the raw materials are extracted from the surrounding soil through the roots. In this way the roots supply the leaves of the plant, which are really small chemistry laboratories, with water and the necessary minerals to produce organic substances.

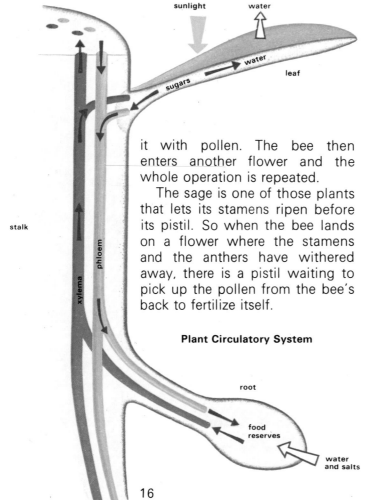

Plant Circulatory System

There are two basic types of roots: the taproot which consists of a single large axis from which fine hairs grow, such as the radish or the turnip, and the fasciculated root which is composed of several axes each of the same size, as in the dahlia.

In each type of root there is a root-cap at the end of each root. This cap protects the growing part of the root organism and helps it to dig into the soil. When viewed through a powerful magnifying glass these caps are seen to be covered in very fine hairs. It is through these hairs that the roots suck in water and certain mineral salts from the soil.

How the inside and outside of leaves are built

Leaves are usually made up of two parts. One of these parts is long and slender and called the stem or petiole. The stem joins the leaf to the main stalk of the plant. The other part of the leaf is flat and open and known as the blade or lamina. The blade is covered in veinings which represent the skeleton of the leaf. These veins link all the tiny 'laboratories' with other parts of the parent plant. If we hold a leaf up to the light we can see that underneath the main veining there is another denser and much smaller set of veining. These tiny veins contain the channels through which the water drawn in from the roots is distributed throughout the leaf.

The surface of the leaf is covered with many microscopic pores called stomata. The stomata absorb carbon dioxide from the air which is then used to build up carbohydrates, and allow water to evaporate.

How plants produce organic substances

By using water, air and some mineral substances obtained from the soil, plants produce sugar and starch which are the basis of all organic matter. This transformation is made possible by chlorophyll which takes the energy of

How plants feed

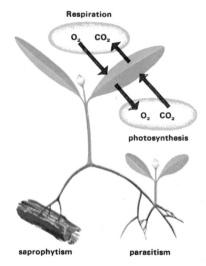

Respiration

O_2 CO_2

O_2 CO_2

photosynthesis

saprophytism   parasitism

Diagram showing the photosynthesis of chlorophyll

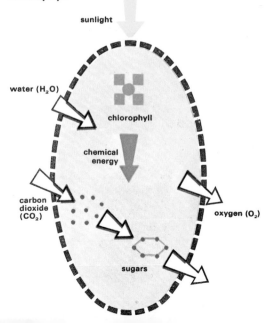

sunlight

water (H_2O)

chlorophyll

chemical energy

carbon dioxide (CO_2)

oxygen (O_2)

sugars

sunlight. Chlorophyll then uses this energy to separate the atoms of oxygen, hydrogen and carbon which make up air and water and re-joins them in a different way to produce organic matter.

This process of photosynthesis is an extremely delicate and complicated operation. So far scientists have been unable to carry out the process artificially.

How plants defend themselves from drought

Plants that grow in dry regions are known as xerophilous, a word which means they love dry places. The roots of these plants spread out horizontally close to the surface of the soil. In this way the roots can soak up whatever rain falls before the heat of the Sun evaporates all the moisture. Sometimes the roots of xerophilous plants go down deep into the soil to reach damper places or even a supply of water.

The stalks of xerophilous plants have no leaves and they are covered with a waxy material which prevents moisture from evaporating from the plant. These plants are also covered in sharp thorns or spines to stop animals from eating them.

In dry, desert areas these plants, and especially the cacti, are a precious source of water as well as food for living creatures. If they had no thorns to defend them they would all be eaten up by hungry and thirsty animals.

Many of these plants produce beautiful flowers and fruit after rain. The fruit can be eaten both by people and animals.

How the poison of stramonium acts

Stramonium, or the Jimson Weed is also known as 'the Devil's grass'. The plant got this name because its poison seems to drive the victim mad as if he were possessed by the devil.

The alkaloids in the plant can also cause serious distortion of the eyesight. In small doses, however, these poisons can be used to treat certain illnesses.

Stramonium found in certain drugs is extracted from the leaves

Philocactus

Lobivia

Neoporteria aspillaga

Opuntia microdasys

18

of this plant. It acts as a sedative and eases nerve and rheumatic pains. Stramonium leaves are also used to make special cigarettes for the treatment of asthma. The seeds of the plant provide an oil which is used in lotions to be rubbed on the body.

How the leaves of the prickly pear are made

The prickly pear grows wild in warm Mediterranean regions. It anchors itself to rocky, barren slopes and forms large areas of scrub that grow to about 3 metres high. On cultivated land the prickly pear is often cultivated as a hedge. It is enough to plant just one leaf for a whole bushy shrub to start growing.

'Leaf' is not really the correct word to describe the green, fleshy vegetation of this plant. The leaves are really parts of the plant's trunk which measure from 15 to 40 centimetres long and 15 centimetres wide.

The actual leaves of the prickly pear are very small and are shed almost as soon as they have appeared on the plant. They leave behind them thick tufts of thin needles. One of these needles grows outwards and becomes very sharp.

Since the prickly pear has no leaves the task of producing chlorophyll, without which no plant can live, is carried out by the trunk.

The prickly pear was introduced into Australia at the end of the eighteenth century as a food plant for cochineal insects. It spread and by 1870 had become a pest in Queensland and New South Wales. Its growth was controlled by the introduction of a little moth, the cactoblastis.

How truffles are found

The truffle is a strange fungus that grows from 5 to 10 centimetres below the ground. It can only be located by the peculiar smell it gives out and the best way to find it is to use a pig or a dog which has been trained in truffle hunting.

The dog or pig is taken to the place on a lead. As soon as it smells a truffle the animal is released and runs to the spot. The pig digs the truffle up with its nose; the dog uses its paws. The animals are rewarded with something to eat.

Some truffles are as big as a clenched fist but others are much smaller. There are two main types of truffle: the black and the white. The white truffle is much more sought after for its pungent and penetrating taste. It is a pale, dirty yellow in colour.

Astrophitum myriostigma

Trichocereus candicans

Mammillaria zeilmanniana

Hawarthia margarantifera

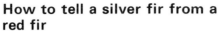

Cone of the
Picea abies

Cone of the
Abies alba

Picea abies

How to tell a silver fir from a red fir

The red fir or *Picea excelsa* is a native of northern Europe and also grows on the upper slopes of the Alps. The silver fir which has the botanical name *Abies alba*, grows on most mountain ranges of southern and central Europe at altitudes ranging from 800 to 1,500 metres.

The silver fir has a pale grey bark which is quite smooth when the tree is young, but it becomes roughened and darkened with age. The red fir has a rough, reddish-brown bark. The two trees have differently-formed cones: in the red fir they are pendulous and soft to the touch, but the silver fir's cones are hard and stick up vertically. Moreover, the needle-shaped leaves of the red fir grow in a spiral arrangement round the stem, whereas those of the silver fir are arranged in two files on the same level of the branch and the underparts are marked with two broad white lines. Many silver firs grow to more than 40 metres high.

How the rose of Jericho survives in the Sahara

The rose of Jericho, or resurrection plant, is a shrub consisting of several branches that lie on the ground to support the plant. These branches produce small leaves and flowers. When the burning desert Sun dries up all traces of moisture, the branches of the rose of Jericho roll up into a ball to protect the small fruit that contains the seeds.

When the rain returns the rose of Jericho unrolls its branches and scatters its seeds which are then ready to produce new plants.

How to tell the age of a tree

If we examine the trunk of a tree that has been chopped down, we will see first of all the outer ring of the bark which acts as a sort of waterproof coat for the tree. Inside the outer covering come a number of concentric rings.

Each one of these rings represents a year in the life of the tree. The space between the rings is the wood which the tree produced during one year.

By counting the number of rings we can tell when the tree was born. These rings also indicate the dry periods the tree lived through as well as wet periods. In dry times the rings are very thin. In heavy rainfall years the rings are thicker.

Slender cores of wood can be taken from a tree, from the bark to the centre of the trunk; these samples reveal the same information and are taken with a borer that does no significant damage to the tree.

How the pineapple grows

The pineapple plant produces large fruits and has a stalk that grows under the ground. This stalk pushes out a tuft of fleshy leaves which are up to a metre long and are prickly at the edges. From the centre of this crown of leaves there grows a stem which also has leaves growing on it. At the top of the stem there is a cluster-like flower of bluish blossoms.

When these flowers have bloomed the stem underneath them swells and produces the fruit which is sold fresh or in tins. Pineapple fruit can weigh up to 4 kilogrammes.

The top of the fruit has a tuft of leaves known as a crown. If the pineapple is placed in the ground in warm, moist conditions, this tuft of leaves will produce a new plant. This is one of the most common methods used to reproduce the fruit.

It was once fashionable to grow pineapples under glass in England, but this practice has now died out. Most pineapples are grown in Hawaii. They are gathered unripe and allowed to ripen on the journey to their destination.

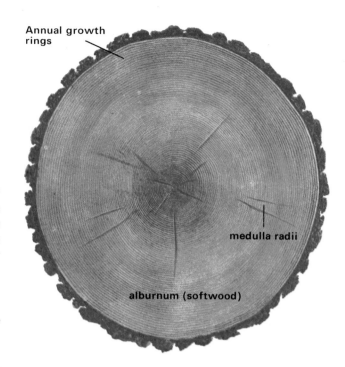

Annual growth rings

medulla radii

alburnum (softwood)

How to tell ebony from other woods

There are many trees that produce ebony. They belong to a family known as the Ebenaceae which grows in West Africa and in tropical Asia including the East Indies, Malaysia, India and Ceylon. In Asia forests with trees of the Ebenaceae family are found up to altitudes of more than 1,500 metres.

The ebony tree has broad leaves and is very large. Its wood is exported throughout the world because of its many uses, but the tree also provides fruit which is quite pleasant and eaten locally.

The most commonly used ebony wood is black. It is also very hard and durable. But there are red and banded varieties of ebony, too. African ebony is brown with even black veining.

Ebony is used in making good-quality furniture, carvings and arts and crafts. These include black piano keys, walking sticks, golf club heads and knife handles. As ebony is a very hard and fine-grained wood it can be smoothed and polished to a high degree.

It is this polish that distinguishes ebony from such imitations as pear-wood that has been dyed black.

Timber prepared as props at a coal mine

21

THE HOW OF ANIMALS

How remoras can follow sharks

The remora, or shark-sucker, has always excited the wonder and curiosity of seafarers. This fish has a flat, oval disc on top of its head which it uses to fasten itself firmly to flat surfaces. This habit has earned the remora a certain reputation in legends.

In olden days sailors thought the remora had tremendous strength and could slow down and even stop a ship by fastening on to its keel. But these are only legends. The remora is about 40 centimetres long and could never stop any craft no matter how small.

Remoras merely use their suckers to be carried along by large fish. They usually choose sharks and stay attached to their underside during hunting expeditions. The remora then eats whatever is left over. Sometimes remoras swim along on their own power and hunt for food.

In some parts of the tropics fishermen have used remoras with a line attached to their tails to catch larger fish.

Remoras belong to the family Echeneidae. There are about seven species found in all tropical and temperate seas.

How animals are classified

In zoos the popular names of the animals on display are written on a label in front of their cages. The label also carries the animal's scientific name in Latin. For example, on a lion's cage, the Latin name is *Panthera leo*; on a tiger's cage the name is *Panthera tigris*; and on the cage of a leopard the name is *Panthera pardus*.

Latin is the language accepted by scientists and zoologists throughout the world to avoid confusion. The Latin name for any animal consists of two words because the scientific classification of animals still follows the basic principle laid down by the botanist Carolus Linnaeus. In the examples we have already quoted the first part of the names is the word *Panthera*: this refers to the genus of the animal. The second part of the name refers to the species. Members of an animal species that have many features in common come together in a genus. The *Panthera* genus, for example, includes the large cats which are unable to purr. Smaller cats, which can purr but do not roar, belong to the genus *Felis*. Both genera are in the family Felidae.

A number of genera form a family and several families form an order. The orders come together under classes and the classes fall into types. The total of all these forms the animal kingdom.

A remora attached to a shark

The ocean sunfish belongs to the family Molidae and can often be seen sunning itself or resting in the surface waters of temperate or tropical seas. Like the remora it belongs to the class of Teleostei.

Ocean sunfish

How the ocean sunfish is made

The ocean sunfish was known in ancient times but the first fishermen who caught these animals thought they were mutilated. This is because the sunfish has a very large head and appears to have no body.

On closer examination it can be seen that the sunfish does, in fact, have a body even though the tail has practically disappeared and the tail and anal fins have grown together into one unit.

The sunfish is a large animal and can measure more than 3 metres in length. It is flat and round in shape and can weigh as much as 2 tons.

Despite its large size it is not an animal of prey, feeding on small fishes and boneless creatures. It has a small mouth and does not swim very well, preferring to drift along in a current.

Classification of a dromedary

Kingdom	Animal
Phylum	Chordata
Class	Mammal
Order	Artiodactyla
Family	Camelidae
Genus	Camelus
Species	Dromedarius

How the condor became a symbol of freedom

There is an old tradition among the Indians of Lake Titicaca that dates back to the Spanish conquest of South America. It concerns the fight between a condor and a bull. The condor was the emblem of the Indians while the bull represented the Spanish conquerors. According to the story the condor was put into a sack with only its neck and head left free and the sack was then tied to the back of the bull. The condor began to peck savagely at the bull's head so that the bull lept about madly to get rid of its attacker.

The battle ended in victory for the condor to the applause of the Indians who saw in this duel a way of showing their dislike of their conquerors.

Condor of the Andes

How to tell seals from sea-lions

Many varieties of seals live beyond the Arctic Circle. All these animals have short necks and no external ears. It is this latter feature that distinguishes true seals from sea-lions which have prominent ears.

Seals range in size from the little fresh-water seal of Siberia, about one metre long, to the enormous sea elephant of the subantarctic regions, which can grow to 6 metres in length.

The most common type of seal, however, grows to a length of just over 2 metres. Its fur is brown or yellowish with dark patches. The seal's hind legs are part of its tail and cannot be used for walking. For this reason it moves by lunging its body along in a clumsy manner when on land.

On the ice the animal is not so awkward and it slides along for considerable distances. But the seal's true element is the sea for this animal is an extremely skilful swimmer and dives at the slightest sign of danger.

How turtles swim

It seems impossible that tortoises that move in such a slow, cumbersome manner should have relatives that swim fast through the ocean. Turtles, which very closely resemble tortoises, are sometimes as quick as fish in moving through the water, despite their heavy shell.

These turtles can weigh up to 250 kilogrammes but they have adapted wonderfully to aquatic life. Through living in the sea for millions of years, their bodies have become streamlined and their paws have turned into flippers.

**Sea turtle
(Chelonia mydas)**

It does this by leaping out of the water, bending itself almost double to do so. Many salmon die of sheer exhaustion while others are caught and devoured by such animals as bears.

When the fish has finally reached the fresh, clear waters of its destination, the female digs a pit in the stream gravel into which she lays her eggs. The male immediately fertilizes them and the female covers them with

Turtles come ashore only to lay their eggs. They drag themselves on to deserted beaches where they dig holes for their eggs.

Their home is the sea and that is where they find their food. Turtles eat meat or plants according to their species. The meat of the turtle itself is regarded as a delicacy, especially the green turtle of the Atlantic and Pacific Oceans.

The scientific name of turtles is Chelonia and they belong to the reptile class.

Pacific salmon

How the salmon passes waterfalls

The salmon lives near the coastline in the Atlantic and Pacific Oceans in the northern hemisphere. In the month of June it leaves the ocean and swims up the river to the place where it was born. The salmon looks for fresh water with plenty of oxygen in it. Nobody knows what makes the fish undergo such tremendous difficulties to complete its journey, but the salmon goes on and many of them die before their journey's end.

In its journey upstream the salmon has to get past waterfalls.

gravel. The Pacific salmon dies soon after spawning, but many Atlantic salmon return to the sea and may spawn again. Most spawning takes place in the late summer; the young are born about two or three months later and swim to the sea after about two years.

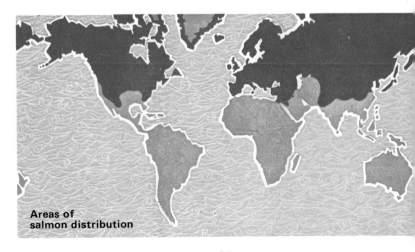

**Areas of
salmon distribution**

25

How the earthworm digs its tunnels

Earthworms cannot stand dry conditions in the soil: their bodies must always be in contact with damp earth and even a few minutes' exposure to the sunlight makes them dry up and die.

Earthworms spend most of their lives digging tunnels in the soil. It is quite surprising how they can burrow their way into even hard ground simply by using the strength of their muscles, for earthworms do not have any special physical equipment for digging.

They contract and expand in a rhythmic manner to force an aperture in the ground and then they push on with their head.

The earthworm swallows some of the soil he moves through. From it, the animal extracts food in the form of vegetable waste. The earthworm then expels the 'digested' soil and leaves it as a worm-cast. It has been estimated that the yearly deposition above ground of soil by earthworms is between 7 and 16 tons per acre in England.

Earthworms can grow up to 15 centimetres or more in length. In tropical countries some earthworms are as long as 2 metres.

How the buffalo defends itself from insect bites and stings

The buffalo likes to make its home in marshy places where it loves to roll in the mud and stay there for hours at a time. It does this for a very good reason: the mud dries into a hard crust all over the buffalo's skin and acts as a shield against the sting of insects and the burning rays of the Sun. This muddy protection allows the buffalo to live in the unhealthy atmosphere of marshes and swamps where no other type of cattle could survive.

The buffalo needs complete freedom. It could never work as a draft animal or live in a barn like domestic cattle.

Male and female Banteng (Bos banteng)

How beehives are organized

A large beehive can contain up to 80,000 bees but there is never any danger that such a vast number of insects will lead to confusion or chaos.

There is only one queen in a hive and her sole task is to keep on laying eggs. There are several hundred male bees, known as drones, who do no work except fertilize the eggs. But as soon as a new queen is born these drones are massacred by the worker bees who are all females, though incapable of laying eggs.

The worker bees form the overwhelming majority of the population of a beehive and collect all the nectar and pollen.

Bees suck the nectar from the flower through a special nose-tube and then carry it in a sack which contains up to 50 milligrams. The pollen is carried in two little baskets on the bee's hind legs. The worker bee delivers these ingredients and other worker bees in the hive mix them together into a sort of paste which is fed to the larvae so that they will develop into adult insects.

How the gardener-bird builds its nest

Little is known about the peculiar habits of the gardener-bird which has a marked liking for colourful objects and for what seems to be gardening. This bird lives in forest clearings in New Guinea. It builds an elaborate nest shaped like a little hut and surrounds it with a

Gaur *(Bos gauria)*

Water-buffalo *(Bubalus bubalis)*

Crestless gardener bird

sort of garden which it decorates with flowers, shells and various colourful objects. These objects are not just thrown together haphazardly: the gardener-bird very carefully arranges everything and tries it out in different patterns before deciding how the garden will look.

Some species of this bird can decorate the interior of their nests by painting them with colours which they make with their own saliva and various materials. Sometimes these birds even use 'brushes' made of small bunches of leaves.

How the ancestor of the horse developed

The illustrations on this page show the various stages in the evolution of the horse. The earliest ancestor of today's animal was *Eohippus* which lived about 50 million years ago. It stood only about 25 centimetres high and lived in the American prairies migrating from there to Asia and Europe where it bred rapidly. The *Orohippus* and *Mesohippus* appeared some 20 million years later and were bigger animals. But the first of these animals to look like today's horses was the *Parahippus*. The *Pliohippus*, which first appeared on Earth about 10 million years ago, bore an even closer resemblance to the horses of today.

How penguins hatch their eggs

During the mating season penguins gather together by the tens of thousands along the coasts of Antarctica. The female penguins lay one or two eggs which they place in a hollow in the ground. They take turns with the male penguin to sit on the eggs, clutching them tightly between their legs and their downy stomachs.

With the eggs covered like this, the penguins can still move from place to place although they look extremely odd when they do so.

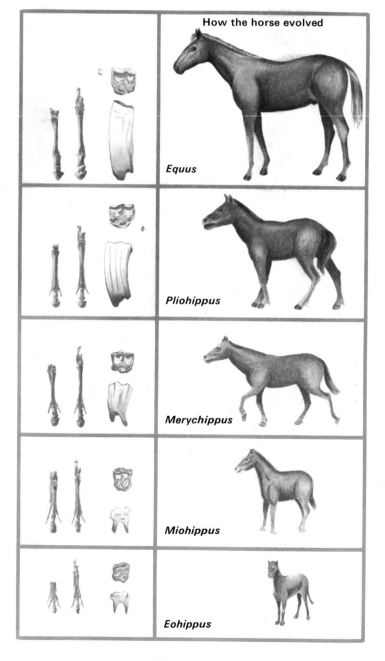

How the horse evolved

Equus

Pliohippus

Merychippus

Miohippus

Eohippus

When the female is sitting on the eggs, the male bird feeds her. He continues to do so for a time after the young birds are hatched.

There are seventeen species of penguins. They vary in height from 40 centimetres to more than a metre. They all live in the southern hemisphere and go on long migratory swims to escape severely cold weather.

How the praying mantis tricks its victims

The mantis can often be mistaken for a grasshopper but more careful observation will reveal that this creature is very different from that harmless insect.

The mantis has a soft, green colour which makes it difficult to see in the undergrowth. To trick its victims the mantis stands up straight and perfectly still, looking like a blade of grass. It holds its front legs with their powerful claws up in front of itself as if it were saying its prayers. This stance has won it the name of praying mantis although one of its American names, Devil's horse, might be more appropriate, for this is a ferocious insect. If any small creature comes too close, the mantis's front limbs suddenly spring forward and seize the victim which is dead within seconds.

How animals further the advance of science

To establish how effective a drug is it must be tested carefully and accurately and its effect on a living organism meticulously studied and noted. This is the task of pharmacology, a science which has made tremendous advances in less than a century.

The work of pharmacologists is often related to biochemistry, since they study the effects of

Praying mantis

Colony of Adélie penguins

29

foreign substances on cells or chemical systems of the body; and to psychiatry, for they also study the effects of drugs on the brain and behaviour.

The most significant stage in the discovery of a new drug is when the active substance that has curative properties is isolated. These substances are then checked for the effect they have on living tissues. This could be dangerous on a human being and even the curative properties of any drug can prove fatal if they are administered in wrong doses.

To overcome these difficulties scientists carry out their experiments on animals such as dogs, cats, mice, guinea pigs, rabbits and monkeys. Many such animals are sacrificed daily in the laboratories of the world, although most countries have strict laws which forbid the infliction of unnecessary pain on them.

One of the most common experiments is to infect these animals with germs to develop diseases. Sometimes various organs are removed from these laboratory animals for detailed study of their functions.

How plankton is formed in the sea

The surface of the seas and oceans is inhabited by hundreds of millions of tiny animals that are almost invisible to the naked eye. These little creatures float about in the ocean currents; their bodies are transparent and most of them can be seen properly only through a microscope. They are known as plankton and they provide many fish and other sea-animals with food.

The movement of plankton in the seas and oceans is very important because these small animals are always followed by shoals of fish. When herrings migrate by the million, they do so to follow the plankton which is about the only food the herring eats. The amount and distribution of plankton can effect the success or failure of a fishery.

Plankton can be gathered from the sea with special fine-mesh nets which were formerly made of silk but today are produced mainly of man-made fibres. On closer examination it is seen to be composed of animals and plants. The plankton comes under two main groups: macro plankton is large enough for the individual pieces to be seen with the naked eye; microplankton is microscopic. Some scientists also include a third category known as meso-plankton which comes somewhere between the two other groups in terms of size.

Microplankton contains many tiny algae. These are plants which reproduce themselves by simply splitting up. Macroplankton consists mainly of a vast range of tiny crustaceans which form the only food of whales. Microplankton also includes the larvae, or young, of crabs, crayfish, molluscs, starfish or the roe or eggs of large fish such as the tuna.

The algae also carry out the important task of putting oxygen into the sea water in the same way as plants do on dry land.

Plankton grows and multiplies at a tumultuous rate. It provides an abundant source of food for both fish that swim near the surface and those that live in the depths. This is because the plankton drifts down into the oceans when the animals of which it is composed die.

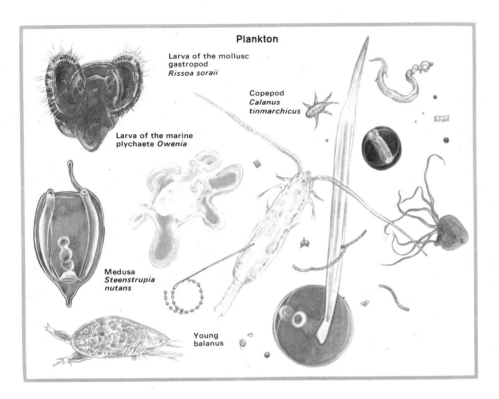

Plankton

Larva of the mollusc gastropod *Rissoa soraii*

Copepod *Calanus tinmarchicus*

Larva of the marine plychaete *Owenia*

Medusa *Steenstrupia nutans*

Young balanus

How the ant-eater feeds

The body of the ant-eater is covered in long hair that prevents ants from reaching its skin. For this reason it has no cause to fear insect bites when it tears the homes of ants apart with its strong claws.

The ant-eater makes its meal by shooting out its long, sticky, worm-like tongue and scooping up the ants that swarm all over the ground after their home has been destroyed. It has highly developed salivary glands which secrete the sticky substance that coats its tongue and traps the insects.

Giant ant-eater

How the squirrel flies

The American flying squirrel is one of the most unusual and beautiful of these animals. It is a nocturnal creature with large eyes, and feeds mainly on berries, seeds, nuts and insects. It does not have the thick, bushy tail of European squirrels, but it has a special fold of skin down both sides of its body.

When the flying squirrel leaps from tree to tree this fold of skin spreads out between its front and rear legs to form a sort of parachute which enables the animal to glide over quite long distances, sometimes covering more than 65 metres in a glide. The squirrel's flat tail acts as a sort of rudder.

There are also other varieties of flying squirrel in Africa and tropical parts of Asia. The best-known of these include the flying phalanger and the African scaly-tailed squirrel. The Australian possums are members of the same family.

How bees produce wax and honey

The wax produced by bees is used in making honeycombs consisting of six-sided cells into each of which the queen bee lays an egg that will eventually give birth to an insect. Other cells in the honeycomb act as storage places for honey.

Bees produce wax in very thin sheets from eight glands on their abdomens. It takes some 1,250 of these sheets to make up one gramme of wax. We can imagine the amount of hard work that goes into the construction of a honeycomb. Not only does the bee produce the wax, but it also shapes it into the hexagonal cell.

The honey is nectar from flowers which has been gathered, concentrated and digested by the bees. The honey still has the scent of the flowers where the bees first found it.

How the queen bee lives in her hive

The queen bee is an extremely fertile animal. This insect is no more than 2 centimetres long but lays an average of 2,500 eggs a day at the rate of two eggs every minute. It does this throughout its entire life, accumulating a total of 2 million eggs.

Each egg is placed inside a hexagonal cell. If the larvae, as the infant bees are called, are fed on a substance known as royal jelly, they too, become queens. If they are just fed on pollen they grow into ordinary bees. But a beehive can contain only one queen. So the first queen bee to emerge from the cells kills all her potential rivals still in their cells and drives the old queen out. The old queen leaves with a swarm of bees still loyal to her to start another hive elsewhere.

Once the new queen begins her reign she carries out what is called her nuptial flight. As she flies through the air she is accompanied by male bees known as drones. The queen bee flies higher and higher and only the strongest of the drones can catch her and mate with her. The queen bee returns from her nuptial flight fertilized and sets to laying eggs assisted by a group of bees who feed her and look after all her needs.

How the prehistoric winged lizards flew

Perhaps we shall never know why reptiles should suddenly try to fly at a certain time in the history of the Earth. One thing is certain: in the rock layers formed about 130 million years ago, scientists have found the remains of many winged reptiles lying next to the bones of

Bees:
a) worker,
b) drone,
c) queen,
d) cell of the queen

dinosaurs. The first to leave fossilized remains behind were the pterosaurs. The front limbs of these reptiles ended in a sort of hand with a highly developed fourth finger. Along the sides of their bodies they had a fold of skin, rather like the membrane of a bat's wing, which was joined on to the front legs at the fourth finger to form a primitive wing.

These reptiles avoided moving about on the ground because the rough terrain could seriously damage their rather delicate wings. They spent most of their time gliding in the skies, and rested perched on rocks or trees so that they could launch themselves into flight again. If they fell on flat ground they had great difficulty in getting back into the air, for if they beat their wings too much they risked damaging them. So these winged reptiles would scramble up to some higher position on rocks, using their front limbs to climb with.

One of the earliest of the winged reptiles was the *Dimorphodon*. It looked like a monster bat and it was a large creature: its skull alone was about 22 centimetres long. Its mouth was lined with teeth that were large at the front and smaller at the back of the beak. The beak itself had a large pouch at the throat, rather like a pelican, and in this the reptile stored insects which it gathered during its flights. The *Dimorphodon* had powerful rear limbs which indicate it was a bird of prey.

How the female hornbill is imprisoned while she hatches the eggs

Like the toucan, the hornbill has an extremely large beak, but the two birds must not be confused. The hornbill's beak is different because it continues above the bird's head to form a sort of knob that looks like a helmet.

The male hornbill which feeds its 'imprisoned' mate

There are forty-five different species of hornbills, with loud, croaking voices and flapping wings. Their strong beaks can break the shells of the hardest nuts, but hornbills will also eat insects and small animals.

Most hornbills build their nests in a hollow tree. The male bird imprisons the female inside her nest by walling her in with dried mud while she hatches the eggs and cares for the young until they can fly. He leaves a small slit in the mud wall and through this he feeds his mate during the whole period she is sitting on the eggs.

How the lobster carries its eggs

Lobsters live along rocky coastlines of the Mediterranean and north Atlantic. They are crustaceans and related to shrimps, prawns and crabs. Like the shrimps, the female lobsters carry their eggs stuck to their abdomens for about ten months until they hatch. The eggs cling to the mother's body by means of a sticky substance and the animal also protects them by covering them with her fan-shaped tail.

The lobster has ten jointed legs, including two with strong claws. The spiny lobster has no large claws but uses its prickly limbs to defend itself.

The main food of lobsters is fish, alive or dead, and the invertebrates which live at the bottom of the sea. They also occasionally eat sea plants.

Lobsters look like prehistoric monsters that should have died out millions of years ago. They are not dangerous to man and because they are delicious to eat, they are the basis of important fisheries. Usually they are caught in quite shallow water by the use of lobster pots, creels or frames covered with netting.

How walruses use their tusks

The tusks of a walrus can grow to a length of almost 70 centimetres and are much sought after by ivory hunters. Walruses use their tusks for several purposes; as a weapon in their fierce battles to win a wife against rivals; to help them climb up rocks and ice when they come ashore; and to dig up clams from the seabed. These tusks are therefore very valuable to the animal but they are, in a sense, also its ruin.

One reason why walruses are not so numerous today and are confined to a few regions in the northern Pacific and the Atlantic, is that, since the ninth century A.D., hunters have slaughtered them for their ivory tusks. The Pacific walrus has longer, more slender tusks.

It was among the Eskimos of the arctic and subarctic regions that the art of carving ivory was most highly developed. Even the most everyday objects, such as harpoon heads, needle cases and the toggles for the dog harness, were decorated.

Male and female spiders of the genus Nephila

Walruses

How the bee-eater makes its strange nest

The nests of bee-eaters are strange constructions, like those of the fishing martin. The bee-eater uses its long beak to dig out deep tunnels on the steep banks of rivers. The tunnels open on to a room under the ground, which is the bird's nest. The floor of the nest is covered in butterflies' wings and the remains of insects.

These remains do not make a very comfortable bed but the young bee-eaters seem to like it.

The bee-eater is a tireless flier. From morning until night it goes in search of insects. While other birds help farmers by eating up grubs that live on plants, the bee-eater prefers to catch its victims as they fly along.

The only damage this bird does in hunting is to kill many bees and this angers bee-keepers.

The bee-eater with its brilliant plumage and pointed wings is related to the kingfisher. It is found in Europe and Australia.

How spiders use their venom

There are about 40,000 species of spiders and nearly all of them have poison glands. Fortunately, in most cases the venom is very weak and has little or no effect on man. The bite of the tarantula was once thought to cause a disease called tarantism when the victim wept and danced wildly. Now it is known that the bite is not dangerous to man.

A few spiders, however, can injure people. One of these is the black widow which lives in North America. Its bite can cause intense pain, severe illness and even death, though this is rare.

Merops rubicus or bee-eater, so called because its food includes bees and wasps

In actual fact the mouth of a spider is made in such a way that it cannot really bite. These animals use their venom as a chemical to paralyze their victim. Scientists have found that the venom of spiders in some species breaks down the tissues of the victim and turns them into a sort of jelly which the spider then sucks up because it has no means of chewing its food.

If a spider is not hungry it does not kill its victim immediately. Instead, it imprisons it by wrapping a thick web of threads round it, waiting for the right moment to inject its venom.

Lampropelma, a genus of giant spider also mistakenly known as the tarantula

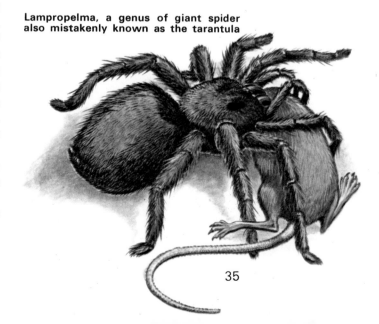

THE HOW OF THE EARTH

How wind and rain can make pyramids

Erosion is a constant natural process by which rocks are worn away. This process is effected by the amount of rainfall and the strength and direction of the wind.

Sometimes the effects of erosion are so weird and wonderful it seems as if a magician has been at work. Some of the strangest effects can be seen in pyramids which resemble a series of pinnacles each surmounted by a rock.

These pyramids are the result of the softer underlying material being worn away while the harder rock at the top remains. The hard rocks act as an umbrella and protect the soil underneath from the attacks of rainfall. These rocks mark the former level of the ground before it was worn away by erosion.

The most famous of these formations include those in Monument Valley in Utah in the United States.

Various coral structures

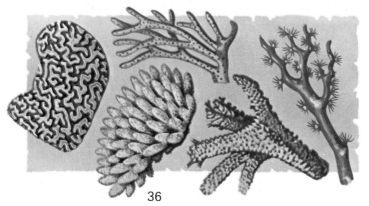

How coral forms in the sea

At first sight coral looks like some fossilized plant. But coral is the 'skeleton' of a mass of small animals known as polyps. The polyps emerge from their coral structure, waving their little tentacles to catch scraps of food. They look like small white blobs and have delicate whiskers on the ends of their tentacles which they use as fingers to take the food they catch to their mouths. The polyps are always ready to slip back into their coral shelter at the slightest sign of danger.

How lava goes hard

Lava is one of the substances that a volcano produces when it erupts. It consists of a material called magma which is a molten rock that rises from the depths of the Earth. The temperature of molten lava reaching the Earth's surface ranges from about 700° to 1,200°C. Most lava is thin and fast-moving and can spread out to great distances.

When the volcano has stopped erupting and the lava has been exposed to the air, it begins to cool, becoming hard and rocky on the outside while remaining soft and even liquid inside. If the sides of the volcano are steep the bottom layers of lava run off while the upper sections go hard. This process causes what is known as a lava tunnel.

Soil which began its life as lava is extremely fertile. For this reason people have always lived near volcanoes despite the danger of periodic eruptions and the risks involved.

How to recognize a glacial valley

When a glacier moves through a valley it exerts a tremendous force on the hillsides. The friction, or rubbing, of the ice mass is also increased by the large number of rocks which are frozen fast inside it and which act as abrasive or scouring elements. The glacier therefore scoops out great masses of soil and rock. When it has retreated or melted the marks of the rubbing or abrasion can be seen on the rocks. These rocks have rounded tops and are known as *roches moutonnées*, which means 'rocks shaped like sheep'. These rocks show heavy scratches known as striae, caused by the rubbing force of the glacier.

Glacial valleys can also be recognized in another way. In a river valley the flow of water is concentrated at one part of the valley's floor, so that a river valley is V-shaped. In a glacial valley the glacier is spread out all over the valley floor and a glacial valley is U-shaped.

Examples of glacial valleys include the fjords, the long sea inlets, of Norway. The sea now fills these long narrow bays but at one time they were completely locked in ice.

To the north of glacial valleys where the great glaciers are formed as a result of the accumulation of snow, there are cirques. These are vast hollows scooped out of the side of hills or mountains by ice and snow when they melt and fall away. In Scotland cirques are known as corries and in Wales as cwms. Sometimes two cirques are formed together and separated only by a narrow ridge called an arête.

A typical Chilean river valley

How rocky walls of mountains crumble

Rain, wind, frost and ice are the tools that nature uses to make even the largest mountains gradu-

Columnar basalt in the Auvergne, France

ally crumble down. This process is known as erosion and takes millions of years to complete its work. Some of the erosion results from the chemical decay of rocks caused by various substances in the atmosphere, and can be seen, for example, in the flaking of basalt. When this happens the rain breaks up the rock even more and washes it away.

The atmosphere also has a physical effect on rocks. Changes in the air temperature is one such effect. Rocks expand in heat, as any solid does, and contract or shrink in cold. This constant expansion and contraction eventually helps to crumble the rock.

Another physical force is the continual freezing and thawing of ice. This is a powerful factor because the water often freezes after running deep into the rock through a crack. The ice then acts from within the rock to break it up.

How hot mineral springs are formed

One of the best-known effects of the great heat that lies inside the Earth can be seen in hot, mineral springs that gush out of the surface of the Earth. These are rich in minerals such as common salt, which gives rise to 'bitter springs', and iron, sulphur and magnesia, giving medicinal waters.

Scientists differ in their opinions on how these hot springs began. Some believe they come straight up from underneath the ground where they were trapped millions of years ago during earth movements. Other scientists think the water began as rain which seeped through the soil, became heated and then rose again.

Perhaps both opinions are correct. It is certain, however, that the waters of these springs have flowed under the soil, become enriched with mineral salts and been heated to boiling point.

How fertile farm soil is formed

Air contains certain chemical substances which are present in greater quantities when the atmosphere is moist. These chemicals attack even the hardest rocks. To see how rocks can be affected one only needs to pick up a pebble from the sea or a river. On the outside the pebble is smooth and rounded: this is the result of the work of water and the air's chemical action. The inside of the pebble is still rough because it has not been reached by the external forces.

The chemical action of the atmosphere is extremely important. It can break down rocks and put oxygen into them by oxidation. The result is farm soil without which we cannot grow our food.

However, we must not think that agricultural soil is merely a collection of tiny particles of rock which have been crumbled away. Such a mixture does not contain many of the ingredients necessary to sustain plant life, and only certain primitive plants, such as lichens, can obtain any nourishment from it.

Soil becomes fertile when these pioneer' plants like lichens die and decay. Their decomposed bodies enrich the soil with their chemical substances to form a material known as humus. It is this humus, which is a mass of dead and decaying vegetation, which makes soil fertile.

How rapids are formed

Rapids in a river are a waterfall that has reached its old age. They are the remains of what was once a vertical fall of water such as the

Foz de Iguacu Falls, Paraguay

Niagara Falls. After millions of years the waterfall has worn the cliff away to a sloping bed of rocks.

The water still flows rapidly and tumbles about over the broken surface of the stream. It is dangerous to boats, sometimes making it completely impossible to sail up a river. But rapids are very useful in helping to produce electric power.

Shooting the rapids in canoes or kayaks is a popular sport in America and is also one of the events of the Olympic Games. At the Munich Games in 1972, a long stretch of artificial rapids was built specially for this sporting event.

39

How an animal becomes fossilized

Men have been attracted to fossils since the earliest times. Even today we read with great interest any report about the discovery of the skeleton of some prehistoric animal.

The question arises: how can the fragile bones of any animal have stayed preserved for such a long time?

Much depends on the type of soil in which the bones came to rest. If the soil was damp and with a strong acid content, then the bones would not have lasted for very long: the chemicals in the soil would soon have broken them up into a powder.

But a damp soil with no harsh chemicals in it, often acts as a preservative. In this kind of soil the bones are gradually petrified, which means they are turned into stone.

When soil is moist and acid and completely without air, then even the soft tissues of an animal can be preserved through a process similar to mummification.

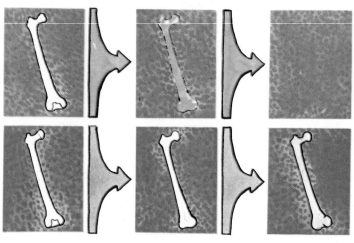

Acid-moist soil: matter disappears

Alkaline-moist soil: complete fossilization

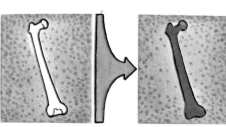

Alkaline-dry soil: partial fossilization

Acid-moist soil with no air: soft tissues also preserved

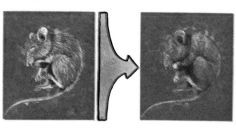

How the Earth's internal heat is used

The internal heat of the Earth is seen on the surface of the planet in volcanic activity. These manifestations of heat include *soffioni*, an Italian word to describe a hole in the earth through which jets of hot steam or unpleasant-smelling gases shoot out. These blow-holes are a sign of volcanic activity under the ground and the gases they release into the air come from molten rocks known as magma which lie at depths of between 5,000 and 6,000 metres.

Scientists found boric acid in these vents and an industry to extract this chemical substance was founded in Italy in 1818. Later it was discovered that the power of these gas jets could be harnessed for other tasks, including the production of electrical power, and the first geothermal electricity was generated

Electric-powered train with overhead cables

at Landarello, in Italy, in 1904.

There are four kinds of geothermal power: dry steam, as at Landarello; hot water, as at Reykjavik, in Iceland, where it is used to heat most of the city; low temperature areas in basins of sedimentary rock, containing water between 40 and 100°C which is used for agricultural purposes such as heating glasshouses; and high pressure zones found by petroleum drilling deep in sedimentary basins.

How life is possible in underground caves

Many strange animals live in the gloom of underground caves. Some of them were completely unknown until relatively recently when the science of speleology developed.

Speleology is the scientific study of caves from all points of view. These include, amongst other things, the discovery and exploration of caves; the study of their geological and chemical problems; and a study of their animal life.

It is difficult to imagine how any living creature could exist in these conditions but despite this there are many cave-dwelling animals under the ground. Most of them are tiny animals which, because of the lack of light, have no positive colour. They are either very pale or even transparent.

Since there is no plant life in the caves they live in, these little animals live on the flesh of other animals.

How underground rivers are formed

When rainwater which contains a certain amount of acid falls on limestone rocks, a strange process can take place. The limestone begins to break up and caverns, some of them enormous, start to form under the ground.

Such a terrain is known as karst. This term was first applied to the Carso, a limestone area along the Dalmation coast of Yugoslavia, but is now used to describe any area with these features.

Karst represents a limestone rock which is honeycombed with tunnels and caves through which the rainwater runs, seeking a way out. As the water moves along it wears away more and more of the surrounding rock to produce long tunnels which turn into underground rivers. These rivers eventually reach the sea after appearing at the surface in places.

Speleologists have tried to follow the course of some underground rivers but many passages are too narrow for a man to get through.

One way of following their course is to place dye in their waters whenever they appear at the surface. They can then be recognized when they break through again.

How stalactites and stalagmites are formed

Even people in ancient days knew that the constant dripping of water could wear away the hardest rock. Geologists have since discovered that these little drops of water not only wear away rocks but form others just as hard. It takes hundreds of thousands of drops of water to wear away one millimetre of stone; but it takes millions of drops to build up the same amount.

To see water which has turned into stone one has to go into a karstic cave. The first striking sight is of stalactites and stalagmites, stone pillars that descend from the ceiling or rise from the floor. Then there is the spectacular draped effect of the rock on the ceiling and walls of the cave. All these wonders have been created by dripping water. Each drop of water contains a microscopic piece of calcium: through the constant dripping these tiny specks of calcium have turned into rock pillars of dazzling beauty.

How a glacier is formed

Snow that falls on low ground does not lie for long and soon melts away in the first warmth of early spring. On higher ground snow remains for a longer time but even there it is usually all

melted away by May. But there are places where even the summer sunshine cannot banish the snow. This is on mountains like the Alps at heights of more than 3,000 metres.

This height is known to geographers as the snowline or the limit of persistent snow. It varies

The level of permanent snow varies with the latitude

The equivalent of 1 measure of rain is 10 of newly fallen snow

=

Height in metres

4,500

3,000

1,500

Mt. Kilimanjaro 3°S

Mt. Blanc 46°N

Mt. Erebus 78°S

according to location on the globe: in the tropics, for example, the snowline is much higher, at about 5,500 metres, and in the polar regions it is practically at sea-level.

If all the snow that falls on the Earth were to stay on the ground winter after winter, all the highest mountain-tops would be covered many times over. But snow only stays on valleys and hollowed-out mountainsides to form snow-fields.

When snow falls it is light and feathery. A piece of snow of this type measuring a cubic metre weighs about 75 kilogrammes. But as the snow heaps up on the ground its weight causes the bottom layers to freeze into a hard glassy mass and the weight of a cubic metre rises to about 900 kilogrammes. The upper slopes of all the world's mountain ranges are covered in these masses of snow. Once it finds an outlet this frozen snow begins to move slowly like a gigantic river of ice and a glacier is born.

How weather forecasts are made

It was already known in the last century that when the barometer showed a low air pressure bad weather could be expected and when the arrow pointed to a high pressure good weather was on the way. When all the air pressures of a region are known a map can be drawn up to show them. On these maps are drawn lines to join places which have the same air pressure: these lines are called isobars. When all these lines are drawn they reveal various systems of air pressures.

The anticyclones are areas of high pressure which usually bring good weather. Cyclones, or depressions, are low-pressure areas and usually bring rainy or stormy weather.

Today meteorologists use satellites and highly accurate equipment to predict the weather with a precision that would have seemed unbelievable not many years ago.

Stratocumulus

Nimbostratus

Cumulus

Cumulonimbus

Stratus

Altocumulus castellanus

How clouds form

The moisture in the air is the result of the evaporation of water by the heat of the Sun. The amount of evaporation depends on the quantity of water and the intensity of the Sun's heat. Another factor that contributes to the increase of atmospheric moisture is the breathing of living creatures.

All these factors combine to produce enormous quantities of water vapour which are continuously rising from the surface of the land and the sea and condensing in the atmosphere. When this happens the vapour turns into clouds of various types.

It was not until 1803 that clouds began to be classified scientifically. Luke Howard published a paper on clouds and the Latin terms which he used became the basis of the internationally accepted cloud classification. Further work was carried out towards the end of the century and the development of aviation stimulated further research.

Clouds have been classified into three main groups by international agreement. The classification depends on the height of the clouds above sea-level. The groups are: cirrus, cirrocumulus, cirrostratus, between 5,000 and 14,000 metres; altocumulus, altostratus, nimbostratus, between 2,000 and 7,000 metres; stratocumulus, stratus, below 2,000 metres. There are clouds that build up like pillars from the land into the sky to a height of over 6,000 metres. These include cumulus and cumulonimbus.

When the condensation of water vapour in the atmosphere goes beyond a certain limit, it turns into rain or snow.

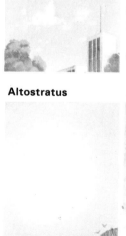
Altostratus

Altocumulus

Cirrus

Cirrostratus

Cirrocumulus

How snow forms

When a cloud meets a very cold current of air, the tiny drops of water vapour that make up the cloud can suddenly turn into very thin pieces of ice. This can happen before these droplets have had time to condense into water, as occurs during rainfall.

In winter it is common for clouds in the sky to be full of minute pieces of ice instead of water vapour. These ice particles are tiny crystals that are long in shape and lighter than air so that they remain suspended in the air.

Snow falls when a certain number of factors are present. These are a combination of low air temperatures and air currents. The tiny particles of ice are then brought together; they become larger and heavier and fall as snowflakes.

When seen through a magnifying glass, snowflakes reveal a complicated and beautiful pattern based on a hexagon. Although snowflakes appear similar in size and structure there is a great variety in shape, size and pattern. It has even been said that no two snow crystals are the same.

How hail is formed

Much of the hail that falls on Europe occurs in summer though scientists believe it is caused by cold temperatures. Some meteorologists believe hail is formed when a current of hot air rises to about 1,000 to 2,000 metres and collides with a cold air current that is descending. The sudden lowering of the temperature in the warm air current freezes the moist air it contains into the little pellets of ice that form hail. This process may be repeated several times, the hailstone gathering more and more coatings of ice, until it becomes heavy and falls.

Other meteorologists think that hail is produced by electrical processes.

Whatever the cause hail is a constant threat to farmers who for centuries have sought ways of defending their fields from it.

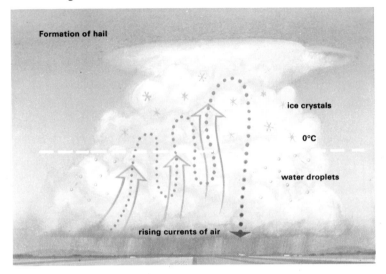

Formation of hail

ice crystals

0°C

water droplets

rising currents of air

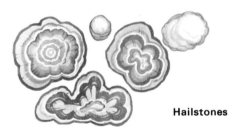

Hailstones

Hailstorms do not usually affect large areas, but they can be so concentrated and intense that they destroy an entire year's crop wherever they strike. Vineyards are frequently affected in this way.

Occasionally huge hailstorms can fall and cause enormous damage. In November 1889 hailstones the size of cricket balls fell in the streets of Louth in New South Wales.

THE HOW OF SCIENCE AND TECHNOLOGY

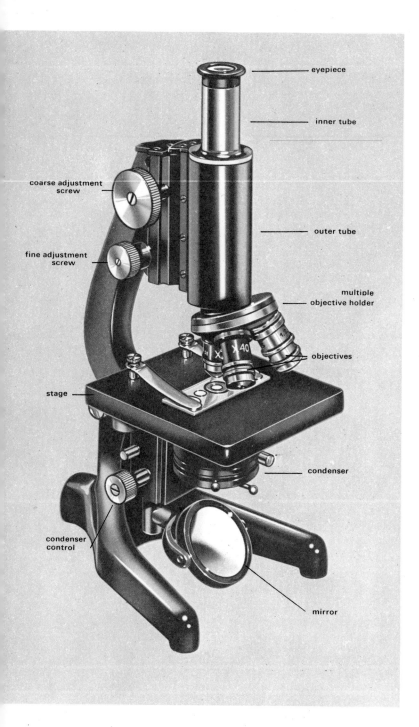

eyepiece

inner tube

coarse adjustment screw

outer tube

fine adjustment screw

multiple objective holder

objectives

stage

condenser

condenser control

mirror

How the microscope works

We do not know exactly when man first discovered that objects seemed much larger when seen through a specially shaped piece of glass. There are some very old stories but they are all vague. The known history of the microscope begins in the seventeenth century when the Dutchman, Anton van Leeuwenhoek, invented a simple microscope consisting of a single lens with a relatively high magnification. The first compound microscope was devised in 1590 by Zacharias Janssen.

The word microscope comes from the Greek *micros* meaning 'small' and *skopeein* meaning 'to look'. The instrument works with two lenses or discs of glass. The upper lens is the eyepiece and the lower one is the objective. The objective lens magnifies the object and the eyepiece lens enlarges the magnification. In modern instruments both the eyepiece and the objective consist of several lenses, so arranged that they rectify the distortion caused by the curvature of the glass.

The objects to be examined are placed on a glass slide. These objects are cut very thin so that light shines through them. In a microscope the light is reflected through the objects by a mirror. Scientists also use electronic microscopes which can magnify objects millions of times.

The basic parts of a microscope are the condenser which illuminates; the focusing mechanism operated by coarse or fine adjusting screws; and a variable diaphragm that controls the amount of light that goes into the condenser.

hunters' such as Koch, Pasteur, Bang, Schaudinn, Eberth, Loeffler and others. Microbes cause the body to produce a substance called antibodies which defend the body. These antibodies were first produced artifically in bodies through vaccination.

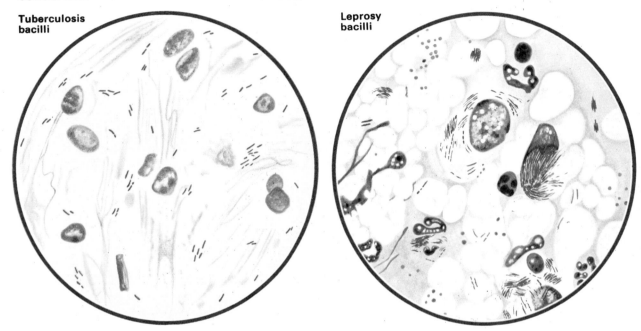

Tuberculosis bacilli

Leprosy bacilli

How disease microbes are fought

The victories of modern medicine are linked with the researches carried out by scientists into the causes of disease.

Microbes are tiny plants like microscopic fungi which enter our bodies in the air we breathe, with the food we eat and the drink we swallow. When they enter our bloodstream they can cause infection and make us ill. Every disease has a microbe as its cause. The microbe can sometimes pass from person to person causing the disease to spread.

Today we know how to cure many diseases and we owe it all to various famous 'germ

The first vaccination ever carried out was done by the British doctor, Edward Jenner (1749–1823), against smallpox. Jenner's experiment was a complete success. Later chemical substances were discovered to kill microbes. These included the arseno-benzoles of the German, Paul Ehrlich (1854–1915), and the sulphonamides of another German, Gerhard Domagk (1895–1964). But it was only during the Second World War that antibiotics were discovered. Two scientists played a leading role in finding these drugs. One was the British scientist, Sir Alexander Fleming, who discovered penicillin, and the other was the American, Selman Waksman, who discovered streptomycin.

How electrical power is transported

One of the great advantages of electricity is the ease with which it can be transported. All the same some major operations are necessary to carry, or transmit, electricity from one point to another. This involves machinery, cables and other equipment used in the generating industry.

The three main parts of the system are: the centres of production; the transmission system through which electrical power is carried from power stations to the main sub-stations which transform it from high to lower voltage; and the distribution system which takes electricity to every user.

Most modern systems use alternating current known as A.C. This is because it is simpler to vary its intensity and requires less complicated generators to produce.

Electrical systems must be as efficient as possible which means they must carry electricity without losing any of it on the way. The quantities of electricity carried today are very large and require high tension.

The highest tension used is 750 kilovolts, though 380 kilovolts is usually the peak in most countries. These high tensions create certain problems which have to be solved through better insulation of the current to prevent leaks or losses as it is being carried along the cables.

One type of power loss is known as the crown effect. It can be seen at night when a bluish haze glows round the high tension wires. Power losses can be considerable and lessen the power that eventually reaches the consumer at the receiving end of the system.

Most transmission lines have a tension ranging from 115 to 175 kilovolts. The tension in the distribution of electricity is lower ranging from 220 volts monophase to 400 volts three-phase. Electric power is supplied with a constant frequency except in the United States and in some regions of Japan where 60 Hz is used as a frequency. The world standard is 50 Hz.

To provide for emergencies duplicate circuits and apparatus

tried to travel along a bad conductor the latter would resist so much that it glowed until it became white-hot.

A carbon filament, for example, gave out a good deal of light; but the light did not last very long because the carbon would

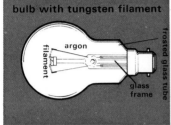

bulb with tungsten filament

filament
argon
frosted glass tube
glass frame

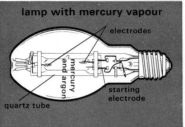

lamp with mercury vapour

electrodes
mercury and argon
quartz tube
starting electrode

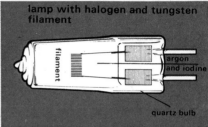

lamp with halogen and tungsten filament

filament
argon and iodine
quartz bulb

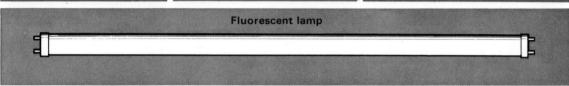

Fluorescent lamp

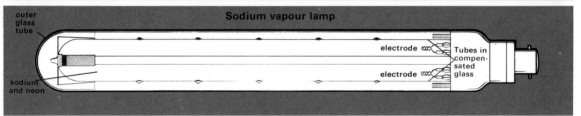

Sodium vapour lamp

outer glass tube
sodium and neon
electrode
electrode
Tubes in compensated glass

are provided, resulting in many circuit arrangements or systems. At least two main transmission circuits are normally provided from a main generating station to each major sub-station, each capable of supplying the load for a time if the other is out of service.

How the electric light bulb was born

Thomas Edison had discovered in his experiments that there were certain bodies through which electric power flowed more easily. He called these good conductors and other bodies that resisted the flow of electric power he called bad conductors. When electricity

soon burn itself up as it was in contact with the oxygen in the air.

Edison then carried out an experiment inside a glass bulb from which he had removed all the air. This time the light of the glowing filament lasted much longer and the first electric light bulb was born.

Carbon filaments have now been replaced by tungsten wire as its high melting point, low rate of evaporation and low electrical consumption make it most suitable for use in light bulbs. A further improvement has been the introduction of an inert gas into the bulb. This was at first nitrogen but is now a mixture of 88 per cent argon and 12 per cent nitrogen.

49

The *Times-Herald* racing car of F. Duryea, 1895

How the first motor cars were made

The word 'automobile', which is another way of saying motor car, means 'moving by itself'. The motor car travels without being pulled by a horse or any other animal and with no visible force to make its wheels go round. For a long time inventors and engineers wondered how such a machine could be produced. One of the first attempts to produce an automobile was made during the eighteenth century. It was a very ramshackle affair and can still be seen today in the National Museum in Paris. The machine was designed by the French engineer, Nicholas Joseph Cugnot.

Cugnot's idea was to exploit the steam engine invented by Watt and use it to power a vehicle. He drew up plans which he submitted to the War Ministry since the machine was meant to carry heavy artillery. Cugnot was authorized to make a prototype. The machine he produced was a large, heavy, steam-powered tricycle. His model of 1769 was said to have run for twenty minutes at just over 5 kilometres an hour while carrying four people. Cugnot then built a larger vehicle. During a test run at Vincennes the machine got out of control and crashed into a wall, demolishing it.

The accident gave ammunition to Cugnot's opponents and the experiments stopped. It took many more years before attempts were resumed to make a motor car.

How the internal combustion engine works

The combustion engine seems a complicated piece of machinery but it consists of the following basic parts: the combustion chamber, the piston, the connecting rod, the inlet and exhaust valves,

The first Michelin tyres were tested on a Peugeot of 1895

The Obéissante of 1873

the carburettor, the sparking plugs and the crankshaft.

The piston travels into the combustion chamber in an up-and-down motion. The motion of the piston is transmitted to the crankshaft by way of the connecting rod and then on to the other parts of the mechanism that turn the wheels.

The movement of the piston begins electrically from the car's battery. As the piston moves up into the compression chamber the inlet valve opens and admits a mixture of air and petrol vapour from the carburettor. The top, or head, of the piston compresses this mixture until it becomes explosive. At that point an electrical spark jumps from the plug and causes the mixture to ignite. The resulting explosion pushes the piston down again causing it to turn the crankshaft which then turns the wheels. When the piston travels back into the combustion chamber the exhaust valve opens and the burnt gases are expelled. This whole process is repeated thousands of times a minute in four basic stages: induction, compression, combustion, expulsion.

How the internal combustion engine is lubricated and kept cool

The component parts of any engine must be lubricated or oiled regularly. Lubrication provides a film of oil which reduces the friction that would quickly destroy rubbing parts. The lubricant commonly used is refined from crude oil and is improved with additives that reduce oxidation and corrosion and act as cleaning agents.

In a motor car there is a basin, known as the sump, or oil pan,

underneath the engine. This contains the oil which is pumped round the engine while it is running.

The internal combustion engine must also be kept relatively cool. This can be done with air or water. Air-cooling is produced by the pressurized inlet of air into the cooling fins of a cylinder and other parts designed to get rid of excess heat. Water-cooling is produced by water being pumped constantly round the engine from the radiator, which is kept cool by the airstream and by a fan which also works the water-pump.

In winter anti-freeze liquids are added to the engine's water jacket to prevent it from freezing and damaging the cylinder block.

How the differential works in a motor car

When a motor car goes round a corner or a bend the inside wheels have a shorter distance to travel than the outside wheels. For this reason the inside wheels have to travel more slowly than the outside ones. This difference in wheel speeds is made possible through the differential.

The differential is a mechanism that consists of an axle that joins two wheels, usually the rear ones. In the middle of the axle there is a round shell that contains a series of geared wheels including the crown wheel. The pinion, which is part of the propeller shaft that runs from the gear-box of the car, sets these geared wheels into motion. When the car turns a corner the geared wheels of the differential vary the speeds of the wheels until the car is on a straight path again and both rear wheels travelling at the same speed.

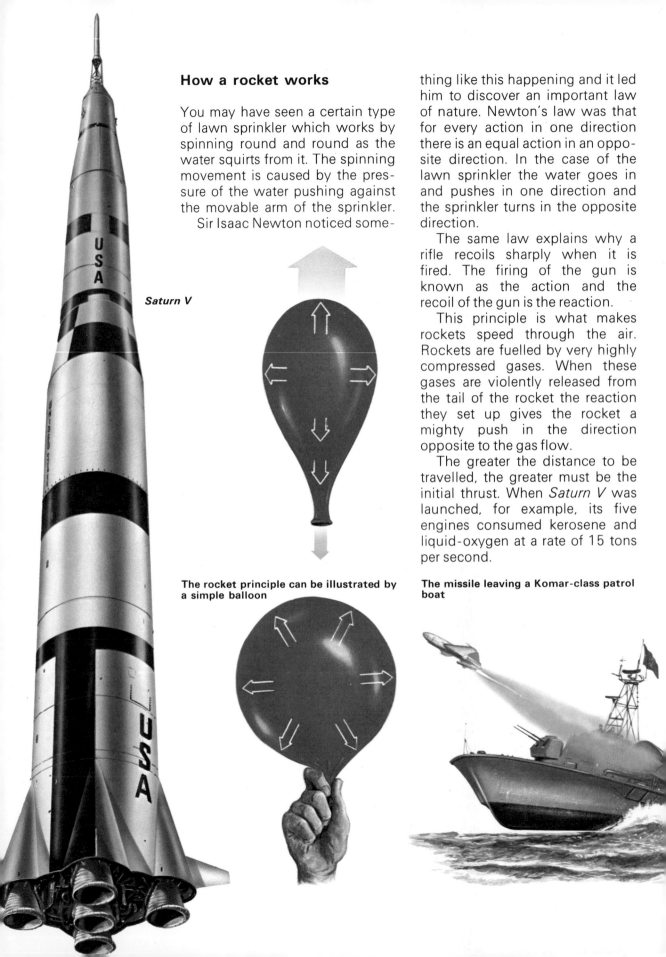

How a rocket works

You may have seen a certain type of lawn sprinkler which works by spinning round and round as the water squirts from it. The spinning movement is caused by the pressure of the water pushing against the movable arm of the sprinkler.

Sir Isaac Newton noticed something like this happening and it led him to discover an important law of nature. Newton's law was that for every action in one direction there is an equal action in an opposite direction. In the case of the lawn sprinkler the water goes in and pushes in one direction and the sprinkler turns in the opposite direction.

The same law explains why a rifle recoils sharply when it is fired. The firing of the gun is known as the action and the recoil of the gun is the reaction.

This principle is what makes rockets speed through the air. Rockets are fuelled by very highly compressed gases. When these gases are violently released from the tail of the rocket the reaction they set up gives the rocket a mighty push in the direction opposite to the gas flow.

The greater the distance to be travelled, the greater must be the initial thrust. When *Saturn V* was launched, for example, its five engines consumed kerosene and liquid-oxygen at a rate of 15 tons per second.

Saturn V

The rocket principle can be illustrated by a simple balloon

The missile leaving a Komar-class patrol boat

How radar works

We have all at one time or another heard the echo of our own voice. An echo is caused by sound waves being bounced back from a solid obstacle, rather like a rubber ball bouncing off a wall. The same thing happens to radio waves which are sent out by a powerful transmitter. When the waves collide with a solid object they bounce back and can be picked up by a receiving set which is usually located at the same place as the transmitter. Since the speed of these waves is known we can tell how far away the obstacle is by calculating how long the waves take to cover the distance. This is how radar works.

The word 'radar' is an abbreviated form of the name 'radio detecting and ranging'. Radar is now used everywhere: at airports, missile bases, space centres for following and tracking satellites and on ships and aircraft for automatic navigation. A simple form of radar is used by police to detect speeding vehicles.

A battery of Sander rockets using solid fuel was used by Fritz von Opel, the German motor car engineer, to reach a speed of 152 kilometres an hour in a glider. In 1928 Opel reached a speed of 200 kilometres an hour using rockets in his experimental car *Rak 2*

The tail-first *Ente* sailplane which was the first rocket plane to fly successfully

How to guard against atomic radiation

Nuclear power was first unleashed in a wave of destruction at Hiroshima and Nagasaki in 1945. As a result of the explosion of the atomic bombs over these Japanese cities, hundreds of thousands of people lost their lives. Many of them were killed by the radioactive waves released by the bombs and even in peacetime people can still be killed by this radiation.

The seriousness of the effect of radiation depends on various factors. These include the size of the radioactive dose received by the body, the duration of the exposure to the radiation, the type of radiation involved and the part of the body affected.

Normally the body can restore and repair any damage done to it but when radiation destroys the cells and tissues they cannot be replaced.

For this reason people who work in scientific laboratories and industries dealing with radioactive materials must be carefully protected with special clothing and equipment and have frequent health checks.

Radioactive materials in research reactors must be handled at a safe distance and with remote-control devices

After taking a shower (above) a technician is checked with a Geiger counter (below)

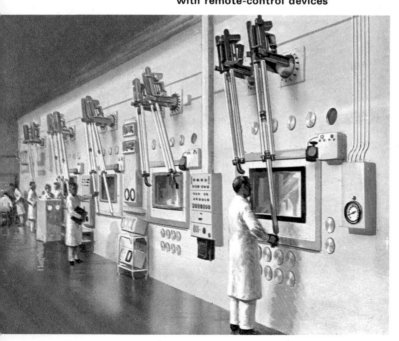

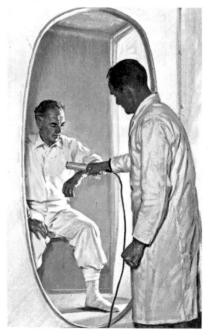

How a nuclear reaction takes place

We speak of a nuclear reaction whenever the nucleus of an atom undergoes any change in its properties. For example, this could be the loss of a proton which becomes detached from its orbit round the nucleus and collides with neighbouring atoms. In nature this process can take place spontaneously in certain substances and gives rise to radioactivity.

Radioactivity was discovered in 1896 by the French scientist Henri Becquerel who proved that pitchblende, a mineral that contains uranium, could darken photographic plates even if they were wrapped in dark paper. It became evident to Becquerel that a very penetrating form of radiation was involved.

We now know that this radiation consists of alpha particles and that radioactive materials also give out two other types of radiation: beta and gamma. Alpha

several centimetres of metal thickness is needed to reduce gamma radiation to an acceptable level.

It was not simple to produce these rays artificially and it took many years of difficult research and complicated experiments. In the end the scientists succeeded. They bombarded the atoms of certain materials with particles taken from naturally radioactive material. By increasing or decreasing this bombardment, the scientists were able to break apart the protective shell of electrons and reach the nucleus of an atom.

In this way nuclear fission, or the splitting of the atom, was achieved. Under such bombardment the atomic nucleus splits into two smaller nuclei. As this happens the atom's electrons are driven outwards from their orbits and collide with the nuclei of neighbouring atoms. This sets off a chain reaction, releasing enormous quantities of energy which can go out of control with disastrous results.

When a neutron (1) and a uranium nucleus (2) collide (3) the uranium nucleus becomes unstable (4) and divides into

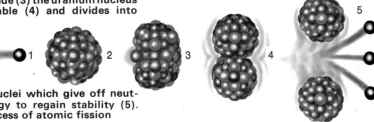

two smaller nuclei which give off neutrons and energy to regain stability (5). This is the process of atomic fission

particles are not very powerful and they can be stopped by a thickness of a few sheets of paper or by a few centimetres of air. Beta rays are more penetrating but can be stopped by thick cardboard, a few metres of air or thin sheet metal. Gamma rays, like X-rays, are extremely penetrating and can be very dangerous to plant and animal life. To stop them

How nuclear reactors are fuelled

Nuclear reactors are complicated structures in which the chain reaction from atomic fission can be set off, continued and kept under control. In this way, an atom can be split without the risk of a terribly destructive explosion. Instead, the process is done gradually and a large amount of energy is produced.

Nuclear reactors are fuelled in different ways. Nuclear fuel must always be a substance which can set off a chain reaction when bombarded with neutrons. The most commonly used elements in fuelling reactors are uranium, plutonium and thorium.

At the heart of the reactor there is the moderator which is a substance that slows down the speed of the neutrons and regulates their flow. The reactor is called fast if it uses fast neutrons and thermal if the neutrons have been slowed down, thereby transferring much of their energy to the moderator.

Fast reactors burn plutonium produced in thermal reactors. They can also generate plutonium from natural uranium or from used uranium

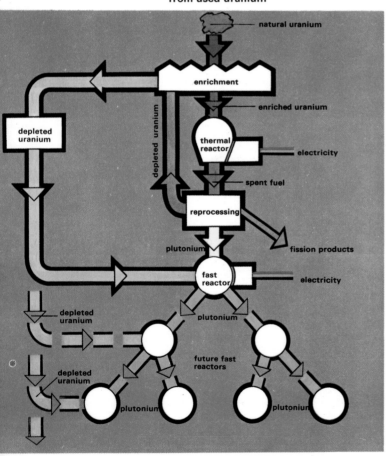

How uranium for nuclear reactors is produced

Uranium in its natural state is found in quantities that average about 4 grammes to every ton of rock. It is an extremely expensive process to extract this mineral from the rocks that contain it even when the deposits are relatively rich.

The best material for nuclear fission is Uranium 235, but natural uranium has only one atom of this structure for every 140 atoms of Uranium 238. So even when the uranium has been extracted from rocks, the element has to be further processed to get the portion with the atomic structure needed for nuclear reactors.

Once the atomic reaction has been set in motion, the energy which is released mostly takes the form of heat. This heat is led to a type of boiler where it generates steam that is later put to several uses. One kilogramme of uranium yields as much energy as 3 million kilogrammes of coal.

How nuclear energy can be used

The splitting of an atom produces a huge amount of energy and scientists from the very beginning have studied ways of harnessing this power to serve mankind. It was from such studies that the first atomic piles or reactors were built.

In 1942 Enrico Fermi and his colleagues became the first to make this major conquest. But a world war was raging and the first use that the energy from nuclear fission was put to was the atomic bomb. Later, however, this new source of energy was placed in the service of man.

Today the heat produced in atomic reactors is used to generate electric power. Soon, whole cities will be heated by nuclear power stations, the waters of the seas will be desalinated and made fresh by atomic power and the world's deserts irrigated so that they become fertile. Nuclear power has already been harnessed to power the engines of ships and submarines.

The various radioactive materials produced in reactors are now employed in many ways to aid mankind. They have helped doctors to treat dangerous diseases and farmers to produce more and better crops. Atomic science can also be used to explore the Earth and help us find its still hidden stores of riches.

Another use of atomic power is to preserve foodstuffs for longer periods and this will help man to deal with the problems of world hunger in the future.

The splitting of the atom has opened up a new era for the world.

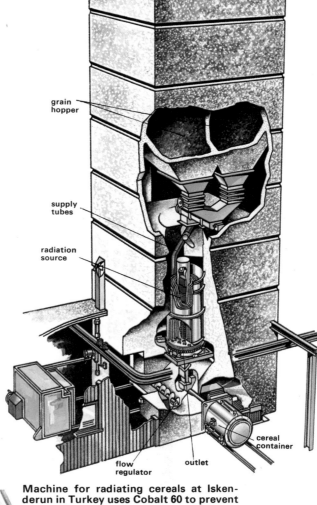

grain hopper

supply tubes

radiation source

flow regulator

outlet

cereal container

Machine for radiating cereals at Iskenderun in Turkey uses Cobalt 60 to prevent insects from breeding in the cereals

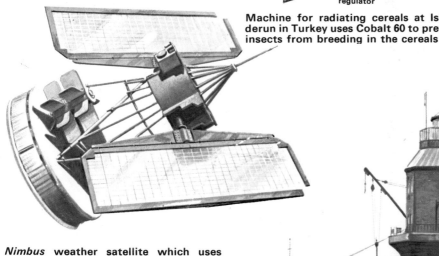

Nimbus **weather satellite which uses solar batteries as a source of power**

The lighthouse at the entrance of Baltimore harbour is powered by 225,000 curies of Strontium 90 and is automated

How computers are used in industry

The electronic computer is used in many fields of activity and is extremely valuable in doing complicated work accurately and quickly. It has removed much of the drudgery from such routine tasks as telephone switchboard operation, the working of lifts, and book-keeping.

How do these wonderful machines work? We can see in the simple example of checking the stocks held by a warehouse.

The diagram on this page shows the various operations that take place one after the other. In large-scale industries it costs a great deal of money to keep a large number of goods in store. Nevertheless a company must always know how many goods it has at a given time in case it runs out of any item. So there must always be a reserve level below which stocks must not go. When that level is reached the company orders more goods to be delivered.

One way of keeping a check is to use a punched-card system. Each article which is delivered to the warehouse has its own card punched with the required information which may relate to style, colour, price, size or other relevant details, and this is fed into the computer.

When the article is sold and leaves the warehouse the computer is fed with this information too. At any time the computer can show exactly how many of those articles are in stock and if the stocks have to be replenished. The computer does this job with great speed and accuracy and can give an account of exactly how many articles of many different types are in stock.

The initial effect of computers is as an efficient means of performing complicated or routine tasks. In the long term, however, they will make new and different activities possible. For instance, education and many occupations will be greatly affected as methods of storing and retrieving vast quantities of information are further developed.

Flow chart for computerized stores

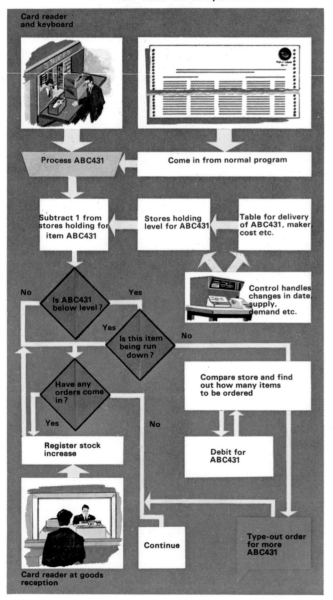

How computers work

There are two basic types of computer: digital and analogue. Both types use highly complex systems of electrical circuits to carry out complicated calculations or to solve difficult problems. The hybrid is a third type which consists of a combination of the other two.

The digital computer is basically a counting machine. In its simplest form it would be a counting frame with beads. A more complicated form would be a cash register. There are small digital computers able to multiply, divide, subtract and add, all at high speed, which are electrically powered and operated by hand like typewriters. Larger digital computers receive their information or data on punched-cards, magnetic tape or perforated tape. This information is read by a unit called the reader which converts the data into a form usable by the computer.

Analogue computers also use complicated electrical circuits but they are specially designed or programmed to deal with particular problems such as guiding Moon rockets or controlling the movements of trains.

Computers have a memory unit which stores information and provides it whenever it is requested. These memory units consist of magnetic drums, discs or tapes which store the information in the form of electrical impulses. When a computer has solved a problem or finished a complicated sum it gives the answer on a teleprinter.

Computers must therefore be able to accept information, store it and all the intermediate processes and results, and present the final results to the user in an understandable form.

How the various chemicals got their names

The complicated but accurate system of naming the various chemical substances that we use today was first drawn up 200 years ago by a brilliant French scientist, Antoine Lavoisier, who is generally regarded as the father of modern chemistry.

Lavoisier was the first scientist to recognize the importance of

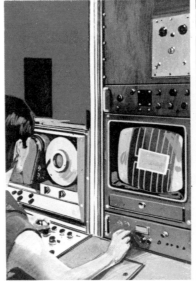

Computerized systems can be used in the design of components

oxygen in the process of combustion or burning. He laid down the principle of the conservation of matter which stated 'nothing is created, nothing is destroyed'.

But the work of Lavoisier did not end there. In collaboration with three other scientists, he devised a reformed system of chemical terminology in 1787, giving a precise name to every known chemical substance. To him we owe a name like 'ferrous oxide' which tells us immediately what substances are involved, in this case iron and oxygen. Before Lavoisier, early scientists had used peculiar and fantastic names to identify the various chemicals.

How timber is transported through forests

Today huge trees can be felled with special tools that work very quickly and the entire operation is carried out by teams of specially trained lumbermen according to well organized plans. Methods of felling trees and converting them into logs are much the same in all forested areas.

One important consideration in lumbering is not to destroy an entire forest, but to cut down only mature trees and leave room for the younger ones to grow. In this way forests, which are part of our priceless heritage, can be kept alive.

Once a tree has been felled, the branches are removed with axes or special saws. The trunk is then cut into sections of the desired length and the bark stripped. The wood should then be left to season in the forest for a period ranging from three months to a year. Seasoning allows wood to dry gradually and thus avoids much of the cracking and splitting which can spoil it.

After the seasoning comes the problem of transporting the timber from the forest. Wood can be carried by lorry, railway trucks or river craft. But large pieces of timber are extremely difficult to transport, particularly if there are no roads and the terrain is rough.

One old method was to cut out 'channels' through a forest which followed steep slopes. The big logs would then be pushed along these channels and slid down the slopes.

This method damaged much of the wood and today timber is carried through forests by means of overhead cables. These are expensive to instal but they move considerable quantities of timber quickly and thus recover their initial cost.

How the electric battery was invented

The first electric battery was born as a result of one of the most famous scientific disputes. During the eighteenth century the Italian doctor Luigi Galvani of Bologna carried out a series of interesting experiments on dead frogs. Galvani obtained vibrations in the muscles of the animals hung from copper hooks over an iron rod. From these twitchings Galvani deduced that the frog possessed electric properties. He was mistaken in thinking this.

But Galvani's work was valuable even though it produced faulty conclusions because it opened the way to the study of electricity by such scientists as Alessandro Volta, another Italian. Volta turned Galvani's theory on its head by saying

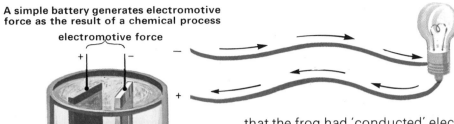

A simple battery generates electromotive force as the result of a chemical process

electromotive force

+ —

carbon
zinc
electrolytic solution

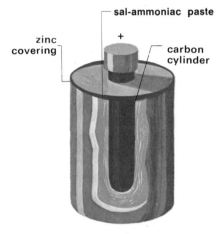

sal-ammoniac paste

zinc covering

+

carbon cylinder

Commercial dry battery

Car battery (accumulator)

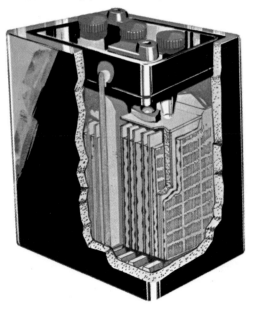

that the frog had 'conducted' electricity which had been generated in the contact between the two metals.

After many fierce arguments Volta won the day. Using his own theories he went on to invent the electric battery by placing zinc and copper in a bath of acid water and so provided a source of continuous current.

Modern physics has revealed the real nature of electricity, a mysterious force which has been known to man since the earliest times. All substances in which the atoms have been placed out of balance because they lack certain electrons or because they have too many electrons, are either positively or negatively charged. Positive charges are composed of atoms or molecules which have lost one or more electrons. Negative charges consist of atoms which for some reason have more than their normal number of electrons.

Electrons which pass from one atom to another inside a material such as a copper wire, form an electric current. This current flows extremely fast from one end of the wire to the other.

When the current flows in the same direction it is known as direct or D.C. This is the type of current generated in a battery. When the electric current changes its flow to a well defined frequency it is known as alternating or A.C. A.C. current is used for lighting and for domestic and industrial purposes.

THE HOW OF ANCIENT PEOPLES

How the hanging gardens of Babylon were built

According to the stories of the time the hanging gardens of Babylon began as a gesture of love and affection. Nebuchadnezzar, king of Babylon from 605 to 562 B.C., had married a Mede princess who was very homesick for her native land and its greenery. To please her the king created the most beautiful gardens on the terraces of his royal palace.

The ancient peoples considered these gardens as one of the seven wonders of the world. Archaeologists have never found any trace of them but some writers who saw the gardens have left behind detailed descriptions. They were not literally 'hanging' but were 'up in the air', that is roof gardens laid out on a series of terraces. These terraces were supported on strong vaults and were filled in with soil in which many kinds of trees grew.

The biggest danger to these gardens was rain which in that region occurs in downpours at certain times of the year. To protect the gardens from the torrential rain the vaults were covered in bitumen or resin and clad in sheets of lead.

During the dry season the gardens were irrigated by pumps from the river Euphrates. The water was brought from ground level to a tank placed on the highest terrace.

How old chemist shops developed

Today a chemist shop is not much different from any other shop. It has shelves which display a wide variety of goods in packets of various colours. Many of the prescriptions which a doctor gives us can be dealt with by an ordinary assistant in the chemist shop.

It was not always like this: at one time a chemist shop was a real workshop or laboratory where medicines were made by mixing together carefully all the various ingredients named in the prescription. These establishments were known as apothecaries. Their shelves were lined with elegant pots of glass or porcelain which contained medicines or poisons. In the rear of the premises the apothecary would pound herbs and grains of medicine together with a pestle and mortar. He measured out the correct doses on a set of scales, made up pomades or pastes and ointments, prepared elixirs or poultices, pills and laxative powders.

Many of the drugs used were of plant origin and are still employed today. But some of the cures were absurd and revolting and used only by gullible patients.

A highly educated woman like Madame de Sévigné, for example, still believed at the end of the seventeenth century that the blood of a female adder purified and toned up the human organism.

The adder's blood, together with dozens of other ingredients, provided a very famous antidote which appears to have first been made up in the days of the Emperor Nero and used until modern times.

How the ancient Germans lived

The peoples who lived between the Rhine and the Danube were considered by the ancient Romans to be barbaric and were called Germans.

The Germans were of mixed Slavic and Teutonic origin. They were divided into numerous tribes, many of which were nomadic while others lived in squalid little villages. Most Germans lived by breeding animals such as sheep and cattle but they also looted and plundered. Their social system was rough and ready. There were three classes: the freemen warriors, the half-free and the serfs or slaves.

Tribal chiefs were elected by the warrior class. This class also declared war, ordered migrations, shared out booty. The Germans had no written laws or judges. Whoever had a wrong done to him had the right to personal revenge and the blood feuds which arose could be passed on from father to son. Disputes could also be settled by payment of an amount considered to be appropriate to the offence involved.

The religion of the ancient Germans was also primitive. They worshipped the forces of Nature. They had great respect for warriors and warlike deeds and force.

Our knowledge of the ancient Germans comes from Julius Caesar's *De Bello Gallico* (The Gallic War). Another extremely valuable source of information is *Germania*, a book published in A.D. 98 by the Roman historian Cornelius Tacitus.

Ancient coins were usually cast by hand around the time of Caesar, and many of these have since been found all over Europe

How the tombs of the pharaohs became known as pyramids

Much of our knowledge about the ancient Egyptians and their way of life comes to us from the ancient Greeks who travelled up the valley of the river Nile. The word 'pyramid' itself comes from Greek. The early Greek travellers saw that these royal tombs resembled in shape the cakes made of flour and honey which they presented to the winners of races in athletic events. These cakes were called *pyramis.*

How the Colossus of Rhodes was made

In about the year 312 B.C., King Ptolemy of Egypt was waging war against King Antigonus of Macedonia. The people of the island of Rhodes were fighting on the side of Ptolemy and were a loyal and brave ally on the sea. Antigonus decided to punish them. In 307 he dispatched against them his son

The pyramids of Giza

Demetrius at the head of a huge fleet which transported a large army.

The people of Rhodes defended themselves heroically for twelve months, but without any help from outside the island was doomed to fall. Ptolemy arrived in 300 to the rescue and forced Demetrius to withdraw. To commemorate the event the people of Rhodes built a huge statue near the entrance to their harbour and it became one of the seven wonders of the ancient world. The statue represented the god Apollo and was made of the metal from the weapons left behind by Demetrius.

The statue was built by the sculptor Chares of Lindus who worked on it for twelve years from 292 B.C. The statue was over 30 metres high. Its huge bronze legs were strengthened by masonry in the inside and people could climb to the top of the statue up a winding staircase inside.

At night the statue was lit and acted as a lighthouse for shipping. In 225 B.C. the Colossus was broken off at the knees in a severe quake and it was never rebuilt. When the Arabs attacked Rhodes in A.D. 653, they had the fallen Colossus broken up and the bronze sold for scrap. It was said that it took 900 camels to remove the debris.

How the ships of the adventurous Vikings looked

Excavations have made it possible for us to know how the Vikings built their ships. The fighting ships or longships were shallow, narrow in the beam and pointed at both ends. They had a single large, square sail, although they used oars as well, a high prow and a projecting stern. The figurehead of the ship of about A.D. 800, unearthed at Oseberg, was a coiled snake with its head upreared. Another Viking ship, found at Gokstad, dates from about A.D. 900.

Longships had about ten oars a side and seem to have carried twice as many men for fighting as for rowing, that would be a total of some sixty men.

The most famous of the longships was the 'big dragon' of King Canute, built in A.D. 1004. It looked like a huge sea serpent, with a dragon's head at the prow and a high-coiled tail at the stern.

The Viking *hafskip* had fewer rowers than the longship and was sometimes more than 21 metres long and 6 metres wide. On voyages of colonization it would carry wives, children, livestock, stores and as many as thirty men.

The naval power of the Vikings was greatly helped by their levy system which allowed them to call up men to form one of the greatest war fleets of their day.

How the ancient Egyptians practised their religion

The religion of the ancient Egyptians was inspired by nature and by the fertility caused by the flooding of the river Nile. The Sun, the wind and animals that helped man in his labours on the land were also objects of worship.

The chief god was Ra who represented the Sun. Ra was the protector of the pharaoh who was known as 'the son of Ra'. Another important divinity was Osiris. This god was killed, according to a legend, by his brother Set who was jealous of his popu-

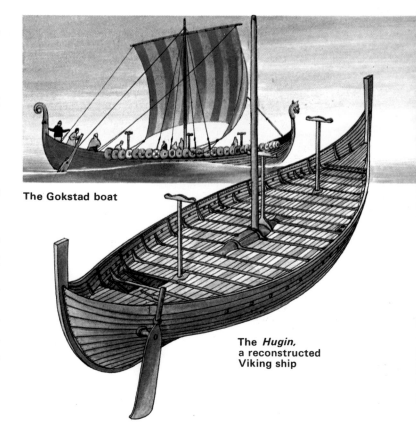

The Gokstad boat

The *Hugin,*
a reconstructed
Viking ship

The Oseberg ship, an
example of a Viking
longship

Ra as a scarab beetle on the ship supported by Nun. From the Anhai papyrus in the British Museum, about 1150 B.C.

scribes, had the head of an ibis or a baboon.

The Egyptians believed in an after-life in which man was rewarded or punished by Osiris. They thought the soul, Ka, could live on in the after-life if the body was embalmed.

larity among the people. Horus, son of Osiris and of the goddess Isis, avenged the death of his father who rose again and became the ruler of the dead.

The ancient Egyptians worshipped many gods who had the heads or even the whole body of animals: Anubis, the god of graveyards, had the head of a jackal; Apis was a bull which bore the Sun between its horns; Apopis was the wicked serpent, an enemy of Ra and a symbol of the clouds that tried to hide the face of the Sun. Bast was the mistress of love, of matters feminine and of fashion and had the head of a cat; Haket, the divinity that watched over births, had the head of a frog; Kheferi, the scarab god of springs, was represented as a beetle; Khenum, who had a ram's head, was the patron of potters because he was supposed to have fashioned the first man from clay; Mut the goddess was represented by a vulture; Sebek was the crocodile god; Selket was the scorpion goddess; and Thot, the god of

The cat-goddess Bast or Pasht

How the dead were embalmed in ancient Egypt

The word 'mummy' comes from an ancient Egyptian word meaning 'tar' or 'bitumen'. Egyptian embalmers used many products in their craft such as bees-wax, cassia (a type of cinnamon), juniper oil, onions, palm wine, resin, salt, sawdust, pitch, soda and bitumen to keep the corpses of the rich and the mighty from rotting.

The bodies were wrapped in linen bandages, clothed in funerary garments and adorned with necklaces and amulets. On the face of the deceased there was placed a mask made of rough canvas and chalk, but for dead pharaohs and high dignitaries this mask was made of gold. Poor people were mummified in any haphazard way and paupers were simply thrown without ceremony into a common grave.

The embalmed body of the deceased was buried together with objects which that person had used during his earthly life and which he might need in the next. Naturally, the graves of the dead reflected their social status during life. The tombs of the pharaohs were magnificent structures full of precious treasures and costly objects.

How bell-towers were first made

Bell-towers were first built to contain a bell to summon people to worship in the church or to ring the curfew or a danger signal. They were constructed in such a way that the sound of the bell ringing could be heard as far away as possible.

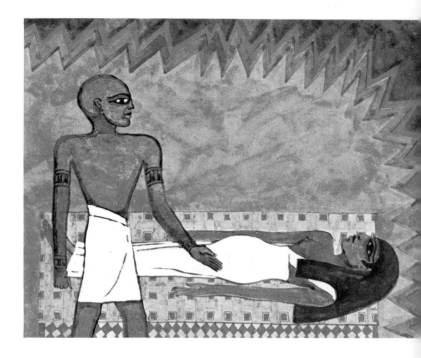

In the past, church bells used to mark all the main stages of the day such as dawn, dusk and the passage of the hours. Farmers working in the fields would regulate their lives to the sound of the church bells.

Bell-towers are usually tall structures. They can be round, square or many-sided. Gothic bell-towers, also known as steeples, have a long, sharply tapering top called a spire. The great spire of Salisbury Cathedral, built in 1250, is about 125 metres high.

In Italy, most bell-towers are square and are known as campaniles. The earliest are dated between the seventh and tenth centuries and are plain, round towers with a few small, round-arched openings grouped near the top. Round campaniles occasionally occurred in later periods, as in the famous leaning tower of Pisa (begun in 1174) which is a more elaborate version of this type.

How dress fashions were in the Middle Ages

The Middle Ages were a period of European history which occurred approximately between the fall of the western Roman Empire in A.D. 476 and the discovery of America in 1492.

During the first three centuries of the Middle Ages, the way people dressed underwent many changes. In the early stages they dressed in the Byzantine fashion: the emperor and the empress wore long tunics in brocade covered with a pallium, a sort of heavy square mantle that had a religious significance. Men let their beards grow and women never cut their hair.

During the Middle Ages, punishment for forgery was savage. Here, a forger is about to have his hand chopped off

When knights prepared for battle they put on a thick, woollen tunic over which they donned their coat of armour or chain mail. They had a broad belt or buckler round their waist from which hung a broad sword. The bandolier went on the right shoulder. On the head was worn an iron helmet, usually with a nose guard, and at the end of the twelfth century the great cylindrical helmet was introduced.

The soldier's dress was completed with a large convex shield on which the knight had his coat-of-arms painted or carved. These arms also decorated the linen surcoat which after about 1200 was worn over the mail shirt.

How women dressed in the sixteenth century

The centre of Europe's fashion for women in the sixteenth century was Italy. It was at this time that gloves became a standard item of dress for women and rich, ornate gloves developed, influenced by the taste of Queen Elizabeth of England. They began to be made in silk or soft leather and decorated with embroidery.

Jewellery was made by such great artists as Benvenuto Cellini. Women wore strings of pearls and ivory combs in their hair. Ladies in other countries impatiently awaited the latest news of the Italian fashions. There were no fashion magazines in those days and models of dresses were shown on dolls.

One of the great fashion designers of this period was Isabella d'Este, Marquise of Mantua. She built her models with the help of famous painters, and the great Leonardo da Vinci is supposed to have given her some ideas. All this luxury was for the nobility and the wealthy, but even the ordinary people dressed smartly enough and the women made themselves up and had their hair styled.

How people dressed during the Renaissance

Dressed in damask and silks, the men of the Renaissance preferred bright colours and often wore costumes of several hues. Towards the end of the fifteenth century, the coat or jacket became shorter and the hose or leggings were elongated. During the sixteenth century men wore a short belted jerkin over a type of skirt.

The novelty for women was the two-piece dress, consisting of bodice and skirt. The skirts were long and wide, edged with ribbon, embroidery or fur.

Wealth was displayed by exaggeration in clothes. Sleeves, sometimes detachable became wider and were often puffed and slashed. The ruff became the most striking feature of both men and women's costume in the second half of the sixteenth century. It was a frill of folded linen worn round the neck and as time passed the ruff grew larger and larger.

During the 1500s women began to wear farthingales. These were underskirts or petticoats made of a stiff material fitted with a hoop round the bottom. They were worn underneath the outer skirt and gave it a wide bell-shape.

How people travelled in coaches

The coach became a widely used form of transport during the eighteenth century when travel was a craze for those who could afford it. They wanted to see new countries and people and were prepared to cover long distances.

Kings, noblemen and the rich had their own personal coaches which were always elegant and comfortable. Their suspension was based on leather straps and later steel springs were introduced which were stronger and more comfortable. Another improvement was the introduction of

This Italian Renaissance interior has a fine chimneypiece with heraldic decoration. Some of the furniture has characteristics of earlier styles, such as Gothic

69

Coach pulled by Cleveland bay horses

How the mysterious Etruscans lived

The Etruscans are the most interesting and the most mysterious of the peoples who lived in Italy before Rome became a mighty empire. They may have come to Italy in about 1000 B.C. from some far region and settled in what is now Tuscany. From there their influence went out to neighbouring regions.

The Etruscan men usually had short beards that came to a point. They wore short, tight-fitting jackets and over these a *tebennus*, a type of cloak that was always brightly coloured and was the precursor of the Roman toga. They had pointed shoes and their caps, known as *tutuli*, were also pointed.

Etruscan women, who were elegant and refined, also wore pointed shoes and caps and long narrow skirts under a pleated mantle. They loved to wear sparkling jewels, earrings, pins, bracelets and pendants of various kinds, often of great beauty and exquisite workmanship, and to comb their hair into various styles.

Etruscan women did not live apart like the women of ancient Greece or, to a lesser extent, of Rome. They took part in gymnastic events and attended banquets.

The guests at an Etruscan banquet were often entertained by musicians playing on flutes and lyres.

The way of life of these people appears to have been happy and carefree. We can tell this from the wall paintings and friezes they left on their tombs and from their sculpture. But we know nothing about the life of the simple Etruscan people who must have worked hard.

windows so that the travellers could see and be seen.

These old coaches seemed to have room for everything. Apart from the passengers there was the baggage, their food, crockery and even a library of books to read on the journey. During the eighteenth and nineteenth centuries a large variety of coaches were built, some had two wheels, others had four. One of the best known was the landau. This was a large, open carriage with four wheels and special seats for footmen and it had hoods which opened in the middle of the body and folded back to either end. The landau was used mainly to travel through the city or on short journeys. It was named after the German city of Landau where it was first made.

People who could not afford the luxury of a carriage of their own travelled with the postal services on coaches called diligences. These were public vehicles that could carry several passengers and ran on regular routes.

How the Etruscans practised their religion

The Etruscans were a very religious people. Their chief gods were Tinia, Uni, Minrva, the trio worshipped by the ancient Romans later under the names of

Two warriors: from an Etruscan wall painting

Jove, Juno and Minerva. Only some of the Etruscan gods had the power to launch thunderbolts. Tinia was one of the more powerful of the divinities.

Religious ceremonies were conducted by priests who formed a very powerful class in Etruscan society. These priests were the only persons permitted to divine or guess the will of the gods and to tell the future. They did this in various ways: by examining the entrails of sacrificed animals; by bird watching; by observing lightning and other weather phenomena; and the ebbing and flowing of streams.

Of all the entrails the liver was studied with the greatest care. A bronze model of a liver found at the city of Piacenza is divided into forty-five areas, each with the name of a presiding deity written in it. The priests who studied birds traced the will of the gods from the way birds flew, cried and ate. The signs seen by these priests were known as auguries which

Apollo of Veii

could be either good or bad.

The Etruscan religion comprised a complicated set of beliefs and ceremonies for every act in public life. The laws relating to the foundation of a city were particularly strict.

The Etruscans believed, especially in their early days, that when they died they passed on to another life similar to the one in this world. They provided the dead with many objects of everyday life and the statues on their tombs depict people sitting at table with guests or playing music, singing or even hunting.

How the Etruscans wrote

The origins of the Etruscan language are wrapped in mystery. The Etruscans have left thousands of examples of their writings but most of them are brief inscriptions on their tombs. There have been a few other texts found which were longer and were probably prayers. One of these was discovered on the wrappings of a mummy found in Egypt.

These writings do not tell us very much. The alphabet is similar to the Greek one but the meaning of most of the words is hidden. The main difficulty is that Etruscan does not resemble any other language known to us.

A few words are known: *ati* meant 'mother', *clan* meant 'son', *lautn* meant 'family', *thura* meant 'brother', *sech* meant 'daughter' and *nefts* meant 'nephew'. Other meanings, though not known for certain, were *avil* (year), *mestrev* (magistrate), *spur* (city), *tinsi* (days), *tiv* (moon) and *usil* (sun).

How King Hammurabi became famous

King Hammurabi, ruler of Babylonia, is remembered in many documents as a great lawmaker and warrior. He reigned for some forty years, from about 1792 to 1750 B.C., and made his capital into a city of great splendour.

By using both force and diplomacy Hammurabi extended his rule gradually over all Mesopotamia. His code of laws was a great achievement and gives us an insight into how justice was administered in Assyria and Babylonia.

Hammurabi was also a great soldier and a ruthless leader with a fiery temperament. He loved war but as soon as he had unified his realm he devoted himself to peaceful pursuits and brought great wealth to the nation. His court was frequented by artists, scholars and philosophers. Babylonia became a land of beautiful palaces and buildings such as the temple to the god Marduk which Hammurabi had constructed.

Bas-relief dating from 600 B.C. showing an Assyrian king on horseback

72

How justice was administered in Babylonia

We know exactly all the 282 laws in which King Hammurabi included the entire legal traditions of his day because they were found on a stele (stone slab) discovered at Susa in 1901 and now preserved in the Louvre Museum in Paris. The laws were written on the slab in a writing known as cuneiform. The slab also has a fine piece of sculpture depicting Samas, the god of justice, looking into the eyes of King Hammurabi as if to inspire him.

Babylonian society was divided into three distinct classes: the patricians, the plebeians, and the slaves. Justice depended on the class to which a person belonged. For example, an article in Hammurabi's legal code said: 'If a patrician takes the eye of another patrician, one of his eyes also shall be taken. If he breaks the bone of another patrician, one of his bones too shall be broken.'

If, however, the person hurt was a plebeian, matters were different. The law said: 'If a patrician takes the eye or breaks a bone of a plebeian, he will pay a mine of silver.' Of course, the penalty was smaller if a slave was involved.

These laws seem very unfair to us today but the penalties inflicted are midway between the brutality of the Assyrian laws and the comparative leniency of the Hittites. We must remember that in the social conditions of Hammurabi's day such laws were needed to curb the vices and passions of the Babylonians.

Hammurabi died but his dynasty, or family, continued to rule for another 150 years although it never reached the same peak of glory as it had in his day.

How the people of Assyria and Babylonia wrote

The people of Mesopotamia, that is the Sumerians, Babylonians and Assyrians, created a system of writing that was quite different from that used in Egypt. The difference was because the people of Mesopotamia used clay to write on instead of papyrus as in Egypt.

It is difficult to make curved lines on clay with a stylus so the Mesopotamians invented a handwriting based on straight lines that resembled nails or wedges. For this reason, their handwriting was known as 'cuneiform', a word meaning 'wedge-shaped'. Cuneiform was later used on other materials, such as stone or metal. This writing was ideographic, as in Egypt, and used pictures instead of words.

How the Carthaginians practised trade

The Carthaginians had the reputation of being dishonest and thieving but this does not seem to be borne out by accounts written by Herodotus, the ancient historian. According to him, the Carthaginians would leave their goods on the seashore along the coast of Africa and would then retire to their ships and wait until the natives came along to inspect the goods. The natives looked at the goods and left a quantity of gold behind. The Carthaginians would then gather up the gold and value it. If they did not think it was enough, they would leave it there and withdraw again. Then the natives would come back and add more gold. If this was enough the Carthaginians would take it away and leave the goods behind.

THE HOW OF MAN

How the American Indians came to know the horse

The Indians who lived in North America had been hunters since time immemorial. They were used to wandering across the vast prairies in pursuit of wild animals. But these Indians only became really nomadic after the coming of the Europeans.

We have often seen on western films how the Indians galloped along bareback on their horses, so it is quite surprising to learn that before the Europeans came in the fifteenth century, no horses had existed in the New World. The horse revolutionized the life of the Indians and changed their ways greatly.

Horses were brought to America by the Spanish conquerors and settlers. Some of these animals escaped and began to breed in the wild, multiplying into the numerous herds of the prairies and pampas. Soon there were tens of thousands of them throughout the continent. The Indians caught and tamed them and then learned to ride them. It was then that life changed for the Indians. This horse, known as the mustang, brought enormous advantages: the Indian tribes could now move more easily from place to place and hunting became more effective and profitable.

How the Indians sent smoke signals

The American Indians used to pass on news from one tribe to another over great distances by using smoke clouds. This system was developed as a result of the vastness of the prairie, the flatness of which also helped to make the smoke visible from far off. There was a code of signals which consisted of a combination of long and short puffs of smoke. But smoke clouds were not the only means of communication among the American Indians. Sometimes they used lights flashed from mirrors reflecting the Sun. The Indians also had a system of writing using ideographs or pictures that resembled the ancient Egyptian hieroglyphs.

Victorio, an Apache Indian chief who sowed terror in the south-west around 1880

Sound did not play a major part in the Indian system of communication as it did in the tom-tom system of drumming in Africa. The Indians, however, imitated animal sounds at night to recognize friend from foe.

How the wandering Indians lived

The typical dwelling of the American Indian was the tepee. This was a cone-shaped tent usually made of animal skins stretched over a strong wooden framework based on a three- or four-pole foundation supporting other poles. A hole was left at the top of the tepee to let the smoke out. During the summer hunt tepees were pitched in a large circle, each family in its allotted place.

Another type of Indian house was the wigwam, a kind of domed hut with a frame of flexible poles covered in skins, mats or bark, which was not as comfortable as a tepee and was usually erected in the hunting grounds. The shape of the wigwam varied according to the region.

The tents and the implements of the Indians were made in such a way that they could be carried from place to place easily as the tribe went on its wanderings.

How the Indians spent the winter

The winter was by far the worst time of the year for the Indians. During this season food often became scarce, especially the herds of bison that wandered in the prairies in summer.

Many tribes would therefore split up and each section would go off on its own. Indians usually spent the winter near forests and rivers: the forests supplied firewood and the rivers, some of which were frozen, contained plenty of fish which was an easy food to catch.

The Indians were very skilful at catching large fish even with their bows and arrows. They could often catch and dry enough fish to last from one season to the next, and if not, some species of salmon could be caught at most times of the year. They preserved much of their meat by smoking it in the same way as bacon, but these smoked supplies often ran out before the end of the winter and then fish became valuable.

In winter the Indians also hunted small game animals. A variety of nooses, snares, traps and pitfalls were used and the peculiarities of the animal to be caught were carefully studied.

Indians used their bows and arrows to catch fish

Pre-Columbian peoples

How Pueblo villages are built

In the more remote and isolated valleys of the Rocky Mountains, in the south-west of the United States and in northern Mexico live the last descendants of the Pueblo Indians. The Pueblos are a peaceful but proud people, devoted to farming and the crafts, especially pottery and weaving. Their civili-

zation reached its greatest peak in about the thirteenth century.

The Pueblo Indians are called after their villages (*pueblo* is the Spanish word for town). In about 1300 they moved south in search of more secure farmlands along the Rio Grande. They built their villages and created the way of life they had lived previously.

The Pueblo villages were built in two different positions: the first type was carved out of the rock of mountain-sides; the second was built in the valley, shaped as a semi-circular citadel or fortress. The cliff dwellings were the more impressive, built as they were out of the solid mountain rock. They often had three or four storeys built in stepped-back fashion so that the roofs of the lower rooms served as verandahs for the rooms above. They were communal buildings, usually quite small, consisting of between one and fifteen domestic rooms, with one or two ceremonial rooms. The lower inner rooms were used mainly for storing crops, while the upper rooms were for sleeping and living and also for the grinding of corn. They were reached by ladders or, occasionally, by staircases. The Indians built their villages in such remote places, which were uncomfortable and often far from water, for defensive reasons.

The Pueblo villages built in the valleys were more like the towns and villages we live in today.

How the Mexican Indians obtained alcoholic drinks

The Yuma, Pima and Papago were tribes of American Indians who lived mainly by farming, growing maize, beans and a kind of gourd called squash. They were so skilful at their work that they had learned to irrigate their fields during the dry season and since A.D. 1 had used flood water for this purpose. Their society was based on the clan system.

One of their main feasts was the annual ceremony celebrating the ripening of the giant cactus (saguaro) and the coming of the summer rains. During this feast the people drank a beverage made from the fermented juice of cactus fruit. The beverage was very potent and those who drank it soon became intoxicated.

The saguaro ceremony had a magical significance, the beverage representing rain soaked in the soil.

How women were treated in Pueblo society

The Pueblo Indians lived in a matriarchal society which meant that the woman was honoured and was the true ruler. The clans, or family groups, were based on descent through the mother and not through the father. Property therefore belonged to the women and when they died they left it to their daughters. The farmland was also the undisputed property of the women.

When a man married he went to live in his wife's house. If his wife had no home, the husband had to build her one.

This structure of society, however, did not mean that men were the victims of the whims of the women and that they had no rights of their own. They were respected for their working skills and also for their contribution to the wealth of the whole Pueblo community.

How the Pueblos obtained water

Pueblos lived in arid regions and water was one of the most precious of their commodities. The Pueblos regarded rainfall as a sign of benevolence on the part of the gods. When it rained, the people in the villages, especially the children, would roll around in the muddy puddles in sheer joy. Villages usually had a large hollow scooped out in the rock or in the ground to hold water for as long as possible. The strictest of the Pueblo laws were those that governed the use of water during the dry season. When water supplies ran out the men of the village travelled to distant springs to obtain new supplies. Even the dew that appeared on plants during the night was gathered.

Drought in these regions could be very prolonged. Examination of tree rings has shown that one such period existed from 1276 to 1299.

How the Polynesians drive away ghosts

The Polynesians believe that the souls of the dead, before they find their way to paradise, wander to and fro playing unpleasant tricks on the living. In spite of the teachings of Christianity the Polynesians are very much afraid of the *tupapau*, as they call these ghosts, and believe that they heavily out-number the living people.

For this reason few Polynesians will go out alone at night, even with a lantern, and no Polynesian will sleep without a light by his bed. Throughout the islands of Polynesia there are specially furnished houses for the ghosts to meet.

According to the Polynesians most of the ghosts simply make a lot of noise by chattering away to one another. Some *tupapau*, however, are thought to be dangerous. These ghosts can cause illnesses and assume the strangest of shapes. The Polynesians believe they are protected from the *tupapau* by spirits called *varua-ino*. These spirits are evil and they come to life whenever a comet is seen in the skies. At such times the *varua-ino*, who are the sworn enemies of the *tupapau*, attack and destroy the ghosts.

Polynesians have learned to live with these ghosts and to keep them at bay by flailing the air with a bamboo pole from time to time and by calling the name of a *varua-ino* to come to their aid. This is enough to drive any mischievous ghost away.

How the Polynesians practise their religion

In Tonga, one of the island groups of Polynesia, there is a legend which has a striking similarity to the story of Cain and Abel in the Bible. Tangaroa, the fisherman-god, one day threw his fishing line badly and his hook caught the ocean bed. Tangaroa pulled and tugged with all his might and main and brought to the surface a number of islands which included Tonga.

The islands were deserted and the god felt lonely so he said to his sons: 'Take your wives and make your home in Tonga.' The two sons obeyed their father and

Ornamental mask from the Caroline Islands

Maori sculpture

A wood carving done by the head-hunters of New Guinea

Polynesian sculpture from Rarotonga

Easter Island sculpture

shared out the island between them. Yaka-Ako-Ouli, the younger brother, was a hard working man who knew how to make axes and necklaces. Tubo, the elder brother, was an idler. He was filled with envy against his brother and one day he killed him.

Tangaroa immediately cursed Tubo and all his children. He summoned the family of the dead man and told them: 'Sail out to sea in your canoes and go to the islands in the east. Your skin will be as white as your soul but the children of Tubo will have a black skin.'

So, according to the Polynesians, Tangaroa populated the islands of the Pacific and much of the world with both good and bad people.

How the Polynesians build their huts

In Polynesia the construction of a house is accompanied by a ceremony that combines politics with religion. The building contract has to be drawn up with the *tafugas*, a guild of skilled craftsmen regarded as the guardians of the art of the god Tangaroa.

Once the contract has been agreed the whole village celebrates the erection of the main pole. This part of the house symbolizes the link between the world of mankind and that of the gods. The rafters of the house are fixed to the main pole and to the poles that form the outer sections of the house. The dome-shaped roof is then placed on this framework.

Polynesians use no precision instruments and do all the building by eye. Their accuracy is amazing. Every house has an individual design reflecting the *tafugas* who built it. When the house is finished the *tafugas* puts his own special mark on the timber and the end of the job is celebrated by feasting.

How the Polynesians cook their native dishes

Taro is a staple food of Polynesia. It has been extensively cultivated for its large, spherical, underground tubers, rich in starch. It grows on open hillsides and when harvest time comes the various family clans leave the villages early in the morning, carrying baskets and knives. The villagers split up into groups. The men do the heavy work, such as pulling the taro out of the ground and lopping off its root and putting it into the baskets. Some of the stems of the plants are specially chosen and re-planted for future crops. The women cut the grass and leave it laid out to dry and become fertilizer for the soil.

During important feasts the job

Above: Commodore Perry
Left: a Japanese print showing 'the black ships'

of cooking is left to the men of the tribe. The men prepare the ovens which consist of flat stones heated until they are red-hot. The food is cooked on these hot stones according to a traditional order of the menu: suckling pigs, vegetables, fish, turtles and breadfruit cut into four. The most expert of the cooks prepare the *poi,* a thin paste of taro starch wrapped in banana leaves. All the food is wrapped in leaves, served in wooden bowls or platters and eaten with the fingers.

The whole oven is covered in leaves and matting to keep the heat in.

How Japan became a modern country

Until July 1853 Japan had been a land closed to all contacts with the West. No ports were open to Western ships, missionaries who tried to convert the people to Christianity were killed and all forms of Western culture were banned. But time did not stand still outside Japan. The early steamships that sailed across the Pacific Ocean needed places where they could replenish their fuel supplies and Japan was the ideal place for this. Despite much pressure from Western countries, however, Japan still remained closed to all their shipping.

The United States government then decided to send a squadron of naval ships under the command of Commodore Matthew C. Perry. Perry was told to persuade the Japanese to sign a treaty opening up some Japanese ports to Western ships. With two frigates and two sailing vessels he entered the fortified harbour of Uraga on 8 July 1853. He refused to obey Japanese orders to leave and demanded that a suitable person be sent to receive the documents he had brought. The Japanese finally complied.

Perry made a great impression on the Japanese dignitaries by his firm and dignified bearing. He returned with a larger force the following year and on 31 March 1854 the first treaty between the

United States and Japan was signed.

By this treaty shipwrecked seamen were promised better treatment and American ships were able to obtain fuel and supplies at two Japanese ports. Japan's traditional policy of isolation was broken and from that moment it established contact with the West. It was destined to become the leading country in the Far East and one of the world's great powers. Only some fifty years later it subjected the Russian fleet to a crushing defeat.

How Papuan canoes are built

In Papua and the surrounding islands the people still use a sea-going craft which is made of three or more canoes joined together by strong pieces of timber. The individual boats form a single vessel on which a strong bamboo deck is placed. There are two masts in the middle, very close to each other, and from these are hoisted rather strange looking sails that resemble the claws of a lobster.

The double canoe of Hawaii and the Tongan *calie* are examples of a twin-boomed craft. The Hawaian craft was first developed in the south seas and consists of two canoes of the same length. The canoes are joined together by curved pieces of timber which also support the single sail.

The Tongan *calie* is more complicated and interesting. The *calie* consists of two canoes of different length joined together by thick timber that supports a platform or deck. Apart from the main mast this deck also carries a sort of cabin large enough to take several persons. The *calie* was used both for fishing and carrying goods and passengers.

How bamboo wood is used

In the countries where bamboo grows this wood is used in an incredible number of ways as it is cheap and plentiful. Bamboo stems are used to build bridges, houses, boats, irrigation pipes and receptacles of all kinds. One of the best known uses of bamboo in its flexible state is in fishing rods. This wood is also used to make garden furniture because it is light and strong and stands up to the weather. The shoots of the bamboo are also delicious to eat.

Bamboo belongs to the gramineous family of plants, which means it is a sort of grass. It has a rhizome, or root part, which grows from year to year and produces new stalks. Sometimes these stalks are enormous, growing to more than 30 metres high.

The stalks are hollow and jointed, with knots from which branches grow. These branches become covered in leaves and the bamboo resembles a tree. Most bamboos flower very rarely and are thornless, but a few kinds have sharp spines.

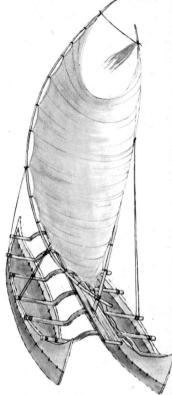

Hawaian double canoe

Japanese bamboo eel-trap

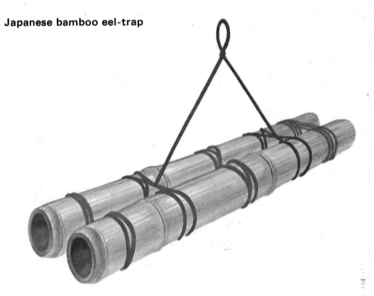

Man wearing a *burnus*

Kabylia

Tuareg

Berber nomad

Algerian costumes

How the Tuareg dress

The picturesque dress of the Tuareg people is also extremely functional because their voluminous clothes offer the best protection against the scorching heat of the desert Sun. The Tuareg wear two tunics made of light wool over trousers which are very broad and fastened round the ankles. These trousers give the Tuareg greater freedom of movement when they are riding. They also wear a broad leather belt designed to regulate the breathing during camel races.

The most important feature of the dress of these nomadic people is a band of dark-blue cloth slightly more than 3 metres long, which is light and looks like a veil. It is worn round the face as a mask, covering the mouth and nose, with a slit left for the eyes, and prevents sand and dust from harming the breathing passages.

The colour of this veil and of the clothes is not accidental. The blue offers protection against the rays of the Sun. To avoid bad sunburn the Tuareg keep rubbing their blue veils on any exposed skin. The blue dye stains the skin and that is why these nomads are also known as 'the blue people'.

How Bedouin tents are made

The wandering Bedouin who live in the Arabian peninsula live in black tents which are usually about 10 metres long and 4 metres wide. These tents consist of several strips of cloth sewn together which can be added to or reduced according to the needs of the family. The tent is pitched on three parallel lines of poles. Usually, one side is left open and it is always anchored firmly enough with taut ropes to stand up to the fiercest winds.

The material for the tent is thick and hard-wearing. It is woven by the women on rough looms from goat and camel hair.

Inside the tent the women's compartment is often divided off

by a shoulder-high screen. The side nearer the entrance is reserved for the men and for receiving guests. The part occupied by the head of the family has a fireplace and everything necessary for the ceremony of making and drinking coffee.

The furniture consists of cushions, rugs and leather pouffes. The most important item is a copper tray on a folding wooden table which is sometimes elaborately carved and decorated with inlaid ivory.

How dromedaries behave in the desert

The dromedary is the most precious piece of property that the desert nomad has but it is not an easy animal to handle. It never becomes friends with its masters or anybody else Every night, these animals have to be forced down to their knees on the ground and tethered firmly.

The dromedary is extremely strong. With one heave it can throw off all its load and gallop madly off, sweeping everything aside that lies in its path. To lead them the nomads use long reins tied to an iron ring driven through the right nostril of the animal.

Camels can flourish on thorny plants, leaves, twigs and dried grasses that other animals would refuse. When the feeding is good, they accumulate stores of fat in their humps which, in emergencies, they can use for sustenance and for the manufacture of water. They are thus able to fast and go without water for several days.

There is one variety of dromedary known as the *mehari* which is extremely swift and the Tuareg tribesmen often owe their lives to the speed of this light-coloured camel. All dromedaries are fast and they are used whenever a journey is a matter of life and death, when a well has to be reached before the water runs out or when an important prey has to be caught.

A nomad can carry in the roomy saddlebag of his *mehari* everything he needs for his lonely desert life: food, clothing, tobacco, salt and the leather containers for butter and tea.

Every Tuareg tribe owns large herds of these camels. The young animals graze by themselves near the camp. When the mothers come together to feed them with their milk, the camels are milked by the tribe's servants. Camel's milk is rich and frothy and is best drunk immediately because it curdles easily and clots if it is heated. The Tuareg drink considerable quantities of this milk.

Lapp costumes

How the Lapps protect themselves from the cold weather

The diet of the Lapp people is not very varied but it is rich in calories and helps these nomads to stand up to the rigours of their difficult climate.

Lapland is a region of northern Europe stretching across the north of Norway, Sweden, Finland and Russia from the Norwegian coast to the White Sea. The climate is dominated by winter: in some places, the Sun does not rise for six or seven weeks in winter, but stays continually in the sky for a corresponding period in summer. Rivers freeze in November and thaw in May, and snow depths vary greatly.

The staple food is reindeer meat and fish eaten fresh during the summer and dried or smoked in winter. The Lapps cook their food on fires lit by the women every day in the centre of the tent beneath a hole which acts as a chimney. Once the meal is over the fire is covered very carefully and the women wash the dishes and the dogs eat the left-overs. Lapps keep their tent-homes scrupulously clean.

Apart from their household tasks the women also make the leather clothing which Lapps wear summer and winter alike. In winter Lapps wear trousers made of reindeer-skin with the furry side turned inwards. In summer they discard these clothes for lighter ones in leather or rough cloth.

Lapps walk a great deal and shoes are an extremely important part of their dress. They wear soft boots, stuffed with grass which is changed frequently.

The holiday costume is covered in hand-embroidery and decorated with shawls, hoods and, for the men, with a cap the shape of which indicates to which tribe he belongs.

How reindeer migrate

In spring the Lapps leave behind the woodlands of the south where they spend the winter and set out for the pastures in the northern mountains. The Lapps move in small family groups, leading their herd of reindeer along established tracks which usually follow the courses of rivers. The rivers are still frozen and the Lapps use them as safe roads for their sledges, laden with provisions. The reindeer are used to following the same route and move along slowly, feeding as they travel.

Half-way through the journey, when spring breaks, the Lapps pitch their tents for a period lasting several weeks. It is at this time that the baby reindeer are born and the tribe has to wait until they are able to walk by themselves. The young reindeer do not take long to learn how to trot about and the herd moves on once more. The destination is the far north where the tundra, the 'cold desert' of northern Norway, Sweden, Finland and Iceland, ends and the Arctic Ocean begins. The reindeer herd spends the short summer on the grassy shores and on the islets along the coast before travelling south once more.

Lapps consume large quantities of reindeer milk and use it to make delicious cheese. When the icy north wind blows and the family is gathered together in the tent, the mother prepares a hot drink by dissolving chunks of reindeer cheese in hot water. This drink provides a great deal of energy and warmth.

Lapps have hunted reindeer since the earliest times and have kept small numbers, but breeding them in large herds is comparatively recent.

Costumes of certain countries of the Asian part of the Soviet Union

Siberia

Uzbekistan

Kirghizia

How the Kurds live in their encampments

The Kurds were once pure nomads, driving their flocks between the Mesopotamian plains and the highlands of Turkey and Iran, but today they prefer to live in one place for considerable periods.

A Kurd encampment, known as a *kissla*, usually consists of four or five tents. The tents are made of

85

goatskin sewn together and held up by wooden poles. The site of the encampment is chosen by the sheikh or leader. Life in the encampments follows the rhythm of the daily tasks connected with the breeding of sheep and cattle.

The men come out of their tents early in the morning to take the animals to the grazing grounds which are located in nearby hollows. The animals are left there until the evening. During the day the men make leather goods which they sell to local markets. The women weave carpets with which to decorate their homes and cloth for their own use.

The main duty of the women is to milk the animals. From the milk they make, cheese, butter and yoghourt which, mixed with water, produces *ayran*, their main drink.

An Inca road in Peru with the Andes in the distance

How the Indians use llamas

The typical beast of burden in the Andes region of South America is the llama. These animals are mostly bred by the Indians for their milk and their thick wool. Usually white, the animals can vary in colour to solid black, with any combination of brown or black spots.

The llama is a stolid and tough animal, able to endure thirst and to exist on a wide variety of vegetation. It is often used to carry loads up steep mountain paths and in places where there are no roads, travelling slowly but safely even in the most difficult and dangerous places. It can carry a load of about 60 kilogrammes for about five days on end without resting. When overloaded or exhausted, however, it lies down, hisses, spits and kicks, refusing to move until relieved of some weight or adequately rested. Only the male llamas are used as beasts of burden. The females are kept in the grazing grounds, and although they do not yield very much milk the Indians put it to a number of uses. Llamas are also bred for their meat which resembles pork.

How the floating gardens of Lake Titicaca are made

The shores of Lake Titicaca which is situated amid the Andes mountains 3,812 metres above sea-level, are covered in vast stretches of reed beds. These plants provide the Indians with the raw material to build their boats and their floating gardens. These gardens are large rafts, rectangular in shape and made of reeds tied together. A layer of soil is placed on the rafts, furrowed according to an ancient tradition and then planted with vegetables. The result is a floating garden. The raft is then towed to a sheltered part of the lake shore where the vegetables can grow. The lake is very deep (about 370 metres) and so the water temperature remains quite constant. Due to the great altitude the plants do not grow as well as they would lower down.

Every so often these rafts are towed back to the shore, laden with ripe crops which are gathered and shared out by the Indian families.

The Indians also cultivate the area surrounding Lake Titicaca, planting potatoes, quinoa, barley and maize on terraced fields around the shores.

How *curare* is prepared in the forests of the Amazon

In the dense jungles of the river Amazon the Indians can immediately recognize the plants that contain the deadly poison known as *curare* which can kill within a few minutes.

The process of preparing this poison is one of the most sacred traditions of the tribe and carefully passed on from warrior to warrior. The Indians use a special knife to scrape the bark of certain trees. They then put a large pot on the fire and when the water comes to the boil they put in the bark scrapings. The water evaporates slowly until there remains a thick, dark and gummy paste, smelling like tar. This is the poison. Before it cools, the hunters dip their arrows in it and pour the rest into small flasks which they carry from their belts. Once the *curare* has dried it becomes extremely hard and has to be diluted.

How marriages in Kashmir were arranged

Kashmir is a large territory situated between Pakistan and India. It is rich in beautiful and picturesque valleys and high mountains. The inhabitants of this region are usually sturdy and robust. They have fine features with expressive and intelligent faces. The women of Kashmir are renowned for their beauty. They have a very sweet, and yet very wilful, character.

The Kashmiris had a particular custom regarding marriage. The young man could not obtain the hand of his beloved without first 'earning' or 'deserving' her. He did this by working in the house of his future father-in-law. The poorer the young man was, the longer he had to work and quite often this service could last for several years.

Amazonian peoples

Mboyes

Charrua

Guarani

How edible birds' nests are gathered

The birds' nests which the Chinese use as an ingredient to make their famous birds' nest soup are built by a swift belonging to the group of birds known as *Collocalia*. This bird closely resembles the swallows of Europe.

Gathering birds' nests

These swifts are great fliers. They make their home on steep cliffs that rise out of the sea in the islands of eastern Asia. The birds build their nests among these rocks and two or three times a year the nests are gathered to be sold in Chinese markets.

The work of gathering these nests is quite dangerous because very steep cliffs have to be scaled to reach them. Once a colony of nests has been reached they can be removed quite easily. The shelf-like nests are made of the saliva of the birds, which goes hard rapidly. It is this saliva, softened by soaking and then cooking, that is used in making the delicious soups.

How the people of Formosa lived

Formosa, known in Chinese as Taiwan, is the largest of the Chinese islands. It is separated from the mainland by a stretch of water called the Formosa Strait. The oval-shaped island has an area of 35,834 square kilometres. The sixty-six small islands that lie scattered about Formosa are not much more than rocks in the ocean. Their combined area is only about 127 square kilometres.

Far inland, in the mountains of Formosa (now Taiwan), lived a tribe of aborigine people descended from the first inhabitants of the island before the Chinese came. These tribes, numbering about 200,000, refused to have any contact with modern civilization. They had a reputation for being fierce, and some of them were thought to be cannibals. The aborigines often fought among themselves, but their battles were more part of a religious attitude than a display of hatred for one another.

Before they went into battle they used to free a bird, which showed by the direction of its flight where the warriors had to go. This ceremony showed that there was no hatred for any particular enemy, and the custom of fighting, regrettable as it may have been, was pure ritual. It was through fighting that one group of aborigines asserted its right to live rather than another.

In this sense the ritual had a social significance as well as a religious one. Every member of the village took part in the campaign against the enemy.

How the legend explains the origin of the Veddas of Sri Lanka

In some of the mountain regions of the centre and the east of Sri Lanka (formerly Ceylon), amid dense forests that make life difficult, lives a very ancient people who have found shelter in this wild region and continued their old way of life: the Veddas.

The way of life of the Veddas is thousands of years old. Little is known about their origin, but there is a verse chronicle written by Buddhist monks that tells part of the story. The chronicle is called the *Mahavamsa* ('Great History'). It relates that the first king of Sri Lanka was called Vijaya. The origins of this king are buried in legend but his existence is more or less certain. One story says he was the child of a princess and a lion. Vijaya's first wife ran away with the children to the mountains, and the Veddas were the descendants of those refugees.

This legend may be pure fantasy, but one theory is that the Veddas are a people who fled from the Aryans who invaded northern India in about 2000 B.C. and took refuge in the territory where they now live.

Today the Veddas have been largely absorbed into the population of Sri Lanka and have adopted its language. In 1911 they were reported to number about 5,300, but in 1964 the government of Sri Lanka listed their population at about 800.

Costumes of Sri Lanka

89

THE HOW OF DOMESTIC ANIMALS

How to bring up a little bird that has fallen from its nest

Quite often in spring newly born birds fall from the nest and lie helplessly on the ground. What can we do to aid these poor little creatures?

First of all they need a warm nest. A small box or basket stuffed with woollen rags is perfect for this. If the little bird is only a few days old it will have to be kept warm. This can be done by keeping a 25-watt bulb alight over the box. The bulb should be shaded so that the light does not distress the bird. The box is best kept in a quiet corner, preferably in sub-dued light, and away from draughts and gas fumes. It must be placed well out of the reach of domestic pets.

The biggest problem is how to feed the fledgling. If it gets the wrong food it will die. A young bird also has to have certain quantities of food given to it at certain intervals. In normal conditions nestlings are fed about every ten minutes by their parents. If they go for more than one hour without food they begin to be ill.

As to the kind of food, birds normally eat insects, grubs and worms. They enjoy maggots but they will also take flies. Use a pair of tweezers with rounded ends to feed the bird.

How to stop kittens from scratching the furniture

It is quite easy to stop kittens from scratching the walls or the furniture. They do this for exercise and to sharpen their claws, rather as we file our nails. The cat has to keep trimming its nails or they become too long and that is why it scratches wooden objects such as the furniture, trees and wooden fences.

Many cats are given special scratching posts, a block of wood or an old box. They soon learn to sharpen their claws on these and to leave the furniture unmolested.

How to wean kittens

To wean kittens away from their mother's milk, add the beaten yolk of an egg to some milk or a few spoonfuls of broth which is not too salty, and some honey or sugar. Another method is to use boiled rice and put it in the kitten's milk or broth with some grated cheese. Minced raw beef, liver or boiled fish can be given later on. By the time that it is one month old the kitten should be able to eat any food suitable for the cat family. It should be fed three times a day up to two months of age, then twice a day to four months, then once a day.

How to bring up a guinea pig

The cavy or guinea pig is one of the most charming household pets. If you want to make friends with one of these little animals always approach its cage with gentle gestures and avoid all sudden movements. If you pick one up hold it in the way shown in the illustration.

Give the guinea pig plenty of fresh vegetables, but make sure you remove all the leftovers in case they go bad for it is important that the bottom of the cage is clean.

The guinea pig loves maize, fruit, vegetables (especially carrots), lettuce leaves, and the core and peel of apples. If it gets plenty of vegetables it does not need to drink. It also likes a little bran.

The cage must be quite big so that the guinea pig can run up and down, and it should have a raised platform where the guinea pig can make its bed. The sawdust on the floor should be changed daily and the whole cage cleaned every week and disinfected about once a month.

During the summer the guinea pig can be put in a fenced-off part of the garden, but make sure that the fence is strong enough or the guinea pig will run away. Whenever it is allowed to wander freely about the house or in the garden, always make certain there are no cats or dogs about because they will attack it.

When guinea pigs are born they are already highly developed, furry, open-eyed and able to eat solid food. After only a few hours they can run about with their mother and are weaned in about two weeks.

The best way to hold a guinea pig (above) and a cat (below)

91

How to look after a dog when it sheds its fur

It is always an awkward time for dogs when they shed their fur. At such a time they should be treated gently and taken for long walks in the fresh air so that they can roll about in the grass and get rid of their loose hair. The dog should also be groomed with a metal comb so that it won't have to scratch itself too much, and brushed to remove loose hair and burrs. Short-haired breeds require little grooming but the longer the dog's hair the more it has to be combed. Some breeds have to be clipped regularly to maintain their health and good appearance.

The moulting period, when dogs shed their old hair, usually lasts about two weeks. During this period the dog should be given fatty foods containing butter, cooking fat or bacon fat. An average-sized dog can eat between 100 and 150 grammes of fat a day without being harmed but a safe fat limit is about 15 per cent of the dog's total daily food intake.

Cocker spaniel puppy

How dogs should be fed

The teeth of a dog are the teeth of a carnivorous, or meat-eating, animal, like those of the dog's wild cousin, the wolf or the fox. For this reason the more meat we give to a dog the longer it will live and the healthier it will stay. But we can also vary its food so that it receives two-thirds meat and one-third vegetables.

Dogs should be given nourishing meat either raw or cooked, in lumps or minced. The meat can be liver, tripe, fish, rabbit or chicken. Other food suitable for dogs includes broth, cheese grated over other food, an occasional raw beaten egg and a few teaspoonfuls of honey. At least once a week a dog should be given a lump of unsalted butter or fat. This fat in the diet helps to keep a healthy sheen on the dog's coat.

Dogs need large bones to gnaw from time to time for they are easy to digest and keep their teeth healthy. They should never be given splintery bones, though, such as those of chicken, rabbit or game. Neither should dogs be given salt but they need vitamin drops in their food.

Most commercial dog foods contain a balanced diet with all the necessary nourishment. If this is the dog's basic food it should be supplemented with small amounts of meat and fat.

Vegetable-based foods recommended for dogs include: rice broth seasoned with olive oil, vegetable broths or rice and milk broths, bread in small quantities and a little macaroni, carrots finely grated on to the rest of the food and occasionally fruit such as apple or pear. A few drops of orange or lemon juice can be added to the dog's drinking water.

Hamster

An ideal cage for a hamster

How to look after hamsters

The golden hamster, which is reddish-brown above and grey underneath, is one of the most popular household pets. It adapts very well to cage life but it is so tame that it can be let out to wander about the home freely. The hamster will let itself be picked up and stroked and will also answer when called by its master. In fact, it can be a real friend to children and keep them amused.

Twice a day the hamster cleans itself very carefully. A healthy hamster has thick, soft fur and no unpleasant smell.

The hamster also keeps its nest very clean. It always leaves its droppings in the same spot and throws them out of the cage if it can. When it finds food it stuffs it into the roomy pouches inside its jaws and then hides it in his nest.

When buying a hamster make sure the animal is young. Always buy two males unless you want them for breeding. Hamsters are very prolific, the female producing several litters a year. A young hamster has very flexible ears covered in fine hairs, bright eyes, a smooth, soft coat with no scars or discolorations.

The following are some rules regarding the care of hamsters.

If the animal's cage is small it must be fitted with a treadmill so that the hamster can exercise itself at night. A hamster needs to move around a lot and it can run as much as it likes on the treadmill.

A hamster will eat almost anything: bread, biscuits and small pieces of meat. But it also must have vegetables rich in vitamins such as carrots and lettuce. Another important item is grain food, including sunflower seeds.

It is not necessary to put a lot of food in the hamster's cage, especially if the food is perishable. The hamster hoards food in its nest and these reserves can go bad and cause infection.

How to prepare a bird-table

If you like birds and do not like to see them shut up in cages, you can still have the pleasure of watching them live in their natural state by setting up a bird-table for them.

To make a bird-table you need a long pole which is driven into the ground near a tree or shrubbery. Next you get a small box with low sides and nail it to the top of the pole to form a flat, horizontal surface for the birds to land and perch on. Some barbed wire wound round the bottom of the pole will stop cats from climbing up to the table.

What sort of food should be put on a bird-table? Breadcrumbs are not enough. There are two menus, one for birds that eat seeds and another for birds that eat insects. For the seed-eaters you need millet, barley, rice and breadcrumbs. For the insect-eaters you must have fat or minced meat, margarine, bread soaked in milk and bacon rind.

Perishable food such as meat, fat and milk should be changed frequently. Care should be taken not to frighten the birds because they may never come back again. Some insect-eating birds have the strange habit of eating in an upside-down position. For such birds put the food into a net which can be hung from a fence or a tree.

Birds need water to drink and to wash with and dishes of water should be put in safe positions so that the birds can splash about and enjoy themselves. Make sure you replenish the water supply every day or as often as possible. This is especially important in winter when natural supplies of water may be frozen.

How to make covered bird-tables for the winter

A small roof to the bird-table can stop food being covered by sudden snowfall in winter and provide birds with some shelter in cold weather. A similar roof can be built on the ground to cover the place where birds' food is usually put.

It is not too difficult a job to make such a roof and ordinary materials can be used. The easiest to make is a simple sloping roof and for this you need a piece of a broad plank. This can be kept in a sloping position on the ground by placing a pair of wooden supports at one end. The plank will provide a sheltered area for the birds and for their food.

Another simple type of roof can be made from two wooden boxes from which two sides have been removed. One of the boxes can act as a roof if placed at the top of a pole and the other as a platform or table.

The linnet has a light beak and therefore eats small seeds such as millet

The greenfinch has a strong beak which it uses to open up large seeds such as sunflower seeds of which it is very fond

How birds' food should be enriched in winter

Many people believe that breadcrumbs and a few grains of rice, corn or bird seed are enough to keep birds fed in winter. This is wrong. In winter birds need food with a high calorie content to fight against the cold.

When you put out food for birds in winter make sure you supplement it with nuts, bits of fat or bacon rind. You can make a sort of seed cake by mixing together the seeds, crusts of bread and other kinds of bird-food and binding it with animal fat. These seed-cakes can be placed on a window sill or in the garden. If you want to watch the birds eat you must not let them see you or they may be too frightened to come. Some birds, however, become very tame with regular feeding and will come every day and wait at the usual feeding place. Robins in particular are friendly birds who will approach people readily.

It is useful to sprinkle some sand around the food as it makes a more natural surrounding for the birds. Sand is also useful because birds usually swallow a few grains to help them digest harder seeds.

How to look after white mice

White mice are rarely longer than 10 centimetres from nose to tail. They keep moving about the whole time and you can watch them scampering about for hours in their cages without ever showing any signs of tiredness. One stops occasionally to nibble at some food but it soon starts moving restlessly about again. It likes the company of other white mice especially when it is young.

If you buy a male and female mouse make sure you have enough room for their young when they are born or else arrange to give them away or sell them to a pet dealer. You must avoid having too many of these animals and not knowing where to put them. As a rule, a male and female mouse can produce up to ten litters a year with about ten baby mice in each litter. In addition mice mature young, at about two or three months after birth, and then start producing litters of their own. This means that, in a relatively short time, your two original mice can found an extremely large family.

White mice will eat almost anything. Their best food, however, is a mixture of oats (ten parts) and millet (one part). This mixture should be made into a paste with water, and occasionally a small spoonful of cod liver oil or some vitamin drops can be added. Once a week give the white mice some fruit, lettuce or chicory. Do not give them any cheese. All waste matter connected with white mice must be removed regularly to avoid infection and disease.

How to look after terrapins

If you are going to have terrapins as pets it is essential that they are kept in a warm enough temperature. For this you need the kind of tank used for tropical fish. It should hold at least 20 litres of water for too little water can cause sudden temperature changes that may result in the terrapin catching pneumonia. A good temperature is between 20° and 27° Centigrade for many of these young terrapins are brought from

Right: male (right) female (centre) and baby (far right) Elegant Slider terrapins
Below: Cooter terrapin

the southern United States where they are used to a warm climate.

Water from the tap is chlorinated and although it is harmless as far as humans are concerned it is not good for terrapins. So tap-water must be kept in a bucket or a tank for a day. Chlorine is a gas and it will slowly evaporate from the water. You can also treat tap-water with filtration equipment.

Terrapin can eat the specially prepared food sold in pet shops but you must also give them chopped herring and raw, finely minced meat mixed with bone-meal and cod liver oil, but only a little at a time or it will rot in the water. Terrapins also like lettuce leaves and carrot tops. Give them a few drops of vitamin oil to help them stay healthy.

How terrapins can become ill

One of the most common diseases affecting terrapins causes their shells to soften. This is due to wrong feeding and the result is that the horny shell of the animal becomes soft and pliable and sinks in at the top. This disease can be treated by giving the animal a varied and plentiful diet with lots of minced meat and vitamins.

Another illness in terrapins causes their eyes to become inflamed. This is often the result of the bottom of the tank being covered in sand instead of gravel or pebbles. As the terrapin swims around it stirs up small clouds of fine sand which go into its eyes and irritate them, sometimes blinding the animal. So always have gravel or pebbles at the bottom of a terrapin's tank to avoid this danger.

Baby terrapins are far more subject to these illnesses than adult animals. You should remember when buying terrapins that when fully grown they reach a length of between 17 and 20 centimetres.

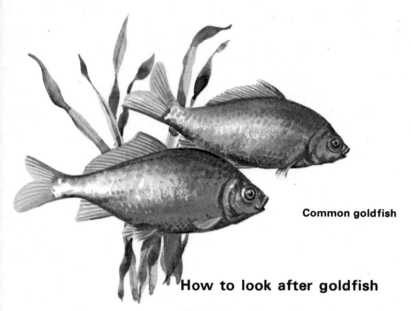

Common goldfish

How to look after goldfish

Goldfish make extremely popular pets. They are not difficult to look after providing you follow a few simple rules.

The first serious threat to a goldfish is when it is taken home from the pet shop. It should be swimming around in quite a lot of water and you should not take it in one of those small plastic bags. If you must use a plastic bag take the goldfish out of it as soon as possible or it may suffocate.

A second danger to goldfish is the tank it swims in. Tap-water contains chlorine which is poiso-nous to goldfish. This water is also too cold and might kill the pet.

A third danger is feeding which is all too often wrong for goldfish. These fish do not require much food, but what they do eat must be carefully chosen. Never give gold-fish breadcrumbs: use the special food sold in shops but be careful to give it only in small quantities. Occasionally you can give gold-fish a small amount of finely minced raw beef or the crushed yolks of hard-boiled eggs.

The larger the tank the happier the fish will be. The ideal tank is an aquarium but a large bowl will serve. Do not forget that even a goldfish can become bored and pine away living alone, so you should give it a companion, either male or female.

Goldfish were originally natives of eastern Asia but were later introduced into China, Japan, Europe and the United States. They have been known to live for twenty-five years in captivity, but the average life span is usually much shorter.

How an aquarium should be equipped

Only a few fish can adapt to life in the restricted space of a tank, but even these will die if they are not given the right surroundings.

The aquarium must be carefully prepared. On the bottom there should be a mixture of sand and pebbles to give a realistic look. Underwater plants are useful be-cause they help to keep the water pure by absorbing waste products and providing oxygen. The water must be neither too cold nor too warm and it must not contain any harmful substances. It should sel-dom be completely changed or

replenished. A glass cover to the aquarium is often used, to reduce evaporation and prevent the fish from jumping out.

How frogs can be born at home

You have probably often seen frog-spawn in a pond. This spawn is a jelly containing tadpoles which are small creatures that grow into frogs. If you gather up some of this spawn and keep it in a large jar of water taken from the pond itself, the tadpoles will continue to grow by feeding on the microscopic plant life in the pond-water. You can add a few pieces of lettuce to the water as extra food.

When the tadpoles are a month old, little hindlegs develop and grow, and then forelegs appear. As the legs grow the tail gets smaller and at last disappears.

When the tadpoles reach the final phase of their development, put a sloping surface such as a board into the water. This will allow these animals to climb out of the water when their lungs develop and they have to breathe air.

It is extremely interesting to watch the tadpole gradually turn into a frog about 2 centimetres long. But be careful: frog-spawn is very much like that of other amphibians and the tadpoles might turn out to be toads or newts.

American leopard frog

European frog

Bull-frog with its spawn and tadpoles

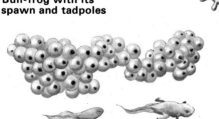

99

WHEN THE WORLD BEGAN

Millions of stars are to be seen scattered in the sky on clear nights. There are many more, however, which are invisible to the naked eye and can only be detected with powerful telescopes. The millions and millions of bright dots everywhere in space are really vast numbers of stars called galaxies.

Our world also belongs to a galaxy. The Sun, around which the Earth rotates, is a small star travelling at high speed on the edge of the spiral-shaped galaxy called by the ancients the Milky Way. The other stars which travel

About 4,500 million years ago, in a spinning cloud of gas and cosmic dust, some of the nuclei condensed. As they rotated they gradually gathered up the surrounding matter, growing larger and larger and more and more solid.

with us in the universe and which therefore belong to the same galaxy, form a broad band in the sky, so thickly scattered with lights that it makes a milky glow in the dark. It is from this that it takes its name, the Milky Way.

When and how were all these stars formed? It is difficult to give a precise answer but it seems that they all originate from the condensation of white-hot gases, the first and oldest 'matter' in the universe. The solar system, that is the Sun and the planets in orbit round it, was also created from a spinning cloud of gas. This itself was a tiny part of the enormous cloud of white-hot gases from which all the stars in the Milky Way originated.

According to recent discoveries, our Milky Way began to form some 10,000 million years ago. As time passed the gases of which it consisted condensed into a great many nuclei, or cores, each of which became a star.

The Sun, which is the nearest star to us, began to form 4,500 million years ago. From the outer portions of the gaseous cloud which formed the Sun the planets were born, including the Earth.

When the Earth was born

If we look back through the history of the Earth, we come to a time, hundreds of millions of years ago, when there was no sign of life on our planet. If we go back still further in time, we reach a mysterious period when the Earth emerged like a ball of fire from a mass of white-hot gases and moved away into space, turning continuously round the shining Sun. Perhaps we will never know exactly when and how our planet was born but it most probably did begin like this.

About 4,500 million years ago, in a spinning cloud of gas and dust, some of the nuclei condensed. As they rotated they gradually gathered up the surrounding matter, growing larger and larger and more and more solid. The central nucleus became the Sun while the others gave rise to the various planets of the solar system.

Under the influence of the force of the Earth's gravity and the enormous atmospheric pressure, the cosmic dust (high speed radioactive particles) falling from space to form the Earth heated up until it became white-hot. The inner core of our planet is still white-hot today.

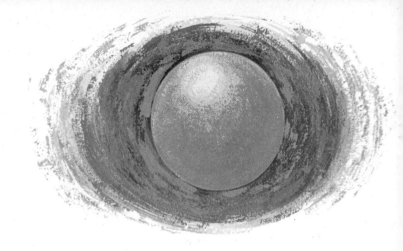

The Earth emerged like a ball of fire from a mass of white-hot gases

If we could cut the Earth in two we would see that it is formed of a rocky outer crust, some 40 kilometres thick, of a second inner mantle of iron and magnesium silicates 2,900 kilometres deep and of a central core of white-hot, molten iron 6,700 kilometres across. This core probably produces the Earth's magnetic field.

The vertical and horizontal projection of our galaxy. The arrows show the position of the solar system.

When the Earth solidified

One of the most difficult tasks of geology (the science or study of the Earth), has been to establish the age of the Earth. Until about fifty years ago the scientists had little information to help them with this problem. By careful observation they could discover whether one rock was older than another, but the further back they went in time, the more hazy and uncertain their knowledge became.

It was only with the discovery of radioactivity that geology made a great step forward in this field.

By studying certain radioactive substances, it was discovered that, in the course of time, they lose

their radioactivity at a steady, invariable rate. The element uranium, for example, loses its radioactive properties over a very long period of time and changes into lead. We know that one gramme of uranium takes a thousand years

to produce 1/7,000,000 of a gramme of lead. With this knowledge it is possible to calculate the age of a rock containing uranium by comparing the amount of lead produced in it with the amount of uranium still present.

Tests made on radioactive rocks all over the world have shown that the oldest were formed about 3,500 million years ago. It would therefore appear that the Earth's crust solidified about 4,500 million years ago.

When the first rocks were formed

In the violent beginnings of our planet the surface of the Earth looked a terrifying place. White-hot magma, formed of molten rock from the Earth's interior, boiled on the surface with constant explosions. At the same time showers of meteorites and cosmic dust, attracted by the pull of the Earth's gravity, made the sphere grow bigger and bigger as it rotated in space.

Huge spirals of gas and water vapour rose out of the magma to darken the sky and keep the light of the Sun from falling on to the Earth. The gloom of the night was continually shattered by flashes from the explosions and eruptions of the Earth's surface.

Millions of years passed before the first islands of rock, derived from cooled magma, appeared on the sea of lava. As it solidified, the white-hot magma, which formed the Earth in the beginning, gave rise to a basic rock type known as igneous (from the Latin *ignis,* meaning fire). There is little trace left of these rocks today, however, at least on the surface: corroded and wasted away by the forces present in the atmosphere, they have been transformed into gravel, fine sand and dust.

These substances, washed away into the large sea-basins by rivers and floods, have been deposited there in layers. The weight of the upper layers exerted tremendous pressure on those beneath, squeezing out the water and then cementing the fragments together again, forming new rocks. By the action of intense natural forces, they have then undergone other fundamental changes. The layers, or strata, have been folded, curved or broken. The distorted layerings of the rocks on our mountains give some idea of what happened to the Earth's crust.

When the first mountains were formed

As it gradually cooled, the magma solidified on the surface and the Earth became covered with a crust of primeval rocks, mainly consisting of granite and basalt. These rocks encased our globe like a rigid shell, while inside it continued to be burning hot.

When the Earth cooled still more it shrank, and the rocky layer which covered it had to contract, like an apple whose skin wrinkles as it withers.

The shell of primeval rocks wrinkled and folded under the strong lateral pressures caused by this shrinking. In some places it sank into the underlying magma; in others it rose up towards the sky.

That is how the first mountains were formed but there is no trace of them left today. Countless disturbances over the ages have completely destroyed them. The mountains we admire today are from later periods and in some cases are comparatively recent.

When coal was formed

The first living beings to succeed in leaving the sea and adapting themselves to life in the air were the algae, simple water-dwelling plants. From these more complex plants were then evolved.

Once they had adapted to their new surroundings, the plants developed quickly. They invaded the land and covered it with green. The period which saw the greatest growth of the forests was the Carboniferous, so called because it was then, 300 million years ago, that the large coal seams were formed.

The black pieces of coal still used today in industry and for heating many homes therefore have a history dating from that time. They were formed by the decomposition of the forests which then covered the surface of the Earth. As time passed, the enormous trunks, felled by age or storms, formed thick layers of wood which were then buried under layers of mud and sand. Instead of rotting, the wood changed completely, partly because it was no longer in contact with the air and partly because of the tremendous pressures and heat of the Earth.

All that remains of the ancient forests are the seams of pit-coal under the ground.

There are several types of coal, depending on their age and the conditions in which they were formed. The most important are bituminous coal and anthracite. Coal-gas and gas for domestic purposes were recovered from bituminous coal. Coke is a by-product. Anthracite gives great heat with little ash and is therefore mostly used for heating systems.

When oil was formed

Today coal has lost the lead it once enjoyed among the fuels. First place has been taken by oil, the precious substance which gushes out of the depths of the Earth, bringing wealth and prosperity to the countries where it is found.

In his search for oil, man has managed to make even the desert habitable, to build enormous platforms to float on the sea, to drill through rock strata down to depths of some 5,000 metres, and has spent enormous sums in doing so.

These are always handsomely repaid once an oil-field has been reached, however, for tons and tons of 'black gold' (as oil is called) stream out of the well. The oil is taken through pipelines to refineries or tankers.

Oil is generally younger than coal. Its formation dates back to a more recent period in the history of the Earth, to the Mesozoic Era, which lasted 225 million to 65 million years ago. This era saw the rise and fall of the great dinosaurs.

Even in the Mesozoic Era the folding and settling of the Earth's crust continued. Thick deposits of sea and lake sediment accumulated in different parts of the globe. The way in which these deposits are layered shows that the land and seas were successively rising and falling in this period.

The Cretaceous Period, from 130 million to 65 million years ago, takes its name from the French word *craie*, meaning chalk, which was actually formed in those distant times. This period is one of the longest in the history of the Earth. It lasted for over 65 million years, during which animal-life on land developed in profusion.

Some of the most important oil

and natural gas fields discovered in Canada and the United States are to be found in the rocks of the Cretaceous Period. Because of the unsettled conditions on Earth, enormous masses of organic substances, perhaps derived from decomposing animals, were imprisoned in the ground where they were gradually transformed until they became the mineral oils of today.

The rock strata of this period are very important, partly because they contain large deposits of copper, aluminium and other minerals but mostly because they also contain fossil traces of the first flowers, a sign that great progress was being made in the plant kingdom.

When the present continents were formed

At the very time when oil was beginning to form, an enormous shift took place in the Earth's crust, which slowly resulted in the formation of the present continents.

Numerous studies, even in recent years, confirm the theory that the great continental mass pushed out of the sea in the earlier periods and then split apart into several pieces which drifted about the Earth for hundreds of millions of years. Finally, between the middle of Cretaceous and early Tertiary Periods (100 million to 50 million years ago) these pieces split up again to form land masses recognizable in form to the continents of today. These sections are still drifting apart.

This interesting suggestion, first put forward by the German meteorologist, Alfred Wegener (1880–1930), is known as the theory of 'continental drift'.

Wegener, who was also a daring explorer and experienced geologist, published his ideas in a book printed in 1912. It naturally created a great stir in scientific circles, which soon split into two

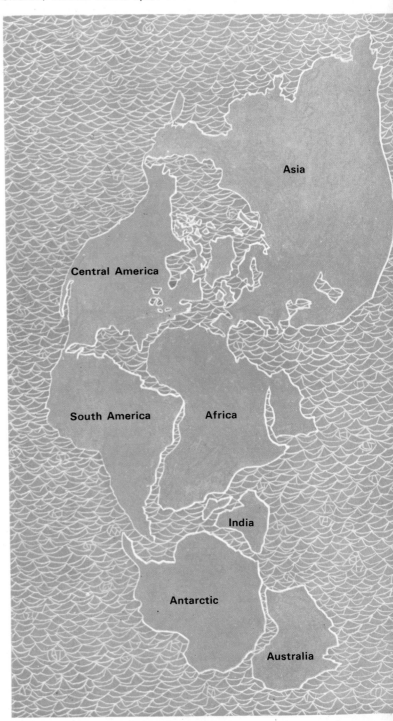

groups, one of his supporters and one of his opponents. They were both eager to prove or disprove his theory.

In a few words, Wegener's idea was as follows: in dim, distant times the continental masses were joined together in a single block (or shield), which Wegener called Pangaea. The rest of the Earth was covered by a primeval mass of water, the Panta-laxia.

During the Eocene Period, about 50 million years ago, a slow but steady movement then began. The Pangaea cracked and, pulled apart by the rotating movement of the Earth, the bits began to drift away from each other as if they were floating on a heavier, more elastic base.

According to Wegener, it was because of this shifting that the folds occurred in the Earth's crust which lifted up the loftiest mountain chains still existing in the world today.

When America broke away from Africa

A careful look at the maps in an atlas will help support Wegener's theory. A map of the Atlantic Ocean, for example, shows a striking similarity in the shape of the two coastlines, one on the Eurafrican side and the other on the American. It almost seems as if the pieces would fit together.

If we believe that the land was once adrift in a single piece on the surface of the Earth, then Eurafrica and America must have slowly floated away from each other.

Apart from the geographical proof, which could be attributed to a vivid imagination, there is surprising geological evidence based on careful study of the rocks. The structure of the minerals both on the Atlantic coast and on the other coasts concerned in the drift theory, shows that not only do they have the same properties but there are even signs of events which occurred before the fracture (folds and ridges).

The animal-life also has strangely similar features: certain animals, like the earth-worms, the snails and some shallow-water fish, lived along both the Eurafrican and the

Extent of the Arctic ice-cap today (above) and in the Great Ice Age (below)

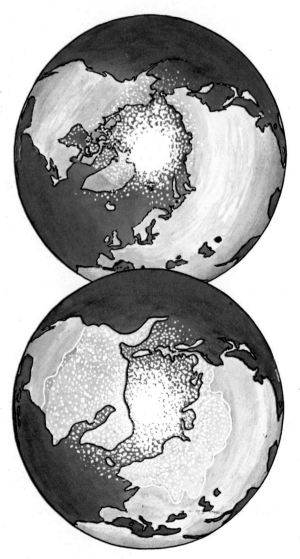

American coasts. The same applies to certain plants.

There is even indisputable geodetic evidence (geodesy is the science of measuring the shape and size of the Earth) to show that the drift is still continuing today. As late as the last century it was suggested that Greenland was moving. It is now known that it is drifting away from Europe at about 2 centimetres a year. The other 'suspect' lands are also continuing to be measured. It is believed that a crack in Africa is working its way along the line of the river Nile and the Great Lakes. Perhaps in hundreds of thousands of years Africa will have broken off, too.

How the Earth may have looked in a cold, glacial period and a warmer, interglacial period of the Pleistocene Era

When the ice invaded the land

About 38 million years ago, when the first large mammals were living on Earth, the climate underwent a great change. In the Oligocene Period, 38 to 27 million years ago, it was still warm and temperate but in the Miocene which followed it grew colder, affecting the spread of the plants. Many tropical or subtropical types of plant disappeared and even the woods shrank, to be replaced by immense grassy plains.

The effects of this change on animal evolution were far-reaching. Many mammals who had been used to feeding on the shoots of trees and bushes had to adapt to feeding on grass. This led to their gradual transformation, which was particularly noticeable in the

shape of their teeth and the structure of their feet and necks.

In the Miocene Period, the mountain chains which had begun to emerge in the earlier periods continued to be lifted up. New land surfaced above the sea, with the result that the oceans shrank. These movements were completed in the Pliocene Period (the last in the Cenozoic Era), which lasted 8 million years. By the end of it,

Glacier (based on a sketch by Agassiz, who did much research into glaciation in the 1840s).

the shape of the continents was as it is today. The fossils discovered in Pliocene soil show animal forms which are in many ways similar to those of the present. Other fossils belong to. species which are now extinct but it is easy to imagine the exact shape of their bodies.

The strangest of these were certain forms of proboscidea, such as the Amebolodon, with long, flexible noses.

Animal-life had already attained the variety of modern times when, about a million years ago, new changes in climate occurred, upsetting the pattern of life on the continents. The cold became intense and large ice-caps covered the globe as far down as our latitudes, driving nearly all the living beings towards the tropics.

Some animals, however, managed to adapt to the new climatic conditions and continued to live in the regions of the North. A typical example of this is the mammoth, a large woolly elephant, remains of which have even recently been found in the frozen sands of Siberia.

The severe cold froze vast stretches of water, particularly around the North and South Poles. Water vapour froze in the clouds and fell as snow, covering the continents so thickly that it did not melt. This made the flow of the rivers dwindle so much that many of them disappeared and the seas were no longer fed as they used to be. Yet the oceans continued to evaporate, although the vapour did not return to them as rain. The level of the oceans thus gradually dropped and the floors of the seas were revealed. Even the deep trench of the Bering Strait was left dry, after several million years under water.

When America was joined to Asia

When the deep trench of land of the Bering Strait was left dry, the two continents found themselves joined together again, as they had been in earlier times. The animals then began to migrate in profusion across the 'bridge' of Bering, particularly in the direction of America.

This migration had disastrous results for American animal-life. The herbivora (grass-eating animals) had lived on the plains of South America, completely cut off from the rest of the world, for at least 75 million years. With no great enemies to struggle against, these animals had gradually become lazy and had reached gigantic proportions which made their movements slow.

When the ferocious carnivora (flesh-eaters) of the old continent arrived from the North along the Bering Strait and down the chain of Central America, a mass slaughter took place. Nearly all the prehistoric American herbivora, incapable of defending themselves, were destroyed by the stronger, more intelligent newcomers.

When the ice retreated

The effects of the Great Ice Age and the retreat of the ice made a deep impression on the surface of the Earth. As they moved slowly along, the glaciers eroded and scoured, digging out valleys and gradually stripping the walls of rocks.

The trails of waste they removed piled up at the base and sides of the glaciers, where it eventually formed huge hills of rock debris.

Vast deposits of rock waste,

left behind by the glaciers, are to be found around lakes, such as the Italian Lake Maggiore and Lake Garda.

There is another, more important aspect of the retreat of the glaciers. The enormous quantities of water, collected on hill-tops in the form of snow, rushed down into the valleys as the temperature rose. There they formed raging

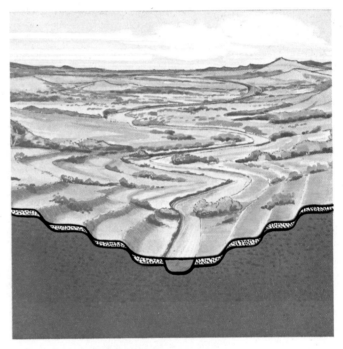

As the sea and rivers successively rose and fell in the Great Ice Age, river—terraces were created

torrents and rivers which swept away all that came in their path. The mountains were eroded away but, at the same time, vast heaps of debris built up in the valleys. This action was particularly strong in the Alps.

The Po River Basin, which had been covered by the sea up until then, was formed in the Quaternary Period (which covers the last 2 million years) by the loads of debris carried down into the valley by the rivers.

WHEN LIFE BEGAN

Pseudomonas fluorescens

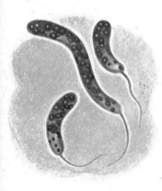

Thispirillum

Nitrosomonas

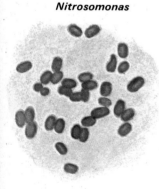

The first plants did not grow on dry land but in the water. They were not proper plants but microscopic living beings which reproduced by splitting up. They gradually progressed through various stages of evolution until they became more complex beings, both animals and plants.

As these first living creatures (the flagellates) were so tiny and like jelly in consistency, they left no trace of their existence in the rocks. They have therefore given us no clues as to the exact period in which they appeared in the waters of the seas.

The oldest rocks, dating back to the dawn of life on Earth, have no traces of fossils in them at all. Scientists are nevertheless agreed that life must have begun on Earth about 3,000 million years ago and that it then evolved at a very slow rate.

The rocks belonging to the end of the Archaeozoic Era, which are therefore about 600 million years old, contain the first few fossil remains of blue-green algae, or sea-weed.

Although these remains are too scanty to enable us to make an exact reconstruction of the animal and plant life in those times, they are extremely important because they suggest that life must have begun long before that.

The algae were highly developed organisms compared with the primitive flagellates, and the gulf between these and the later living beings is tremendous.

According to the scientists, it took a very long time for the primitive little balls of jelly, half plant and half animal, to develop first into more advanced single-celled beings, distinctly either animals or plants, and then into beings with many cells.

The flagellates joined up at some point into colonies. They formed gelatinous masses of individuals, at first independent but then gradually more closely connected, until they became a single, more complex individual capable of reproducing, multiplying and dying.

It took nearly two and a half thousand million years of slow transformation for the very first living beings to reach such well-developed plant-forms as the algae.

The algae were, in fact, the first plants with well-defined vegetable characteristics to spread all over the globe but, of course, only where the surface was covered with water. The fossil imprints found on rocks formed 500 million years ago record the

The sequence from left to right illustrates how an area of bare ground can be colonized by a succession of plants

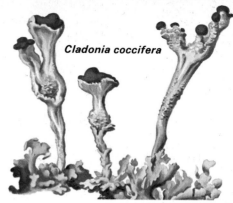

Cladonia coccifera

Thamnolia vermicularis

existence of a great variety of algae at the bottom of the sea, similar in every way to the modern sea-weed.

On dry land, however, there was still no trace of life, either animal or vegetable. The glare from the many volcanoes lit up a desolate landscape consisting solely of solidified lava, disintegrating rocks and huge mountains of sand and gravel washed up by the torrents of water.

When the algae left the water

About 435 million years ago, in the Silurian Period, a great upheaval in the crust of the Earth lifted the floors of many seas out of the water. This is probably what made the sea plants transform themselves, in order to survive. For hundreds of millions of years they had gone on vegetating in the water. When the basins dried up and they found themselves out in the air, they had to change their shape and organs in order to adapt to the new surroundings.

Once started, the evolution of the plants progressed rapidly. In little more than 150 million years the simple, almost microscopic algae became the gigantic trees which formed the immense forests of the Carboniferous Period.

To survive in the open air, the plants had to modify the organs on which they depended for life. The initial transformation was rather lengthy and we know little about it in detail but, as soon as the plants had acquired the ability to use the oxygen in the Earth's atmosphere, they found that conditions were perfect for developing new forms, more and more suited to their surroundings.

The bottom of the sea is always rich in the remains of plants and animals and these form quite a fertile soil. When large areas of land emerged from the sea as the waters retreated, they were therefore already covered with a thick layer of humus, or fertilizer, and could provide the plants with the ideal surroundings in which to develop. So the first land plants thrived and within 100 million years they had reached enormous proportions, forming the first forests.

When the giant sea-snails were alive

The traces of fossil animals in the rocks of the Cambrian Period, dating back to 550 million years ago, confirm that the trilobites were some of the first animals to have armour to protect the soft parts of their bodies. As time passed, however, many other sea-dwellers learned how to produce limy shells.

Among these were huge giants nature evolved in an unexpected way. It appears that the first nautiloids had a very long, perfectly straight, cone-shaped shell but, as time passed, this folded back on itself, curling up in a spiral and becoming very like the shell of a snail.

The reason for this development is that it is easier to carry something rolled up than it is to drag the same weight on the ground. So the first nautiloids to be born with coiled shells had the advantage

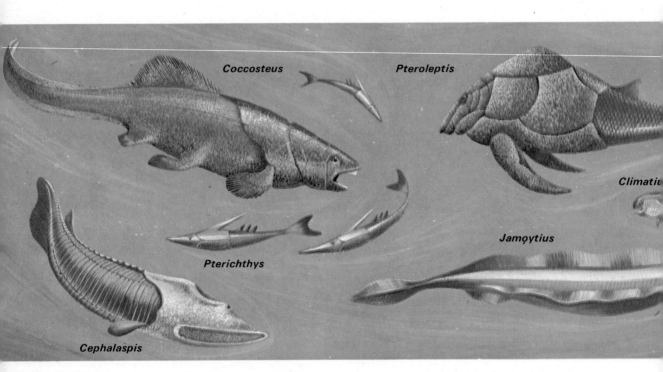

Coccosteus

Pteroleptis

Climatiï

Jamoytius

Pterichthys

Cephalaspis

like the nautiloid, an enormous snail with tentacles. Its shell was shaped like a brightly coloured, elongated cone and grew up to 4 metres long. It was a predatory animal which crawled along the bottom of the sea, ready to snatch at its prey with long tentacles. The modern octopus and cuttle-fish were later evolved from it.

It is interesting to examine the fossils of nautiloids in rocks of different periods and see how over the others. The straight-shelled nautiloids gradually suc-combed to the hazards of their environment and disappeared, while the spiral-shelled ones spread more and more.

In rocks of the Silurian Period (430 million years ago) only fossils of nautiloids of the spiral-shell group are to be found, while traces of the long, conical shells have completely disappeared.

When animals with backbones appeared

The arrival of the vertebrates—animals with backbones—is important because it marks the start of the development of all the higher orders of animals, up as far as man. The vertebrates, too, first appeared in the sea.

The first being with a skeleton with a backbone was probably the *Ainiktozoon*, of which some fossil remains have been found. Its head was in one with its body and

The oldest traces of primitive fish forms date back to the mid-Ordovician Period. Fragments of bodies have been discovered in the Colorado and Wyoming districts. The most interesting of the fish illustrated here are the *Cephalaspis* (on the left) with a bony, flattened head-shield and a scaly body, and the torpedo-shaped *Jamoytius* with fin-like folds half-way down its sides.

The Coelacanth (on the right) is an example of a living fossil. It was discovered off East London, in South Africa, in 1938, proving that the Coelacanthids had survived for more than 70 million years. Since then, other similar specimens have been caught, telling us a great deal about them.

strata of the next periods.

When the *Ainiktozoon* appeared, the waters of the seas were brimming with life. Shellfish with shells in two parts, like the modern oyster, were already in existence and the primitive corals, which looked quite different from those of today and were more like transparent-petalled flowers, flourished. They lived and died on top of each other, piling their shells in huge layers. These were later transformed into rock from which mountains were formed.

Coelachanthus

its backbone was fairly elementary. The first vertebrate fish which lived in the water were probably evolved from it.

They were armoured animals, without jaws, who rummaged in the mud at the bottom of the sea with their mouths wide open, looking for food. They quickly evolved into their present shapes, so that many fish which look much the same as the modern species are to be found in the

When armoured fish lived in the sea

While the forests which gave rise to the coal seams were thriving on dry land, new species of vertebrate animals were developing in the sea.

The first fish, like the *Ainiktozoon*, were jawless so could not chew. With their mouths permanently gaping, they were only able to swallow tiny prey.

113

About 400 million years ago, however, new forms of fish, with jaws and teeth, made their appearance.

Their long heads were covered with a great many bony plates, decorated with small knobs, called tubercles. Their bodies, too, were protected at the front by a bony sheath, while the tail was free.

On the whole, these animals were tiny but there were also some which were gigantic, like the *Dinichthys*, which measured up to 6 metres long. There were also strange-shaped armoured fish similar to turtles and crabs, like the *Antiarcha*.

Fossil larvae of branchiosaurus, similar to salamanders

The amphibians had strong limbs and could move with equal agility on land and in the water

Later, unarmoured fish also appeared, which could breathe with both their gills and their lungs.

This ability proved extremely important, as it allowed some of these animals to leave the water from time to time, so becoming amphibious.

When the first land animals appeared

We have to wait until the Earth was invaded by the plants to find the first traces of animals capable of living out of the water. This is natural because the plant-eaters come before the meat-eaters in the chain of life. Without the plant-eaters the meat-eaters would have no food and, before the plant-eaters must come the plants, which are their essential food.

About 400 million years ago the Earth was covered with green. Even where the ground was rocky and barren, algae and lichens had managed to squeeze into the cracks, creating a base for the development of more advanced plants. The land was eventually ready to support the first animals and provide them with food and shelter. So they came.

We know for certain, although we do not know when, that they came from the water, leaving the bottom of the sea to venture on to dry land. The first land animals were probably scorpions, spiders, cockroaches and millepedes, all descendants of the sea-scorpion and all quite similar to the modern species.

The wings of the cockroaches were the first to beat in the air. Soon other little animals learned to fly. For the most part they were small insects which were quite different from the present ones, such as the six-winged *Steno-dictya*, fossils of which have come down to us preserved in clay and loam from the Carboniferous Period. The insects were often predators, who roamed the primeval forests, hunting for other little animals.

When the fish became amphibious

Over 350 million years ago, just before the great forests of the Carboniferous Period, some of the fish belonging to the primitive groups were born different from their ancestors. As well as gills, they found they had rudimentary lungs which allowed them to breathe the atmospheric air directly, instead of filtering the oxygen in the water through their gills. As a result, these fish could keep their heads out of the water for short spells, inhaling the air and passing it into their lungs.

One of these, darting in and out near the bank, was washed up on the dry beach by a sudden wave. Had it been a normal fish, it would have quickly died of suffocation, but its lungs helped it survive until it managed to crawl back into the water.

This was the vertebrate animals' first experience of a new, completely hostile environment, and the time spent out of the water was soon to prove invaluable.

These creatures were the ancient ancestors of the lung fish which are still found today in Australia, Africa and South America.

When the continents were raised again, many lakes dried up. Enormous numbers of fish died in the parched mud. Only the few fortunate species which were also provided with rudimentary lungs could survive. To keep alive, they dragged themselves laboriously along on their fins from puddle to puddle. Some, however, stayed on dry land, in the shade of the nearest bush, first for a short while then for longer and longer. This was probably the origin of the first amphibious animals, ideally suited to life on the marshy ground.

The amphibians who left the oldest fossil imprints on the rocks were the stegocephalians, who retained obvious signs of their close relationship with fish. We do not know if they still had traces of fins, but they definitely had a scaley cloak round their bodies, like fish. Sometimes, in some of the species, the scales thickened on their stomachs, knitting together to form a hard shell. This effective protection proved to be very useful when the stegocephalians crawled along the ground to get from place to place.

The development of these ancient animals and their gradual adaptation to new needs is an excellent illustration of the natural process of evolution.

Fossils of these first amphibians are to be found in rocks of the Devonian Period but there are many more in those of the Carboniferous and Permian worlds. The shape of their skulls, particularly their jaws, is strangely similar to that of the crossopterygian fish which, like the coelacanth, had stayed in the water.

Ranging from a few centimetres to many metres long, the stegocephalians came in a great variety of shapes. It was as if nature, after so long confined to the water, had at last exploded and was

Darwin was one of the first to put forward theories on the evolution of the species. They were explained in 1859 in his book, *On the Origin of Species by Means of Natural Selection*

115

enjoying suddenly creating a variety of different shapes from the same basic model.

These animals spent part of their lives on dry land and part in the water: the adjective 'amphibious' is therefore highly appropriate in their case, as it comes from a Greek word meaning 'leading two lives'. They crawled along the ground like the modern lizards, wandering among the trees and bushes of the ancient forests, hunting for insects and other little animals.

They never went far from the water's edge because they had not yet learned how to make hard-shelled eggs which could be laid straight on the ground, so they were compelled to return to the water when they were ready to reproduce. The young spent their early life there, perhaps because suitable food was more readily available in the water.

When the fish began to resemble modern varieties

In the days of the huge reptiles of 200 to 100 million years ago, life in the sea became very different. The armoured fish disappeared, perhaps destroyed by the voracious selachii, ancestors of the modern sharks.

The cartilaginous, or gristly fish (sharks, rays, chimaeras) whose skeletons are not made of bone but of a softer substance called cartilage, multiplied considerably and grew to enormous sizes. The bony fish then spread gradually, too, and branched out into a great variety of species.

They became widespread mainly because of the great skill they developed in swimming and obtaining food. By then they looked very much like their modern de-scendants.

Practically all the kinds of bony fish which inhabit the oceans today had already appeared about 100 million years ago and there has been little change in them since. There are more species of bony fish in the world than of any other vertebrate animal; 30,000 is probably an underestimate. They vary greatly in structure as well as in size and colour.

Nor have the giant turtles, which are fished in the sea today, changed since those days. Their origin is unknown but by the middle of the Triassic Period turtles were numerous. They are exactly the same now as the great *Archelon,* fossil imprints of which have been found in rocks 100 million years old.

The only sea-creatures to experience any new changes were the selachii. Many species disappeared, others were completely transformed until their scales looked like those of today.

When the Great Age of Reptiles began

Dinosaurs were gigantic reptiles which lived on the Earth in the Mesozoic Era for nearly 100 million years. They had evolved from the small amphibians who had so laboriously left the sea in the Devonian and Carboniferous Periods.

As soon as some of the amphibians learned how to produce hard-shelled eggs, they were able to do without the water where they had originally been compelled to lay their eggs. That was when the first reptiles were born and it happened about 300 million years ago, in the Carboniferous Period of the Palaeozoic Era.

The first reptile was probably the *Seymouria*, quite a small animal. A geological expedition in 1969 discovered that it had spread as far as the area which is now the South Pole. The most ancient reptiles also included the first giants, such as the *Moschops*, which was some 2 metres long.

The reptiles quickly multiplied all over the Earth, splitting up into numerous different groups. One of the most important was that of the small *Saltoposuchus*, the first reptile capable of walking on its hind-legs. From it, all the great dinosaurs were later evolved.

The tortoises and other small reptiles also made their appearance in this period. Their inconspicuous shapes would have passed unnoticed had not another extremely important group of animals—the lizards and snakes of today—been derived from them.

Some of the major groups of animals which have come down to the present day therefore have their forerunners in the start of the Mesozoic Era. Even the mammals have a direct ancestor in those far-off days. It was the *Cynognathus*, which was probably the first animal to have warm blood in its veins.

Cretaceous dinosaurs

When the ancestor of the carnivorous dinosaurs appeared

When the reptiles appeared the Earth was bustling with activity. Each new reptile may be regarded as another experiment by Nature. Some of these experiments were successful and the new species developed, multiplied and stayed. Others failed and the new animals, ill-equipped to face the perils of their environment, gave way to their betters and the species became extinct.

Pteranodon

Pterodactylus

Dsungaripterus

Certainly one of Nature's most successful experiments at the start of the Mesozoic Era was the *Saltoposuchus*. It was only a small reptile, but it was very lively. It had also learned how to stand up and walk on its muscular, springy hind-legs which were perfect for sprinting. Its front legs, ending in strong, clawed fingers, were therefore free for grabbing at prey. So, in addition to its sharp, needle-shaped teeth, this reptile had two new offensive weapons. Indeed, it was so well equipped that, despite its size, the *Saltoposuchus* was not afraid to attack even very large prey, frequently getting the better of it.

Within a comparatively short space of time, all the dinosaurs had originated from this animal and, from the sub-branches, came all the modern birds and crocodiles.

When the largest reptiles became extinct

About 75 million years ago, almost without warning, the largest reptiles disappeared from the face of the Earth. The rock strata formed in later periods do not contain a single fossil of these animals. What brought about such an unexpected disappearance? How could the huge dinosaurs, who had dominated the Earth undisputed for nearly 100 million years, suddenly vanish without a trace?

Scientists have often tried to explain what happened, but none of their suggestions seems wholly convincing, although there are three which are more acceptable than the rest.

Firstly, the change of climate. As so many mountain chains were lifted up the climate changed completely. The differences in the seasons became very noticeable and the dinosaurs, used to an even temperature, succumbed to the cold, dry weather.

Secondly, the evolution of the plants. The forests became overgrown by large, wood-trunked trees which replaced the herbaceous plants. As these had been the dinosaurs' favourite food, they died of hunger.

Thirdly, the appearance of the rodent mammals. These small, intelligent animals began to feed on the dinosaurs' eggs. The dinosaurs did not protect their eggs after they had laid them and buried them, and so the eggs were easy prey for these little animals. They gnawed at so many dinosaurs' eggs that they made the giants extinct.

When the reptiles flew

Perhaps we shall never know for what mysterious reasons some of the reptiles suddenly tried to take to the air and conquer the sky. The fact is, however, that traces of numerous winged reptiles are to be found next to the fossils of the great dinosaurs dating from more than 130 million years ago.

One of the most widespread and the most ancient was the *Dimorphodon*. It looked like a monstrous bat and its size was remarkable: its skull alone measured 22 centimetres long.

The large-skulled *Dimorphodons* disappeared quickly, to be followed by other winged reptiles of various shapes and sizes. The *Rhamphorhynchus* was very common, with its peculiar tail ending in a diamond-shaped rudder, and there were various pterodactyls. The name means 'winged fingers' and refers to the very long little finger which kept the whole flap of flying-membrane taut.

In the course of time the winged reptiles grew bigger and bigger and better and better at flying. The largest and the best at flying was probably the *Pteranodon*, fossils of which have been found in North America and Russia.

It had a wing span of a good 7 metres and spent its time skimming over the water, catching fish and shellfish. Its incredibly wide wings prevented it from walking comfortably so, on the ground, it was probably compelled to crawl on its stomach but, in the air, with its light weight of only 12 kilos, it was amazingly agile.

Like the land dinosaurs, the winged reptiles, too, disappeared from our globe almost without warning, about 75 million years ago. The reason for their sudden extinction still remains a mystery.

Diatryma (above)

Phororhachus (below)

When the ancestors of the birds appeared

Strange as it may seem, the first birds did not evolve from the winged reptiles. Their forerunner was certainly a reptile but a different kind from that of the flying *Sauria*. The first of these creatures to leave us a clear picture on the rocks was the *Archaeopteryx*, which lived with the great dinosaurs over 130 million years ago.

The fossil imprints of this primitive bird are so complete that they tell us exactly what it looked like.

About as big as a pigeon, it was a strange mixture of half bird and half reptile. Obvious signs of its close relationship with reptiles are the movable, clawed fingers on its wings, its tail of twenty individual joints and its toothed jaw. Yet its body was covered with a fringe of feathers, which was something completely new.

Its wings were no longer a sheet of skin but a fan of feathers which spread out and beat the air as it flew. It was still a very simple flying machine, in need of a great many improvements and, indeed, the *Archaeopteryx* was a poor flyer, but its appearance marked an important stage in the history of evolution.

The first bird was definitely not a predator because its jaws were too weak. Perhaps it only fed on fruit, berries and small larvae. To take off, it clambered up to the top of a tree and launched itself out into space.

After this first laborious performance, the birds multiplied rapidly. Their ability to fly improved and they became the only true lords of the sky.

There was a time, in the evolution of the animals, when the fiercest predators of the plains were not mammals but enormous birds with savage beaks. They could not fly but ran with great speed. All derived from the primitive *Archaeopteryx*, they soon increased in number, sometimes reaching gigantic proportions, and competed for the hunting field with the carnivorous mammals.

Elephant

Mastodon

Mammoth

Trilophodon

Dinotherium

Moeritherium

Holocene

Pleistocene

Pliocene

Miocene

Oligocene

When the giant birds appeared

About 70 million years ago, on the plains of South America, lived the *Onactornis*, a giant running bird nearly 3 metres tall.

It had a very strong, hooked beak nearly 40 centimetres long. Fierce and cruel by nature, it, too, swooped down on the large mammals of the plains, trying to tear their stomachs open to make them bleed to death and so provide itself with a plentiful supply of food.

Many other meat-eating birds lived at that time and were equally fierce and dangerous, although smaller in stature. Some lived until comparatively recently, like the legendary *Aepyornis*. Skeletons discovered in the swamps of Madagascar show that this was an enormous bird, 3 metres tall, weighing some 500 kilos, which walked on two strong runner's legs.

According to the tales of some early travellers, this bird was still living in Madagascar a few centuries ago, particularly in the swampy regions of the south, and it only disappeared quite recently.

When the first mammals appeared

The appearance of the first mammals on the Earth went almost unnoticed, at the time when the dinosaurs were at their peak. Strange new animals, small but very active and much more intelligent than the dinosaurs, gradually came to live in the forests and glades. Unlike the reptiles, they were warm-blooded and therefore not affected by climatic changes. Continually circulating through their bodies, their blood kept their body temperature at a constant heat. This suddenly proved to be extremely important because it allowed the new creatures to cope with seasonal changes in climate without being affected by them too much. These changes became more and more noticeable towards the end of the Era and eventually made the great dinosaurs disappear.

Another feature of the new animals was a more highly developed maternal instinct, which

Early examples of plant-eaters: the *Phenacodus* (below) had small hooves but its skull and teeth were ill-suited for grazing; the *Coryphodon* (centre) was bigger and had longer teeth; the biggest was the *Uintatherium* (above) which had bony bulges on the top of its skull which must have made it look rather odd.

led them to look after their young, while the dinosaurs could not care less, once they had laid their eggs. The young of the warm-blooded animals were born alive and nursed by their mothers until they were ready to eat other food. This, too, is a very important characteristic and one of the mammals' most distinguishing features. In fact, they are called mammals because they have the mammae, or milk glands, with which they feed their young.

We know very little of the first mammals who dwelt in the forests at the time of the last dinosaurs because their fossil remains are rather scarce. Certainly one of the most ancient was the *Morganucodon*, which lived about 160 million years ago, in the Great Age of Reptiles. It measured 10 centimetres long and had a remarkable resemblance to the modern shrew-mouse. Other ancient mammals were the *Prodiacon*, a primitive hedgehog, and the *Taeniolabis*, one of the first to feed on plants. The others ate mainly insects, slugs and snails.

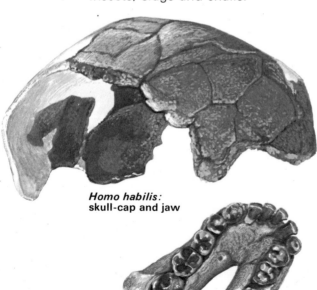

Homo habilis:
skull-cap and jaw

When the giant mammals were alive

At the same time as the dinosaurs disappeared, about 75 million years ago, the mammals made a great advance. Numerous branches developed from the primitive stock of mostly small rodents and became carnivores or herbivores. The herbivores, or grass-eaters, quickly multiplied and in 10 million years had greatly increased in size and were much bigger than the modern sheep.

Some of the most interesting grass-eaters of the period were the *Pantolambda*, 115 centimetres long, and the *Barylambda*, almost 3 metres long. Both of them were already provided with hooves at the end of their legs, like their modern descendants.

With the plentiful food and the pleasant climate, the grass-eaters grew to be gigantic. Proof of this are the fossil remains of the *Baluchitherium*, a huge rhinoceros of the Oligocene Period, without doubt the largest land mammal which ever existed. It was five and a half metres high and rested on four enormous legs like tree-trunks. The first fossils of this animal were found in Baluchistan at the beginning of this century.

In strata of earth formed 38 million years ago, there are also many fossils of the *Brontotherium*, a group of grass-eating animals some 4 metres long.

Perhaps these animals were crushed by their own weight. They became weaker and weaker and finally disappeared, to be replaced by more agile, stronger types. Cases such as this are frequently met with in the evolution of animals, when over-specialization leads to the extinction of a species.

When the first mammoth was discovered

The mammoth is not a true fore-runner of the present-day elephant. Both derive from the same older ancestor.

The mammoth lived in the Quaternary Era and was therefore a contemporary of the first men. Complete examples of this animal, which disappeared tens of thousands of years ago, have been found, perfectly preserved, in the frozen ground of Siberia.

The first discovery of a frozen mammoth was made in Berezovka, in Siberia, in 1899. This was one of the most complete mammoth carcases ever discovered. Perhaps it had fallen into a deep crevasse in the ice, because its right fore-leg and the bottom of its back were broken.

As it fell, the mammoth triggered off an avalanche of snow which covered it, wedging it in a grip of ice. For many centuries it stayed buried there like that, until the ice melted. Its body then began to decompose and the foul smell attracted the attention of some passing fur-trappers' dogs.

When the first experts arrived they found that the hair, the skin and even the blood of the mammoth had been perfectly preserved.

Since then, many other bodies of mammoths have been discovered intact in the ice. These discoveries have told us all about the great proboscids with their huge curving tusks which lived in the Great Ice Age but which were very different from the modern African and Indian elephants.

Many stuffed mammoths are to be seen in museums today.

When the hominids made their appearance on the Earth

The Neozoic Era is usually divided into two periods: the Pleistocene, which included the Great Ice Age, and the Holocene, which saw man assert himself over all other creatures in Creation. According to most geologists, traces of the first men date back to the start of this era, although there are some who claim that a primeval species of human being was already in existence at the end of the previous era. During the whole of the Pleistocene Period man spread very slowly over the Earth. With only his physical strength to help him, he had to fight for survival against difficulties and dangers of every kind.

The worst danger lay in the fierce, great animals with which primitive man had to battle for control of the woods and plains. Many of these animals, like the sabre-toothed tiger and the cave-bear, disappeared long ago; others, like the lion, the hyena and the leopard, retreated from our regions

The hominids, as they are called, were very different from *Homo sapiens*, our ancestor

in historical times but still live today in hotter, more congenial climates.

The mammoth still lived in the colder regions and was certainly stalked by the first tribes of huntsmen. A slaughtered mammoth meant an enormous supply of meat for the whole tribe, so the primitive hunters devised ingenious traps to catch these huge beasts. For in their fight with the mammoth and the other terrible wild animals which threatened them, their most effective weapon was their intelligence.

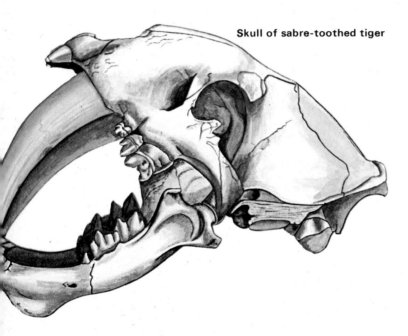

Skull of sabre-toothed tiger

Where had this new creature come from, who was patiently extending his dominion over all the other animals? By which evolutionary process was he born? The answer is easy, yet very difficult. Although many fossils point to the direct evolution of man from more primitive beings, themselves evolved from certain families of apes, the same fossils cannot explain how, at a certain moment in the history of evolution, a miraculous spark of intelligence was kindled in the brains of our ancestors.

In the development of animal life, the most surprising discoveries have been about the evolution of the apes. They, too, appeared in dim, distant times and then gradually split up into different groups, some of which looked quite like man.

Numerous fossil discoveries made in the last decades have shown that some extinct branches of the family of apes had learned not only how to walk upright, like man, but how to make and use primitive tools. In particular, they had rough weapons for fighting their opponents. These were the hominids—animals of the family of man—but they were still very different from *Homo sapiens,* who was our direct ancestor.

According to the most recent discoveries, the hominids lived between the end of the Tertiary Era and the start of the Quaternary. At one time it was thought that human life was only 600,000 years old but now many scientists are inclined to think that we must go back to over a million years ago to find the early hominids.

Throughout the Quaternary Era subman continued to progress, going through various stages which are recorded by fossil discoveries of skulls and other parts of the skeleton.

These discoveries link the important steps in the evolution of man: *Pithecanthropus* was followed by Neanderthal Man and then *Homo sapiens. Pithecanthropus* is the most ancient being: his name means 'ape-man' and that is just what he looked like, although his skull was slowly growing bigger to make room for a larger and more complex brain.

When Neanderthal Man appeared

Pithecanthropus (*or Homo erectus*) was already able to make simple stone tools. His favourite weapon was a large stone chipped into an oval shape like a large almond, which he clutched in both hands or tied to a stick, so making the first axe.

A variation of this subman was *Sinanthropus*, or Chinese Man, who had an even more developed skull and whose fossil remains date back to 500,000 years ago.

Over 400,000 years then passed before the appearance of Neanderthal Man, the creature who finally gave up the wandering life and a diet of plants, slugs and snails to become a hunter, starting to eat the meat of his prey.

He takes his name from the Neanderthal Valley, near Düsseldorf in Germany. There, in 1856, in a small cave, the first fossil remains of a new race of human beings, far more complex than *Pithecanthropus,* were discovered. There was only the top of a skull and a few bones but soon many other discoveries were being made in various parts of Europe—in France, in Belgium, in Gibraltar and in Yugoslavia—and so it was possible to understand the habits of these men, who already knew how to work flints with great skill.

Neanderthal Man was quite small. His average height was only 1·55 metres but his body was broad and his muscles were strong. He had an ape-like skull, with heavy, arched eyebrow-ridges which met in the middle. His face was long with wide cheekbones and a broad, flat nose.

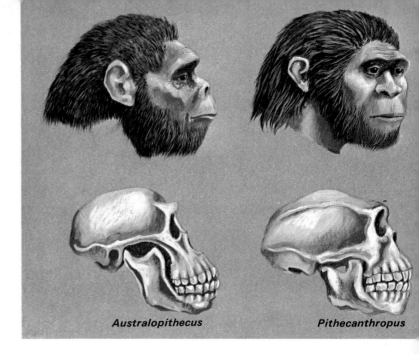

Australopithecus *Pithecanthropus*

His forehead and chin were receding, and he had a short neck.

With his hairy body and ape-like face he looked brutish and savage. Yet his brain was as big as that of modern man. Neanderthal Man already possessed a remarkable degree of intelligence, which we can tell by the artistic workmanship which he put into making numerous objects from wood, bone and flint.

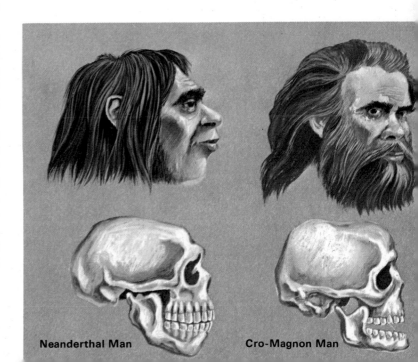

Neanderthal Man **Cro-Magnon Man**

WHEN CIVILIZATION BEGAN

The people who lived thousands of years before us left many traces of their existence. They are mostly objects of every day use, such as charms, weapons, tools, coins or even ruins of their homes, all revealing the history of the people.

Archaeology is the science which tries to collect enough information from the remains of the ancient peoples to find out how they lived.

The work is extremely difficult because it requires both enthusiasm and patience, inspiration and method. Very rarely does the archaeologist have the good fortune to come across particularly valuable and significant remains and his work seldom makes the front-page story.

It is more a labour of love, painstaking determination and perseverance which hardly ever fire the imagination of the general public.

The archaeologist loves beautiful things of the past. He is an enthusiast who finds his work sufficiently rewarding to make up for its difficulties. For archaeology is a science which needs dedication and great perseverance.

When archaeology began

The enthusiasm which inspired the scholars of the Renaissance during the fourteenth, fifteenth and sixteenth centuries, and their love for anything to do with classical Greek and Roman art, led to the first archaeological excavations. The lack of any precise methods of research and adequate scientific means was compensated for by the eagerness of the excited diggers.

The results, however, were of little importance. Anything which was brought to light nearly always ended up in the noble mansions of whoever had financed the excavations. They thus came to form the first great private collections of archaeological treasures, which can still be admired today.

Renaissance archaeology was not therefore supported by any notable follow-up. It was only towards the middle of the eighteenth century that an interest in the past was awakened in the world of Western culture. For example, the discovery of Herculaneum, buried by the famous eruption of Vesuvius on 24 August A.D. 79 was started in 1709.

Any sensible, well-organized methods of excavation were still a long way off, however. The men employed to do the actual digging were often so clumsy that they seriously damaged the works of art they were uncovering.

The archaeologists who worked in the second half of the eighteenth century and the whole of the nineteenth may be regarded as the true pioneers. Their enthusiasm filled the obvious gaps in their preparation.

The most important were Winckelmann, Schliemann and Pitt Rivers.

After them came a second generation of archaeologists, better prepared both from the educational and the archaeological point of view. The most famous of these were the Frenchman, Henri Breuil, the Englishman, L. S. B. Leakey, and the Chinaman, Pei-Wen-Chung. With them archaeology became a true science.

The science of archaeology employs some extremely complicated techniques which require highly specialized knowledge. Today archaeologists have to be scientists, teachers and organizers. Sir Mortimer Wheeler, R. Braidwood and R. Heizer were the first of this type of archeologist. The work is done under the closest supervision, with almost mathematical precision. Many features of the pioneer days of archaeology have changed but the modern scientists reveal the same enthusiasm which has been the solution to so many problems.

But archaeology is not concerned only with buried treasures from lost cities. Archaeologists often spend most of their time on simple objects of daily use.

L. S. B. Leakey (above)
Sir Mortimer Wheeler (below)

Below:
A. Pitt Rivers (left),
H. Schliemann (centre)
H. Breuil (right)

When Archaeology became a comparative science

Archaeological investigations often used to specialize in the old days by going deeply into the discoveries they had dug up and so reconstructing the life of a people. This type of specialization has today been replaced by a more modern approach, which involves the comparative study of the discoveries.

What is 'comparative archaeology'? For example, the primitive dwellings so far discovered all over the world and belonging to a particular period are studied in detail. The results of this research are compared and provide useful pointers for understanding the people and the different aspects of their lives: society, trade, art and so on.

So the archaeologist today is no longer an inspired detective with a clever knack of uncovering clues to the past, but a painstaking scientist ready to work with other scholars to achieve a common aim. We must hope that the archaeologist of the twenty-first century will have the widest back-up support: skilled workers, technicians, photographers, recording staff, helicopters for checking localities, laboratories (mobile, permanent and central) for the analysis of remains found during excavations.

When the first boats appeared

One of the most fascinating archaeological trails is that left by boats. Who were the first people brave enough to launch boats capable of making trips along the coast?

Our evidence shows that the people of the island of Crete were the first navigators of the sea. This achievement is thought to have been made in the Neolithic Age. It is known for certain that by 3000 B.C. the inhabitants of Crete were expert seamen and were travelling to and from Egypt. There they sold their cargoes, which were mostly of obsidian, a black, glossy volcanic flint, which was in great demand for making sharp tools and weapons.

The Cretans even ventured as far as the Lipari Islands to stock up with materials which were in short supply on their own island.

Gallery grave at New Grange, Ireland. In these monuments there is a gallery or chamber built of stone slabs, sometimes with several compartments.

When the first villages grew up

In the Near East, roughly where Palestine is now, recent archaeological investigations have unearthed the rich remains of a Neolithic civilization which flourished 9,000 years before Christ.

The structure of the houses is remarkably advanced. Both the outside and inside walls are built of stone and each room in the house is separate. Although the roofs are thatched they are supported by solid rafters.

Even the furnishings, ovens, stone pots and mats are evidence of a civilized culture. The houses are not isolated but grouped together in villages of about fifty dwellings each.

When evidence of megalithic culture occurred

At one time it was thought that megalithic (or huge stone) monuments belonged to a particular culture which was especially widespread in Europe. Later discoveries have shown that the use of vast stones, some of them really colossal, was common to the primitive peoples all over the world.

There are many kinds of megalithic monument, from the megaliths of Japan to those of Holland, from the stone heads of Easter Island or Spain to those of India, from the carved blocks found in Ireland at the entrance to enormous graves to the the tombstones still in use by the African peoples.

Some particularly interesting examples of megalithic monuments are the gallery graves to be found in the west of England and Ireland.

An Australian limekiln (above); Medieval markings on brick (below); Inca wall (right)

One of the most fascinating archaeological trails is that left by boats. The photograph shows an ivory model of a boat, discovered at Knossos, Crete.

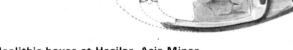

Neolithic house at Hacilar, Asia Minor

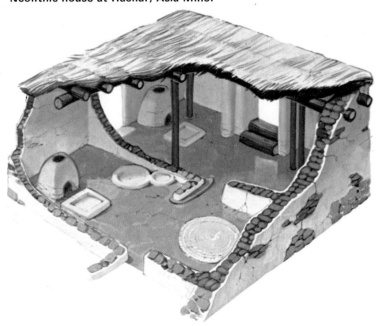

When the Neolithic Age developed in Europe

The archaeologist has to explain many problems, for the discoveries he makes with such patience are not always easy to interpret.

A mound in which several pots have been stacked, for example, might have been a tomb or it could really have been a shop or a store. Signs of burning could mean houses, places of worship or public places where skins were smoked. Even some large monuments and complicated architectural constructions are sometimes so puzzling as to remain unexplained. This is the case of Stonehenge, in Wiltshire.

It consists of large circles, approached down a long avenue. Seen from above they look like a giant keyhole. The whole area is bounded by a low, unfortified bank with all the houses on the outside. The most complex structure is in the middle. It comprises a circular colonnade of enormous stone uprights with lintels, also of stone, linking the ring of uprights. Inside this a second row of twin posts, again linked by lintels, dominates the structure which altogether seems like a temple or a place kept for funeral ceremonies.

Archaeologists are still uncertain why it was built, although they are inclined to believe it was used for religious, perhaps astronomical, purposes. Some experts have associated it with the Druids. It was almost certainly built during the late Neolithic to Early Bronze Age (1800–1400 B.C.)

Henges are common throughout Europe and date back to the end of the Stone Age and up to the Bronze Age.

When the Neolithic Age ended in Europe

Archaeological discoveries are sometimes amazing, like the discovery of some beakers, apparently commonplace objects, called bell beakers because of their shape.

The people who made these beakers in their millions, all more or less alike although with different decorations, spread over much of Europe at the end of the Stone Age. They were the same people who built the great henges.

Traces of these people have been found in eastern Europe in Czechoslavakia and Hungary, and in western Europe in England, Spain and Sicily. Many bell beakers have been found in tombs, together with ornaments of gold, amber, jet, a greenish-blue stone, probably turquoise, and flint and

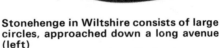

Stonehenge in Wiltshire consists of large circles, approached down a long avenue (left)
    Neolithic objects from England: copper daggers, flints and pitchers (above and below)

131

Two-handled jar of pale green Lung Ch'uan celadon

copper weapons: daggers, arrow tips and spears.

The origin of these beakers and the way in which they were made are still subjects for discussion among the experts. Some say they originated from Spain, others from Holland, others again claim the influence of the area which now corresponds to France.

One fact, however, is clear: the prehistoric people who made them had a great influence on European civilization, throwing it into such a state of activity that it quickly progressed towards a more advanced way of life.

Their importance becomes all the greater if we remember that the ancient civilizations of the Near East, such as the Egyptian, were already flourishing. So, on this side of the Mediterranean, the Stone Age was still acting as a brake on more advanced forms of culture. The people of the henges and the bell beakers took Europe into the Bronze Age about 1,000 years behind the times.

When the Mesolithic Age flourished

Historians separate the Palaeolithic from the Neolithic by another age which they call the Mesolithic. Mesolithic culture did not appear among all the peoples of the times but its special features are evident in some of them.

One distinction of the Mesolithic Age was a marked improvement in hunting and grain harvesting methods. The biggest animals had died out after the last cold spell. The smaller game was extremely plentiful but even more difficult to catch than its predecessors. If the mammoth had presented hunting problems because of its enormous size, the deer, wild boar, fish and birds proved to be in some ways more difficult prey because they were more agile and cunning.

Mesolithic Man knew how to invent baited traps for the fish and snares, bows and arrows for catching animals. Two separate archaeological excavations, one in Europe and one in Asia, are particularly enlightening about the life of the men who lived in the Mesolithic Age. At Star Carr in Yorkshire flake tools, scrapers, harpoon and lance heads made from red deer horn have been unearthed and a wooden canoe paddle has been found intact.

At Belt in Iran examples of different stages of Mesolithic culture, dating from 9500 B.C. to 6600 B.C. were found in one single cave. The relics left by the ancient inhabitants of this cave show how their activities progressed: bows and arrows for catching seals from the earliest occupants, weapons for catching gazelles from the next.

Ko dish netted with a fine crackle (above)

Ju dish with petal foot (below)

When the Neolithic Age flourished

The Neolithic Age is usually known as the New Stone Age, referring to stone which man had polished. Yet historians and archaeologists agree that the two most important features of this period are the transformation of man from a hunter to a breeder and from a gatherer to a cultivator.

It was in this period, that man learned how to take care of animals, to use them for food, work and clothing. In his use of plants, too, man took an important step by giving up his habit of living off nature and starting to work together with it.

All this helped to stem the traditional wanderings from place to place. The first well-populated villages were born with the first forms of craftsmanship and the first tribal organizations. Archaeologists have unearthed implements used by Neolithic men in the first forms of agriculture.

When the most beautiful porcelain was made

One of the most interesting chapters in archaeological discoveries deals with cups, bowls and pots. From the rough stone bowls of the Palaeolithic Age to the delicate Chinese porcelain, the history of ceramics vividly records man's progress and his gradual artistic refinement.

The civilization which far outshone any other in this art was without doubt the Chinese.

The perfection which these articles attained in the course of a thousand years did not substantially alter the original ingredients: kaolin and petuntse.

A great civilization grew up in the Indus valley with beautiful cities and its own writing. The most famous city is Mohenjo-Daro in the Sind (today West Pakistan) where the bath-house illustrated here is to be found.

133

Kaolin is a white clay and petuntse a feldspathic rock which takes on a glassy sheen when heated to 1,450 degrees C.

The period of greatest splendour of Chinese porcelain coincided with the famous Sung dynasty (A.D. 960–1279).

When the Egyptian civilization began

Largely due to the work of the archaeologists, we have been able to know one of the most splendid civilizations of all time. Priceless treasures of culture and art have been dug up from the Egyptian civilization which flourished on the banks of the Nile 3,000 years before Christ.

Perhaps no other ancient civilization has been so rich in the information it left behind it: from the temples to the tombs, from the jewels to the writing, all reflects a life of the greatest refinement.

Today we have a detailed picture of ancient Egypt, not just the important personages, the Pharaohs and priests, but also of the humbler people. This reconstruction has been made possible by the patience and skill of the archaeologists, particularly in the last two centuries. The tombs of the Pharaohs, with their friezes of the daily life, are a marvellous collection of pictures from which we can visualize how the ancient Egyptians lived.

Work and play, activity and repose, life and death speak to us clearly from the pictures which decorate the Egyptians' last resting places.

The picture language is a record of bustling activity in all walks of life, from the thousands of slaves condemned to build enormous pyramids, to the more powerful and refined who ruled like gods over a whole race.

The ideal life of the Egyptians, as recorded by the numerous written descriptions, the paintings and the objects which have come

Gold dagger of Tutankhamen (about 1350 B.C.), Cairo Museum

down to us through archaeology, was a simple existence. Pleasant and beautiful things were enjoyed but not to excess. The brick-built houses were owned by the state officials, the court dignataries, the merchants and the people in high places.

There were often charming oases where the master enjoyed the pleasures of family life. The slaves, the hunting and fishing, are all well documented by the inscriptions and paintings.

Funeral temple of Hatshepsut

When the temple of Hatshepsut was built

The great Pharaohs have always been famous in the history of Egypt. Man-gods, they were surrounded by great pomp and ceremony. But the history of ancient Egypt was also written by the mighty Queens, about whom the archaeological evidence is impressive and vivid.

One of the most important examples is certainly the temple built by order of Hatshepsut, the first woman destined to rule Egypt.

This sovereign of the eighteenth dynasty of the Pharaohs, reigned from about 1503 to 1482 B.C., shortly after her predecessors had succeeded in driving out the Hyksos, the Shepherd kings who had occupied Egypt.

Her funeral temple, rising at the feet of the towering cliffs near Thebes and built by the architect Senenmut, demonstrates how colossal and perfect the art of ancient Egypt was.

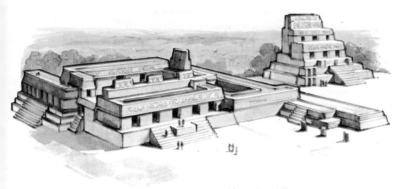

When the Aztec civilization flourished

Another great civilization which flourished at the same time as the Mayan was the Aztec. Both of them were situated roughly where modern Mexico is now.

The impressive buildings which survive them are all that is left of a splendour which will never die. It seems impossible that such greatness should have been ruined by civilized Europeans. Ignorant and fanatical, the Spanish conquerors gave vent to their greed and, for the sake of plunder, broke up a priceless treasure.

The archaeological remains tell us that one of the most beautiful cities of all the pre-Columbian civilizations was Tenochtitlan, which means 'stone rising in the water'. It was founded by the Aztecs on an island in lake Texcoco. The magnificence of its buildings and the richness and splendour of their decorations made this the capital city of an empire.

Not only the temples were built of stone at Tenochtitlan, but also the houses. Coated with a dazzling whitewash, they were graceful and attractive. Their terraces and gardens were gay with flowers and each neighbourhood was served by a network of navigable canals. The private houses were the fabric of the whole city, the heart of which was an immense square resplendent with the large, gold-decorated temple.

When the Inca civilization was brought to light

The third great civilization of America before Columbus, that of the Incas, grew up in the area now covered by Peru and its surrounding territories. It is more difficult to date it, as the Incas had no system of writing and so archaeological excavations have been the only means of reconstructing their history.

The most reliable estimate of the start of the Inca civilization puts it at about A.D. 1200. The most important discoveries and the ones which have provided the most information were made by an American archaeologist, Professor Hiram Bingham, of the University of Yale.

In 1911 he was lucky enough to find the remains of an Inca city, Machu Picchu, which means

Bingham discovers Machu Picchu in 1911

'Ancient Peak'. It lies about 100 kilometres from Cuzco, ancient capital of the Inca empire at the height of its splendour. Perched on an almost inaccessible mountain top, it was the last hideout of the fleeing Incas during the Spanish occupation. For four centuries it remained unknown and forgotten, even by the Indians of the Andes, the Incas' descendants.

One of the unsolved mysteries is how the Incas managed to transport the enormous blocks with which their walls, houses and stairways were built. They were hewn from quarries about 600 metres lower down the mountain. How they managed to carry them up to the top with the kinds of transport available in those days is still unexplained.

Most of the Inca people were farmers but every man had to serve periodically in the army or on building or mining. They built not only cities but suspension bridges, irrigation canals and fortresses.

When the ancient temples of the East grew up

The archaeologist who examines a site used for religious ceremonies normally expects some extraordinary surprises. This is what happened, for example, to the scholars who explored the gorgeous temples of the East with their extravagant architecture.

The uninhibited symbolism revealed in the countless statues, spires, turrets and other architectural embellishments, is a hard test for the scholar who wants to find the collective and individual meaning of these unusual works of art.

It is an oriental characteristic to express emotions as dramatically as possible whether in paintings, sculptures or architecture. The sculptures of the fantastic animals which decorate the temples are world-famous for their grotesque, terrifying faces.

A magnificent but by no means

unique example, is the famous temple at Madurai in India. Built in the shape of a rectangle measuring 260 metres long by 230 wide and surrounded by an arcade supported by 1,000 columns, the gigantic temple soars up, thick with spires and turrets, like an inaccessible mountain. The nine pyramid-shaped towers are mirrored in an inner pool of clearest water. Here is a whole world waiting to be interpreted by the archaeologist.

Temple of Minaksi at Madurai. It belongs to the seventeenth century and guards a collection of priceless jewels.

When the city of Zimbabwe arose

An ancient African city which still puzzles and fascinates the archaeologists is Zimbabwe, in the south east of Zimbabwe Rhodesia. The enormous stone walls, dating back to between A.D. 1100 and 1500, suggest a civilization which was certainly African although mixed with outside influences.

Recent research into the question has disproved the ancient legend which claimed that Zimbabwe was the last trace of the fabulous kingdom of Ofir and the site of King Solomon's mines.

Its reputation had attracted the attention of a private society which, towards the end of the nineteenth century, had devastated Zimbabwe and the surrounding area in its search for gold and other treasures.

What remains of the ancient civilization is gathered together with the utmost care by the archaeologists. The most usual findings are gold ornaments and pieces of jewellery with engraved patterns. From their discoveries archeologists hope to learn the history of one of the most ancient and advanced peoples of Africa.

When the Moslem civilization began in the Sudan

Africa is an immense, almost untouched field of research which daily proves to be increasingly important for our understanding of unknown cultures and civilizations.

The Sudan is one of the few regions of Africa scientifically explored in the nineteenth century. The German explorer and archaeologist, Heinrich Barth, after years spent in the Sudan, brought back a book of detailed notes. In it he meticulously described the features of the area he had explored.

Nothing escaped his careful investigation: the houses, the villages, the tribal customs, are all listed, together with purely geographical notes about rivers, mountains, vegetation, distances and so on.

With the help of this work Europeans were able to learn about the Sudan at a time when Africa was for the most part still unknown. Around Timbuktu today there are still buildings which are of great interest from an archaeological point of view. Some of these are mosques which are a sign of an active trade with the Moslem Arabs.

Massive wall at Zimbabwe, dating back to A.D. 1500

When archaeology joined forces with atomic science

The atomic scientists who discovered nuclear energy may have been aware of its enormous potential, but they certainly could not have foreseen the infinite uses to which this energy would be put within the space of a few years. If they had been told that nuclear energy would even be used in archaeology, the inventors of the atomic bomb would have had serious doubts.

Yet today this is a tool which has provided definite proof. It all started with the discovery that living organisms contain Carbon 14, which is produced by the neutral particles in cosmic rays penetrating Earth from outer space.

Since Carbon 14 is reduced by half over a period of 5,568 years, archaeological discoveries can be dated by measuring how much Carbon 14 is still contained in them.

The oldest African mosque at Timbuktu to have lasted until the present day is built of sun-baked bricks

Skeleton surrounded by objects (above)
Radio-carbon dating is now used to
ascertain the age of skeletons and other
archaeological discoveries (below)

Cro-Magnon Man   Neanderthal Man

Animal bone
(Palaeolithic)

5   17   15

The apparatus used in this delicate task has only been working for a few years but it has already given invaluable service to archaeology.

Establishing the age of the discoveries, which may date back 30,000 years, has often been essential for deeper and more accurate knowledge.

Although this highly delicate method still has some limitations, it is true to say that it has already introduced the archaeology of tomorrow.

Other recent technical inventions are also being used. The ground containing traces of ancient buried civilizations can be picked out from aerial photographs taken from great heights. Even the artificial satellites are proving to be extremely helpful in this field, with the information and photographs they are continually sending back to Earth.

Special camera equipment helps explore ancient tombs, underground passages and chambers which were the work of man. There is no longer any need for the traditional excavations which often risked permanent damage to the priceless buried treasures.

Even the computer has now been put to use by archaeology. Recently the whole of the Great Pyramid of Cheops was X-rayed centimetre by centimetre by a complex computer capable of revealing not only the composition of the blocks used to build it, but also whether unknown cavities were hidden inside the monument.

This is only one example. The future alone can tell how much computers have to contribute to the development of the science of archaeology.

Enormous strides have been made along the road leading to

the discovery of the ancient civilizations. Archaeology has revealed
the existence of unknown peoples,
their ways of life, their dress and
even the reasons for their disappearance.

It would seem as if little is left
to be told about the mysteries of
the past, as if there could be no
new civilizations to dig up. Yet
the experts insist, with undeniable
proof, that archaeology today is
still in its infancy and that it has
reached a turning-point in its
methods of research.

Scientific discoveries and technical advance provide the students
of the past with an impressive
array of tools. But the archaeological conquests of tomorrow
will be all the greater as an increasing number of specialists go
to work in the field and find
themselves having to work as a
team.

The figure of the romantic
archaeologist is becoming more
and more a memory of the past.

WHEN WAR BEGAN

When did war begin? This is a question which has never been answered. It is probably as old as man and may be older.

According to some scholars,

Mars, God of War

the first war was fought towards the end of the Great Ice Age: two tribes of apes, one vegetarian and living in the forests, and one meat-eating and living on the plains, fought over a territory which was gradually shrinking as the sheets of ice advanced. Although this is pure guess-work, war has existed since the earliest signs of human civilization.

The majority of archaeological discoveries consists of weapons which were not necessarily used for hunting animals. The Bible, Egyptian, Babylonian and Hittite history, the Homeric poems are all full of descriptions of battles and wars, which have influenced the course of history. But, although war is a constant theme in the history of man, his ways of fighting it have altered profoundly. In the Stone Age it was customary for the winners to devour the losers at the end of a battle; today the Geneva Convention controls the treatment of prisoners of war, although it cannot be said that it is always strictly observed. In the Age of Chivalry battles were fought by a rigid code of rules, but today men can fight without even seeing their enemy.

War is therefore an interesting guide to the technological progress, dress and morals of the people fighting it and as such it is extremely important to students. But it is also the most tragic, horrifying and inconclusive act that man can ever commit.

When a handful of men changed the history of the world

Battles which have made their mark on the destiny of the world are rare in the history of man. One of these rare cases is the battle of Gaugamela.

It was the year 331 B.C. Alexander the Great had been sitting on the doorstep of the vast Persian Empire for several years past but now he had issued an historical challenge to his giant foe. The kingdom of the Persian Emperor, Darius III, was so vast that it had taken him many years to call together an army from all his people. But, at last, at the head of an army larger than any previously assembled, numbering more than half a million foot soldiers, 45,000 horsemen, 15 elephants and 200 war-chariots, he hurried to squash finally the annoying mosquito which had dared to bother him.

Against this huge army Alexander pitted a small formation, the spearhead of which was the Macedonian phalanx: 9,000 men armed with very long lances and arranged in eight columns along a one-kilometre front.

The morning of the battle dawned. In the weak October sun the Macedonians watched the huge Persian army launch itself into the attack with a tremendous roar. The wing of the Macedonian army broke under this human sea. Darius was certain of victory. But suddenly the phalanx appeared.

Behind the terrifying iron wall of their lances, the Macedonians aimed at the opposing army. Darius' lines wavered, then broke. It was all over! One of the greatest empires ever to have existed had miserably crumbled.

When proud Rome was brought to its knees

At the Caudine Forks the Romans underwent a humiliating experience. Ambushed by the Samnites in 321 B.C., they were compelled to pass, one by one, under a yoke formed by two crossed swords, as a sign of submission. They were then free to return home.

The only compensation the Samnites demanded was that the Romans should finally decide to lay down their arms for ever. In view of their sorry situation, the Consuls accepted and peace was signed, but the Roman senate, which had not had to go under the yoke, thought it better to reopen hostilities.

And so proud and haughty Rome, having suffered such a humiliating defeat, was further

Roman soldier

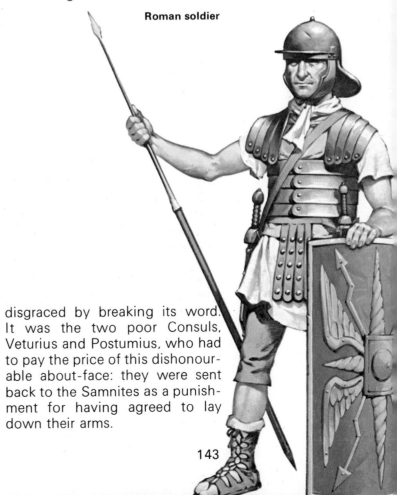

disgraced by breaking its word. It was the two poor Consuls, Veturius and Postumius, who had to pay the price of this dishonourable about-face: they were sent back to the Samnites as a punishment for having agreed to lay down their arms.

When the trumpets of Rome put Hannibal to flight

The battle of Zama, in 202 B.C., was the decisive battle in the Second Punic War. It was an important moment for Roman history because it marked the final defeat of Carthaginian power.

It would be impossible to describe it in a few lines, but there was one strange event which played a big part in the outcome of that encounter.

The armies of Hannibal and Scipio were facing each other; the forces were slightly in favour of Carthage, which had 50,000 men against the 45,000 of Rome. Above all, it had one exceptional weapon: its elephants.

But those very elephants were the ruin of Carthage. The cunning Scipio knew what they were like and, when he saw them advancing, he gave orders to his trumpeters to blow their bugles with all their might.

The awful noise terrified the huge animals who fell back, trampling on the Carthaginian cavalry behind them.

Seeing their confusion and surprise, Scipio sent in his troops to the attack. The Carthaginians were defeated and their might was crushed for ever.

When Europe was saved from the Moors

It was A.D. 732 and the Moorish Empire was at its peak. The Moorish armies, under the command of the Caliph Abder Rahaman, had occupied Spain, crossed the Pyrenees and descended into France. The road to the plains of Central Europe was wide-open to invasion. Against this threat was Charles Martel, grandfather of Charlemagne, at the head of a coalition of the peoples of France.

It was a clash between two different civilizations, different not only in their religions and cultures but also in the way they fought. On one side the Moors, lightly armed, placed their trust in their archers and horsemen, armed with javelins and scimitars. On the other side was the powerful apparatus of war of the tall, strong Franks, completely protected by steel, armed with broad shields and long, heavy swords or terrifying battle-axes; these warriors were mounted on powerful horses which were much taller than the highly-strung Arab ponies.

For several days the Moslems had been trying to provoke the Frankish warriors and make them come down from the hills of Poitiers, where they were drawn up in a long, unbroken wall of steel. They wanted to engage them in hand-to-hand combat, at which they were experts, but Charles Martel did not yield and, on the morning of 7 October, the Moorish horsemen finally took the initiative and launched themselves into the attack.

For hour after hour the Moors battled against the giants without managing to break their array. Then, towards sunset, the Franks suddenly stirred and attacked in serried ranks. The impact of the Christians was so great that the Moslems panicked. As darkness fell the hills of Poitiers were littered with the corpses of retreating Moors and the Empire of the Crescent Moon saw its dream of a conquered Europe crumble.

Charles Martel had broken the Moslem invasion of France, saved Aquitaine, and established his title as defender of Christendom.

When Turkish rule in the Mediterranean was ended

More than 800 years had passed since the battle of Poitiers. The Turks had taken the place of the Arabs in controlling the southern Mediterranean but the old rivalries between Christian and Moslem were not dead yet. One of the greatest naval conflicts in history was about to take place: the battle of Lepanto on 7 October 1571.

The forces in the field were more or less equal: estimates vary slightly, but there were about 240 Christian galleys plus 6 larger galleasses to about 260 Moslem ships. The battle was fierce and lasted many hours. The Christians were suddenly put at an advantage, however, by the arrival of the

of the Turkish galleys were rows of slaves, mostly Christian prisoners who certainly did not look favourably on their masters. The oarsmen in the Christian ships, on the other hand, were mainly volunteers or prisoners who knew they would regain their freedom if the Christian squadron won.

This situation was to the Europeans' advantage for two reasons. Firstly, in the hand-to-hand fighting, they could rely on the help of the oarsmen, who were allowed

Sixteenth-century Venetian galley

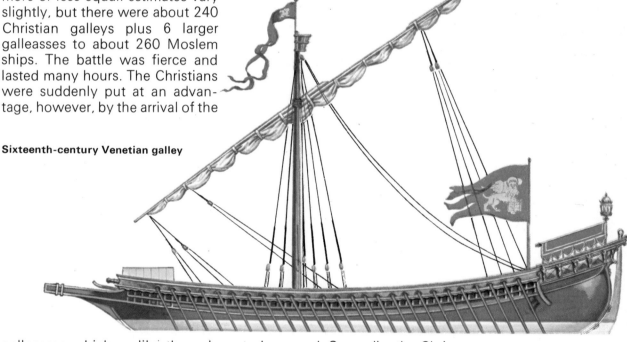

galleasses which, unlike the galleys, bristled with cannons both on their prows and on their broadsides.

This initial superiority was then strengthened still more by another advantage. In those days, although the ships had sails, they were propelled mainly by oars. Altogether there were more oarsmen than soldiers on the ships at Lepanto. But between the two armies there was one great difference: chained to the benches

to be armed. Secondly, the Christians at the oars of the Turkish ships sometimes managed to free themselves, settling skirmishes which were vital to the Europeans. These two factors, combined with the great courage of the fighters, helped Don John of Austria, commander of the Spanish, Venetian, Papal, Genoese, Maltese and Florentine allies, to get the better of the valiant Ali Pasha and finally to break Moslem power in the Mediterranean.

General Wolfe dies

When Canada became a British colony

During the Seven Years War, (1756–63), the Prussians' English allies attacked the French in their overseas possessions. Of these, one of the most important was Canada, with its beautiful city of Quebec on the St. Lawrence river. At Quebec the French had a well-seasoned garrison under the command of General Montcalm. England, however, had already set her sights on Canada.

At the end of the summer of 1759, a British naval squadron sailed up the St. Lawrence, heading towards the city. A strong contingent of troops landed under the command of General Wolfe, who surrounded the city and attempted to attack it from the front. The manoeuvre was unsuccessful and, in the course of a fierce battle, the English were driven back.

So Wolfe made his troops set sail again and head back down the St. Lawrence. The French general, Montcalm, detailed a large number of men to follow the British retreat and General Wolfe seized his opportunity.

He sailed secretly back up the river, landed a little more than a mile from Quebec and climbed the heights of Abraham to the plains above. The French came out of the city to give battle and throughout 13 September the two armies fought bravely until the British troops eventually gained the upper hand. On 17 September the French evacuated and the next day the city surrendered.

At the end of the conflict among the dead were the two generals, Wolfe and Montcalm.

This battle was of great his-historical importance for the Americans. Following it, in 1760, Amherst captured Montreal for the British. France had to give up her claim to Canada, which became a British colony, and French colonial power declined in America.

When a handful of Swedes routed the Russian Army

It happened at Narva, a little town on the icy Gulf of Finland, in the winter of 1700.

The town's small garrison, a thousand of the Swedes' allies, was besieged by an army of 60,000 Russians under General Dolgorovky. The Russians wanted to snatch the base from the Swedish King Charles XII. The story is one of the most glorious pages in Swedish and world history.

The winter was particularly severe that year. The snow had fallen very thickly and made the roads impassable. Nevertheless, Charles XII, aware of the danger threatening his allies at Narva, did not hesitate to march to their aid.

Hindered by the cold, the mud and the snow, the expedition came in sight of Narva on 20 November. Without a moment's rest and deliberately ignoring the superior numbers of its opponents, it moved in to attack the Russians who were besieging the town.

Against the 60,000 soldiers and 145 cannons of the Czar, Charles XII had only thirty-seven cannons and 10,000 men: six Russians for every Swede!

The relief force threw itself into the attack. The besieging Russians, surprised by the vigour and bravery of their enemy, fled in disorder after three hours' hard fighting.

The collapse of a bridge on the road of retreat hampered the Russians' flight and many of the fleeing soldiers died a miserable death in the frozen waters.

Narva and its heroic defenders were saved, while the Russians paid for the bravery of the Swedish soldiers with 18,000 dead. The

Eighteenth-century Swedish grenadier

Swedes, on their part, had only lost 2,000.

This victory gave the Swedes supremacy in the Baltic.

When the power of the United States began

Saratoga, 1777. The American War of Independence was smouldering. The Redcoats, the universal symbol of the mighty British Empire, were completely out of their depth. They were faced not by any regular army but by a collection of colonials determined to defend their rights and ready to drive the English off their land at all costs.

Up until then, however, all that had happened was petty harassing or guerilla attacks. The English were convinced that, once they had forced their opponents out into the open, their superior knowledge of military tactics would triumph.

But they were wrong. They sailed off down the Hudson but were defeated by the rebels for the first time on 19 September in the battle of Freeman's Farm, and again on 7 October at Bemis Heights. Then they were forced to retire to Saratoga.

Nor were they allowed to rest there. The rebels, led by General Gates, laid siege to the town and, after some violent skirmishes, succeeded in breaking the enemy resistance. General Burgoyne had no alternative but to surrender and hope that the Americans would let him withdraw with his troops.

Gates did not hesitate. He knew that the English were men of honour and, as soon as he had their promise that they would never again take up arms against the colonies, he allowed them to return home.

So American power began. It was a power born of a generous, human gesture which did credit both to the victors and the vanquished.

Austrian Dragoons officer (1805)

When the wind joined forces with Napoleon

In the days of the great sailing ships, the direction of the wind or a change in the weather were deciding factors in the outcome of battles. Not everyone knows, however, that the wind played an important part at Marengo, too, where Napoleon inflicted a heavy defeat on the Austrian army.

Resting in Italy after the Egyptian campaign, Napoleon found himself confronted by a strong Austrian army entrenched in Alessandria.

This time the great general disobeyed his own rules. Once in sight of the city, he set up camp near the village of Marengo and dispatched General Desaix with a strong contingent to check that the Austrians were not leaving. His own forces were thus split.

So on the morning of 14 June 1800, when General Melas marched out of Alessandria at the head of 30,000 Austrians, Napoleon had only 19,000 men with whom to oppose him. He quickly sent messengers to Desaix, but he knew they had little chance of reaching him in time.

The battle began at eight o'clock in the morning. By five in the evening all seemed lost for Napoleon. Melas returned to Alessandria to announce his victory. But suddenly, in a cloud of dust, Desaix appeared, after a forced march to help the French. The tables were turned and the Austrians surrendered under the onslaught of the fresh reinforcements.

The French lost about 4,000 men, including Desaix who fell in the attack; the Austrians lost 9,500.

Napoleon won with the help of the wind. Desaix, in fact, had not received the messages but had heard the noise of the shooting carried across to him by the wind, which was fortunately blowing in the right direction!

Soldiers of the nineteenth-century French army

When Nelson fought his last battle

Trafalgar is one of the best known battles in history. It took place off Cape Trafalgar, south of Cadiz, on 21 October 1805, when the English dealt a mortal blow to the might of Napoleon. It was on this occasion that Nelson sent the famous signal to his fleet: 'England expects that every man will do his duty.'

In the middle of the fierce fighting the French vessel *Redoutable* became locked in battle with the *Victory*, Nelson's flag-ship. After a bloody clash the French were driven back, but a shot from a sniper's musket in the *Redoutable's* topmast had mortally wounded Nelson.

If at this point the flag of the British admiral had been lowered, there was a risk that the other British ships would have given up the fight at the crucial moment. So the news of Nelson's fatal wound was withheld from the English fleet.

It was only at the end of the battle that the victorious English learned of the death of their admiral, Napoleon's enemy till the bitter end.

The *Ohio* (above, left); French battleship (above, right); the *Victory* (below)

When Napoleon lost his Empire

The Battle of Waterloo, which brought an end to the Napoleonic Empire, is famous in history for the savage violence of the fighting, which involved hundreds of thousands of men and lasted on and off for three days, from 15 to 18 June 1815.

Napoleon's army was 120,000 men and 570 cannon strong, while the Anglo-Prussian allies had a total of 220,000 men and 500 cannons.

Until sunset on the third day, on the field of La Haye Sainte, Bonaparte had managed to save his empire.

For more than twelve hours, without food or drink, the soldiers of both sides had been slaughtering each other. Yet the initial positions remained unchanged, apart from the piles of dead and wounded mixed with the acrid smoke of the cannon fire and the dust churned up by the cavalry charges.

At seven in the evening, after trying all day, the French broke through. Although pressed in the rear by the Prussians, Napoleon's victory was in his grasp. All that remained was to send in the Old Guard, the pride of his army.

But, for the first and last time in his life, the Emperor hesitated. After nearly an hour, when he ordered the attack, it was already too late. The English troops under Wellington had been reinforced with the help of the Prussians, and the French charge was repelled. The evening of 18 June 1815 saw the massacre of the Imperial Guard and the crumbling of a world. One hour of indecision had changed the course of history.

When the military might of Germany was born

Germany was born one rainy day in July 1866. Prussia and the Austro-Hungarian Empire were fighting for control of the German principalities. After occupying the territories which now make up Western Germany, the Prussian army turned south, divided into three columns. Waiting for it was a strong Austrian army.

The Prussians won and they won because of their own mistake. In command of the Prussian army was Count von Moltke, an experienced, careful strategist who had a very definite plan: to keep the three columns of his army separate on the march and then reunite them for the battle. But Prince Karl, at the head of one of these columns, thought otherwise.

As soon as he was within reach of the enemy he joined up with the nearest column and moved into the attack in a position of weakness.

Defeat seemed certain but Moltke knew how to make the most of even a calamity like that. He ordered the column which had stayed in the rear to advance quickly.

While Prince Karl engaged the main body of the Austrian army, he waited hopefully. Towards evening, when the situation seemed desperate, the reinforcements arrived and the Austrians were defeated.

So a tactical error turned into one of the most brilliant military masterstrokes and marked the start of German power.

Soldiers of the 92nd Highlanders

WHEN EXPLORING BEGAN

Primitive man's daily worry was how to survive physically. Feeding himself, bringing children into the world and providing for them, took up his whole attention for a long time. But every time man worried about his surroundings, he was unconsciously starting to discover the Earth.

What lay beyond the ring of mountains encircling the fertile valley? Where did the river run, from which he drank every day? What secrets were hidden in the vast sea which lapped the shore? What had the countless stars moving across the sky to do with the life of man? Would the Sun which rose in the morning come back and shine again after it had sunk below the horizon in the evening, leaving the Earth in darkness? Would the Moon dare to come out at night to comfort all the living creatures?

As primitive man tried to find the answer to these questions, he was exploring the Earth and making the first geographical discoveries.

The first people whose dress and way of life are well-known to us were comfortably settled on the land, from which they obtained food and prosperity. The farming peoples were often dissatisfied with their surroundings, however, and invented unknown worlds and lands full of riches.

Their stories magnified their desires, coloured them with magic and carried them off to wonderful adventures. That is how the most beautiful legends began. Although interwoven with fantasy, they all contain elements of truth.

The Golden Fleece which, according to legend, the Greek, Jason, travelled to find as far afield as the edge of the Black Sea, is probably a fable grown up round a simple labourers' implement. It was most likely the sheepskin, which gold prospectors used for sieving gold dust out of river sand.

One of the greatest stories of adventure and exploration is of Odysseus' wanderings. After the Trojan War, he visited many strange places and encountered innumerable obstacles before returning home to Ithaca.

When the first explorations were made

The first news of geographical discoveries of any importance dates back to about 600 B.C. It comes from Egypt, where during the reign of the Pharaoh, Necho II, an expedition was organized to sail round Africa, from the Red Sea to the Nile delta.

The Pharaoh entrusted the venture to the Phoenicians. He knew what good seamen they were and was perhaps afraid that the Egyptian boats, built to sail the waters of the Nile, might not stand up to the sudden storms of the ocean. The voyage ended happily but lasted three long years.

Necho not only realized how important it was to complete the voyage round Africa, but also started planning a very forward-looking canal which was to join the Nile to the Red Sea. It was only the terrible wars he had to wage against his country's enemies which prevented him from carrying out his project.

The Egyptians were the people with great ideas but it was the Phoenicians who performed the fantastic feats. They were a people who had settled on a coastal strip of land at the eastern end of the Mediterranean and who had many colonies, the most important being Tyre and Sidon.

In the sixth century B.C. they were already making regular journeys from the coast of Africa to Great Britain, especially to Devon and Cornwall which they called the 'Tin Islands'.

To do this they had constantly to pass the terrible Pillars of Hercules, which stand on opposite sides of the Strait of Gibraltar and were supposed to mark the end of the world.

Primitive Egyptian galley with papyrus sail used on the Nile in 3000 B.C. for carrying grain

Phoenician merchantman

When Africa was first explored

Ever since the earliest times Africa has been a land of promise. It was therefore only natural that the peoples living around the Mediterranean should feel a burning desire to explore it. The voyage round Africa in the sixth century before Christ was not an isolated incident. Other important expeditions preceded and followed it.

The Egyptians, for example, in the reign of the first lady Pharaoh, Hatshepsut (from about 1503 to 1481 B.C.), pushed inland to explore Nubia and the remote areas of Somalia, called the 'land of Punt', the 'land of aromatics and incense' mentioned in ancient Egyptian writings. There they were

The Vikings reached America in the tenth century A.D. and must have met the redskins (left)

lavished with hospitality by the native sovereign.

The main reason for this expedition was a search for precious wood which was known to be plentiful in those lands. The Egyptians must have been amazed to see the lake-dwellings of Punt built on stilts with the same wood that was so valuable to them.

Several centuries later, towards A.D. 150, the Greeks followed the coast of East Africa as far as Zanzibar.

The remains of numerous buildings are proof of the interest which Rome was bound to have taken in the African markets. Concrete evidence of how much was already known about Africa at the turn of the second century A.D. is the map which the great Ptolemy drew, using the wide geographical knowledge of the time.

When the Vikings reached North America

One group of people above all others has the distinction of having discovered an amazing number of new countries: it was the Vikings, with their natural thirst for adventure.

Even today it is not known quite how far they went with their daring expeditions. We know for certain, however, that around A.D. 1,000 they even touched the land which Christopher Columbus only reached 500 years later.

Born sailors, expert navigators, eager for adventure, they had already frequently visited the Mediterranean. They then set themselves to explore the unfriendly regions of the North.

One island which had a special fascination for them was Greenland. The first to reach it was Eric the Red, towards 980.

After a while, as nothing more was heard of him, Bjarni Herjolfsson set forth in search of the vanished sailor. By chance a storm tossed the Viking ships against an unknown coast, that of North America, but Bjarni did not want to land there.

The first European really to set foot on the country now called America was Eric the Red's second son, Leif Ericsson, although he did not realize the importance of this event.

With thirty-five men he had set out from Greenland, passing by Baffin Island, which he called 'the land of the flat stone'.

He then followed the coasts of Labrador and Newfoundland and spent much of the winter in what he named 'Vinland', or 'Wineland', because of the grapes which grew there. Scholars have situated Vinland on the coast of the present North America.

When Henry the Navigator took the first steps towards colonialism

At the time when sea trade was dominated by the maritime republics of Genoa and Venice, and North African trade was monopolized by the Arab merchants, Henry the Navigator (1394–1460) came on the scene.

Son of John I of Portugal, he

felt a burning desire for adventure. When he was only twenty-one years old he conquered Ceuta, the fortified North African port opposite Gibraltar, which had been an Arab possession for centuries. This thorn in the side of Europe had been an important factor in Arab expansion in Spain and Portugal.

For Henry, this early conquest was only the start of a scheme which filled his thoughts. He was

sure that, beyond the immense Sahara, lived rich and prosperous nations with really fabulous gold mines.

Having seen the failures of other explorers, however, he moved cautiously. He encouraged marine engineering, founded a naval academy at Sagres and planned long sea voyages with the eye for detail of someone who knows he is embarking upon tremendous adventures.

Henry, who was called 'the Navigator' because of his passion for the sea, may rightly be regarded as the first conqueror and explorer of modern times.

When the Portuguese rounded Cape Verde

Such whole-hearted enthusiasm and complete dedication as those of Henry the Navigator could not fail to bring amazing results. The Portuguese sailors, although terrified by ancient superstitions and beliefs, ended up by actually wanting to go on the most daring adventures and the most dangerous voyages.

Spurred on by their passion for the sea, they discovered Madeira in 1420 and explored the Azores in 1427.

In 1434 a Portuguese ship commanded by Gil Eanes rounded Cape Bojador, opposite the Canary Islands. But the greatest victory against the ancient nightmares which preyed on the minds of the European sailors was the expedition of Dinis Dias: in 1445 he rounded Cape Verde, the most westerly point of Africa.

Dinis' voyage, which finally opened the doors of the immense riches of darkest Africa to the Europeans, was hailed by Henry the Navigator as the climax of his long, impassioned work. The way was clear and the superstitions defeated at last: the most wonderful opportunities now seemed possible.

The sea charts became more and more accurate and the navigational aids increasingly helpful until, in 1446, Alvaro Fernandes was able to probe his way along the coast of Africa nearly as far as the modern Sierra Leone.

This was the furthest point reached by Portuguese exploration in Prince Henry's lifetime.

When the caravel sailed

The maritime explorations promoted by Henry the Navigator would, by themselves, have been enough to ensure him a place in history. But he had another great distinction: he helped build a new type of ship, the caravel. Developed by the Portuguese for exploring the coast of Africa, the caravel was capable of standing up to long sea voyages and of achieving remarkable speed.

Henry probably guessed that the Atlantic would soon become the scene of the most glorious sea adventures. He certainly appreciated the importance of suitable equipment, capable of taking man to remote, unknown lands.

The caravel was not a completely new ship as it was derived from the carrack, a large ship already in use in the Italian seafaring towns. It was lighter and faster than the carrack and it had more sails and rigging capable of carrying a heavier load.

Originally used for coastal trips, the caravels soon proved to be the most suitable ships for making long voyages and sailing the stormy waters of the Atlantic.

Cross-section of a caravel (below). The caravel was not a completely new ship as it was derived from the carrack, a large ship already in use in the Italian seafaring towns.

The Santa Maria

When the idea occurred of reaching India from the west

In 1460 Henry the Navigator died without having achieved one of his greatest ambitions: to reach India by sailing round Africa.

The price of spices and other oriental products was very high in Europe because of the cost of transport. They came part of the way by sea, as far as the Red Sea, and then by land, as far as the ports of the Mediterranean.

After the death of Henry the Navigator, pride of place in maritime exploration passed from Portugal to Spain, thanks to the work of the Italian, Christopher Columbus, one of the best remembered men in history.

He was born in Genoa in about the year 1451, a natural sailor, brave and imaginative, who became dedicated to the study of geography and astronomy. Helped and advised by the Florentine geographer, Paolo Toscanelli, he reached a conclusion which was the start of his amazing expedition: if the world is round it must be possible to reach the East by sailing towards the West. Instead of sailing around Africa he decided to cross the Atlantic to reach India.

It was a fortunate geographical error that further convinced Columbus that his idea was right. He thought that the circumference of the Earth was less than we now know it to be.

It is interesting to note that not even after Columbus had discovered America did he realize his mistake, and so he did not suspect that between the point where he landed and the coasts of India there stretched an entire continent and the biggest of the world's oceans.

Columbus 1492–3
Columbus 1493–6
Columbus 1498
Columbus 1502–4
Da Gama 1497–9
Cabral 1500
Land known in 1492

Lisbon
Palos
Cadiz
The Azores
Madeira
The Canary Islands
San Salvador
Tropic of Cancer
Haiti
Cape Verde Islands
The Equator
Porto Seguro

When Columbus' plan nearly failed

Columbus knocked on every door, trying to find someone who would give him the chance of proving that his theory was right. He was so confident of his brilliant idea and certain of the success of his venture, that he put up with all kinds of humiliations and awkward situations.

At last he seemed to have found somebody prepared to listen to him: Queen Isabella of Spain. She promised to submit his plan for consideration by a special commission of 'learned men and mariners'. This commission made him wait for four years for its decision.

Columbus almost knew what the experts were going to say: they were going to turn him down. Desk scientists are the last to understand expeditions of this kind, Columbus knew, but he waited in hopes for a word from the Queen, even though the committee had already announced its disapproval, as he had feared. But the Queen inexplicably remained silent.

After a long, futile wait, Columbus left for France, disheartened and disillusioned. Suddenly Isabella made up her mind and called him back, just when he was about to cross the border. Three ships were at his disposal, complete with crews and supplies. All they were waiting for was his order to sail.

For Columbus it was the end of a nightmare and the start of the adventure on which he had spent all his time and energy for so many years. His faith in the success of the expedition was unshakeable and in 1492 Columbus started his journey eager for victory.

When Columbus thought he had reached India

The dawn of 3 August 1492 saw three ships lined up in the port of Palos, about to set sail: they were the carrack, the *Santa Maria*, Christopher Columbus' flag-ship, and the two caravels, the *Nina* and the *Pinta*, three ships fit for the most difficult adventures.

The voyage, with its ups and downs, took longer than Columbus had expected.

A month passed with good and bad weather alternating and the sailors showed obvious signs of exhaustion and discontent. They were afraid they would not reach their destination, India, and only their leader's firmness kept them under control.

But, on 9 October, after more than two months at sea, the crews showed a bad sign of their strain: mutiny was being plotted. Columbus pleaded for three more days' time before giving up the expedition. It was enough. Flights of birds appeared and carved sticks and reeds were picked up, bringing the sailors hope. At sunrise on 12 October the long-awaited shout was raised from the crow's-nest of the *Pinta:* land ho!

The silhouette of an unknown land was looming on the horizon. Columbus and all his men were sure they had reached an island off the coast of western India. When other islands were discovered, they called them the 'Indies'

They could not know that their sea route to India was blocked by a vast mass of land, a land which stretched from the North Pole to the South Pole, a land which would later be known as America.

An account of Cabot's voyage, written shortly afterwards, says, 'In the year 1497, on 24 June, at about five o'clock in the morning, the Venetian John Cabot and his son Sebastian discovered that land towards which no one before them had dared to sail and they called it "First Sight" because, I believe, it was the first they had sighted'.

When Columbus became embittered and disillusioned

Christopher Columbus did not realize he had discovered a new continent but this does not detract from the bravery of his expedition.

On his return to Spain, Columbus was given a royal welcome. He had paved the way to Spanish colonial rule, which was to last for centuries. In the following years Columbus went back to Central America three times. He wanted to find out more about the enormous country he had discovered.

At home, however, the inevitable jealousies, court gossip and the mean ambitions of his rivals had embittered his satisfaction in his achievement. He left for his last expedition in 1502 but returned deeply disillusioned by what he had seen in the conquered lands.

It seemed to him that the natives had been robbed, cheated and, in many cases, massacred by a horde of fanatics driven on solely by their lust for power and wealth. Part of his dream was in ruins, the part in which he had seen himself not as a conqueror but as a civilizer.

When the Europeans reached North America

It was another Italian who landed in North America, this time further north. Like the great Columbus, he was convinced that the shortest way to the East was via the West.

John Cabot was born in Genoa in about 1450 but in 1476 he moved to Venice and became a citizen of that city. About eight year later, he went to London with his family. Henry VII supported him and granted him a contract to sail in search of un-

When he came back from his voyage in 1499, Amerigo Vespucci wrote: 'It is right to call it the New World. The ancients repeatedly said there was no land south of the Equator but my last voyage has proved they were mistaken because in the southern regions I have found a country inhabited by more people and animals than Europe'.

known lands. This was what the navigator wanted. The English ships, too, were very seaworthy and Cabot, who took his son, Sebastian, with him, came in sight of America at dawn on 24 June 1497.

The place where they landed corresponds to the modern Newfoundland. Cabot's journal describes it as full of white bears and enormous deer. The explorer reports that the inhabitants of that country wore furs and skins and that the sea was teeming with all kinds of fish.

In the same year in which Cabot completed his trip on the North Atlantic route, the Portuguese, Vasco da Gama, made his equally epic voyage on the routes to the south. He rounded the Cape of Good Hope and so opened the direct route to India.

Seldom have so many new and historic discoveries occurred within so short a space of time.

When the name 'America' was first used

After Columbus and Cabot there were countless explorers who probed the coast of America but there was one who gave his name to the new continent: Amerigo Vespucci.

The son of well-to-do parents who lived in Florence, Vespucci started off by studying the classics and then commerce. But he kept the precious fund of geographical knowledge which he had learnt from Paolo Toscanelli, the same scientist who had influenced Columbus' ideas.

Vespucci was a man of strong commonsense who also had a great spirit of adventure and he was able to survive some very difficult moments and dramatic situations. The calm he showed, even in times of extreme danger, has remained famous. Storms at sea and outbreaks of madness left him unruffled and in control of events.

When he got back from his voyages, which he made between 1497 and 1504, at the time of Columbus, he described what he had seen in the minutest detail, with special attention to situations involving people.

Even more than Columbus himself, he was convinced that the new lands were a completely undiscovered continent and he repeated this belief over and over again in his writings.

Perhaps this was the reason why in 1507, a year after the death of Columbus, the German mapmaker, Martin Waldseemüller, suggested that the name 'America', meaning 'Amerigo's land', be given to the new country because it had been so clearly described by Amerigo Vespucci.

Vasco Nuñez de Balboa reached the Isthmus of Darien, the old name for the neck of land between North and South America.

The straits of Magellan

When the Pacific Ocean was discovered

The first person to discover the Pacific Ocean was a Spaniard who landed in America in the wake of the explorer, Rodrigo de Bastidas. His name was Vasco Nuñez de Balboa.

His foresight was as great as his open-mindedness and courage. Remembering the information he had collected from all sides, he pushed down as far as the Isthmus of Darien, the old name for the neck of land between North and South America. After nearly two months of forced march through tropical jungle, he came in sight of the new ocean on 29 September 1513.

The expedition was made possible by the enforced help of 600 natives, under the orders of 200 Spanish soldiers. In the name of the King of Spain, Balboa took possession of the new ocean, calling it the South Sea.

In recognition of this expedition the King appointed Balboa governor under Pedro Arias de Avila. The conqueror's boldness, however, aroused the suspicions of his immediate superior who condemned him to death. But by then the ocean which was to become known universally as the Pacific had been revealed to the world.

When the first European ship entered the Pacific

Another Portuguese renewed the glories of Henry the Navigator: he was the nobleman, Fernão de Magalhães, best known as Magellan. In command of the Spanish fleet, he set off to reach India (Columbus' old dream) by crossing America and then sailing further westwards. He had five ships at his disposal and with them, on 20 September 1519, he headed straight for South America.

He calculated that, by sailing south down the coast of the new continent, he would eventually find a passage through to the ocean which Balboa had first discovered.

The hazards he had to overcome were deadly: in the month of June the *Santiago* was shipwrecked; there were few survivors. The other crews were not always prepared to accept the sacrifices which the situation demanded. When Magellan was almost certain he had finally found the long-sought passage, the *San Antonio* mutinied and sailed back to Spain.

At last the three surviving ships, after difficulties and mis-adventures of every kind, rounded the tip of South America. An immense but tranquil ocean finally lay before the disheartened sea-men and for this very reason the new ocean was called the Pacific.

When the first voyage round the world was completed

The ocean crossing lasted ninety-nine days, from 28 November 1520 to 6 March 1521. But Magellan's hopes and those of his men grew greater and greater as they waited expectantly for India to appear on the horizon.

When supplies were running alarmingly low the three Spanish caravels finally reached the lush islands now called the Philippines.

Here on Mactán Island on 27 April 1521, Magellan was killed in a skirmish with natives.

The expedition continued, although only after one ship, the *Concepcion*, had proved unsea-worthy and been burned.

On 6 November 1521 the *Trinidad* and the *Victoria* finally reached the goal of their dreams, India. On 21 December, when the two ships went to set forth again, laden with precious spices, the *Trinidad*, too, turned out to be too rotten to be seaworthy. The *Victoria*, under the command of Elcano, continued alone and alone she carried her men and cargo back to Spain.

On the voyage across the Indian Ocean and round the coast of Africa, scurvy and starvation claim-ed other victims.

In the end, on 7 September 1522, Elcano brought the leaking but spice-laden ship to anchor off Saville. There were only seven-teen other European survivors and four Indians, 'weaker than men have ever been before'. In three years the *Victoria* had sailed round the world, the first ship to do so.

Typical caravel (Portuguese)

When the Niger was explored

Europeans had long wanted to explore the interior of Africa. The obstacles in the way were so insurmountable, however, as to discourage any serious attempt. It was not until 1795 that a young Scottish doctor, Mungo Park, agreed to lead an expedition organized by the African Association of England.

The society had been created for scientific and trading purposes but it also hoped to do some good for the natives. The main task entrusted to Mungo Park was to explore the course of the river Niger.

His expedition lasted eighteen months and met with difficulties and dangers of every kind. He only just managed to find his way back to the English trading station at Pisania and then home.

On his return, Park wrote about his adventures in a book, *Travels in the Interior of Africa*, which was published in 1799 and became

Mungo Park became famous for his journeys down the Niger

Livingstone sees the Victoria Falls for the first time

very popular. After another six years, on 31 January 1805, he set out again for the Gambia, with an even larger party of explorers than had accompanied him in 1795.

He was determined to find the source of the Niger. Very few of his companions reached the banks of the river, however. Out of the forty European members of his expedition, all but eleven were struck down by fatigue and disease.

Park himself was drowned when he was attacked by hostile natives and his boat capsized in the turbulent waters of the Niger. He was not far from the source which he had so doggedly sought.

When Livingstone discovered the Victoria Falls

On 20 November 1840 another Scotsman, the medical missionary David Livingstone, set off to explore Africa. He penetrated into the heart of the Dark Continent, crossing the Kalahari Desert and discovering Lake Ngami and the river Chobe.

In 1852 he sailed a long way up the course of the great Zambesi River, where he was amazed at the grandeur and marvellous beauty of the landscape.

He found a way to fight slavery, which in those days was the 'open sore of the world', as he himself called the slave trade.

For thirty years he did not rest a moment from his religious and medical work. He finally succeeded in crossing Africa, from the Atlantic to the Indian Ocean.

During this expedition he discovered the highest waterfalls in the world, which he named Victoria, after the then Queen of England.

When Stanley found Livingstone

In 1869 the Englishman, Henry Morton Stanley, was sent to Africa by the *New York Herald*. His first task was to search for Livingstone, of whom nothing had been heard for five years. He eventually found him in the village of Ujiji on the west side of Lake Tanganyika, in 1871, and greeted him with the famous words, 'Dr. Livingstone, I presume'.

Stanley then went on methodically to explore the area around the lake. Another epic voyage took him from Lake Victoria to Lake Tanganyika and thence to the Congo.

The newspaper accounts of his travels were followed with great interest all over the world and especially by King of the Belgians, Leopold II. When Stanley returned to Europe in 1878, Leopold persuaded him to work for him towards setting up a Congo Free State under Belgian rule.

Sir Henry Morton Stanley

all subsequent astronomical research, which Ptolemy summarized in his *Almagest* (the Arabic word for 'the greatest') in the second century A.D.

According to these theories, the Earth is in the centre of the Universe with the planets and the stars rotating around it in circular orbits. This belief is known as geocentrism.

When Ptolemy's idea of the Universe collapsed

Ptolemy's theory was regarded as perfect and indestructible until, nearly twelve centuries later, the great Mikolaj Kopernik, known to us as Copernicus (1473–1543), reached the opposite conclusion. From his studies of the motion of the planets he decided that the centre of the Universe was the Sun and that the planets, including the Earth, move round it.

The Polish scientist could not announce his discoveries because they clashed with the official view and he was afraid of persecution. So the new idea was not published until after his death.

Known as the theory of heliocentrism, referring to the Sun as the centre, it was not developed further until the beginning of the seventeenth century, when the German, Johannes Kepler (Keplerus), confirmed it with his three famous laws of planetary motion.

The Italian, Galileo Galilei, then proved the theory scientifically with the use of the recently invented telescope. All these ideas were crowned by the English scientist, Sir Isaac Newton (1642–1727), who discovered the law of gravity, which explains why the planets are bound to rotate round the Sun and cannot drift away from it.

When man began to study the stars

Why does the Sun rise and set? Why does the Moon appear in so many shapes in the sky? Why do some stars look brighter than others? To these and many other questions man tried to find the answers, often mixing scientific facts with fanciful beliefs.

The beneficial effects of the Sun, for example, were thought to be so miraculous that they made primitive man believe in it as a god. The Egyptians and the Aztecs are outstanding among the peoples who worshipped the Sun, dedicating colossal temples to this, their greatest god.

Apart from religious and mythological beliefs, the earliest known studies of the stars date back to 3,000 years before Christ. The first accounts of unusual astronomical events (such as eclipses of the Sun and the Moon) were made then.

It was the Greeks, however, with Eratosthenes and Hipparchus, who first tried to give a scientific explanation to the astronomical happenings of their time. Their theories were taken as the basis of

Sundial

Aztec temple to the sun-god

When radio astronomy began

A new science, perhaps the youngest of all, is radio astronomy. With its help it is easier to understand not only the evolution of the Universe but also the very nature of our own planet.

The father of this new science is generally considered to be Karl Jansky, an American engineer. In 1931 he discovered that the signals on a 14·6 metre wavelength came from a precise point in the sky, in the area of the Sagittarius constellation.

In 1936, an American radio amateur, Grote Reber, using Jansky's directions, started to explore the sky, carefully noting the origin of the signals. The instrument he used was a parabolic dish nearly 10 metres in diameter, which may be said to be the first radio telescope.

Today there are radio telescopes with parabolic reflectors of 50 metres and more in diameter, capable of exploring the Universe thousands of millions of light years away. The telescope at Jodrell Bank measures 76 metres in diameter and was the first fully steerable radio telescope.

When the race to the Moon began

After so many conquests on Earth, man felt ready to conquer space. In this exciting and dangerous race, the boldness of the competitors was no longer sufficient. They had to be backed by the careful preparations of thousands of highly specialized people.

From now on it will become more and more necessary for the whole of mankind to unite all its energies if the exploration of space is to be successful. Proof of this is the race to the Moon, which has involved Russians and Americans in high-level competition.

On 4 October 1957 the U.S.S.R. launched the first of Earth's artificial satellites, the *Sputnik* (or 'fellow traveller').

Four months later, the first American satellite, *Explorer I,* discovered the Van Allen radiation belt above the Earth.

More than three years passed before, on 12 April 1961, the first man was launched into space. He was the Russian, Yuri Gagarin, who made a complete orbit of the Earth in 89·34 minutes.

On 20 February 1962 the first

Two of Galileo's telescopes

167

United States astronaut, John Glenn, was put into orbit. In June 1963 the first woman cosmonaut, Valentina Tereshkova, went into

Yuri Gagarin

The spaceship *Vostok*

The telescope at Jodrell Bank

orbit with her *Vostok 6*, two days after the *Vostok 5*.

Another two and a half years of feverish preparation passed and, on the 15 December 1965, two American spaceships rendez-voused in space, flying together for six hours: they were *Gemini 6* and *7*.

In January 1969 two Soviet spacecraft, the *Soyuz 4* and *5*, linked up in flight and, for the first time, two astronauts changed from one spacecraft to the other.

When the exploration of the Moon began

The success of the Americans in the race to conquer the Moon was given a decisive boost by the launching of *Apollo 9* in March 1969. It was then that the lunar module, the vehicle designed to carry the astronauts on the lunar soil, was tried out. The practice run for the landing on the Moon was entrusted to *Apollo 10*, which gave the astronauts Stafford and Cernan the chance to fly over the surface of the Moon in the lunar module.

The attention of the whole world was then turned to Cape Kennedy: and on the 16 July 1969 the American astronauts, Armstrong, Aldrin and Collins, left in the spaceship *Apollo 11* for the big expedition. After three days of perfect flight, on 17, 18 and 19 July, the lunar module broke loose from the command module with Armstrong and Aldrin on board and, on 20 July, it made a perfect landing on lunar soil.

Early on 21 July, Neil Armstrong became the first creature from Earth to set foot on the Moon. The goal which had seemed such folly had been achieved.

When other inhabitants of the Universe may be discovered

Astronomical research increases with all the new scientific instruments which are always being invented. Nowadays some very powerful telescopes are used to study the sky.

The telescope at Mount Palomar in California, for example, is world-famous for its huge reflector 5 metres in diameter. Radio telescopes have also greatly extended the field of research into the Universe.

The Universe consists of countless other stars similar to the Sun, around which other planets and satellites often move, just as in our solar system.

The similarities between our solar system and other distant systems of stars are amazing. That is why the last great question which man has to ask is, perhaps, the most fascinating of all: do other beings like us exist on any of the countless worlds which fill the sky? And if they do exist, will we be able to communicate with them and find out how they live?

Though there would be enormous difficulties in finding common ground with the cultures of the other inhabitants of the universe, they would be overcome.

It is unlikely that we would be able to exchange literary information with them, but there are certain elementary ideas which must be understandable to any creature that has developed the apparatus needed to receive our radio messages. For instance, the theorem of Pythagoras would be easy to transmit and would be readily understood.

Experiments along these lines are already being carried out.

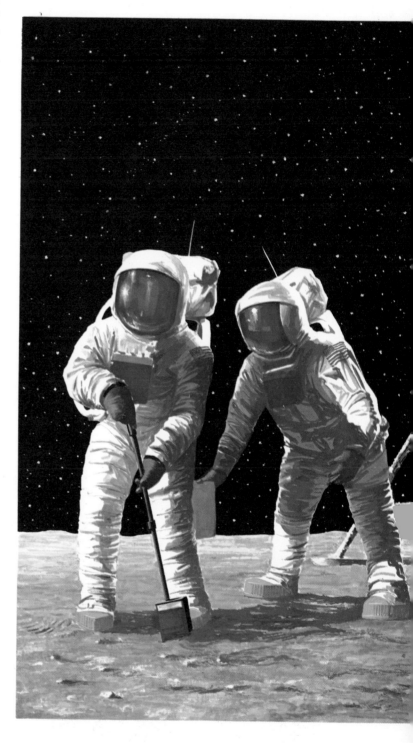

WHEN POWER BEGAN

Today we are always hearing about 'power': electric power, mechanical power, nuclear power. But, although the word seems so modern, it is in fact very ancient, going back to the dawn of man. The only kind of power known to primitive man was that of his own muscles. It was with the strength of their muscles alone that our distant ancestors struggled for what they needed to live and to gain the mastery over nature and the animals.

Soon man discovered that the power he had been given could be increased by special tools: a piece of wood or bone or a pointed stone were better weapons than his bare hands.

In fact one of the main characteristics of man as opposed to the less advanced animals is the ability to put natural materials to precise uses.

Most things that are made are tools or weapons, and they are fashioned in order to make up for man's physical deficiencies. They have played an enormously important part in the evolutionary process. With such instruments man found it much easier to kill his prey.

When primitive man then became a hunter of fast-moving animals and birds, he discovered the spear-thrower and the bow and arrow. These made him feel stronger and better able to secure the food he needed.

Spear-throwers and arrows were man's first real weapons. They marked an important stage in his development. The spear-thrower was a piece of wood with a hook in which a spear was engaged so that it could be thrown with much greater force. It was a kind of continuation of the human arm, a kind of catapult. A weapon very similar to the primitive spear-thrower is still used today by the Australian aborigines.

It was only with the bow and arrow, however, that man became a true hunter. He grew to be such an expert with this weapon that he could hit birds in flight and fishes swimming in the water. The rapid progress which man made after the discovery of these weapons shows how important they were to his evolution.

In particular, through them our ancestors became more aware of the muscular power they had been given. Although strengthened by their weapons, it still remained their chief force.

When animal power began to be used

Some time between 8000 and 5000 B.C. that is, in the Neolithic Age, students of the history of man tell us that he began not only to kill animals but also to breed them.

For thousands of years he had been hunting animals, some of them much larger and stronger than he was, to feed himself and obtain their skins. Now he had realized that it was better to make friends with them and put them to other uses, instead of always catching and killing them.

The first animals which man domesticated were probably the ones he needed for food. Quite soon, however, he learned to domesticate other, bigger animals which could help him till the fields.

The animals have helped tremendously in human activities.

Think, for example, of the many services they have carried out for farmers over the centuries: from ploughing to sowing, from watering the land to clearing it of trees, they have worked side by side with man.

Ancient horse-drawn 'locomotive': the horse walked on a moving track

When man began to use the forces of nature

Man had found his first urge to progress in the basic need to survive. As his life gradually became free of the burden of hunger, he began to take note of his surroundings.

Many of the things which he had discovered out of necessity were thus enriched by many others which he discovered out of curiosity.

For example, what was it that drove primitive man to move away from the place where he was born? What made him venture forth on the treacherous waters of the rivers and seas? What made him use the mysterious, powerful forces which nature had to offer? It was partly need but also curiosity, the two big incentives which have spurred on the progress of man in every age.

This spectacular 'flying fish' catamaran makes use of the power of the wind

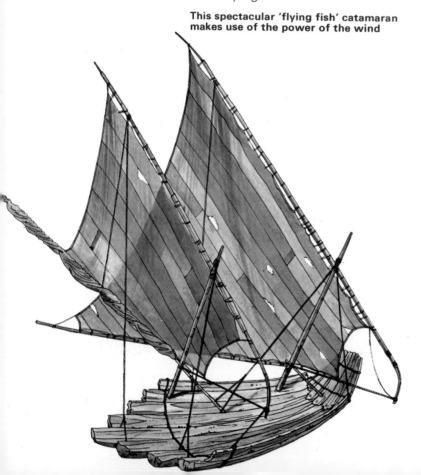

When man discovered the force of the wind

Exactly when the wind was first used by man for his own ends is uncertain but it may have happened at the beginning of the Neolithic Age.

In 1929 the archaeologist, Sir Flinders Petrie, excavating at Al Fayyum in Egypt, found a stone model of a sailing boat which he claimed had been made a good eleven thousand years before.

Sailing ships became widely used until, in the eighteenth century, they reached the height of their splendour. With their huge sails spread to the wind, they caught as much of it as possible and so were blown along at high speed.

The date when the first windmill made its appearance is also uncertain but it was probably introduced into Europe in the twelfth century. Windmills became increasingly widespread until the early nineteenth century when the development of steam power caused their slow decline.

The windmills of Holland are the most celebrated of all.

When man began to use solar energy

The Sun's energy, which gives life to all the creatures on Earth, is perhaps the one kind of energy which man has not yet learned to harness properly. Even in the field of bodily health, it is only in the last few decades that medicine has discovered how to use the health-giving powers of the Sun's rays for treating certain diseases.

If we remember that the Sun is emitting an astonishing amount of energy all the time, so much that it is quite beyond our grasp, and

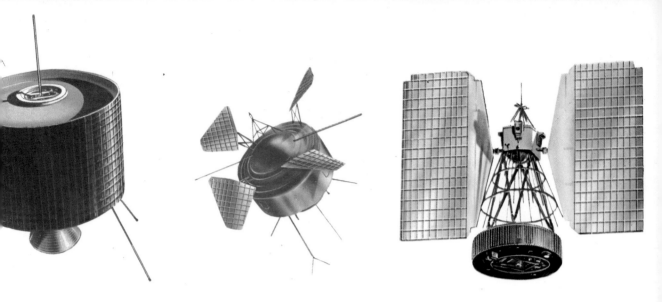

Early Bird, the first commercial communications satellite (left). The gigantic Russian satellite *Proton* (centre) The *Nimbus* (U.S.A.) (right)

that life about us is thriving because of it, we will have some idea of its potential uses.

Some very complex devices are already being worked by solar energy. There are, for example, the Orbiting Solar Observatories (O.S.O.) with special solar cells on their outsides to produce electric power. Other similar devices are mounted on space exploration equipment.

Or there is the solar furnace, consisting of a series of reflective mirrors to produce electricity from the heat of the Sun. The largest example of this is at the Laboratoire de l'Energie Solaire at Mont Louis in the eastern Pyrennees in France.

A recent invention is the electric car, operated by batteries charged by solar cells.

Electric vehicles are nothing new: they were used for the first time a century ago, and the first practical use of them dates from about 1900.

Among their obvious advantages is their silent running and the absence of fumes that pollute the atmosphere.

When man began to use the water of the rivers

The greatest civilizations grew up on the banks of rivers. Their water provided drink for men and animals and irrigated the fields.

River water was therefore used first of all to sustain life. Then man soon learned how to sail on the rivers, following the current. Even today, in densely wooded countries, lumberjacks use the currents

The train was invented in the nineteenth century. To the more old-fashioned it seemed an invention of the devil, destined to be very short-lived, but in fact it revolutionized the entire world of transport. Even today trains pulled by steam engines are still in use.

With the invention of electric power, industry was quickly radically transformed. Machines hitherto worked by steam were now worked by electricity.

to carry timber to the sawmill or port.

But the water of the rivers was a source of power which was to be more widely used. As soon as man invented the millstone he realized that the flow of the rivers could turn the millstones faster than a man or animal could by its own strength. Until quite recently nearly all rivers had their own watermills.

There was one point, at its falls, where the current became even stronger. There nothing could stop the rushing waters as they hurtled down with a deafening roar.

Yet, once again, man managed to find a way of harnessing this force. When the tranquil flow of the rivers was no longer sufficient to set his inventions going, the violent force of the waterfalls had to be called upon. Even today much of our electric power is produced by the water of waterfalls. Where there are no natural falls we build them artifically with weirs and dams.

When steam power was discovered

If we had to put an exact date on the beginning of the age of modern progress, we might well take 1690. This was the year in which Denis Papin put forward his conclusions on the study of water vapour in his thesis known as the *Acts of Leipzig*. His boiler, which he called a steam digester, was the mother of all the steam engines later used for converting the force of vaporized water into movement.

The use of hydrothermal power, that is power produced by superheated water, made rapid, successful progress. Steam power was one of the main causes of the

Industrial Revolution of the eighteenth century. Steam-driven looms gave rise to the first industrial boom of our times.

It was not until the nineteenth century, however, that the more ingenious use of steam gave birth to the train. To the more old-fashioned it seemed an invention of the devil, destined to be very short-lived, but in fact it revolutionized the entire world of transport.

Steam engines were in universal use for over 100 years, but after the Second World War, they dwindled in favour of diesel and electric traction. They are still used to a limited extent in some European countries but are rare in mainline service.

The power obtained by heating water was so great that sea transport, as well as land transport, was soon driven by special steam boilers. These turned enormous paddles, like watermill wheels, which propelled the ship along. The old Mississipi paddle-steamers which were a major form of transport on that river during the nineteenth century, are still famous.

When the power of the sea was harnessed

The sea is a deep, largely unexplored mine full of riches. The surprises in store for us in the future must be quite fantastic, considering that oil, gas, diamonds, cobalt, and manganese all abound in the sea.

The force of the tides is already being used to produce electric power. A famous example of this is the wave-power electricity generating station on the estuary of the river Rance in Brittany, France. It was opened on 26 November 1966 and is capable of producing 544 million kilowatt hours a year. The use of the temperature of sea currents to produce other types of power seems near at last.

Fresh water, however, is in short supply, acutely so in some places. This has led scientists to design and build plant for taking the salt out of sea water and so turn it into fresh water for drinking or industrial purposes.

In these days of the use of natural power, we look to the sea as one of our riches.

When electric power was discovered

Today we think nothing of pressing a switch and brightening our lives with warm light, turning a knob and watching a television show, moving a lever and starting up a whole factory. All this is made possible by a powerful and beneficial source of energy which we call electricity.

Not two centuries have passed since the discovery of Count Alessandro Volta who, with his battery, gave birth to the age of electricity in 1801. Yet electricity has become the indispensable force which makes the world go round.

The New Yorkers became only too aware of this when, on 9 and 10 November 1965, a city-wide black-out threatened their whole way of life.

The need for electricity is increasing rapidly and is used as a yardstick for the development of a community. But the production of electricity is meeting grave difficulties because the thermal variety poisons the environment, the hydro type has already expanded as far as it can go, and the nuclear sort is still too expensive.

When electrical energy was first used

One way of producing electricity is in generating stations operated by the force of water moving enormous turbines, or rotary motors. When connected to generators, they produce electric current.

Another kind of generating station is the thermoelectric station. Instead of the force of water it uses the force of heat produced by fuels like oil, coal or gas. This kind of generating station is on the increase because of the present shortage of water to feed hydroelectric stations. Tides are now being used to generate electricity, too.

The two essential pieces of equipment in a generating station are the turbine and the generator. The turbine is set going by the action of falling water or by steam produced by burning fuel.

hydroelectric station

dam

generator

penstock

turbine

waterflow

It then starts up a movement in the generator which converts this movement into electric current. The size of the turbines and generators varies according to the production capacity of each generating station.

Electric power is certainly the chief source of power in the twentieth century. We find it everywhere: there is not a machine which is not operated, directly or indirectly, by electricity. The production and consumption of this type of power is increasing at a tremendous rate.

For a rough idea of how much electric power is needed at the moment, we only have to realize that it takes one kilowatt of electricity to wash a few kilos of clothes in a washing machine but it takes a good 375 kilowatts to make a ton of steel and as much as 15,000 kilowatts to make a ton of aluminium.

The consumption of electric power in Europe is doubled every ten years. In 1970 it was 1,090,000 million kilowatt hours and it is estimated that it will be 1,692,000 million by 1976.

With consumption rising at this rate, production of electricity will have to grow just as fast, otherwise all human life will be thwarted by the inability to expand.

As the hydroelectric stations are inadequate, however hard they work, and the thermoelectric stations need coal and oil, supplies of which are slowly being exhausted, it is essential to find other sources of energy for making electricity.

The water collected in a reservoir is carried to its destination through various sizes of pipe. Similarly, electricity is carried by special copper cables which conduct a greater or lesser amount of power, depending on their thickness.

The huge cables are held up by pyramid-shaped framed steel pylons and the thinner lines supported by wooden or cement poles. Even thinner wires form the electrical circuits in our houses. As water runs from the biggest pipe into the smallest, so electricity is transmitted from the thickest cable to the thinnest.

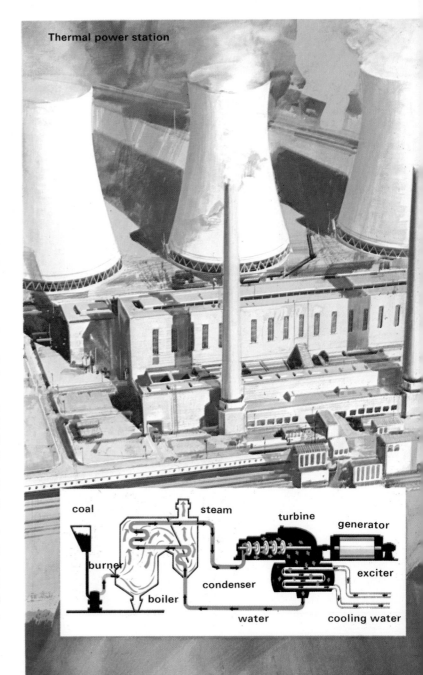

Thermal power station

coal   steam   turbine   generator

burner

boiler   condenser   exciter

water   cooling water

When electricity began to be used in industry

With the invention of electric power, industry was quickly transformed. Machines worked by steam were now worked by electricity. It saved time and was more practical and economical. Steam boilers were slowly replaced, although they remained the undisputed leaders in the field of transport: the electric train was still a long way off.

The invention of the hydraulic, or water-driven turbine, which made for better use of water power, was the work of the Frenchman, Benoît Fourneyron, in 1827.

Hydraulic turbines reached a high degree of perfection and it became possible to produce as much as 90 per cent of the theoretical maximum amount of power.

When the turbine came to be connected to direct current generators (dynamos) or alternating current generators (alternators), more electricity was produced more cheaply.

If we compare the earliest generators with the extremely powerful, sometimes colossal dynamos of the modern electricity stations, we will see how much progress has been made in this field, which is one of the most important industries of the present day.

When drilling for oil began

It seems certain that oil has been known about since the earliest times and that the most advanced peoples, like the Chinese, for example, used it in the normal way for lighting their homes.

It was only at the beginning of the nineteenth century, however, that scientists and technologists started seriously to investigate the use of oil as a source of power. The experiments proved that it was possible and oil was forecast as an indispensable source of energy in the very near future. Nearly all the oil which had been used up until then had been from natural outcrops on the surface but drilling for oil under the ground now began.

The first drilling took place on 27 August 1859 at Titusville, Pennsylvania, in the United States, when a 21-metre well was drilled. It was directed by Colonel Edwin Drake, a pioneer in oil prospecting in America. With the successful discovery of oil the area boomed and the first oil refinery was also built at Titusville.

High-speed 150 megawatt generator rotor (above)

50 megawatt generator stator (below)

When the internal combustion engine was invented

One invention destined to succeed was the internal combustion engine. In engines of this type, a fuel-air mixture is burned so that the hot gases produced exert a force on moving parts of the machine.

In the last years of the nineteenth century many attempts had been made to develop an engine of this type. Above all, it was the work of Lenoir, Schmidt, Beau de Rochas and Daimler which brought about the internal combustion engine, the father of all the millions of vehicles now travelling on the roads of the world, propelled by the same device.

Oil was used to run the new engine right from the start. If supplies of this precious liquid were to cease today, many of our activities would stop at once. The discovery of more and more petroleum deposits has therefore become a problem which concerns all the countries in the world.

When the use of petroleum spread

The rapid acceptance and spread of the internal combustion engine, particularly at the beginning of this century, made it all the more necessary quickly to increase the exploitation of existing petroleum deposits and find new ones.

The problem of transporting the crude oil, as petroleum in its natural state is called, from the wells to the refineries became more and more critical, too.

It is in the refineries that petroleum is transformed into liquids more suitable for fuels: petrol for cars and aeroplanes, liquid gases such as butane and propane, lubricating oil for engines, diesel oil and naphtha, used for heating.

One of the most recent developments is that of providing protein for use in animal feedstuffs.

Oil deposits are scattered over the surface of the Earth so the crude oil has to be transported in a variety of ways. The most common are road, rail or ocean tankers and pipelines.

Oil tankers of 160,000 tons or more now form the largest vessels in use in the world. They are known as V.L.C.C.s (very large crude carriers).

Pipelines are the most recent method and the most likely to be used in the future as it is the most practical and fastest.

It is only in the last few decades that deposits of natural gas have been discovered in

Electric car

Europe. This is used both for domestic purposes, such as heating, and as a fuel, instead of oil, in many industries.

It is a precious source of power, particularly for a country like Britain which previously had to rely on oversea supplies for oil.

Britain now obtains natural gas and some oil from the North Sea. The gas is piped inland, direct to where it is needed.

179

When nuclear power was discovered

Nuclear power is entirely the result of highly scientific research. With the splitting of the atom at the beginning of the twentieth century, it became possible to set off reactions which produce a powerful supply of energy. If not properly channelled, however, this energy can prove lethal to man. It is therefore true to say that the most recent of the sources of power discovered by man is by far the strongest.

This immense force, which made its first unhappy appearance

during the Second World War, today has peaceful applications of far-reaching importance. It is used both in medicine and in transport, in industry and in daily life.

Nuclear-powered ships, for example, can make a quick response to calls for help: they can sail to the sites of natural disasters and supply them with all the power they need. Nuclear reactors can give power to orbiting laboratories for the exploration of space. Cobalt 'bombs' can help medicine in its vital work of curing diseases, such as cancer.

In the field of agriculture, radio-activity can help make some important discoveries about plant foods and the use of different types of soil and fertilizer.

If radioactivity, that is the force released by an atom when its nucleus is split in two, can be controlled and harnessed by man for purposes of peaceful progress, it will prove to be an incomparable source of energy and a power for good.

But tragedies like the atomic bombing of Hiroshima and Nagasaki when hundreds of thousands of people were killed in Japan in August 1945 must not be repeated.

When atomic power was used for producing electricity

A practical application of nuclear power for peaceful purposes is the production of electricity. Since the late 1940s, the years immediately after the Second World War, scientists and technologists have managed to develop equipment for producing electric power from nuclear energy.

The first atomic power station in the world was built in 1956 at Calder Hall in Cumberland. The plant's present output is 180 megawatts, or 180 million watts, of electricity.

The world's largest atomic power station is the Ontario Hydro's Pickering Station. This reached its full output of 2,160 megawatts in 1973. The biggest single nuclear reactor is at present the Browns Ferry Unit 1 on the Wheeler reservoir in Alabama. Opened in 1973, it has an output of 1,098 megawatts, but it is due to be overtaken by the Grand Gulf Nuclear Station at Port Gibson, Mississippi.

The world's natural fuel resources such as coal and oil, now used to generate electricity, may well be exhausted in about 100 to 200 years. However it is estimated that the resources of nuclear power are approximately 100 times as large as the energy available from existing fuel reserves.

It is hard to predict exactly what technological and scientific developments will be brought about by the use of nuclear power. We can, however, take a quick look at some of the more extraordinary aspects of an invention which will certainly change the face of the Earth.

At Farsta, on the edge of Stockholm, the whole town's heating is provided by one nuclear reactor. In the nuclear power station at Chinon, in France, as much electricity is produced by a ton of uranium as is produced by 10,000 tons of coal. This is only considered a modest achievement, however, for the same quantity of uranium can in fact produce three times as much electricity. In the not-too-distant future 'rapid neutron' reactors will be able to achieve some really staggering results. A ton of atomic fuel will produce as much power as is obtained by burning 600,000 tons of coal.

In the field of propulsion, nuclear-powered ships and submarines have already been tried. The American aircraft carrier, *Enterprise,* is equipped with atomic reactors which make it completely self-sufficient. Nuclear submarines can stay submerged for months on end and quickly change their position, which makes them more useful and independent.

In the field of space travel, plans for the next ten years involve the use of nuclear power. It is probably with this kind of propulsion that man will succeed in conquering the enormous distances of space.

The first nuclear reactor at Chicago (above)
Calder Hall: the first atomic power station (below)

WHEN INVENTING BEGAN

Our daily lives could not proceed normally without the valuable help of metals.

Copper was one of the earliest metals used by man. Implements and weapons dating from 5000 B.C. have been found in graves in Egypt. There are also records of the working of copper mines on the Sinai Peninsular in about 3800 B.C. It took more than a thousand years for the appreciation and application of copper to spread through Europe. Few inventions can have been as important as this great discovery of our ancestors.

Man soon learned how to make copper harder by alloying it, or mixing it, with tin, so producing bronze. It is the discovery of bronze (5,000 years ago) that is generally said to mark the beginning of the history of modern man.

With the discovery of metals, man had taken a big step forward towards civilization. His evolution naturally progressed more rapidly from then on. At first little bronze was used but by the late Bronze Age there was a great development in the use of metals for tools, weapons, utensils, shields, trumpets and coins. These were shaped by the blacksmith, who soon became surrounded with mystery by his fellowmen.

To their minds, anyone capable of drawing these marvels out of the fire must surely be a kind of wizard blessed with supernatural powers. Yet, despite the belief that his art was magic, the blacksmith was really just a skilful, intelligent craftsman who knew how to master the forces which nature put at his disposal.

Even thousands of years later, when the blacksmith had become a familiar and commonplace figure, he still aroused a feeling of respect and wonder in the unskilled layman.

Today the iron and steel works continue the ancient art of iron-working on an industrial scale. Using very advanced techniques, they achieve some amazing results.

When cast iron and steel were obtained

Cast iron, a mixture of iron and carbon, has occupied a position of great importance in the industrial world since the eighteenth century. It was in this century too, in 1740, that Benjamin Huntsman produced steel at Sheffield and the modern age of metals began. His process is still used, especially in the Sheffield area, for making high-grade steels.

Both cast iron and steel are produced in blast-furnaces, which are quickly becoming fully automated units.

The blast-furnace, with its chimney stack 35 to 40 metres high, is filled with layers of coke and iron ore. The very high firing temperature, of between 1,600 and 1,800 degrees, produces cast iron which is, in fact, a compound of iron and carbon.

Steel, too, is a compound of iron and carbon but the amount of carbon it contains must not be more than 1·7 per cent.

When aluminium was isolated

The most plentiful metal in the Earth's crust is aluminium, although until a century ago no one knew of its existence. This is because aluminium does not exist in the pure state, like gold, but is always combined with other minerals, such as bauxite and kaolin. Aluminium was first discovered by Sir Humphrey Davy in 1807 and first produced in 1827 by Hans Christian Oersted. Afterwards Wöhler improved on Oersted's methods and succeeded in obtaining the metal in a purer form.

Today aluminium is used in the manufacture of all kinds of

tools and vehicles, from kitchen utensils and electric wires to train, car and aircraft parts, as it is the basic ingredient in the light alloys or metal mixtures, from which they are made.

When the telescope was invented

It was 1609 when Galileo Galilei, Professor of Mathematics at the University of Padua, heard about the invention of the telescope by a Dutch spectacle-maker. By putting one lens on top of another he had discovered that the objects at which he was looking seemed bigger. Galileo decided to build a telescope for himself. Although

small, his instrument enabled him to see the mountains and craters of the Moon, the spots on the Sun and the satellites of Jupiter. He also established that the Milky Way is nothing but a collection of myriads of stars.

In fact, although the telescope was invented by the Dutch spectacle-maker, Galileo was the first to use this wonderful instrument for scientific purposes. He therefore deserves his reputation as one of the inventors of the telescope, the instrument for 'seeing at a distance'.

Galileo's first telescopes, treasured as priceless antiques, are preserved in the Galileo Museum at Florence.

(Above) fragment from Hero's Pneumatics, published in Urbino in 1575. (Below) part of Villard's rope mechanism

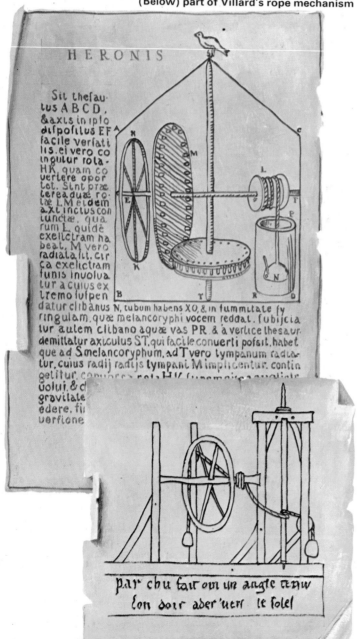

When Leonardo da Vinci designed his amazing machines

Since the earliest times man has done his best to invent labour-saving machines.

It was only with the many-sided genius of Leonardo da Vinci, however, that plans were made for revolutionary machines which are quite amazing in the way they anticipate modern devices.

Leonardo's projects included a machine gun and numerous other pieces of military equipment; a helicopter worked by a spring called an airscrew; very light bridges; even parachutes and boats with paddle-wheels. His inventions were not just drawings in his notebooks. He completed the construction of the canal at Martesana and two other important navigation and irrigation canals, the Naviglio Grande and the Naviglio Interno. He also designed musical instruments, such as lyres and violas.

When printing was invented

It is true that the Chinese had already 'printed' a book in A.D. 868, but the invention of printing as we know it was made in Europe in the 1450s.

Many people claimed to be the originators of the movable ·type from which books are printed. The invention is generally attributed to Johann Gutenberg, however, a master craftsman of Mainz on the river Rhine, in Germany.

The first type used by Gutenberg was made of wood and his printing presses were worked by hand. Today, automatic printing machines can run off thousands of books in a few minutes.

When the first clocks were made

Even people who had no form of writing had their own special way of noting the succession of the days, the seasons and the years. Among the earliest instruments used for measuring time were sundials, sand-glasses and water-clocks.

The clock as we know it did not appear until the end of the thirteenth century. Before that the Arabs had built devices similar to the clock but not as efficient.

The first clocks were enormous and were nearly always placed on church or bell-towers so that everyone in the town could see them. Their movements were simple and noisy but they worked for many years, although they did not always tell the correct time.

The earliest English turret clocks still in existence were installed at Salisbury Cathedral, Wells Cathedral and Dover Castle.

When the first reflecting telescope was invented

After the first scientific telescopes of Galileo, the study and design of instruments for exploring the mysteries of the Universe made steady progress.

The first reflecting telescope to be built was Sir Isaac Newton's. It was 1671 when he developed this special new instrument in which light was reflected by a concave (curved inward) mirror

A very early wooden-frame chamber clock, dated 1643

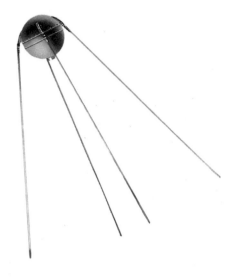

The Russian satellite *Sputnik I,* Earth's first artificial satellite

within the focus of the main mirror. The image produced was observed on an eyepiece at the side of the telescope. Newton preferred using a reflecting telescope because it was free of the coloured fringes which nearly always make images in refracting telescopes look blurred or out-of-focus.

Because it is so easy to use and so cheap, the Newtonian type of reflecting telescope is still widely used today.

When the first large telescope was built

In 1947 an enormous mirror was carried up to the top of Mount Palomar in California. It was the essential part of what was then the largest telescope in the world. It has a diameter of 5 metres and weighs about 15 tons.

Making such a large mirror presented some almost insurmountable problems, as the pure quartz which it had been intended

to use lost its brightness and smoothness when it cooled. It was decided to use Pyrex, which took a whole year to cool in perfect conditions. The polishing alone took another eleven years, by the end of which only 15 out of the original 20 tons were left which shows the enormous amount of high precision work entailed.

Visitors to the telescope are kept at a safe distance, because just the heat of their bodies could upset the balance and accuracy of this complex and sensitive apparatus.

When radio astronomy became important

It is only in the last twenty years that radio astronomy has become one of the most important sciences. Yet in 1931 an American engineer, Karl Jansky, had already discovered the existence of radio waves. These waves come from the centre of our galaxy and are at least ten thousand times longer

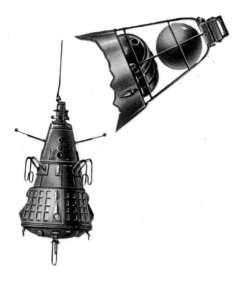

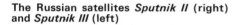

The Russian satellites *Sputnik II* (right) and *Sputnik III* (left)

than light waves.

To catch the very weak signals coming from outer space, enormous telescopes have had to be built to collect sufficient radiation for a signal to be detected. The telescope at Jodrell Bank is probably the most famous of these.

A special type of radio telescope is the radio interferometer. It detects the position of radio sources in the sky and shows the effects of interference of the radio waves coming from different directions.

When the first satellites were launched into space

It was 4 October 1957 when the Soviet Union launched Earth's first artificial satellite.

After this, a race began which brought an American triumph on 31 January 1958, when *Explorer I* discovered the famous Van Allen Belt. The discovery of this broad zone of radiation, named after the man who launched the instruments which found it, Dr. James

Van Allen, had some far-reaching consequences. It made possible the design of equipment capable of shielding future astronauts from the danger of radiation.

Since that time many artificial satellites have been placed in orbit for military, scientific and communication purposes..

Man's landing on the Moon on 21 July 1969, owed much to these artificial satellites which orbit the Earth, revealing the secrets of space with their special instruments.

When the first microscopes appeared

The very small and the very large have always fascinated the human mind. Since the earliest times, men of science have tried to build instruments to investigate these two extremes.

For the infinitely small, or 'microcosm', as it is called in Greek, the microscope was invented, to magnify anything which cannot be seen with the naked eye.

187

The first microscopes appeared in the seventeenth century. They were extremely simple instruments, consisting of two fixed lenses in two sliding tubes. Magnifying and focusing were made possible by sliding one of the tubes inside the other.

Only opaque objects (objects which cannot be seen through) could be examined with these microscopes, however. It was not until the end of the seventeenth century that Campari, an Italian inventor, managed to overcome this difficulty by building a microscope for looking at transparent materials.

A modern electron microscope

When the compound microscope was invented

Human research never admits the word finished. This applies to all branches of science and is therefore also true of the world of microscopes.

The magnification achieved with the simple microscope was limited, and so the compound microscope with two principal lens systems was developed. In 1624, Galileo saw one of Cornelis Drebbel's instruments in Rome, and immediately introduced several improvements to it. He called his instrument a spyglass and made a present of it to some of his friends.

In this microscope the image enlarged by the first system is seen and enlarged again by the second system. Useful, that is clear, enlargements of up to 2,000 times are possible.

An instrument of this kind is of tremendous assistance in the study of certain bacteria and viruses, and the analyst is greatly helped by its magnifying power.

If new remedies are discovered for wiping out the many diseases which still threaten mankind, it will no doubt once again be thanks to the microscope, as it has been in the past.

When the use of the microscope spread

The microscope has been a useful instrument in all branches of science ever since it was invented. But it is only the rapid evolution of science and technology in the last twenty years that has brought about its wider use.

Work cannot even be carried on in some spheres of activity without the microscope.

In hospitals doctors use it to diagnose and then treat diseases; surgeons use it to perform delicate operations on complex and sensitive parts of the body such as the eye or the ear.

In the electronics industry the microscope permits high precision work which would otherwise be impossible.

Where the microscope is the most essential piece of equipment, however, is in research laboratories. The examination of botanical and animal cells takes place with the help of the microscope. It is also used in the sciences of petrology and metallurgy to obtain information on rocks and metals.

The microscope takes part in all kinds of complicated investigations, without which many stages in the progress of man would be lost.

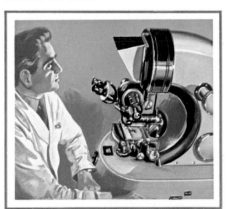

When the electron microscope was invented

The first electron microscope was built by M. Knoll and E. Ruska in Berlin in 1932. Its development was rapid and in a few years its magnifying power had been increased from 17 to 400 times.

Its inventors despaired of the instrument ever working properly, as it was so difficult to keep the vacuum needed inside the optical column for all the electrons to multiply easily and produce an image.

In 1936, however, the electron microscope was at last demonstrated as an instrument of practical use.

Nowadays, electron microscopes have reached such a degree of perfection and are so useful that they can make enlargements of hundreds of thousands of times.

It was a French physicist, Louis de Broglie, who was the true father of the electron microscope. In fact, in 1924 he had managed to detect the wave-like nature of electrons, which move about in the air like light or sound. It was therefore de Broglie who put forward the basic theory for what, some years later, became the electron microscope.

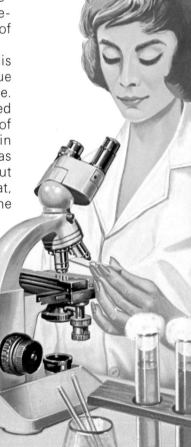

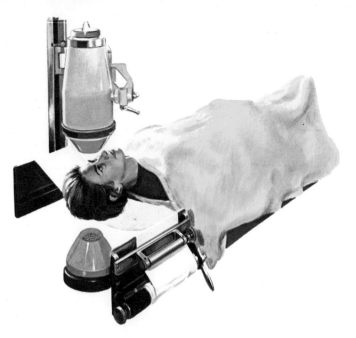

When X-rays were discovered

In 1803 John Dalton put forward his theory that matter is made up of indivisible particles called atoms, and another ninety-two years passed before the German physicist, Wilhelm Conrad Röntgen, discovered X-rays.

The contribution X-rays have made and are still making to many branches of the biological and physical sciences, is a measure of the importance of this discovery. With X-rays it has been possible to build a super-microscope which can not only see atoms but can also see inside them. Röntgen's discovery, in fact, was the start of modern atomic and molecular physics, which is the study of the structure of matter and its constituents.

Although X-rays have so many uses, they are best-known in the field of medicine. They help diagnose the early stages of diseases and then assist in the treatment of them by killing cancerous cells in biological structures or stopping the cells from splitting up and spreading. They are of invaluable use in hospitals today.

When radioactivity was discovered

Radioactivity was discovered by the French physicist, Henri Becquerel. In 1896 he was examining uranium salts when he noticed that they emitted radioactive rays. Then in 1898 Pierre and Marie Curie succeeded in separating radium. This gives off rays so powerful that they can penetrate solid surfaces.

The first nuclear reactor was built in the United States in 1942. The first experimental nuclear bomb exploded in New Mexico in 1945.

When the peaceful uses of atomic energy began

The military use of nuclear power calls to mind the horror of Hiroshima and Nagasaki. But nuclear power also has a great potential for good which can be used when its force is released.

The atomic age began on 2 December 1942, when Enrico Fermi made the first controlled nuclear chain reaction. It already has many peaceful applications to its credit.

In 1956 the first nuclear power station in the world was opened at Calder Hall, in Cumberland, to produce electricity commercially.

On 10 December 1967, a tremendous explosion was set off 1,300 metres under the ground in New Mexico. New ways of using nuclear explosives for peaceful purposes were being tested.

In 1957 the International Atomic Energy Agency was created under the auspices of the United Nations. The aim of the I.A.E.A. is to ensure that nuclear energy is used for peace to finance research projects for peaceful purposes.

When the first atomic submarine was built

The appearance of the first nuclear-propelled submarine in the history of navigation dates back to January 1955. The *Nautilus,* named in memory of Jules Verne's famous imaginary submarine, could sail twice round the world using only 4 kilos of Uranium 235.

But perhaps the most spectacular adventure of this American submarine was its voyage under the ice-cap of the North Pole in 1958, a feat which met with complete success.

Following the successful trials with the *Nautilus,* the U.S. navy embarked on an extensive building programme of nuclear-powered submarines of several different types.

When the first rails were used

English miners were the first people to think of tracks for guiding the wheels of their coal wagons.

The idea probably came to them from the furrows made by the continual trundling of the wagons through the underground tunnels.

The furrows were eventually edged with wooden lines, kept apart by sleepers, also of wood. As they wore down, the lines were repaired with iron face-plates but these did considerable damage to the wagon wheels so that, in time, they too had to be made of iron.

The first 'railroads' were built in England for horse-drawn coaches.

Finally, in 1797, the first real rails were made. They were cast iron rods, 90 centimetres long and weighing 22 kilos each, produced at the Coalbrook Dale

foundry by Richard Reynolds.

The first vehicles to travel on rails were pulled by animals or men.

Even after the steam engine had been invented, animal traction continued for many years.

For example, the first public railway was operated by the Surrey Iron Railway Company which had been created through an Act of Parliament passed in 1801. The railway was opened in 1803 and ran between Wandsworth and Croydon, drawn by horses.

Trevithick's *Catch-Me-Who-Can*

When the steam engine replaced the horse

On 21 February 1804 the first self-propelled locomotive, built by Richard Trevithick, was demonstrated in Penydaren, Glamorgan.

When perfected, the engine managed to pull up to five wagons with a load of 10 tons of goods and seventy passengers. Running along at speeds of up to 8 kilometres an hour over a distance of 16 kilometres, it seemed to many people a wonder hardly to be surpassed.

There were many others who did not like the new machine, however, and who were convinced it would not work. They insisted that as the rails and the wheels rubbed against each other they would create such friction that it would stop the train. So Trevithick organized a kind of train circus as a publicity stunt, calling his locomotive *Catch-Me-Who-Can*. He chose a site near London's Euston Road and, at 24 kilometres an hour, his little train chugged round and round to the enthusiasm of the assembled crowd.

When Stephenson built his *Rocket*

Trevithick is generally regarded as the father of the steam train but the most famous figure of the pioneer days of railways is George Stephenson who was born in Newcastle upon Tyne in 1781.

An enginewright and mechanic at the Killingworth colliery in Northumberland, he managed to find the money to build a locomotive which he called *My Lord* and which was successfully tested on the tramroads of the colliery in 1814.

Various kinds of locomotive were designed by Stephenson and they were all remarkably successful.

The young engineer became so enthusiastic about the new means of locomotion that he decided to launch himself into the exciting task of providing steam engines for public railways.

In 1822 Stephenson was appointed engineer of the Stockton and Darlington Railway. On 27 September 1825 the first steam passenger service in railway history was inaugurated. Speeds of up to 24 kilometres an hour were reached.

Conclusive proof of the efficiency of Stephenson's steam engines came on 6 October 1829.

Five locomotives entered for trials set by the directors of the Liverpool and Manchester Railway but only Stephenson's *Rocket* passed and so won the competition and a prize of £500.

It travelled at up to 39 kilometres per hour, fully laden.

On 15 September 1830 the railway age began. That day the Liverpool to Manchester line was opened, the first to be operated entirely by steam.

When steam replaced sails

The nineteenth century is also known as the steam age, which reflects what an important part steam played in every sphere of life.

At the same time as the steam train was making its trial runs, the American, Robert Fulton, was designing and testing his first river boat propelled not by the force of the wind but by two big wheels worked by a steam engine.

His steamboat, as Fulton called it, made its maiden voyage on 9 August 1807 and, eight days later, it started a 240-kilometre trip up the Hudson River, from New York to Albany. It took 32 hours to accomplish this journey, a speed which was soon considerably increased.

In the war of 1812–14 against Great Britain, Fulton built the first steam warship.

The new ships were so successful that they soon began to supplant sailing ships, despite the fierce struggle which the owners of the sailing ships put up against the 'dangerous' new invention.

In May and June 1819 the first ocean-going steam ship, the *Savannah*, crossed the Atlantic from the United States to Ireland.

The voyage cannot be said to have been a complete success, however, as the engines only took over from the sails for 85 hours because supplies of coal ran out.

The early steam ships still depended partly on sails for auxiliary power. It was a long fight between sail and steam, and at the beginning of the twentieth' century there were still plenty of sailing ships plying the oceans. But they were now economic only for transporting non-perishable food-stuffs over long distances.

Stephenson's *Rocket*

When iron was first used in shipbuilding

Up until the 1840s the vast majority of ships were made entirely of wood. There were very few iron bits and those were non-essential. Although the hull had changed shape, it differed little in construction from the way shipbuilders had worked for thousands of years.

The first important composite ship, that is one constructed of wood and iron or steel, was the *Great Britain*, built at Bristol in 1845. It proved its strength and endurance when, in 1846, it ran aground in Dundrum Bay in Ireland. Although it remained aground for eleven months, it was then refloated and continued in existence until 1937.

News of the system spread far and wide because it marked an important advance in shipbuilding. It combined the flexibility of wooden planking with the strength of an iron framework. The iron's main advantage, its solidity, was happily married with wood's best feature, its flexibility.

The greatest obstacle to be

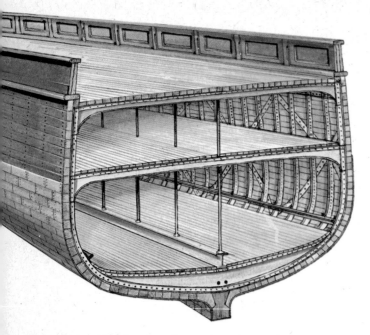

Composite ship (made of wood and metal)

When the first motor cars appeared

The first automobile, or self-propelled vehicle, in history was invented in 1769 by Nicolas Cugnot, a French military engineer. It was a kind of tricycle with a strong frame on which a two-cylinder steam engine rested. It could pull a load of 5 tons at a speed of 5 kilometres an hour.

This ancestor of the motor car is now to be seen in Paris but looks more frightening than exciting to ride on.

By 1862 steam engine exhibitions were being organized. The bulky machines looked no different from the ones which ran on rails.

Among the few successes at the first exhibitions were the machines of Amédée Bollée, who was determined to make a 'practical horseless carriage'. In 1873 his first vehicle was ready. He called it *Obéissant*, the French word for obedient, because it was so easy to steer. It was a kind of bus with steering-gear on its two front wheels. The success of the *Obéssiant* was so encouraging that Bollée continued his series of 'automobile' machines.

An important event in the progress of road transport was the discovery of the internal combustion engine.

Following this, in 1876, the German, Nikolaus August Otto, patented a kind of four-stroke engine based on a design by the Frenchman, Beau de Rochas.

But it was not until 1882 that Gottlieb Daimler, another German, built the first light engines. Three years later, Daimler's son drove 3 kilometres with one of these engines installed in a four-wheeled carriage.

Another motoring pioneer was

overcome was the galvanic action which the sea water set up between wood and metal, causing them to rot.

It is a well-known fact that contact between two heterogeneous bodies (bodies of a different kind) produces electric currents which may be very destructive.

In the case of ships the trouble was accentuated by the presence of salt water.

The remedy was found by insulating the points of contact between wood and iron with rubber. This type of mixed construction was used for about twenty years, particularly in the cargo-carrying clippers.

Towards the middle of the nineteenth century, the first giants of the ocean were built for long, fast voyages. One of the most famous was the *Great Eastern*, launched in 1858, and one of the strongest ships ever built. It was the first ocean liner, with a crew of 400 and able to carry 4,000 passengers.

the German, Karl Friedrich Benz. In 1885 he built a car which was to prove highly successful.

French manufacturers were the first to realize the importance of these inventions. Using the patents of Daimler and Benz, they laid the foundations of the huge industry which is still flourishing today and has known such names as Panhard, Levassor and Peugeot.

The first Motor Show was held in Paris in 1887.

When the first underground railway was built

In 1863 London must have already been having its traffic problems because that was the year when the first underground railway system in the world was opened. It had been specially designed to reduce the city's traffic, which had become too congested and noisy.

It was a steam railway which soon became very popular with Londoners who made regular use of it. The line was about four and a half kilometres long and linked the stations of Paddington, Euston, King's Cross and Farringdon Street.

The trains were quite comfortable and travelled at remarkable speeds for those days. They could carry 27,000 passengers a day.

This first underground railway was extended to form an inner circle in 1884.

In 1890 the 'tube' was built by boring through the earth from underground working sites. It was the City and South London Railway and ran from the City to Stockwell. For the first time an electrified line was used which set going small electric locomotives.

It was the forerunner of the modern high-speed underground.

Yarrow and Hilditch's motor car

Obéissant, 1873

Hewetson's Benz *Victoria*, 1895

When the rack railway was invented

It is very difficult for smooth steel wheels to grip smooth steel rails. This soon became one of the disadvantages of railways. Even today, the steepest slope which train wheels dare attempt has a gradient of only one metre in every eleven.

Several people tried to overcome this problem. In 1812 the Englishman, John Blenkinsop, invented an engine with special toothed wheels which engaged with a rail, also toothed, fitted to the track.

The rack railway is still widely used for short distances in hilly areas. It passes through mountainous regions such as the Alps and goes to the summit of Snowdon in North Wales, and Mount Washington and Pike's Peak in the United States.

A special kind of railway is the funicular, or cable-railway, in which trains are pulled by metal cables. These railways are used in mountainous countries, such as Switzerland, to transport skiers and tourists.

When the first monorail was built

It is widely believed that the monorail is a recent achievement. Yet the first design was patented in 1821 and built in 1824.

A German monorail which has been operating regularly since 1901 is the famous *Schwebebahn*, which means 'suspension-railway', and runs on an overhead rail from Wuppertal Barmen to Wuppertal Vohwinkel.

The Alweg monorail system was tested in Germany in 1952 on the Cologne-Fuhbingen line. This is a track system except that only one rail is used, the carriages travelling over a concrete beam.

Another monorail system, called Safage, was tested in Texas in 1956. The cars are suspended from trolleys with rubber-tyred wheels driven by diesel motors.

In the 1960s supporters of the monorail claimed it as the answer to large-city transport problems. It is cheaper to construct than underground railways, but has the disadvantages of unsightly overhead rails, and the difficulty of changing cars.

Alweg-type six-car monorail train in Japan

When the first automatic railway was opened

In 1927 the first train to operate without a driver or guard went into service in Britain. It has continued to carry London's mail ever since. Its wagons have now covered more than 80 million kilometres. A similar completely automatic mail train is operating in Brussels.

A very recent invention is a kind of vehicle which has almost no friction, or resistance to motion, because it does not rub along the ground. It is the hovercraft, which originated from an idea for travelling on water. It moves along, raised off the ground by the cushion of air which special motors create underneath it. By using the hovercraft principle on a track, it is hoped to produce a vehicle which will combine the advantages of the air cushion with those of accurate control.

When the Montgolfier was invented

It proved so difficult to beat the force of gravity, that many inventors turned their attention to machines which would fly by using gases lighter than air.

The problem was eventually solved by the Montgolfier brothers, the sons of a French paper merchant. Employed by their father in his business, they had learned about the different kinds of paper. Their enthusiasm for science did the rest: on 4 June 1783, at Annonay, a village near Lyons, the first balloon in history rose into the sky and became known as the Montgolfier, after its inventors.

The two brothers had worked from a simple theory which proved to be correct: if hot air rises, it must only need to be sealed in a light-weight envelope for the envelope to be pushed upwards, too. The hot air was produced by burning straw and wool in a brazier slung beneath the balloon.

When the first man rose into the air

The first man to rise into the air was a scientist, the French physicist, Jean-François Pilâtre de Rozier. It was 15 October 1783, a few months after the first balloon had taken off.

A 'flight' of only a few minutes seems laughable to anyone who is used to seeing supersonic jets streaking across the sky. But if we remember that those early balloons were something completely new and that the first balloonists were

Montmartre funicular railway up the hill to the Sacré Coeur

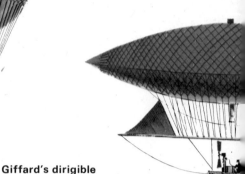

Napoleon wanted to use balloons to invade England (left)

The balloon of Pilâtre de Rozier and the Marquis d'Arlandes (left)

Giffard's dirigible

faced with innumerable dangers, their achievement seems quite staggering.

Pilâtre de Rozier's flight attracted so much attention that the Montgolfier brothers were encouraged to continue their experiments. The daring French physicist who was the first to venture into the sky may be regarded as the forerunner of the modern astronauts.

When the first cross-Channel balloon flight was made

A few weeks after de Rozier's historic flight, two balloonists took off. De Rozier was accompanied on his ascent by the Marquis d'Arlandes, and King Louis XVI himself was present at the launching. The admiring crowd watched a flight of 8 kilometres which took about half an hour.

News of the event quickly spread all over the world and was widely imitated. More and more modifications were introduced: an air-tight fabric envelope to reduce gas leaks; the use of

hydrogen as it is lighter than air; more comfortable cars better suited for the purpose.

On 7 January 1785 Blanchard and Jeffries crossed the Channel, a highly difficult and dangerous feat. The following June de Rozier and a friend were killed during their attempt to repeat this achievement and fly from France to England.

When airships were invented

Every day it became increasingly apparent that balloons could not rely on unpredictable air currents but would have to be made more manageable, with an engine and a rudder to steer them.

In 1852, again in France, the first airship was launched. It had been made by Henri Giffard who had risen from being an ordinary railway worker to becoming an excellent engineer. He called his invention *Giffard I*.

Steerable airships, or dirigibles as they were known, made some memorable achievements. They took a major step forward in 1872

The dirigible of Santos-Dumont (above) Zeppelin perfected the rigid type of airship (right)

when their steam engines were replaced by internal combustion engines. This innovation was the work of a German engineer, Paul Haenlein.

The two main features of the dirigibles were their rigid envelope and their engine. They soon became so easy to handle that they were used commercially for carrying goods.

Steerable airships flourished over a period of 85 years, from 24 September 1852 (the *Giffard I* at Paris) to 6 May 1937 (the *Zeppelin LZ 129* at Lakehurst, U.S.A.).

The most famous airships of all were the Zeppelins. They appeared on the flying scene in 1900, when the German officer, Graf Ferdinand von Zeppelin, flew over Lake Constance in an 126-metre-long airship which he named after himself.

Another Zeppelin closed the history of the airships when it burst into flames in the sky over Lakehurst on 6 May 1937. Thirty-six people lost their lives in the fierce explosion.

When 'heavier-than-air' machines beat the 'lighter-than-air'

Leonardo da Vinci's flying machine was built so that the pilot moved the wings with his hands and feet, and the tail with his head.

Leonardo had designed machines for flying but, apart from their curiosity value, his plans did not produce any concrete results.

For over three centuries, brave and sometimes fanatical men continued to make attempts to fly.

This is the period which spans Leonardo's inventions and the first serious efforts made by modern technology to break through the barrier of the pull of the Earth's gravity.

One of the best remembered is William Henson's aerial steam carriage. This was designed in about 1850 and owed much to the work of Sir George Cayley who had made a model glider in 1804 and later built a full-sized glider.

By the time airships had reached their peak, the aeroplane was born. Clément Ader and Otto

Leonardo's flying machine

Lilienthal are generally accepted as the founders of aviation.

In 1890 Ader succeeded in lifting his propeller machine a few centimetres off the ground and making it fly for 50 metres: this was the first real human flight.

Lilienthal, on the other hand, decided against a steam engine like Ader's in favour of the wind and natural air currents. He de-

Spiral wing of Leonardo da Vinci's helicopter

signed a kind of glider with fixed wings which was meant to slide off the top of a hill.

Lilienthal's experiments continued successfully for a number of years, and as a result of his studies aeronautics became an exact science.

Lilienthal experimented himself with his gliders and it was on one of the flights that he crashed and was killed in 1896.

At the time of this fatal accident he had already made about a hundred launchings.

When the first aeroplanes were invented

In the field of aeronautics, each step forward brought the conquest of the air that much nearer attainment.

As ballooning had had two brothers, the Montgolfiers, so mechanical flight had as its originators another two brothers, the Americans Wilbur and Orville Wright of Dayton, Ohio. Their machine was a biplane, or an aeroplane with two pairs of wings, similar to Lilienthal's glider but powered by a 16 horse-power internal combustion engine and weighing about 62 kilos.

On the morning of 17 December 1903, the Wright brothers made their first flight in this machine. It took place near the Kill Devil Hills, Kitty Hawk, North Carolina.

The flight only lasted 12 seconds but, at a later attempt, they travelled more than 500 metres. Many people think of 17 December 1903 as the true date of the start of modern aviation.

Wilbur Wright went to France and first flew in public near Le Mans in August 1908. By the end of the year he had made over one hundred flights in Europe, had broken every record and had even made a flight lasting two hours and twenty minutes.

On 25 July 1909 Louis Blériot, flying a machine powered by an engine designed by the Italian, Alessandro Anzani, crossed the Channel from Calais to Dover.

On 7 January 1910 Hubert Latham climbed to a height of more than 1,600 metres.

Again in 1910, on 23 September, Geo Chavez, a Peruvian living in Paris, crossed the Alps on a tragic flight which cost him his life, just as his journey was ended.

Henson's Aerial Steam Carriage, 1842

When aeroplanes were first used in war

In the ten years following the Wright brothers' flight, aeronautical conquests went from strength to strength.

On 29 September 1913 the Frenchman, Maurice Prévost, succeeded in reaching 200 kilometres an hour in a French-made monoplane. It was an amazing record which heralded even greater and more spectacular progress within a short space of time.

For the First World War then broke out and to many it seemed that the aeroplane must become a first-rate war machine.

Manoeuvrable, high-speed aeroplanes were quickly built, more for reconnaissance flights than for actual combat.

The Italians, who had already experimented with aeroplanes in action in the Libyan war of 1911, were also the first to use them in the new conflict.

By the end of the war there was an active aircraft industry in several European countries.

Great progress had also been made in training pilots, who had had a wonderful opportunity to gain experience on active service.

In the field of civil aviation, aeroplanes were used from 1914 both for carrying passengers (in Florida) and mail (in Italy). Their use as a civil transport grew steadily from 1919. Scheduled routes were established in Europe and in local regions throughout the world, and special designs of airliner came into service.

The seaplane, which could take off and land on water, had been invented in 1911 in the United States. It, too, was greatly improved during the war years.

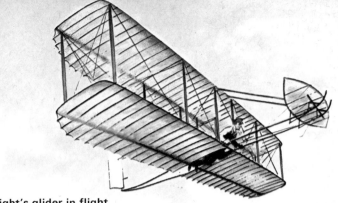

Wright's glider in flight

When the first transatlantic flight was made

In 1919 the first Atlantic crossing was made from Newfoundland to Ireland by the Englishmen, Alcock and Brown.

In 1926 Commander Richard Byrd of the United States Navy became the first person to fly over the North Pole.

1927 brought the most famous of the flying achievements when Lindbergh crossed the vast expanse of the Atlantic Ocean in a solo, non-stop flight from New York to Paris.

In 1930–31 a squadron of Italian seaplanes flew from Orbetello in Italy to Rio de Janeiro in Brazil.

In 1938, on the eve of the Second World War, the Italian, Pezzi, set up his altitude record of 17,083 metres, a record which has still not been beaten by a piston-engined plane.

The wind tunnel where the Wright brothers experimented with different kinds of wing

Engine built for a 1909 aeroplane

Orville Wright's first historic flight on 17 December 1903

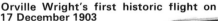

When the first photograph was taken

Although the invention of photography is comparatively recent, the camera obscura, which is the darkened box with a hole in one wall which forms the essential part of a camera, has been known since about the year A.D. 1000.

Documents of that period record that an Arab, Alhazen, had described the principle of the camera obscura.

It was not until 1812, however, that the first lens for taking photographs was made. It was a concave-convex system (curved inward on one side and outward on the other) and was invented by the English chemist, William Hyde Wollaston.

This invention led to the start of photography, which was the work of another chemist, the Frenchman Joseph Nicéphore Niepce. He succeeded in fixing the image transmitted by the camera obscura on a sensitive metal plate.

Compared with the rapid ex-

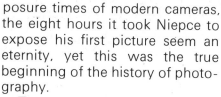

posure times of modern cameras, the eight hours it took Niepce to expose his first picture seem an eternity, yet this was the true beginning of the history of photography.

The camera was invented by Louis Daguerre, who in 1829 formed a partnership with Niepce. In 1839 Daguerre succeeded in putting together a camera with a lens. The photographs taken with this first camera were called 'daguerreotypes', after their inventor.

When photographic film was introduced in 1875, replacing the heavy plates of the daguerreotypes, modern cameras came into being.

When the cinema began

Photography was well advanced when the cinema began.

Attempts to animate pictures date back to the magic lantern, but it was not until the end of the nineteenth century that the cinema arrived.

The Americans, Germans, English and French had all been racing against each other to be the first to produce a 'movie'.

Victory went to two brothers, Louis and Auguste Lumière, who projected their first film to the public in a Paris hotel. It was 28 December 1895 and in a short while the news of the Lumière brothers' invention had spread all over the world.

At that time few people realized that a new art-form had been born. The majority thought of the motion picture as a piece of technical gadgetry intended for the few. But it soon became the most popular form of public entertainment.

The cinema was born silent, the actions generally being explained

by captions. In the most up-to-date cinema halls all that could be expected was a pianist paid to accompany the events on the screen with appropriate background music.

In October 1927 Al Jolson appeared in *The Jazz Singer*, a silent film with four talking or singing interludes. This was the start of sound in films.

All-talking pictures followed in 1928 with the film *The Lights of New York.*

Colour films, wide screens and cinerama are recent technical innovations but have added little to cinematography from the artistic point of view.

When television began

The first inventor of television was the Scottish engineer, John Logie Baird. After years of painstaking research and experiment, he succeeded in making the first television transmission in 1926. By the outbreak of the Second World War in 1939 television was being broadcast in England, Germany and the United States.

It was not until 1950, however, after the war had finished, that the industry began to function efficiently again and in 1953 there were regular television programmes in many countries.

By 1960, programmes could be viewed for most of the afternoon and evening.

Although experiments in colour television have been carried on since the early days of television, regular colour broadcasting has only become widespread in the last few years.

In 1954 Eurovision began. It is a system for exchanging programmes between the various European television networks.

When the transistor was invented

In 1918 a thermionic valve, which is the kind of valve most used in radios, was as big as a milk bottle. This shows how important it was to the development of modern technology when the size of these instruments was gradually reduced.

By 1935 valves had been made much smaller and measured about 10 centimetres over all; during the Second World War this measurement was halved and in December 1947 the transistor was invented by John Bardeen, Walter Brattain and William Shockley.

The transistor is the component which replaces the cumbersome old valves. It amplifies electric currents and voltages so much that it can make enormous savings on size, weight and, above all, power consumption.

The industries which are completely transistorized today are portable radios, ballistic missiles and military equipment in general, various kinds of control systems, electronic computers and telephones.

WHEN THE PLANTS IN OUR LIVES BEGAN

The first men on Earth did not know how to grow plants or breed animals. To get food they spent the day hunting or gathering fruit and seeds which ripened naturally in the woods. In the summer life was easy: game was plentiful and the trees and bushes provided fruit and berries of every kind. But when the snow came the animals hid and the plants were bare and no longer gave fruit.

Even if the women of the tribe had saved food for the winter, it was very difficult for them to preserve it. In time the fruit withered and supplies of meat ran out.

It was then that man discovered that there were other plants which could save him from starving. They were woodland plants with dry fruits which did not wither in the winter: the hazel trees, chestnuts, oaks and walnuts.

In many lake-settlements large quantities of shells and other traces of these fruits have been found, a clear sign that they were an important food for primitive man. The fruit of the dogwood, or cornel tree, another common woodland plant, was also highly prized in prehistoric times, when primitive man had to gather the fruits of the woods because he did not know how to farm.

In the pile-dwellings of Lake Ledro, in northern Italy, incredible amounts of dogwood berry stones have been found, buried in the mud at the bottom of the lake. While it seems that the lake-dwellers probably used this fruit for food, the piles of seeds are so numerous and large that the berries must have been used for something else as well perhaps to produce an alcoholic drink by leaving them to ferment.

Early Grain types and flint sickle

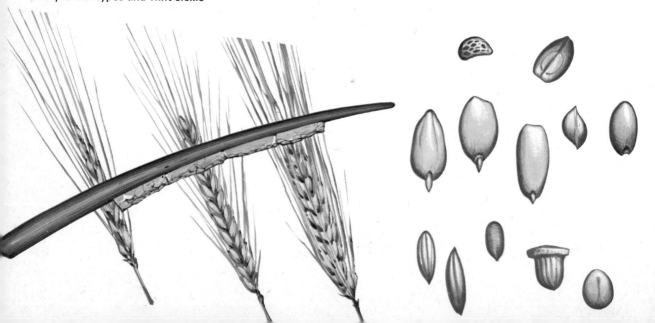

When corn was first grown

What is a grain of corn? It is something very small, only a few millimetres long and weighing only a few milligrammes. But if it is put in the ground in the right conditions, the seed swells, puts out a little root, a small leaf, and gives birth to a new plant.

Within the space of a few months the grain multiplies: it becomes thirty or forty new grains, grouped in an ear, themselves ready to produce new plants and multiply.

This process must have so impressed primitive man that it encouraged him to become a farmer, so that he could have enough corn to eat every year. Corn-growing is very ancient: nobody even knows in which part of the world it began or from which wild species the modern cultivated plant is derived.

According to the most likely suggestion, corn-growing began by chance. In the earliest times the cave-dwellers only gathered the grains of barley, wheat and rye which grew wild in woodland clearings. As this food could be kept for long periods, they filled their hide sacks with it to take with them on their frequent wanderings through the forests.

Before leaving, however, they never forgot to scatter a few grains on the ground, to please the gods.

After the winter, when they retraced their steps, they were amazed to find that the grains they had left on the ground had taken root and had given rise to new plants with swollen ears of corn. Perhaps this was how man learned to sow grain to grow new plants. And so some of the hunters became farmers, cultivating corn for themselves and their families.

The corn was eaten just as it was, in grains, or roasted over the fire. Bread-making was still unknown but it appears to have developed quite soon as cakes of barley have been discovered in Stone Age dwellings. Baking was practised by the ancient Egyptians. The Romans established public bakehouses from which free bread was distributed.

Early and late maize; squash

When cloth began

Textile, Halicar

In the Egyptian tombs paintings have been discovered which illustrate the cultivation of flax and the preparation of flax fibres for weaving into linen cloth. Linen must have been widely used in those days: the shrouds in which the mummies in the Pharaohs' tombs are wrapped are made of this material. The flax plant was therefore known in early times.

The use of hemp for making cloth and ropes also has very ancient origins. This plant was grown in China for its textile fibres as long ago as 2800 B.C. The fibres are coarser than those of flax and so are often stronger, which is why they are also used for making ropes and matting, as well as fabrics.

Hemp is a bushy-looking plant with stems of about 2 metres long and leaves with sharp-toothed edges. The flowers are either male or female and occur on separate plants.

An olive grove with detail of the fruit and leaves

When the olive became known

When Noah, the sole survivor of the Great Flood, saw the dove flying back to the ark with an olive branch in its beak, he knew that God's anger was appeased. So the story in the Bible goes and ever since the olive has been regarded as a symbol of peace.

There are many ancient books which quote the olive as one of the plants best-known to man and most closely answering his needs. This shows that the olive tree has been grown for thousands of years.

In the Palace of Knossus at Crete, dating back to 3,000 years before Christ, enormous jars have been found which were used for collecting and storing oil. The Greeks were great olive-growers and introduced the tree to Italy, along the Mediterranean coast.

The olive lives for a very long time, sometimes for thousands of years, but it never grows very tall. Its trunk is often gnarled and twisted and its leaves are a silvery green in colour because of all the tiny grey scales which shine on their undersides. The fruit of the olive is called a drupe: it is like a small fleshy plum, rich in oily substances, with a stone in the middle. While green the fruit can be bottled in brine. Olive oil is extracted from the ripe fruit.

The warmth of the Sun is vitally important if the olive is to grow. That is why this plant is better suited to southern countries or to a warm temperate climate, and is only rarely found in the northern countries. In California and in Arizona there are vast olive plantations.

Apart from the common olive, there are about fifty other varieties of the olive family.

When men learnt to produce wine

The cultivation of the vine in the Mediterranean basin has very ancient origins, and the art of producing wine is just as old. It is mentioned several times in the Bible, which refers to the grape as one of the Earth's greatest gifts to man.

Particularly expert in viniculture were the peoples of southern Italy, so much so that the Greeks called this part of the Italian peninsular *Enotria*—the land of wine.

It seems probable that in Italy the vine existed in a wild form even before the appearance of man, and it is certain that the first inhabitants of the peninsular ate the grapes they found in the woods, although they did not know how to cultivate them.

There is evidence, almost certainly reliable, of viniculture in Sicily as long ago as 2000 B.C. From Sicily it spread to other regions, and increased rapidly with the expansion of the Roman Empire.

During the Middle Ages it was monks who were the specialists in the cultivation of vines. Then the grapes spread again in the eighteenth century, when the worst vine diseases were identified and combatted.

Today Europe is the main wine producer, followed by a number of States in both North and South America, some parts of Africa, and Australia and Japan. Because there are many types of grape, there are also many wines on the market, of which the European ones are most favoured for their taste and bouquet. They have been produced for thousands of years, and have a long standing popularity.

When the pomegranate became known

The pomegranate bush which can grow to a height of 6 metres, is a native of subtropical Asia.

For thousands of years the strange fruit of this bush has been regarded as one of the most important fruits of the Mediterranean region. It is mentioned in the Bible and also figures in mythology.

Its sweet juicy seeds, like rubies in colour, and its beautiful bright red flowers have been an inspiration to authors and poets. The Italian poet, Carducci, wrote of '... The green pomegranate yonder with crimson blossoms bright.'

In addition to the many varieties of fruit produced and grown, there are some 'full bloom' varieties of the shrub which bear beautiful double flowers but no fruit and are therefore only grown for ornament.

The pomegranate belongs to the Punicaceae family.

The art of viniculture is often depicted in ancient paintings and figures

When tulips were precious flowers

There is a big family of plants called the Liliaceae. It includes not only the lily but 4,000 other species as varied as the buttercup, garlic, onion, hyacinth, aloe, yucca, asparagus, lily-of-the-valley, tulip and aspidistra.

Tulips are among the best known and most common Liliaceae today but a few centuries ago they were rare and were very precious, expensive flowers.

Grown for thousands of years in Turkey, where more than 1,300 varieties were known, they did not arrive in Europe until the second half of the sixteenth century. They achieved their greatest popularity in the eighteenth century, when there was not a garden, however humble or however grand, which did not include them.

Vast sums were spent on acquiring rare varieties of the bulbs. Today tulip-growing is an industry, particularly in Holland, which is the largest producer.

When cocoa was brought back to Spain

It was Columbus who, on his fourth voyage in 1502, took cocoa beans back to Spain. The Spaniards made them into a drink, adding sugar, but it was nearly 100 years before the use of cocoa spread to other parts of Europe.

Cocoa is obtained from the roasted seeds of a large fruit which ripens directly on the trunk or branches of a tropical plant. The Indians made it into drinks, mixing it with vanilla and spices, or made biscuits by kneading it with maize. They even used it as money in trade.

The cacao tree has large oval leaves. It can grow to 12 metres high but is usually pruned to between 4 and 8 metres. Small pinkish, wax-like flowers are produced on the trunk and the oldest branches. From these the pod-like fruit develops. It is up to 25 centimetres long, containing a white or pinkish pulp surrounding the seeds, which are a little bigger than our hazel-nuts. To reach the floury kernel in each seed, the tough pod which protects it has to be broken.

Each fruit may contain about thirty seeds called cocoa beans. They are first separated from the pulp then cleaned before being roasted. The roasting heightens their aromatic flavour and makes it easier to reduce them to powder. Special machines then release the cocoa from the tough skin and grind it up, at the same time separating part of the natural fat or cocoa-butter which is used for making such things as soaps and cosmetics.

Over a million tons of cocoa is produced a year, the bulk of it coming from West Africa.

When Charles V refused a pineapple

One of the most exotic fruits to arrive in Europe after the discovery of America was the pineapple.

Partly because it was so difficult to keep and partly because people were suspicious of it, the pineapple had to wait to conquer Europe until the arrival of rapid transport, the canning industries and mass advertising.

Even the Emperor Charles V of Spain refused to taste the first pineapple offered to him in case it was poisonous. Today, however, it is widely grown in all tropical countries where there is plenty of sunshine and warmth.

The first Europeans to mention the pineapple were Christopher Columbus and Sir Walter Raleigh who found it growing in the West Indies. In America it was already grown by the Indians, who had introduced it into many regions.

About 20 centimetres long, the pineapple looks something like a pine-cone. It grows on spikes rising from the centre of the plant. Botanically, it is a multiple fruit, like the blackberry and the strawberry. The plant, with its elongated, prickly leaves, only fruits after its third year.

When America gave us new food

Before the discovery of America, nobody in Europe had heard of maize. In fact, sweetcorn, which is unripe ears of maize, was unknown over here until it was imported from the New World, where it was intensely cultivated by the Indians.

They were already producing several types of Indian corn but later varieties have increased the number of seeds and improved the quality of the cobs.

Even more important than Indian corn was the arrival in Europe of a strange edible tuber called the potato. A native of Chile and Peru, the plant was found by the Spaniards on their first explorations of the South American continent. They took it home with them, together with other strange vegetables. By the end of the seventeenth century it was a major crop in Ireland and a hundred years later was widely grown in Europe, especially in Germany and in the west of England.

Other important vegetables introduced into Europe as a result of the discovery of America are red and green peppers, certain species of cucumber and beans and tomatoes.

When spices were worth more than gold

The precious spices from which seafaring republics had made their fortunes were known and used in Europe in the earliest times but their origin remained a mystery. Normally it was the Arab merchants who supplied them to European traders, but those cunning adventurers had never disclosed the source of their merchandize.

It was only with the great voyages of discovery that the origin of nutmegs, cinnamon and cloves was revealed.

Cloves were found by the Dutch in the Molucca Islands. For a long time attempts were made to prevent specimens of the clove-tree being 'stolen' for transplantation in other colonial territories, but in the eighteenth century clove-growing spread rapidly to all the other tropical regions. Today there are extensive clove-plantations in Madagascar, where the spice was introduced by the French.

When the plants are in flower, their strong scent can be smelt up to 300 kilometres away from the coast.

Cinnamon-growing is also widespread in many hot countries today.

Cinnamon comes from the bark of a tree which grows wild in India and Sri Lanka. It is the oil of cinnamon which produces its flavour: this is prepared from pieces of bark which are soaked in sea water and then distilled. A few centuries ago it was so precious that powerful nations actually went to war over the control of its production. The island of Sri Lanka passed from Portuguese to Dutch and then to British rule because, for trading reasons, each of these countries wanted to gain possession of its cinnamon groves.

The best known and most used spice is still pepper. In the Middle Ages the black berries of this sharp-tasting seasoning were so valuable that several people suggested using them as money for trade. A native of the moist, low-country forests of Ceylon and Southern India, the pepper plant is a creeping vine which is normally trained up other trees.

Its large leaves, arranged alternately, have almost no stem. Its flowers are joined in hanging spikes and produce round fruits, first green and then red. If picked at the red stage and left to dry, they become black and wrinkled and make black pepper. But if left to ripen fully, the pepper fruits turn brown and produce a single round seed inside them. When husked this seed makes white pepper, which tastes less sharp.

When coffee came to London

Nearly half the coffee drunk in the world today comes from plantations in Brazil but the plant is really of African origin.

It used to grow wild in the regions around the Red Sea and was first popularized in the Middle East by caravans of Arab merchants, although the drinks they prepared from it were somewhat different from the coffee we know today.

Coffee was introduced into Europe during the sixteenth and seventeenth centuries. It gained its first real popularity in the coffeehouses of London, the first of which was established in about 1652.

Coffeehouses flourished in the major cities of Europe and North America later in the 1600s.

By the end of the eighteenth century, the cultivation of coffee had spread to all the tropical regions, particularly America.

The coffee plant is a shrub which does not like the direct rays of the sun when it is growing. For this reason, neat rows of other shade trees, such as the acacia, are normally also grown on the plantations.

When wild the coffee-tree may grow up to 8 metres tall but the cultivated kind is pruned to a height of 2 to 3 metres. It has dark green, glossy leaves, oval in shape, and its white, scented flowers bloom in clusters in their axils. The flowers are replaced by green cherries which ripen to scarlet and contain two beans inside which are the seeds.

When roasted and ground, these seeds produce coffee powder. The drink we make from it contains caffeine, a drug which stimulates the heart and nervous system.

When tobacco was a medicinal plant

'Sovereigne herbe' was what our ancestors called tobacco in the sixteenth century. It had been found in tropical America, where the natives had been growing and smoking tobacco for thousands of years.

In Europe it was valued first as a medicinal plant and only taken as snuff.

Tobacco was also called 'Nicotiana' in honour of the French ambassador, Jean Nicot, who helped make it known by presenting a few seeds of the plant to Queen Catherine of Medici. The habit of smoking tobacco spread fairly slowly, however.

Cigars and cigarettes are prepared from the leaves of the plant, specially dried and cured to improve its properties. Numerous varieties of tobacco are grown today.

WHEN THE ANIMALS IN OUR LIVES BEGAN

In the far-off days of prehistory man's attitude towards the animals was entirely self-interested. He regarded them either as dangerous beasts, to be guarded against, or as precious sources of food, to be procured by hunting and fishing.

In either case, although he had no scientific interest in them, man was compelled to perfect his knowledge of the animals which lived on the plains and in the forests. For he could not avoid the wild beasts nor defend himself from their attacks and he could not catch his quarry without knowing their habits, their weaknesses, what they ate or where they slept.

Then, when man had caught his animal, it had to be cut up for food and skinned for its hide. And so he was taking his first lessons in anatomy.

The tribe's priests and sorcerers were in a way the first scientists, as it was their job to sacrifice the animals to please the gods. So they, better than anyone else, knew the anatomy of the victims they were cutting up on their altars.

A wonderful record of the interest that primitive man took in the animals, is provided by the beautiful rock-paintings discovered in several caves. The artists demonstrate an expert knowledge of the animals they were depicting.

Some animals have been man's faithful companions since the earliest times. Others have been domesticated and bred to produce meat, milk, eggs or skins. Still others have always been hunted as game. It is therefore natural to find frequent mention of animals in history, even in documents dealing with the most ancient civilizations.

Some peoples, however, have attached such importance to these creatures that they were thought to be incarnations of gods or devils, who were propitiated with ceremonies and sacrifices.

The gods of ancient Egypt are famous. A sacred cat was worshipped at Memphis and an ox at Thebes. Other cities worshipped wolves, jackals, lionesses, crocodiles, ibises and various fish from

Cave paintings at Niaux, showing bison wounded by arrows

the Nile. Many of these animals are portrayed in almost human form on the walls of the tombs, on the coffins and on the furniture in the funeral chambers.

Less well-known but equally important are the portraits of sacred animals, such as the plumed serpent, which appear in the sculptures of the ancient Mayan people.

When zoology began

We have to wait until the great Greek philosopher, Aristotle (384–322 B.C.), for the first serious attempt to bring together all the knowledge available on the animal kingdom.

Aristotle's merit is not just that he wrote five hefty treatises on all that was known about the animals in those days. He also made many original comments, discredited legends and described some 500 animals in amazingly accurate detail, even by today's more informed standards.

Yet, over the centuries, scholars became incapable of continuing and deepening Aristotle's work. They even distorted his writings to such an extent that new legends and ridiculous beliefs grew up and were handed on from people to people.

With the Romans the natural sciences made no progress at all. The only scholar to gather information on the animals was Pliny the Elder (A.D. 23–79), but his *Natural History*, written in thirty-seven books, is a mixture of useful comment and absurd legend. It contains many imaginary animals such as winged horses and unicorns and is certainly not of the same standard as Aristotle's earlier work.

The Middle Ages encouraged

the birth of strange beliefs and superstitions still more. It was even thought that one particular goose was born as the fruit of some coastal plants.

It was not until the Renaissance that scientific interest in the animals was revived and descriptive works were written again.

Egyptian god, shown as a crowned hawk

When the first animals were domesticated

Primitive man could not begin to be civilized until he learned how to domesticate, or tame, the animals. Until then, he had to wander through the forests hunting game and tracking prey and he was forced to embark on long journeys to follow the animals which migrate.

As soon as he learned to keep a few animals, to use their milk, eggs, skins and meat, early man was able to build himself a permanent dwelling, to work with his hands and to farm the land around his hut.

The first animals bred by man might well have been birds. It was easy to find broods of baby birds in the trees or on the ground. They were caught and taken back to the hut, where they were fed and grew fat, laying a plentiful supply of eggs before they were killed and eaten.

Taming and breeding birds must have been much easier than catching and keeping a large mammal. The number of domestic species of birds known since antiquity shows that man began early in his history to breed birds.

A theory shared by Darwin was that all the domesticated breeds of poultry were derived from *Gallus bankiva*, a bird which inhabits northern India, Burma and parts of Malaysia. Darwin admitted, however, the lack of good evidence for this theory.

Pigeons, hens, ducks, geese and guinea-fowl all appeared on the table at banquets in antiquity.

Already in Roman times many types of domestic hen were known, and the guinea-fowl was bred by the Greeks who called it the African hen.

The peacock, too, was very highly thought of in Greece, where it had been introduced by Alexander the Great who discovered it in India.

It is also interesting to note that in the last few centuries there have been very few new domesticated animals.

The last large bird that was introduced to our tables, and especially at Christmas time, was the turkey.

In modern times man has shown a greater interest in machines than in animals.

When the dog appeared by man's side

Prehistoric rock carvings and cave paintings show scenes of hunting and daily life in the primitive villages. Often man is drawn with the dog by his side. It is the clearest proof that the dog was the mammal which first became accustomed to living near human dwellings, sharing the fate of the primitive peoples, accompanying them on hunting expeditions, helping them and defending them from the perils of the wild animals.

Several fossil dog skulls have been found near Stone Age camps and among the remains of lake-dwellings. The oldest remains of dogs in Europe have been found at Star Carr in Yorkshire. The breeds are different from the modern dogs but they are definite evidence of their long-standing friendship with man.

The freezes of Egyptian temples are also carved with figures of dogs as too are many early Egyptian monuments.

Cattle and sheep soon appeared near primitive villages, too, providing them with a valuable supply of food. They may have been brought into Europe by people who came from further east. When man succeeded in taming cows and sheep he took the first step towards stock-breeding.

A close companion of the sheep in prehistoric man's pens was the swine, the cousin of the wild pig. Near Stone Age camps in central and northern Europe, fossil remains of pigs have been found, together with those of goats and oxen. This is the earliest evidence of the domestication of pigs in Europe. In China they have been bred since 4,000 years before Christ.

When the cat 'walked by himself'

The cat is such a common domestic animal in our houses that it seems as if its friendship with man must date back to very ancient times, as does the dog's. But this is not so. Primitive man did not know the cat or, if he had occasionally met it in the woods, he thought of it as a dangerous meat-eater, of which he had to beware.

It hid in the trees and in the depths of the forests, living on prey like a tiger or any other fierce animal.

The first signs of its domestication are to be found before 2000 B.C. in the Egypt of the Pharaohs, where the cat was worshipped as a god. Nobody knows how it came

Below: Many mummified bodies of cats have been found in Egypt, a testimony to their religious significance in ancient times

This is not surprising as the beech-marten is a ferocious flesh-eater of the weasel family, which creates havoc in hen-houses and farmyards.

Unlike the marten, a close cousin which lives in woods and kills small wild animals, the beech-marten prefers to live in the open, using some abandoned ruin or old hut for refuge. It may often be found hidden in a stable, barn or wood-pile near the house.

From here it steals forth at night to creep into the hen-house where it goes completely berserk, slaughtering as many animals as it can. When it has finished it makes off, back to its lair, carrying a single fowl in its mouth. So it has no need to wreak such havoc among the poultry but the beech-marten is one of the fiercest and most blood-thirsty of carnivores and is hated and pursued by all farmers.

When the turkey came to Europe

For the people of the United States the turkey is a kind of national dish and is always served at traditional dinners, particularly on Thanksgiving Day. This feast celebrates the harvest and the other blessings of the past year.

The first Thanksgiving Day occurred in 1621. In a letter dated 11 December, Edward Winslow described how, when the harvest had been gathered, 'our Governor sent four men on fowling, that so we might after a more special manner rejoice together.... They four in one day killed as much fowl as . . . served the Company almost a week.' The 'fowl' were a large flock of wild turkey.

It was introduced into Europe at the beginning of the sixteenth century and since then roast

to Europe from Egypt, but we have a definite account of its presence in this continent towards the end of the Roman Empire. It is hardly mentioned in Greek, Roman or Jewish literature and at the beginning of the Middle Ages in Europe the cat was rare and costly. It had been known in China since A.D. 500 but it was not until the fourteenth century that it became a well-known household pet.

There are a number of varieties of domestic cat, an unusual one being the long-haired 'swimming cat' from Van in Turkey. It is chalk-white with auburn head-markings and a ringed tail, and is notable for its apparent liking for water.

When the beech-marten hunted house-mice

Until the fourth century after Christ the Romans did not know of the domestic cat. In its place, to rid themselves of mice, they kept tame beech-martens.

Relations between this animal and man are therefore very old but, apart from the exception of 'domestic' beech-martens, these relations have always been hostile.

turkey has become the traditional Christmas dinner in many European countries. The turkey has gradually increased in size as the breeds have been improved by selection and crosses. Today, a good farm turkey may measure as much as one metre twenty tall if it is a cock and slightly less if it is a hen. Turkey breeding can be a very profitable business and has become a large scale industry.

Wild turkeys still live in the forests of the United States. They are smaller than the domestic ones and live in huge groups, scratching the ground for berries, roots, worms and any other kind of food. They sometimes make long migrations to find new land for undisturbed grazing.

When the legend of the unicorn flourished

The ancient peoples of the Mediterranean believed in the existence of the unicorn, a mythical animal which was supposed to look like a horse with a long horn on its forehead. This story seemed to be confirmed by the first travellers to northern seas who brought back with them strange, spirally twisted 'horns' that they had found on the beaches of the mysterious northlands. Yet nobody had seen one of these mythical animals, dead or alive.

The legend of the unicorn stirred the imaginations of men until the late Middle Ages. Some people even tried to reconstruct the legendary animal by taking the skeleton of a horse and fixing one of those famous spiral horns to its skull.

But, with the beginning of scientific study based on the close observation of nature, these hoaxes were exposed.

In 1655, some sailors fished a narwhal out of the ocean and carried its skeleton back to Europe. It was clear that the long, twisted 'horns' discovered by the ancient travellers really belonged to this aquatic mammal and not to the unicorn at all. For the narwhal, a kind of whale, has a single large tusk, twisted in a left-handed spiral, which juts out horizontally from its mouth.

So the 'horns' found on the beaches were not from unicorns but were tusks of dead narwhals, washed ashore by the sea-currents.

When whales were terrifying monsters

Today everyone knows that the whale is not a fish but a mammal. Until the middle of the sixteenth century, however, even scientists thought it was a huge fish and knowledge of this animal was so slight that the strangest legends grew up.

One of these claimed that when the whale is resting motionless on the surface of the water it may be mistaken for an island, to the great danger of the sailors who land on it!

Whales are indeed exceedingly large but not as large as the ancients described. The sei whale, a small rorqual, or fin-back whale, grows to at most 21 metres long, a third of which is taken up by the head. Its mouth is immense, up to 6 metres long and 3 wide.

To obtain its food the whale swallows a mouthful of seawater and then, with its jaws closed and using its tongue like a piston, it drives all the water out, filtering it through the fringed plates which it has instead of teeth. Small fish and above all plankton remain trapped in the cetacean's mouth.

Turkeys

Chihuahua

Snakes

Grey squirrel

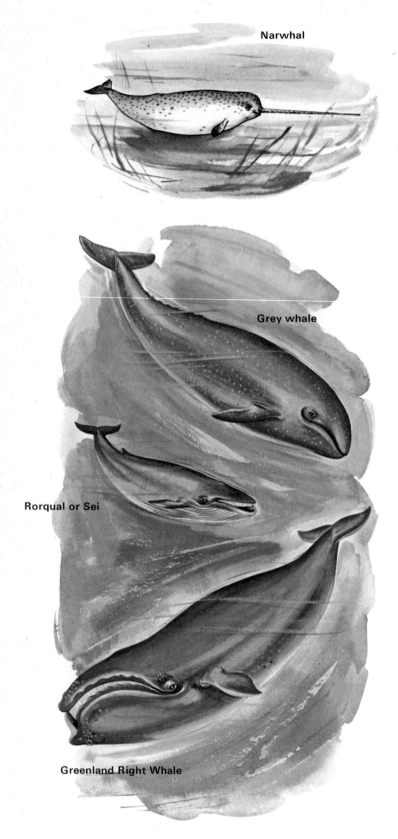

Narwhal

Grey whale

Rorqual or Sei

Greenland Right Whale

The gray whale of the northern Pacific can grow to a length of 15 metres. The beaked or bottle-nosed whale is the smallest of the whale family and grows to a maximum length of only 9 metres.

The female whale normally gives birth to only one baby whale, which is about 7 metres long.

Sei whaling by Europeans began when other whales, which used to frequent our local seas, became very rare because of the wholesale slaughter.

Since the beginning of history the Eskimos and Red Indians have managed to catch a few specimens of this aquatic mammal by a very difficult method. They row up to the animal in flimsy canoes, climb on to its head and drive two sticks firmly between its blowholes, making it die of suffocation.

The whaling ships were 200–300 ton vessels with square sails, a wide main beam and deep holds which could take up to 2,400 barrels of oil. They could be recognized from a long way off by their sails, which became stained by the brick ovens in which the whale fat was boiled to extract the oil. It was essential to have space to cut the whales up into sections, and so the cabin, normally in the prow, was moved astern.

The boats actually used for catching whales, were slim craft made of cedar and so light that two men could lift one. They·could be rowed by five men at a speed of up to 10 knots.

In modern times whale fishing, chiefly of rorquals, has become so profitable commercially that the whale is in danger of being overfished, and international agreements limit the total kill.

When Cook's discoveries amazed the naturalists

In 1770 Captain Cook's sailors penetrated the interior of the Australian continent to look for fresh meat. They returned to the ship carrying some 'game' which astonished and intrigued the whole crew. What they had caught were big kangaroos, which no one had ever seen before.

Only found in certain parts of Australia, these strange creatures had never been heard of by zoologists and it was not until their chance discovery by the sailors that kangaroos became known to the world.

Today they have become the symbol of Australian animal life.

Their best-known feature is their pouch. The baby kangaroo spends much of its time in its mother's pouch, and even when it can run and jump it goes there for shelter and protection.

Kangaroos can grow to nearly 3 metres in length, including the tail. The head is small compared with the rest of the body and tapers forward. The shoulders and front legs, too, are feebly developed, but the hind legs and tail are long and powerful, so that these animals can leap forward and move swiftly.

They are plant-eaters and consume vast quantities of pasture, browsing on grass and various kinds of vegetation. It is for this reason as much as for sport that kangaroos are hunted, for the grass is needed for cattle and sheep.

By nature kangaroos are timid and inoffensive except when cornered and then they defend themselves with their sharp claws and powerful hind legs.

In the wake of Cook's voyages of discovery, incredible accounts of strange, sometimes incredible animals reached Europe.

For example, the skin of the first duck-billed platypus on record was taken to England in 1797. It gave rise to heated discussions, not to say violent quarrels, among scholars who did not know how to classify it.

The duck-billed platypus is indeed a strange mixture of bird and mammal. It has the bill and egg-laying habit of a duck but when the 'chick' hatches out the mother platypus gathers it up and suckles it, like an ordinary mammal.

And this is not all: the platypus has the tail of a beaver, which it can beat at swimming; it is cold-blooded, like a snake; it burrows underground holes like a mole and it waddles on land like a penguin.

Altogether, it seems to be a complete freak of nature.

Yet this creature really does exist and has kept scholars fully occupied, observing its habits and anatomy and looking for links with other creatures, alive or extinct.

The echidna, which is very rare, is a mainly nocturnal animal and lives in the sandy, rocky regions of south-east Australia and Tasmania. It is found in no other area.

Kangaroo

The echidna, or spiny anteater, as it is also called, is another inhabitant of the Australian continent which has attracted great interest and sparked off endless discussions.

It is a mammal but, like the duck-billed platypus, it lays eggs. The female echidna places her single egg in her pouch and suckles the baby there when it has been born.

It, too, is a strange mixture of characters belonging to animals of widely divergent species. It has sharp prickles like a hedgehog or porcupine, an elongated, sensitive snout like no other animal's, padded feet like an elephant's, strong claws and a worm-shaped, sticky tongue like an anteater's.

It has the same eating habits as an anteater, too, as it feeds solely on ants, catching them with its darting tongue. It uses its strong claws to dig up and turn out ants' nests, making the insects run.

This animal, like the porcupine, rolls itself into a ball when disturbed.

When the animals began to be classified

The first scholars to describe the animals living on Earth tried to group them according to certain common characters. They felt they must put the vast quantity of knowledge they had amassed into some sort of order.

Aristotle had already devised an important system of classification, in which he divided the animals into two main groups: those with blood and those without blood. We now know that all animals have blood, even if it is not always red, but in Aristotle's day knowledge of the animals was limited.

For another 2,000 years, scholars who came after him continued to classify animals more or less in the same way. It was not until 1700, with the development of anatomy, that the internal structure of animals began to be better understood.

At the end of the seventeenth century John Ray devised new classifications and these were further improved by Georges Cuvier in the early nineteenth century. These new classifications form the basis of those now used by modern science.

Platypus

Echidna

Since the middle of the eighteenth century, the two-name (binomial) system, devised by the Swedish botanist, Linnaeus, has been adopted for all classifications. In this system, the scientific name of each animal is always made up of two parts, the first indicating the genus, or subdivision of the family, and the second the species, which describes what the animal is like or where it is found.

When the great debate on the origin of the animals began

In the first half of the nineteenth century animal research made tremendous progress. But naturalists were divided into two opposing camps. On the one hand were the scholars convinced of the unchangeable nature of the various animal species. On the other were those who believed in the continual evolution of the animals and the tendency of the species to go on changing to adapt to their surroundings.

Scholars in the first group, called creationists, were supported by Linnaeus' theory that 'there are as many species as the different forms created by the Supreme Being at the beginning of time'.

The chief exponent of creationism was Georges Cuvier (1769–1832), the founder of comparative anatomy. He refused to accept the evidence showing that the animals which lived long ago were not the same as those living today.

When scientists believed in the theory of catastrophism

Cuvier was bitterly opposed to any theories contrary to his own, and his great prestige was one of the reasons why important discoveries were ignored. These discoveries would have shown how the animal kingdom evolved.

However he could not continue to ignore the discoveries of fossil remains of animals which had disappeared millions of years before.

In particular, these remains were always being found in certain layers of rock dating back to definite geological eras.

He explains this fact by the theory of catastrophism. According to this, at certain times in the history of the Earth, immense cataclysms occurred, changing the surface of the Earth and wiping out all sign of life. When calm was afterwards restored, a new act of creation repopulated the Earth with more advanced animal forms.

Following the same theory, another scientist, d'Orbigny, had even worked out as many as twenty-seven creations interspersed with twenty-six floods and universal catastrophes. This explanation could obviously not hold good for long, however.

Even in Cuvier's day, another great scientist, Jean Baptiste Lamarck, had put forward a scientific theory in a pamphlet he published.

It recognized that the animals living around us are the result of a continual evolution of primitive forms, due to the influence of climate, temperature and altitude.

At first his theory passed unnoticed but Lamarck's inspired guess soon became the basis of all modern zoological science.

When evolution became a certainty

Although Lamark's theory of evolution was to a certain extent correct, its weakness lay in its lack of definite scientific evidence.

Then, in 1859, a new event threw the zoology world into complete confusion. Just over twenty years earlier, Charles Darwin had returned from a long surveying voyage to South America and the Pacific. There he had collected some important material, and in 1859 he published his book *On the Origin of Species by Means of Natural Selection*. In it his observations on the slow change of the animals from the ancient primitive species to the modern ones were so well illustrated that the doctrines of the creationists crumbled for ever.

On one stage of his voyage aboard the *Beagle*, Darwin went to explore the Argentinian Pampas and came upon the fossil remains of enormous creatures which were bigger and more strangely shaped than anyone had believed possible. Later, on the Galapagos Islands, thousands of kilometres away from the coast of Ecuador, he discovered that geographical isolation had indirectly given rise to

Charles Linnaeus

Lamarck

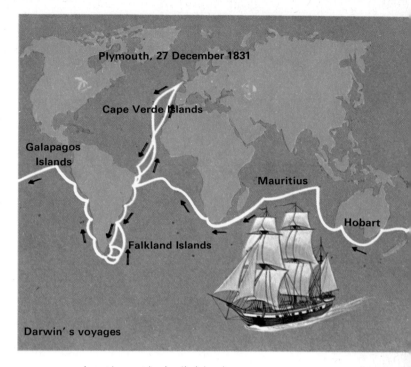

Plymouth, 27 December 1831

Cape Verde Islands

Galapagos Islands

Mauritius

Hobart

Falkland Islands

Darwin's voyages

new animal species.

He noticed in particular that the finches which live there form a family of their own, which is only to be found on the Islands and not on the South American mainland. They most probably all originated from a single pair which went to the Islands a long time ago and adapted to their environment by evolving into five genera and some twenty species. Each of them had developed different eating techniques and therefore differently shaped beaks.

These observations and those made from other animals from geographically isolated regions led Darwin to believe firmly in the evolution of species and to describe the mechanism of mutation.

Basically, Darwin said that in every species the only individuals to survive and reproduce are the ones which are best fitted to defend themselves and adapt to their environment. This means that there is a continual process of natural selection which in time gives rise to new breeds.

Darwin

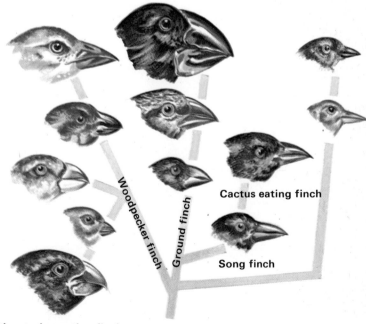

Woodpecker finch

Ground finch

Cactus eating finch

Song finch

Vegetarian eating finch

THE WHY OF THE ROCKS

Why we think of the Alps as young mountains

During the many millions of years of its history the Earth's crust suffered countless upheavals. They resulted in the formation of in-numerable chains of mountains.

No trace whatever now remains of the oldest of these because they were completely eroded away by atmospheric forces. Some remnants of others still persist but they are buried beneath strata, or layers, of more recent rocks. At the present time the highest peaks are the newest ones; they are high just because water and other influences were too late to level them completely.

The Alps, the Himalayas and the Rocky Mountains began to rise about 65 million years ago; they are, therefore, quite old, but to the geologist they are still young because the unit of measurement which he uses to record such enormous natural events is equal to millions of years.

According to modern discoveries the Alps are still rising slowly but the amount which they gain in height is continually cancelled out by erosion.

The chief cause of their upheavals is to be found in the thrust exerted by the African continent. It moved northwards and forced the rock strata of the Mediterranean Basin to pile up against the lands of Europe which had emerged earlier, and to form the present parallel chains of mountains.

The Alps consist of numerous ranges divided by deep valleys. They stretch from the Gulf of Genoa to Vienna and rise between the plains of northern Italy and of southern Germany.

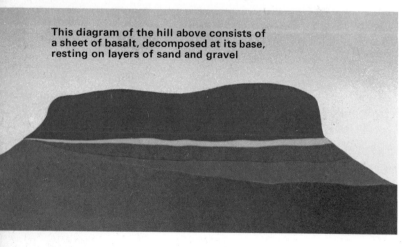

This diagram of the hill above consists of a sheet of basalt, decomposed at its base, resting on layers of sand and gravel

Why mountains die

To anyone who visits the mountains and sees them the same and unmoving year after year, this may appear impossible. Nevertheless day by day the mountains are being eaten away and changed. The erosive action of wind, rain and frost wears them away, little by little, removing from their walls rock particles, which are ceaselessly carried downwards.

The speed of erosion varies with the hardness of the rocks and the intensity of the rain, wind and storms which pound against the face of the rocks. However all mountains finish by being worn away and disintegrating until they are levelled out. Of course this takes hundreds of millions of years to happen. During this time the life of a mountain can be divided into three parts: youth, maturity and old age.

Why some mountains have perpendicular walls

Let us imagine that a huge area of the Earth's crust gradually rises above the surface of the seas and keeps its horizontal position.

When a certain point is reached, an enormous vertical or inclined crack, miles and miles long, appears in this mass of superelevated rocks and part of the mass begins to sink whilst the remainder stays still or continues to rise.

Eventually there will be a great difference in height between the two masses. This will expose the strata of the rocks which remain upright so as to form very imposing mountains with perpendicular walls.

A view of part of the coast of the Isle of Wight

225

The Giant's Causeway with inset showing detail of hexagonal columns

Why basalt rocks are rust-coloured

Basalt, a volcanic rock which is quite common, is very easy to recognize by its colour, ranging from black to dark green, its compactness and its heavy weight. However basalt rocks which have been exposed to the air over a long period become covered on the surface with a reddish coating, very similar to rust. This happens because this rock usually contains various iron compounds which become oxidized by the action of the atmosphere.

Where there are very large and compact deposits of basalt these rocks can be found in the form of columns or pillars. The lava issuing white hot from the bowels of the Earth cools on the surface and forms structures of hexagonal or six-sided columns joined tightly to one another and arranged perpendicular to the surface.

Why some rocks split into sheets

All metamorphic rocks, that is those which have undergone great changes, which have a lamellar or fibrous structure and can therefore be divided into sheets, sometimes very thin sheets, are called schists. This structure is caused by the crushing and parallel arrangement of the components of the primitive rock.

Some very common schists are mica, chlorites and talc which, because of their plate-like formation, can be split along parallel lines.

After being formed schists may undergo other changes by contraction, high pressure or variations of temperature. We then have what are known as crystalline schists.

A great variety of these are found and are named according to the elements of which they are composed. For instance, we have mica schists formed mostly of quartz and mica; quartzites; calcareous schists containing calcite; phyllite composed of quartz and mica in very fine laminations; talc schists, and many others.

The Blue Lias rocks of Lyme Regis are rich in fossils

Why primitive man used flint tools

Flint is fairly common in rocks of all ages. It contains a high proportion of silicate of a special crystalline structure, making it both hard and fragile at the same time.

Primitive man usually found it along the river banks in the form of large pebbles. By striking them in a particular way he broke them into sharp flakes.

These pieces of flint were very useful for scraping, cutting, sawing and polishing. Fixed on the end of a stick, they could inflict serious wounds on the large animals which man hunted.

Until metals came on the scene much later, flint was the inseparable companion of early man because its fine grain and brittleness made it better than any other stone for forming the implements and tools which he needed.

Many different kinds of flint tools were made and innumerable examples of them have been found. It is sometimes possible to trace ancient trade routes by knowing where a particular type of flint was obtained.

Why some rocks split into slabs

As opposed to crystalline shale, argillaceous or clayey shale is of a very fine grain structure.

The schistosity of these rocks is perfect and they can be split into very large sheets and very thin sheets. They are to be found in many parts of the country and have been used for centuries for covering and roofing houses. The most valuable of them, called slate, is still employed for making the large blackboards used in schools.

Sometimes because of the high proportion of mica flakes, the sheets of these clayey shales have a very bright appearance. They frequently contain fossils which are nearly always imperfect and in a poor state of preservation. This is as a result of the same phenomena of pressure and crushing which changed the sedimentary into metamorphic rocks.

227

Why the diamond is a precious stone

Generally speaking precious stones are no more than fragments of minerals which have crystallized in a different way from normal. They owe their value not so much to the costliness of their materials as to their rarity.

There are many types of gem but only four really deserve the title of 'precious': the diamond, the emerald, the sapphire and the ruby. The diamond has been known for at least 3,000 years and is the hardest mineral found in nature. This quality, together with those of beauty and rarity, make it the most precious stone in the world.

In its natural state this precious stone is certainly not one of the most magnificent. On his sixty-sixth birthday King Edward VII was presented with the largest diamond in the world (it weighed 3,106 carats) which was found in the Transvaal in 1905. When he saw the rough appearance and lack of lustre of the stone, he is reported to have said: 'If I had seen it in the street, I would have kicked it away like an ordinary piece of glass.'

A little later this famous 'piece of glass' was cut with the greatest skill by Asscher's in Amsterdam into nine major gems and ninety-six small brilliants. The biggest gem, known as the Great Star of Africa, is the largest cut diamond in the world. That and the second largest gem are part of the British crown jewels and are on display in the Tower of London.

Why some stones were made into amulets and seals

The beautiful rare coloured stones, often of small size, which are found in caves or in the beds of rivers, attracted men's attention from the very earliest times. Our ancestors could not explain where these small sparkling stones came from. The very bright colours were quite unlike any rocks with which they were acquainted.

Being superstitious, they thought they were signs from the gods and that to possess such stones gave them divine protection against all kinds of misfortune. That is why amulets were made and we know from archeological discoveries that they were used in prehistoric times.

In the course of time and with the progress of civilization men began to make these precious stones even more beautiful and sparkling by polishing them, cutting them into regular shapes and mounting them in holders of precious metals such as gold and silver. Someone also had the idea of cutting into them decorative and personal designs, so that the owner could recognize them easily if they were mislaid or stolen.

When stones prepared in this way were pressed on to a tablet of soft clay they left in it the impression of the design. That is how the first seals came into being, and they were used on clay tablets in Babylon some 5,000 years ago. Some of these seals were in the form of cylinders.

(1) Roman garnet engraved with the head of Jupiter Serapis
(2) Persian cylindrical seal
(3) Sassanid engraved onyx

Why some mountains are made of marble

From the geological point of view marble is a calcareous or limestone rock of crystalline structure. Limestone is a sedimentary rock usually formed beneath the seas by the depositing of enormous layers of shells of small sea animals. But normal limestone is not marble. It can be turned into marble in various ways.

For instance, if the limestone layers are covered by lava, the heat of the molten mass changes the surrounding rock by fusion

into crystallized limestone, that is true marble. Sometimes crystallization is the result of very high pressure.

Even the purest marbles contain other minerals such as quartz, colouress or pale yellow mica and dark flakes of graphite.

229

Why water is the enemy of the rocks

If we follow a stream or river from its source to its mouth we can see that from the very beginning it is a great enemy of the rocks and soil.

Whether it comes from a glacier or a spring or merely from flood waters, it attacks the soil right away and carries down with it sand and pieces of rock, which twist and bump here and there like hammers, breaking up the river banks.

This erosive action is particularly strong in mountainous areas where the water flows down steep slopes. Even in the plains where it moves more slowly, however, the river continues to break off and carry away the soil, widening its bed and making twists and turns, particularly during floods.

Why treeless mountains are more exposed to erosion

If heavy rains fall on to a mountain forest only some of the water runs away at once. The brushwood and vegetation retain more than half of it in small pools or merely in scattered drops.

But if the rain falls on a bare mountain, streams and torrents are formed immediately and flow impetuously down the slopes, gouging out tiny valleys and carrying away large amounts of soil.

In this case fast flowing water is one of the most active agents of rock destruction. The work of erosion differs, of course, from one type of soil to another.

In argillaceous, or clay, mountains such as the Appenines in Italy, for example, the water scoops

out characteristic gullies formed of numerous minute valleys separated by dividing walls.

In granite areas the rain loosens and carries away all the oxidized and decomposed rock particles, and creates a landscape of rounded masses of rock.

Finally in mixed areas, pyramids of rock can be formed. The surrounding ground is removed from around the heavier masses which then act as a shade for the earth beneath.

This phenomenon is the cause of the rocky ridges surmounted by huge boulders which are typical of certain scenes in the American West, in the arid zones of the Rocky Mountains.

Why we are sure that the Earth was once covered by enormous glaciers

The surest sign that a glacier reached a certain place is the presence of moraines.

These are always composed of deposits of rocks, loam and mud which a glacier carries with it during its slow movement and which accumulate at the points where the tongues of ice melt. These moraines tell us that over a million years ago in the Pleistocene Period there was a considerable fall in the temperature on Earth. The cold became more and more intense, and immense sheets of ice advanced from Siberia and Greenland and invaded Europe, Asia and North America.

It was like a very long winter which lasted for about 100,000 years, during which there was continuous snow. As the snow collected in enormous layers on the continents, the seas and oceans,

which were no longer being fed by the rivers, began to fall in level. Water continued to evaporate and form clouds but it was not replaced by the rain water which normally returns to the seas.

Some of the glaciers which exist today are left over from the Pleistocene Period when ice covered three times as much of the Earth's surface as it does at present.

Before the Pleistocene Ice Age there were two earlier periods when ice covered areas which are now tropical. The first occurred about 600 million years ago in Pre-Cambrian times, and the other was during the Permian Period, some 235 million years ago.

231

THE WHY OF PLANTS AND ANIMALS

Why fungi are not green like other plants

For their food most plants make use of a special substance by means of which water and mineral salts (absorbed from the soil) and carbon dioxide (absorbed from the air) are changed into the starches which are necessary for growth. This substance, which is what gives plants their green colour, is called chlorophyll and the process of transformation is called photosynthesis because it needs the light of the Sun.

There are, however, some plants which do not have any chlorophyll and are therefore able to grow in the dark. Fungi, for example, can be grown even in caves, and truffles actually grow underground. These plants, lacking any chlorophyll, are therefore not green, and need organic substances produced by other plants. That is why fungi live on the trunks and roots of dead trees.

Why the coconut palm is called the king of the vegetable kingdom

The coconut palm grows along the coasts of Africa and in other tropical areas. Some people call it the king of plants because of the wide range of products which can be obtained from it.

It is a beautiful tree with a strong trunk growing to a height of nearly 33 metres and ending in a tuft of fan-shaped leaves, each of them from 4 to 5 metres in length. Male and female flowers develop in the axils of the leaves and are in small inflorescences or groups.

The fruit which they produce are well known oval coconuts weighing as much as 2 kilos. When they are on the trees, however, the nuts are not the dark brown colour which we know. They are covered with a thick fibrous husk, green in colour, which is removed before the coconut is put on sale. The fibres are used for making matting and ropes.

A palm tree can produce as many as ten bunches of coconuts, each composed of ten to twelve nuts. Beneath the brown woody shell, which is sometimes used for making buttons, we find the coconut 'seed', that is the white pulp, rich in sugar, fats and protein which we love to eat. A drink called toddy is also produced from the sap of the young stalks.

Morel *(Morchella esculenta)*

Sarsosoma globosum

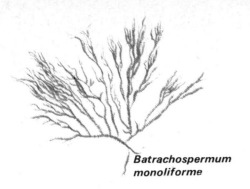

**Batrachospermum
monoliforme**

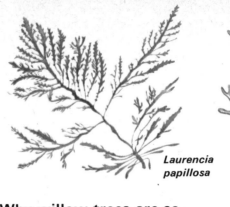

**Laurencia
papillosa**

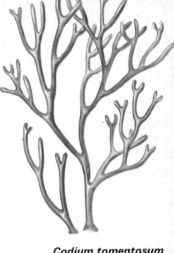

Codium tomentosum

Why seaweed is found in so many different colours

There are many kinds of seaweed living in the sea and you can often find pieces of them on the beach where they have been left by the tide.

The commonest are the green ones which are found in the shallowest parts of the sea and which almost reach the surface. The brown and red varieties of seaweed grow at deeper levels.

It has recently been shown that there is a very good reason behind the distribution of the various types of seaweed in the sea bed. The coloured pigments which distinguish them from one another serve, in fact, to enable them to use the light of the Sun, which becomes weaker as the water gets deeper.

For instance, the red rays are filtered first by the sea water and are therefore stopped at a shallow depth. These rays are practically the only ones used by the green seaweeds which are therefore on the sea bed nearest to the surface.

The brown ones and in particular the red ones, on the other hand, can live below a depth of 100 metres because they are also able to make use of the green rays of the sunlight which can penetrate to such depths.

Each ocean has its own distinct varieties of seaweed and a large percentage of the species in any one ocean is not found elsewhere.

Why willow trees are so common in the country

There are almost 500 species of willow scattered over a large area from the tropics to the northern zones. To the *Salix* or willow family belongs the tiniest tree we know. It is the dwarf willow which is only a few centimetres high and grows in the mountains right up on the snow line.

Willow trees are found everywhere in the country because men have used them for all kinds of purposes since the earliest times. For thousands of years, in fact, these trees with their very pliable branches have supplied the raw materials for weaving baskets and for making furniture.

Corallina officinalis

Deiesseria sanguinea

Why trees change colour in autumn

Every year with the approach of autumn the trees come to their period of rest. Little by little the leaves turn yellow and then curl up and fall to the ground. The tree then remains almost completely inactive until the return of good weather in the spring. It is a sad sight but at the same time a wonderful one, because before dropping the leaves turn to shades of yellow, brown and red.

The explanation of this is quite simple. Plants are living organisms and must have food, and this they obtain by utilizing the organic substances provided by the leaves. At the same time, like animals, they also produce waste matter.

Animals are able to get rid of the waste materials from their food but the plant has to retain them in its tissues until the autumn. When the time comes for the leaves to fall, the plant extracts from them all the products which can be used, leaving behind the waste materials. This is what gives the foliage its yellow, brown and red colours.

Why trees lose their leaves in autumn

In autumn the leaves of many trees change colour and then gradually fall and the branches become bare.

Other trees like the pine, the fir, the laurel and the holly keep their green foliage even in the winter, and you may therefore think that they do not need to change their leaves every year.

This is not so; even the evergreen plants change their old leaves for new ones, but they do it a little at a time throughout the whole year. This can be seen from the layer of dry needles which are to be found under fir trees.

All plants change their leaves, but why?

There are many reasons. In the case of broad-leaved plants there is the problem of defence against the cold. If they kept their foliage during the winter they would expose an enormous area to the frost, equal to that of all the leaves put together side by side.

In addition the plant needs rest and therefore discards all those tiny chemical workshops which evaporate water in large amounts and call on the roots to supply more and more.

But the main reason for the change, even for the evergreens, is that eventually the chemical laboratories in the leaves get old and need to be replaced by new and efficient ones. The shorter days of autumn hastens this change.

When the old leaf has fallen, a healing layer forms on the stem and closes the wound, leaving the leaf scar. This can be seen clearly on many twigs in winter and is one of the marks by which trees are identified.

Why clover makes the land fertile

Clover is easily distinguished from the other grasses of the meadows.

It is a very important plant not only because it is widely cultivated for animal food but also because wherever clover grows the soil becomes more fertile after a certain time.

The roots of this tiny plant have small nodules containing special bacteria which are able to absorb nitrogen from the air and fix it in the earth.

Since nitrogenized substances are among those mostly used by plants, land which has had the benefit of the activity of clover roots becomes much more suitable for cultivation.

Why the fig is not a real fruit

The part of the fig tree which we call the fruit is, in fact, a very fleshy flower closed in on itself like a small bag. Numerous minute flowers with very simple petals open on the inside and can be seen when the unripe fig is opened. Each one of these flowers actually produces a small dry fruit; these are the tiny seeds which we find when we eat the sugary pulp of the fig.

Fig trees are typically Mediterranean plants. They often grow wild and are used to form hedges along the roads and to cover rocky and steep slopes.

The fig is so widely used in Mediterranean countries that it is called 'the poor man's food'. When they are ripe the leaves are gathered and are stored or sold for cattle fodder.

Why leaves exposed to the Sun do not get hot

If during the warmest part of the summer we put sheets of paper or fragments of any material in the Sun, we find after some time that they are very hot. If they are metal they may well become hot enough to burn us.

On the other hand, the leaves on trees are exposed all day long to the Sun but when we touch them they are always fresh as if the Sun's rays had not fallen on them.

Their continued freshness is due to the fact that they evaporate ceaselessly an incredible amount of water, the residue of the complicated chemical changes which take place inside them.

This evaporation causes a fall of temperature so that they always feel cool to the touch.

A cassowary

Why the cassowary kicks the plants it feeds on

Because of this strange habit the cassowary is regarded as having a very bad temper.

It can often be seen giving furious kicks at the trunks of trees without any apparent reason.

In fact the cassowary is thought to be a timid bird but if we remember that it has very strong legs and that it feeds mainly on fruit, we can see the reason for those blows; they are to shake the plant and make the fruit and ripe berries fall to the ground.

The cassowary lives in New Guinea and the nearby islands and one species reaches the north-eastern tip of Australia. With the emu and the ostrich it is one of the largest living birds, growing to a height of more than one and a half metres. It is unable to fly but is a very fast runner and can reach speeds of up to 50 kilometres an hour. On each foot it has three toes, the inner one having a long, straight, stiletto-like claw.

Cassowaries live in family groups or in pairs in tropical and mid-mountain forests. They like to be near water, for they swim readily and are good fishers.

Why some birds have very long legs

Birds with such legs are usually aquatic birds. The long legs enable them to move about in the shallow water of marshes, searching for the small fish and shellfish on which they live.

The plumage of some of these birds, in particular the herons and egrets, is really magnificent. To make it even finer two tufts of feathers stand up from the head like decorative ribbons.

In the egret, which is smaller than the heron, the plumage is completely white. These birds which live in marshy places are nevertheless pursued by hunters who use all kinds of tricks to capture them.

Against their guns the egrets

A heron

can only offer their swift, high flight, but against the hunters' dogs they do not hesitate to use their strong beaks and peck at the dogs' eyes with well aimed blows.

At one time ornithologists, that is scientists who make a study of birds, put all long-legged birds into one class and called them wading birds, but now they think that this classification is too broad.

These birds are now generally divided into three classes: the herons with long beaks and very slender and flexible necks; the cranes which are of various sizes but are all excellent walkers; and the last category comprising many species, mostly marine.

Why some caterpillars move in a long line

The commonest caterpillar in Italy and the one which has perhaps the most feared chemical defence is the processionary caterpillar of the pine woods, which has very irritating hairs.

If you have been on holiday in Italy and walked into a pine wood you may have seen strange processions of caterpillars of a greyish brown colour coming down from the trees and continuing along the ground, always following a precise line of march. There are hundreds of them in close touch with one another, following the leader who guides them in the search for food. Usually these journeys take place at night but these caterpillars are occasionally seen by day going up or down the rough bark of the pine trees.

The reason for this strange behaviour is that the processionary caterpillars are blind.

To find their feeding grounds they have to follow the leader

who moves towards the leaves following his own instinct, and produces a fine silk thread which serves as a guide for the others, like the famous thread of Ariadne.

Why the kiwi has a very long beak

The kiwi's beak is long and thin because it is used for searching in the ground and under dead leaves for the caterpillars, worms and insects on which it feeds.

The kiwi hunts only at night

The kiwi, and (left) kiwi and snipe

and remains hidden during the daytime in thick bushes or in holes in the ground. Alone among birds the kiwi has a fine sense of smell. It is, perhaps, the last descendant of the large wingless bipeds which lived on the Earth in very remote times.

Kiwis mate for life. The female lays large eggs measuring about 7 by 12 centimetres, which are hatched by the male bird who sits on them for about eighty days.

The only living examples of these birds are to be found in the forests of New Zealand, where they are strictly protected to prevent their becoming extinct.

Why bats fly at night

These small winged creatures have no need of sunlight. They swoop at dusk between houses and plants with surprising speed, catching the insects which they devour in large numbers. Every moment they have to avoid all kinds of obstacles but they are always able to do so by quick, deliberate movements.

A mysterious sixth sense guides them at night and enables them to 'see' the dangers and avoid them in time. This sixth sense works on a system something like our modern radar.

In fact, as it flies the bat emits a series of very shrill sounds, so high pitched that our ears cannot pick them up. When some obstacle or object gets in its way these ultrasonic sounds are bounced off it and returned. All this takes place in a fraction of a second.

The bat hears, recognizes, calculates and veers away from the obstacle with a flap of the wings. It does this hundreds of times every night, for its brain is able to interpret complicated patterns of sound and echo with amazing speed.

Long before man was able to do so, therefore, this mammal learned to use the same principle on which radar is based.

But the bat's instrument is more perfect than ours.

The bat, in fact, is able to distinguish whether the object in its path is an obstacle or an insect, and can control its flight as required to avoid or approach.

Why the scorpion is said to eat with its legs

Before putting food into its mouth the scorpion minces it by rubbing it against its shell with its legs and pincers. This method of chewing outside the mouth is the remnant of a habit which was very common in ancient times when the first armoured creatures appeared. We know that the scorpion is a direct descendant of one of the first species of animal which populated the Earth.

From time immemorial these animals have captured the imagination of men by their monstrous shapes and very strange habits. A certain type of cannibalism is very common among scorpions: immediately after mating the female gobbles up the male.

Fruit bats at roost

Why the skunk never runs away

One of the animals which is really feared because of its terrible chemical weapon is the skunk, which lives in America. It is a omnivorous animal, eating both meat and plants, and is closely related to the weasel, ermine and polecat. Like them it has a soft fur.

But whereas the fur of the other animals of this group is of a colour which matches their surroundings, the typical skunk has a shaggy, glossy black coat marked by a white strip running from the back of the head to the tail. In fact this animal has no need to hide away in the woods to avoid meeting other animals. Quite the reverse, it is the others which sneak off as soon as he appears.

The skunk never runs away. When he is threatened he turns around swiftly, lifts up his bushy tail and launches at his enemy with incredible accuracy an evil smelling liquid produced by special glands.

This chemical defence is very

effective. The liquid is sprayed to a distance of several metres and has a really awful smell which it is difficult to get rid of even after repeated washing.

Why the smallest European mammal is also one of the fiercest

The smallest mammal in Europe is the shrew, which can weigh as little as 2 grammes and be only a few centimetres long. Nevertheless, despite its extremely small size this animal is bloodthirsty and fierce and offers fight to any of its own species which it finds on its hunting ground.

It feeds mainly on insects, snails and worms and is said to eat almost continuously, consuming its own weight in food about every 3 hours. With the exception of snakes and some rapacious birds, the shrew has no enemies because no other animal dares to attack it.

Not only does it give off a nauseating smell from a gland on the side of its body when it is in danger, but it unleashes all its ferocity, becomes really enraged and does not hesitate to attack and bite anyone who tries to capture it, with no thought of escape. ·

It is not easy to find a shrew on the ground because of its small size, but if you should find one, do not try to pick it up in your hand or you will be bitten by this tiny, wild creature.

The short-tailed shrews, common to eastern North America, are reputed to have a poisonous bite; the toxin, however, is only powerful enough to affect the shrews' prey.

The tree shrews of southern Asia have bushy tails and look more like squirrels. They are dark olive brown in colour, with long, pointed muzzles. They feed on insects, some plants and the eggs and young of birds.

Etruscan shrew

239

Why the hippopotamus has protruding nostrils

Hippopotamuses live in herds near large African rivers and spend almost the whole day in the water, with only their eyes and nostrils showing. But the nostrils are very prominent on the nose so that the animals are able to breathe even when they are completely covered by water. In this way nature enables them to hide from their enemies.

Their food is exclusively vegetable, consisting of grass and marsh plants which the hippopotamus eats mainly at night when it comes out of the water.

Sometimes these animals become annoyed for no apparent reason and they will then lower their heads and attack even men. Normally, however, they are not dangerous.

The large African hippopotamus is more than 4 metres in length and weighs over 3 tons. In West Africa, however, there are some dwarf hippopotamuses which are only a quarter of the size of the large ones.

Why the fur of the polecat is not much sought after

The very name of this animal indicates the most characteristic feature for which it is known among hunters. It is a close relative of the marten and to protect itself it emits a nauseating smell produced by special glands.

The trouble is that the smell remains on the long, coarse fur of the animal even after being treated in all kinds of ways and for this reason the fur of the polecat is of little commercial value.

And yet the polecat is hunted fiercely because it is a bloodthirsty and ferocious animal feeding mostly on small mammals and any birds it can catch. It often makes its way into farms and slaughters poultry and rabbits. In winter it even takes up its abode close to the hen roosts and hides beneath piles of wood or in hollow trees.

If it did not have this wicked habit, the polecat could be regarded as an animal useful to farmers. Quick and agile, it destroys many rodents during its nocturnal excursions and does not hesitate to attack even vipers.

Hippopotamus

Why the rhinoceros likes to roll about in the mud

During the heat of the day the rhinoceros usually buries itself in muddy water, from which it emerges with a layer of mud on its skin. This dries and forms a protective coating against the bites of insects.

Despite the thickness of its hide, the rhinoceros is afraid of the bite of some parasites which inject it with germs of dangerous diseases. This fear seems very strange in such enormous animals, as much as 4 metres in length and covered with a thick hide like armour, but in the case of the rhinoceros it is another example of the fly beating the lion.

The legs of this beast are short and thick but this does not prevent it from running at a good speed, especially when charging an intruder who has annoyed it.

The African rhinoceros is common, particularly in the area of the great lakes of East Africa, because it prefers moist regions. Its habits are mostly nocturnal.

All species of rhinoceros are vegetarian: some browse on leaves and buds of shrubs and small trees, others graze on grasses.

Rhinoceroses are usually solitary, but a calf may accompany its mother for a long time, even after the birth of a younger offspring.

In former times, rhinoceroses inhabited both the eastern and western hemispheres, but now they live only in tropical Africa and Asia and are in danger of becoming extinct. The Asian rhinoceros has one horn, with the exception of the Sumatran which, like the African varieties, has two.

Rhinoceros

the *Platybelodon,* a mastodon as big as the present elephant, which walked along with its head down and its tusks thrust well into the ground, turning it over in search of the tubers, rhizomes and roots on which it fed.

In fact the name of this animal refers to the special shape of its lower jaw which, because it was used for 'ploughing' the ground was made like an enormous hollow shovel fitted at the sides with large flat incisors with cutting edges.

Why the elephant has long projecting tusks

Today the two enormous projecting teeth are of no use to the elephant, but if we could go back some 20 million years we would find an ancestor of this pachyderm which used its enormous tusks to turn over the earth in search of food. In those far-off days there were long stretches of plains deeply ploughed by long parallel grooves.

The author of these strange furrows in the grassy plains was

African elephant

Asia. This animal is a really blood-thirsty one and it is not content, like the lion, to kill the victim which is going to supply it with a meal. Whenever it can it carries out a massacre among the herds and animals at the water-holes, just for the pleasure of seeing the blood flow.

If often happens that the female tiger, having given birth to five or six cubs, will eat the weak ones and leave only one or two, to which she will teach all the tricks of hunting.

When it grows old and loses its agility, the tiger becomes very dangerous and will even attack man.

Once in India and other parts of Asia tiger hunting was a common sport. These hunts were carried out on a large scale with hundreds of beaters and the hunters riding on tame elephants.

If it is captured young and raised in captivity the tiger can be tamed to some degree and an act with tigers is always a great attraction in the circus. However the tamer has always to be on the alert against any sudden outbreak of ferocity.

Why the tiger has a striped coat

The vertical yellow and black stripes of the tiger's fur act as a camouflage coat. It conceals the tiger among the bamboos and marsh vegetation of the places where it lives, particularly the jungles and lush undergrowth of

Why some animals hibernate

Let us take a look at the ground in the winter. When it is not covered with snow and ice it is hard and bare. There is not an insect to be seen and not a single fruit remains on the bare branches of the trees. Just imagine what a life of suffering it would be for many wild animals if nature had not arranged for them to fall asleep for several months.

And they go to sleep just at the right time. For some animals it is a matter of a heavy sleep with

brief interruptions for the needs of survival: this is what happens to the squirrel, for example, which even at the height of winter finds time to munch the acorns which he stored away in the summer.

In some cases, it is much more than that: the rhythm of life slows down for such animals just as it does for plants, the temperature falls, the blood flows slowly, the breathing slows down and becomes almost imperceptible. This state of almost complete quiet is called hibernation.

For reptiles, amphibians and some fish hibernation is even more total: for them the arrest of life is almost complete in winter.

During hibernation, of course, the animals consume the fats accumulated in the summer and when they awake again they have lost a good deal of weight.

Why the chameleon often changes colour

A close relative of the lizard, the slow-worm and other reptiles, the chameleon is common in the whole of Africa and Madagascar, and is also found in some parts of Asia and Southern Europe, where there are about eighty species. It can grow to a length of 60 centimetres, but the most common variety does not exceed 30 centimetres in length.

The most striking thing about the chameleon is the speed with which it can change colour, from white to yellow, to black, to green, to brown.

It is generally thought that the chameleon changes colour in order to match its background, but in fact these changes are due to the changes of light and temperature of its surroundings and the condition of the animal.

Indeed the chameleon has no need for camouflage because when it is out hunting it is able to deceive its prey by remaining perfectly still on a branch for hours. It is always sure of plenty to eat because of its sticky tongue which can dart out at its prey even to a distance of 10 centimetres.

The chameleon is well adapted for the life it leads in the trees. Its feet and tail are able to grasp a branch and hang there without difficulty when it is reaching out to capture some victim. The large prominent eyes can turn 180° and each one can move independently.

Chameleon

243

Why the buzzard can be distinguished from other birds of prey

In the country birds of prey have a bad reputation for stealing chickens and farm animals. The buzzard is a particular offender but when you get to know this bird better it turns out to be more useful than harmful.

It is about 60 centimetres in length and with a wing span of 120 centimetres; these are the average measurements for a buzzard which, because of its large

Red-tailed buzzard

size, can at first sight be mistaken for an eagle.

The expert, however, cannot mistake it for any other daytime bird of prey, even if it is merely a dot high in the sky. The buzzard has broad wings and a rounded tail and in its flight it traces wide characteristic spirals, searching with its keen eye the countryside below for signs of its prey.

The speed with which it dives down from the sky on to its

chosen victim is really astounding; it falls like a stone, with wings closed, and only opens them again just before touching down. The spectator hardly has time to see a sudden ruffling of feathers before the buzzard is climbing into the sky once more with a small mammal or reptile gripped tightly in its sharp talons.

It prefers mice and squirrels but it likes other small animals and does not hesitate to attack even a viper, although it is not immune against its poison.

For these reasons it should be regarded as a valuable ally of man.

Why the woodpecker remains in the woods during the winter

At the approach of the bad weather insects become scarcer and scarcer. The cold kills them off or forces them to hide away in sheltered places. That is why almost all insectivorous birds migrate in search of more plentiful food.

Common buzzard

Woodpecker

Why it is difficult to see a sloth on the trees

Two-toed sloth

Not the woodpecker, however; he remains in the woods and continues to peck away at the bark with his strong beak in search of food. This bird has a perfect knowledge of how to capture the larvae of insects inside the trunks, where they are hidden, and therefore he does not lack for food even in the winter.

When, by pecking with his beak, he finds that some larvae have made a tunnel, the woodpecker makes a hole with astonishing speed. He puts his long, sticky tongue into the hole and captures the larvae without hesitation so that it finishes in his capacious stomach.

It is easy to see how useful the woodpecker is in removing from the plants a large amount of larvae which are harmful for the wood. For this reason it is protected by law.

The woodpecker's nest is also very interesting; it is dug out in the shape of a bottle inside old dead tree trunks and the bottom is covered with soft wood shavings.

The sloth is a typical animal of equatorial America; indolent, lazy, incapable of any effort or initiative, it spends the whole of its life gripping with its long claws the branch of a large tree and eating all the leaves within reach of its mouth. Sloths move only when there is no more food and they have to find another leafy branch.

The females often rest hanging head downwards with the baby clinging to their rough fur of their stomachs. More rarely these animals sleep coiled up in the fork of a tree.

It is nevertheless always difficult to observe the sloth because its shaggy fur is of a grey-green colour which makes it resemble a shapeless lump of moss.

These creatures do not even come down to the ground to drink. Rather than do something so energetic they quench their thirst with the few drops of dew they can manage to lick from the leaves each night.

Generally silent, they can, when necessary, utter a shrill cry.

THE WHY OF MAN

Why it is possible to find very old skeletons

Archaeologists and particularly those who are interested in the problems of ancient burials, often come across skeletons in a very good state of preservation. This is because human bones are composed for the most part of two mineral substances: phosphorus and calcium. It is in fact the calcium which gives the bones their strength and whiteness.

Skeletons rarely disintegrate completely although not all the 206 bones which make up our bodies remain intact. The parts of the skeleton which are usually best preserved include the skull together with the lower jaw. Other bones which are normally well preserved, in addition to the skull, are the long bones of the limbs, the ribs and the pelvis.

Why complete sets of teeth are rarely found

Although teeth are really bones, perhaps even more solid than the skeleton, it is extremely rare that a complete set of teeth is found among the remains of ancient man.

There can be many reasons why teeth are missing; some will be the result of disease and some the result of accidents and fractures.

We know for certain that the habit which was very common among the ancients of eating certain types of food containing a kind of mould, was the cause of widespread dental decay.

In addition, of course, primitive man was very often in danger of losing his teeth: fights with animals, falls, the effort of chewing very hard foods all contributed to this.

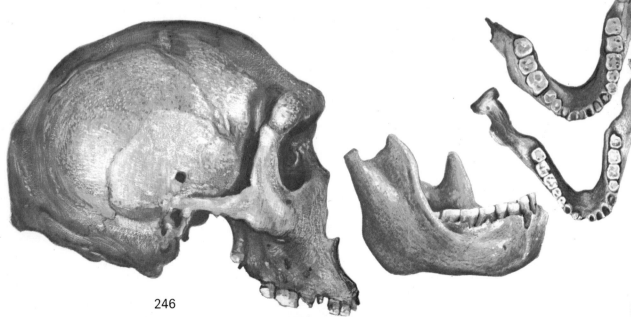

Why man walks on two legs

Walking on two legs is something we do quite naturally, without stopping to think that it is a most difficult thing to achieve. Indeed, it requires a great sense of balance and correct control of the muscles. Standing erect and walking are acts typical of man and of no other animal. Even the apes, which of all living animals are most like man, walk differently.

If we compare the human foot with that of a gorilla, there are two very obvious differences. First of all the human foot, contrary to that of the apes, has a flat base; secondly the ape has a big toe which can be moved opposite to the other toes so that it can grip curved surfaces such as the branches of trees.

The feet, indeed, are an indication of the kind of life that these two creatures lead. Man needs to stand erect and walk and the apes to grip the branches of trees and to leap from one to another.

able to build enormous constructions as well as very small ones, to play musical instruments, to cut, manipulate and to put food into his mouth.

Why the human hand is able to do all kinds of work

It is said that man's first tool is his hand. No-one pays much attention to such an obvious remark, yet if we remember the difficulties we suffer when, for example, we have a hand in plaster, we realize how much we depend on this essential part of the human body.

What makes it possible for the hand to perform such a wide variety of actions is above all the thumb. It can 'oppose itself' to the other fingers and enable the hand to tie things, to grasp and to pick up objects.

Because of his hands man is

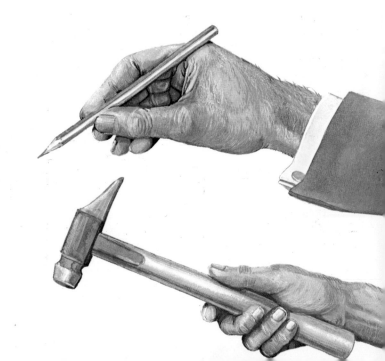

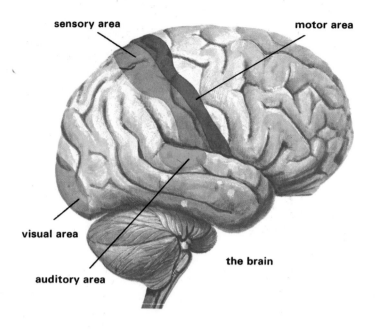

sensory area

motor area

visual area

auditory area

the brain

Why it is the brain which controls the body

According to old beliefs and superstitions the various human emotions were located in particular parts of the body: courage, for

Comparison of the cubic capacity of brains

Gibbon

Chimpanzee

Modern man

Vol. 90 cc.

Vol. 400 cc.

Vol. 1300 cc.

instance, resided in the heart, cowardice was connected with the liver, cunning with the brain, hatred with the bile, and so on.

Although it is possible to find some truth in such ideas, science has definitely established that the brain is the organ which controls all our actions without exception, and the brain is therefore the control centre of the body.

How does this come about?

The brain and the spinal cord, which is the natural continuation of the brain, are made of a very delicate and rather soft material, grey in colour, which occupies the whole of the skull and the long central core of the backbone. Special channels and nerves lead into this very sensitive material and it is their task to transmit to the brain all the sensations received from the various sense organs and then to pass on at once the orders which the brain sends to the organs, even to the farthest limits of the body.

The nervous system, the headquarters of which is the brain, is responsible, therefore, for all our actions: seeing, hearing, smelling, tasting and touching. But it is above all due to the nervous system, and therefore to the brain, that we are able to appreciate and understand our senses.

When we talk about mental health, nervous diseases and depression we are concerned with the nervous system. Nowadays medicine has become very specialized in the field of nervous diseases because it is considered, and rightly so, that as a result of the hectic life which modern man leads, it represents one of the most delicate areas of medicine and one subject to the greatest changes.

The weight of the brain varies

with age, height, body weight, sex and race.

The brain of the adult man is heavier than that of a woman, in this country averaging 1,409 grammes as compared with 1,263 grammes.

The two hemispheres into which it is divided are symmetrical but although they are identical they do not have identical functions: various sense or motor activities are located at different points and sometimes in only one of the hemispheres. For instance, the centre of language, of the association between written words and spoken words, between ideas and the words which represent them, are normally only located in the left hemisphere and therefore these faculties are not impaired if for some reason the right hemisphere is injured.

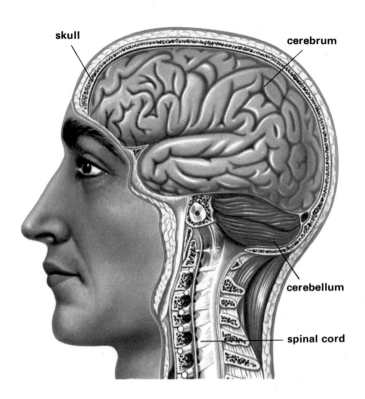

Why we say that an intelligent person is brainy

The current sayings regarding the brain, such as 'brainless' or 'very brainy' to describe people of little intelligence or of great intelligence, may seem to be merely ordinary phrases or old superstitions but nevertheless there is some truth in these sayings. That part of the brain where ideas are formed, where the memory is located and where our free choice is decided is much more developed in man than in any other animal, living or long dead.

The average weight of the human brain is about 1,300 grammes. The animal which in proportion to size has a brain nearest to man's is the chimpanzee with a brain weighing about 400 grammes.

Why it is important to protect the back of the neck

The part of the brain situated at the back is called the cerebellum. Its location at the back and below the skull is a very delicate one as it coincides with the place where the skull and the backbone meet.

Artificial protection of this part of the head has always been a problem; for instance, in time of war special helmets were used to protect the nape of the neck.

Why go to so much trouble? Because the cerebellum has the delicate task of co-ordinating the movements of the muscles and keeping them in a state of readiness to carry out whatever orders they may be given, whether it is a delicate task, some simple operation or the rapid movements of self defence.

249

Why we have a skeleton

The movements of the body are carried out by special bundles of flesh called muscles. However, the complex muscular system would not be able to function at all if it were not supported by a suitable structure. This structure is the skeleton. It is in reality a kind of framework which supports the body.

Although this description is correct to a certain extent it is not the whole story. First of all because the skeleton is a framework which is capable of very complex movements, quite different from ordinary frameworks; in the second place because the function of supporting the body is not the sole purpose of the skeleton. The bones are not only more or less strong supports, well and efficiently jointed together, but they are also living elements of our bodies, organs which are entrusted with delicate tasks.

In the central cavity of almost all bones, for instance, there is a soft tissue known as the bone marrow, which in the long bones has the task of producing the red and white cells of the blood. Although they appear solid the bones are penetrated by a large number of tiny holes through which pass the blood vessels which feed the bones themselves.

Fewer but larger vessels also pass through to collect from the marrow the blood cells just mentioned and put them into circulation.

Since the tasks of the skeleton are so important and delicate it is easy to understand the advice doctors give to all, but particularly to the young, to enrich their diet with calcium and phosphorus, without which the bones would become either too fragile or too hard.

Why a splint has to be put on a broken limb

How can a broken bone become strong and firm again? Because it is a living part of the body and it is therefore unlike metals or minerals which cannot grow together again once they are broken. Human bones are, in fact, made of both inorganic and organic substances and the latter possess the ability to reproduce their cells, albeit slowly, until the damaged tissue is healed.

Sometimes, a further layer of bone is even created at the site of the fracture. For this reconstruction to take place it is essential that the limb or damaged part is immobilized. That is why plaster of Paris casts or splints are applied to the injured limb.

Organic material such as protein (one third)

Inorganic material such as calcium salts (two thirds)

Bone composition

Why sport is good for us

Physical activity brings into play the muscles which develop in various ways according to how we use them. For instance, a boxer will have well developed arm muscles and a footballer will have good leg muscles.

The activity of the muscles also varies with what we do during the day: during the time we devote to study, the muscles of the eyes and hands will be most used but when we are moving about it will be the muscles of the limbs and abdomen, and so on.

Sport is therefore a safety-valve because among other things it is a way of exercising all the muscles of our bodies together and making sure that some of them are not left too long inactive. This is why the so-called complete sports, such as tennis, athletics and swimming, are to be recommended.

Why our bodies can perform such a variety of movements

If the bones of the skeleton were all fixed solidly together the body would not be capable of any movement at all.

In fact, however, we know that we are capable at any given moment of making all kinds of movements. This is made possible by the various joints which we have in our bodies.

Some of these joints permit only a relatively limited movement. In the spine or backbone, for example, each vertebra can only make slight movements because it is prevented by hard ligaments of fibrous tissue which serve as a protective cover.

On the other hand the most mobile joints are those of the legs, arms, hands and fingers: the joints of the knees and fingers are like hinges and those of the elbows like pivots.

The most mobile of all are the ball and socket joints of the shoulders and hips.

FATS

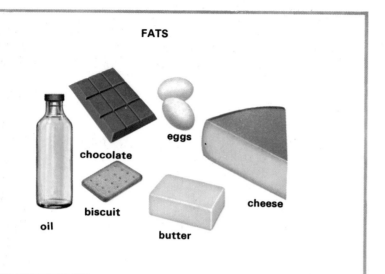

oil

chocolate

eggs

biscuit

butter

cheese

CARBOHYDRATES

sugar

beer

apple

potato

bread

banana

PROTEINS

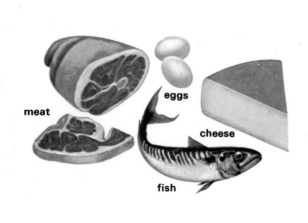

meat

eggs

cheese

fish

Why our bodies need food

In order to be always efficient and do their work properly the cells which form our bodies need certain vital substances: carbohydrates.

These are made up of three chemical elements: carbon, oxygen and hydrogen. The human organism converts the carbohydrates into sugars to enable the cells to utilize them. To make a very ordinary comparison, sugar is for our bodies what petrol is for our cars: fuel.

In addition to sugar our organism needs other very important substances: fats and proteins. The first, weight for weight, supplies twice as much food value as the sugar.

Carbohydrates, fats and proteins are found in plentiful amounts in the foods we eat every day. Eating is therefore a prime necessity for man as it supplies his organism with the energy to enable it to function correctly.

The amount of energy which various foods provide has been measured by scientists in special units called calories. A calorie is the amount of heat required to raise 1 kilogram of water 1°C. The human body needs varying numbers of calories according to the work it has to do. For example, if 3,000 calories are enough for light work, at least 4,500 calories are needed for heavy work.

It should be remembered, moreover, that the nutrition which comes from foods, particularly from fats, serves not only for immediate use but also to provide stores of energy to be used as and when required. To function properly, however, our bodies require regular, well-balanced meals.

Why vitamins are essential to life

There is one type of food which the body cannot do without: the vitamins. They were quite unknown not so very long ago but they constitute an essential part of our daily food and without them the body can suffer considerable damage. The lack of vitamin A, for instance, is the cause of eye diseases and skin diseases; a shortage of vitamin B gives rise to nervous troubles; insufficient vitamin C can cause scurvy and vitamin D deficiency is the direct cause of rickets in young children. Rickets is indeed one of the commonest diseases in those parts of the world where food is scarce.

A correctly balanced intake of vitamins, therefore, provides the body with the best conditions of health and an improved nervous system.

Why alcohol can be harmful

Although wines and other alcoholic drinks are in daily use, often in quite large amounts, it must be remembered that alcohol can be dangerous.

This is primarily because it is not a food and cannot therefore be used for the 'fuelling' of the body, nor is it transformed into a natural reserve like some foods which are converted into reserves of fat.

In addition, even as a source of energy alcohol is an inferior product because it acts as a violent stimulant and has a harmful effect on the balance of the organism.

Alcohol should, therefore, be taken in moderation and at the right times, for instance, with meals.

Some sources of the principle vitamins

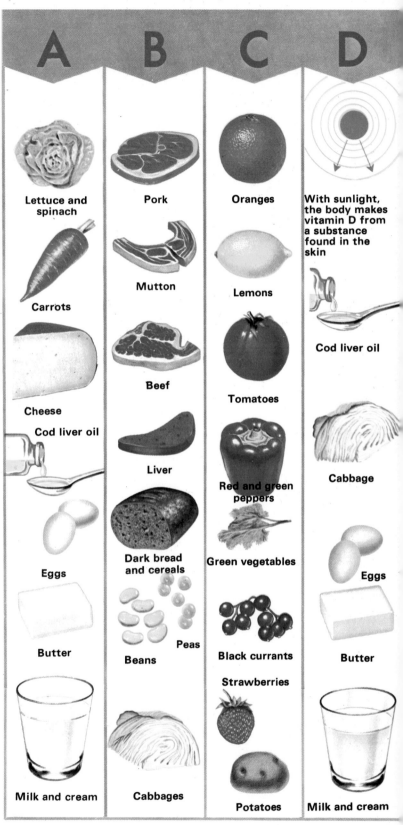

A
Lettuce and spinach
Carrots
Cheese
Cod liver oil
Eggs
Butter
Milk and cream

B
Pork
Mutton
Beef
Liver
Dark bread and cereals
Peas
Beans
Cabbages

C
Oranges
Lemons
Tomatoes
Red and green peppers
Green vegetables
Black currants
Strawberries
Potatoes

D
With sunlight, the body makes vitamin D from a substance found in the skin
Cod liver oil
Cabbage
Eggs
Butter
Milk and cream

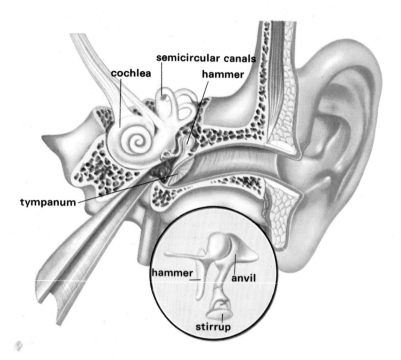

semicircular canals
cochlea
hammer
tympanum
hammer — anvil
stirrup

The stirrup transmits the vibrations to a special fluid which fills the inner ear. In turn the waves in the fluid pass them on to the cochlea which contains the fundamental organ of hearing: the semicircular canals.

Among other things, these canals, in conjunction with the brain, enable us to keep our balance and to stand upright. The sound is finally transmitted to the brain by means of the acoustic nerve.

If the membrane of the ear drum is injured or there is any damage to the delicate apparatus of the ear, the hearing is impaired or lost altogether.

Nowadays, special hearing aids are available to correct defects of hearing.

Why we are able to hear sounds

We are able to receive messages which come to us from the outside world through our senses.

The messages which reach us by means of air waves are captured by the sense of hearing, which is located in the ear. The ear is a system of perfect mechanisms, closely connected with one another, which enables us to appreciate a wide range of tones and sounds.

By what means does this come about?

The sound waves are collected by the auricle, which is the part of the ear you can see, and cause the drum to vibrate; this is a very thin and taut membrane. The vibration produces movements of the tiny bones of the middle ear, which have rather curious names because of their shapes: hammer, anvil and stirrup.

Why we see the shapes and colours of objects

We see by means of the eyes. The eye is a very delicate and complex organ and works more or less like a camera.

Light enters the eye through a hole, the pupil; passes through a lens, the crystalline lens; is projected on to a layer of special tissue, the retina, situated on the opposite wall of the eyeball. The retina functions like a photographic film and is modified by light; it is a very thin layer of nerve cells, called cones and rods, which identify the colour or black and white images. When light strikes the cones and rods the eye transmits to the optic nerve a detailed message of what it sees. The message reaches the brain, which at once gives the necessary instructions. The eye turns the images upside down in the same way as happens in a camera, and the brain reverses them once again so that we see them exactly as they are.

The special shape of the eye and the number of rods in the retina enable us to see the images of the external world in the usual way, but if the number of rods or the curvature of the retina were different, we would see things differently, as is indeed the case with some mammals. For example we know that the cow sees objects much larger than we see them and some members of the cat family are able to see in the dark because of the different shape of their eyes.

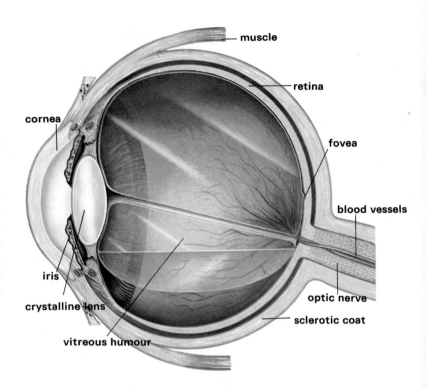

Why some people need spectacles

Quite different from glass lenses, the crystalline lens of the eye has the ability to alter its curvature. In fact it is provided with muscles which make it more spherical when it is looking at near objects and flatter when it has to look at distant objects. It may happen with the passage of time or through some other cause, that the crystalline lens loses some of its elasticity and the muscles are no longer able to change the curvature. The eye then sees near objects in a blurred manner. This defect is called presbyopia.

Whereas normal eyes see well both at long and short distances, there can be two cases where the diameter of the eyeball is not normal: myopia and hyperopia. Myopia is when the distance between the lens and the retina is too great and the eye can see near objects well but not distant ones. The reverse to this is hyperopia when the distance between the lens and the retina is too short and the eye sees distant objects and not those near at hand.

It is only in the last few centuries that the invention of special lenses for correcting vision has made it possible to help those with defective vision. Today a larger number of lenses are available for correcting almost any visual defect. Many people now wear contact lenses: these are invisible when worn and give a wider field of vision than spectacles.

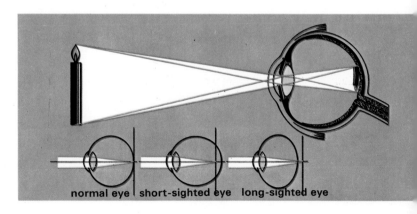

normal eye | short-sighted eye | long-sighted eye

THE WHY OF WAR

Why rich men went to war in armour

Armour was a kind of personal defence, protective clothing made of materials which would withstand the blows of the enemy. The earliest forms of armour were made of animal skins, then of leather and later of metal. In the Middle Ages iron mail armour was introduced which allowed greater freedom of movement and was therefore preferred by those who fought on horseback. The horses were protected by special armour called bards.

It was not until the end of the fifteenth century that armour made entirely of steel came into use. It was at that time in particular that armour became the exclusive privilege of the few. Indeed it was only kings, nobles and rich men who were able to afford armour and have the luxury of being better protected in war; also the limited number of armourers worked only for those who could pay them well.

The head was specially protected by a helmet: it was made of the same material as the armour but fitted better. On the helmet could often be seen the insignia of rank. The face was protected by movable visors which were both strong and practical.

Why old cities had walls

Men have devised means of attack and defence against their enemies since the early days when they first fought among themselves.

One of the oldest methods invented by man to protect not only human life but also his dwellings and possessions, were the city walls. These were massive erections which can measure more than 10 metres at the base and rise to two to three times that height.

They were intended to place an insuperable obstacle in the way of the enemy and were often built very simply without any special embellishment; sometimes they were very rough indeed. They surrounded the city completely or at least the important centre of the city, and were often also surrounded by a deep moat filled with water. The oldest had scarcely any openings other than the entrance gate. At a later date long narrow slits were made in the walls from which the enemy could be attacked while the defenders remained well covered.

On the tops of the walls there were often ramparts where the soldiers could keep watch on the enemy and, in case of attack, occupy a good position overlooking their opponents. People were able to enter or leave the city by drawbridges located opposite the main gates.

These defensive city walls were of such solid construction that even today many of them are still in a perfect state of preservation. The greatest and most famous of all is the Great Wall of China which defends not merely a city but a whole vast country.

Why old cities were besieged

Against fortified cities the methods of attack were above all assault and siege.

Assault was an attempt to occupy the city by force by breaching the walls, by tunnels or by exploding mines. The idea of a siege was to force the city to surrender through lack of munitions or, more often, through lack of food.

For this purpose the first task of the besiegers was completely to surround the city and prevent anyone from entering or leaving. This was extremely important because anyone who left might get reinforcements or escape, neither of which the attackers wanted. Anyone going in could do even more damage by bringing help in some way to the besieged, particularly food and munitions.

The object of sieges was to force the enemy to yield and therefore an essential task of the besiegers was to weaken the resistance of the defenders within the walls.

In the course of history there have been some very famous sieges, some lasting for years. Perhaps the most famous was the siege of Troy which continued for ten years and was only ended by the stratagem of Ulysses, when the Trojans allowed the famous wooden horse within their walls.

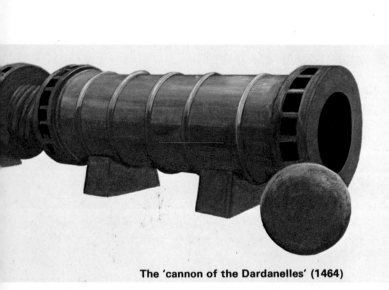

The 'cannon of the Dardanelles' (1464)

The catapult,
an old siege weapon

Why gunpowder was used for war

One of the problems which man had to solve from the time when he first began to hunt was that of finding weapons which could hit a target from a distance. The more afraid animals became of man, the further away from him they kept.

This led to the creation of various weapons which were thrown, and then to the bow and arrow.

The invention of gunpowder, that is a mixture of potassium nitrate, sulphur and carbon which burns very rapidly when it is lighted, led to a whole series of discoveries and finally to the firearm. This was a metal tube

One of the most spectacular self-propelled guns ever built was the German *Mrs Karl 040*. This vehicle was over 10 metres long and mounted a gun of 540 or 660 millimetre calibre. This monster was used at Sebastopol during the Russian campaign and at the end of the war in the unsuccessful German offensive towards Budapest. A special railway truck had to be provided to transport it from one part of the front to another.

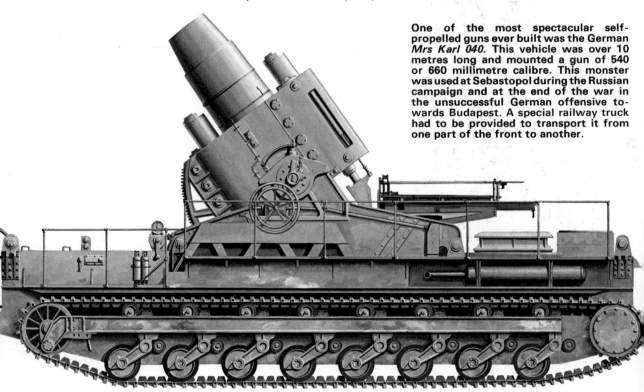

Russian Grenadier (1814)

filled with gunpowder which, when ignited, caused an explosion. Heavy balls were thrown to varying distances, depending on the length of the barrel and the size of the explosive charge.

For about 600 years gun powder was the only explosive; then, in the middle of the nineteenth century, nitroglycerin and nitrocellulose were discovered.

Why every army had drummer boys

The drummer boy is without any doubt one of the best known military figures, thanks to the literature and paintings which have made him famous.

Drummer boys were very young boys who joined the army at only twelve years of age to take up a career as non-commissioned officers. They did not carry arms but were regarded as real soldiers.

It was their duty to beat the drums not only as part of the band during military parades but also during battle or at special moments when the fighting was at its fiercest. Drums were used to give the signal to break camp, advance and retreat.

The drum beats provided a rallying point and gave the soldiers a sense of community and safety. This is essential when men are fighting for their lives.

Why rifle ammunition is called cartridges

Until the middle of the nineteenth century, when you wanted to fire a rifle, you had to prepare the firing device, compress the explosive charge in order to get a more powerful explosion, and then place the bullet in close contact with the powder.

All this obviously took a long time and as the years passed improved systems were developed to permit much faster loading of the weapon.

The explosive charge, the priming device and the bullet were finally combined into a single paper holder, or cartouche, so as to be ready for use.

From this primitive wrapping is derived the name of the modern cartridge, which is made of cardboard, metal or plastic.

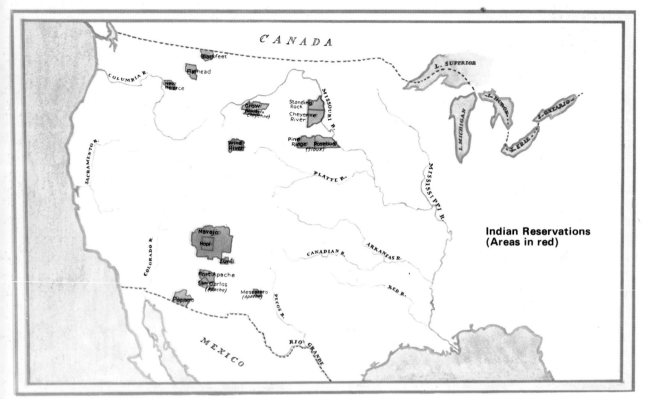

Indian Reservations
(Areas in red)

Why the first American settlers exterminated the redskins

The American government had on many occasions promised the various Indian tribes that they would respect certain territories which would remain areas reserved for the redskins only. These agreements, however, were never respected by the whites. The greatest enemies of the Indians were those who, through need or greed, were driven to occupy those enormous tracts of uncultivated land which promised such rich harvests.

From this arose the interminable conflicts which went on for years and affected many innocent victims on both sides.

Why the Indians now live in reserves

Why the United States are so called

The Signing of the Declaration of Independence, 4 July 1776

It was a black future that was reserved for the descendants of the Indians. The ever advancing waves of the white conquerors demanded more and more space; there could be no place for anyone who left unproductive huge areas of land as big as whole states. The Indians were to be guaranteed their liberty but in a very much reduced territory.

To a very great extent those who had ruled over immense hunting grounds and were forced without hope into small reserves, refused to mix with the white population and preferred to lead a very impoverished life in order to keep their integrity as a nation.

Almost a century has now passed since the decline of the redskins but they still retain the traditions, costumes and rites of their ancestors. They live mainly by their own work as artisans, peasants and tourist attractions.

In 1775 the first conflicts arose between the English settlers in America and the government at home. On 10 June 1776 the so-called Articles of Union were approved; these were the first attempt by the English colonies in America to draw up a constitution of self government.

The Declaration of Independence was approved on 4 July 1776. This act of total rebellion against the mother country was the beginning of war between the English and the new citizens of the Union. They belonged to thirteen colonies which from that moment became independent states but united among themselves in a federation. The Federal Constitution had to be accepted by nine out of thirteen states. On 21 June 1788 the ninth state ratified the Constitution and on 4 March 1789 the United States of America was born.

Why Venice became wealthy as a result of the Crusades

The geographical position of Venice, its magnificent fleet and the political ability of its rulers

were all factors of great importance in a situation such as that created by the Crusades. The First Crusade had shown that to reach the Holy Land by the overland route was a long undertaking beset with many snares. To transport the troops by sea meant a saving of valuable time and a much safer journey.

But transport costs money and the Republic of Venice charged very high prices for the services it supplied. As a result the Crusades became a real gold mine for the Venetians who took advantage of these journeys of the Crusaders to increase their own business.

The greatest profits were made by Venice when she did not ask for payment in money but in help. It happened during the Fourth Crusade (1202–4); the organizers did not have the means of transporting the troops and Venice offered her services in return for a favour, military help against the city of Zara which had rebelled against Venice. The Crusaders kept their promise but Venice raised the price and asked for further military help to put a trusted friend, Isaac d'Angelo, on the throne of Constantinople. This caused a whole series of complications which all turned out to be very profitable for the Venetians. They occupied the main islands of the Aegean and ensured for themselves control of the Bosphorus and the Dardanelles.

Why flags were invented

The story of flags started at sea. From very remote times navigators needed to signal their identity both to people on land and also to the vessels they met at sea. In addition during the Crusades it became necessary to distinguish the combatants and that is why many modern flags originated under such circumstances. A clear indication of this is that the cross is still frequently included in the flags of many nations.

For purposes of signalling and identification flags must fly out in the wind, so they are usually made of a light material with an indentical pattern on both sides.

262

Why the power of Spain declined in 1588

Spain's period of greatest splendour was in the time of the Emperor Charles V (1500—58). Her predominance in Europe was reinforced by the great wealth brought back from the New World.

There was only one power which stood in the way of that supremacy, England. Philip II, the son of Charles V, tried to put down the competition of this rival by an expedition consisting of more than 130 warships. Even before it had engaged in a single battle it was called the Invincible Armada.

The most decisive encounter took place on 8 August 1588 off the coast of Gravelines, in France, and ended in the total defeat of the Spaniards.

Perhaps never before, as in this case, had a single military defeat brought about the overthrow of a great power; the countries subject to Spain began to raise their heads and the supremacy at sea passed unquestionably to the English.

Why tanks were built

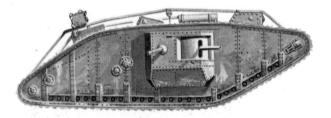

The idea of using a kind of moving and powerfully armed fortress is a very ancient one. Da Vinci designed a tank. The first tanks in the modern sense of the word were the English ones which went into action during the battle of the Somme in September 1916. This type of self-propelled armoured vehicle was given the name tank because of its box-like appearance. In the Second World War tanks were developed to an extraordinary extent: they were provided with armour plate to withstand enemy shells and fitted with bigger and better guns.

Despite the invention of powerful anti-tank weapons, the tank still maintains its original features: mobility (up to 50 kilometres an hour) and power of attack.

Why submarines were used so much in the Second World War

In the two World Wars Germany was in conflict with Great Britain which obtained regular supplies of food and arms by sea from the Commonwealth and the United States. Germany therefore carried out special naval operations aimed at sinking as many British and Allied ships as possible.

In the First World War one form which this took was the use of sea-raiders, mainly surface vessels, which the Germans used with great skill and ability. They met with a certain degree of limited success.

In the Second World War the Germans concentrated more on the use of their U-boats or submarines. From August 1940 to May 1943 they waged furious war against Allied convoys in the North Atlantic and sank hundreds of ships. During these three years of sea warfare the U-boats made use of several forms of attack, the final one being by packs of U-boats which combined to attack Allied convoys.

Why aircraft carriers were built

Many people realized after the First World War that the decisive weapon of the future would be the aeroplane.

Not everyone, however, understood that the air force would have to operate with the navy as well as with the other branches of the armed services.

The countries which were convinced of this need, and in particular the United States and Japan, built ships fitted out specially for the purpose and they were called aircraft carriers.

There were many advantages to be gained by this, two in particular: effective air cover was provided for ships and convoys and by this means air bases could be established in any place required by the progress of the war.

Modern aircraft carriers are colossal ships able to carry, launch and collect again scores of planes in perfect synchronization on several launching pads. The famous U.S.S. *Enterprise* is nuclear powered and has her own guided missile defence system.

Why the V1 and V2 were such deadly weapons

The need to launch deadly contrivances at a distance has always been one of man's basic problems in war.

During the last World War when Germany had definitely lost the air supremacy, the Germans devised new weapons to launch very explosive projectiles over long distances. These weapons were based on the principal of rocket propulsion. The Germans

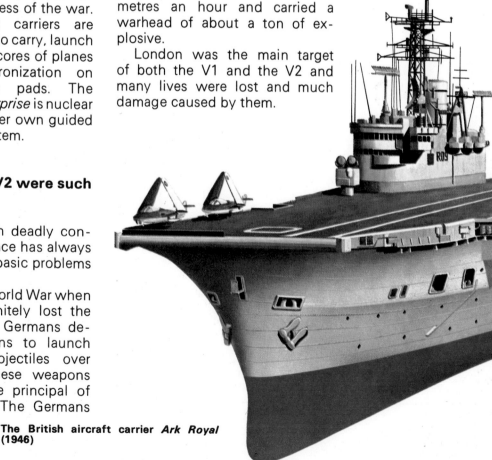

The V2 rocket, the largest and most advanced missile of the Second World War

The V1 flying bomb: its low speed (620 kph) made it very vulnerable

called them *Vergeltungswaffen* (reprisal weapons) and they were therefore known by the letter 'V'.

The VI was a kind of unmanned aeroplane which was intended to fall on predetermined targets. In September 1944, three months after the V1, which was faulty and not very fast, the Germans were able to launch the V2. This rocket reached a speed of 5,600 kilometres an hour and carried a warhead of about a ton of explosive.

London was the main target of both the V1 and the V2 and many lives were lost and much damage caused by them.

The British aircraft carrier *Ark Royal* (1946)

THE WHY OF GEOGRAPHY

Why maps have the north at the top

Ancient cartographers always regarded Ptolemy as the master map maker. He was an Egyptian scientist who had produced the best maps known in the ancient world 150 years after Christ. Ptolemy drew in the centre of his map the part of the world which he considered the most important, Egypt. To the north of Egypt were the Mediterranean Basin and Greece, with which Egypt had frequent contact, and Ptolemy therefore marked the north at the top of his map. Since then all map makers have done the same.

There is, therefore, no exact scientific basis for the origin of this common setting of maps. Indeed in the Middle Ages when the generals taking part in the Crusades and the merchants dealing in spices had to travel eastwards, maps were drawn with the east at the top and the north on the left.

From the practical point of view one system is as good as the other. What matters is that the cardinal points on the map should be indicated in such a way that countries which are really situated to the north of the countries shown in the centre of the map appear to the north on the map, and those which lie to the south are shown to the south of the centre on the map, and so on.

Why we talk about getting our bearings

Suppose that we are about to make a long journey in an unknown and deserted country where there are neither streets nor signposts. What would we do to keep in mind the itinerary we are following and to record the route to follow on the way back? We would look carefully around and try to fix in our memory some specific unmistakable details of the way: curiously shaped rocks, hills, a group of trees, and so on. On our return, when we come to these landmarks we shall know that we are on the right path.

But suppose that we have to travel across the desert or the immense steppes or the sea, what landmarks have we? This was the first problem which had to be solved by the early travellers when they ventured into unknown lands or the open sea. As they had no points of reference on the land they turned their attention to the sky.

They had noticed that the Sun appeared to rise and set at the same places on the horizon. Where the Sun rose they called east and where it set they called west and decided to take the east as their point of reference for their travels. That is why we talk about getting our bearings or orientation, from the word 'orient' which means east.

Why the Pole Star is important

On a clear night it is possible to find the north by looking at the sky. There is one star which always remains in the same place and the others seem to revolve around it. This is the Pole Star which sailors recognize easily; it shows where the north is and from it all the other points of the compass can then be worked out. It is also used in determining latitude.

Although the Pole Star appears to be a single star to the naked eye, it is really a group of three stars.

South of the equator where the Pole Star is not visible we can find our bearings by the Southern Cross, a constellation which indicates the direction of the South Pole.

Why we use the cardinal points

In order to work out correctly which way to go on a journey or the direction of a place, a single point of reference such as where the Sun rises or sets is not enough. For this reason the ancients agreed to fix four basic or cardinal points to which reference could be made.

These points are north, south, east and west. If we know where the east is it is easy to discover the other cardinal points: all you have to do is to stand facing the place where the Sun rises: the north will then be on your left hand, the south on your right and the west, where the Sun sets, will be behind you.

For giving intermediate directions between the four cardinal points, we use the points of the compass.

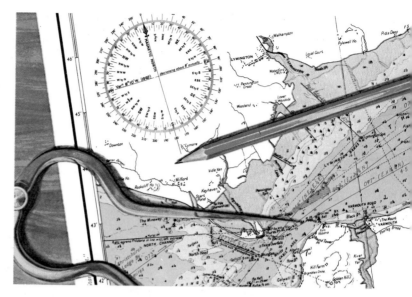

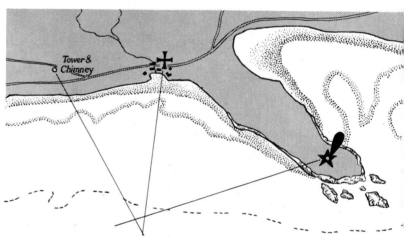

To fix the exact direction for a journey reference is made to the cardinal points fixed by the ancients

Why sea breezes change direction morning and evening

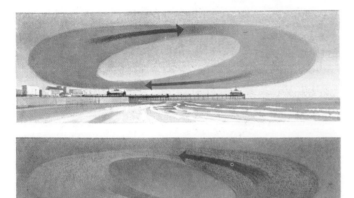

Among regular winds the commonest are the sea and land breezes. These are very light local winds caused by the difference of temperature between land and sea.

Formation of a cold valley wind (above) and a warm mountain wind (below)

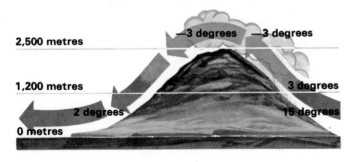

During the day the earth warms up more quickly than the sea and therefore the air above it becomes lighter and rises, creating an area of rarefied atmosphere at ground level. The air above the sea, which is colder and therefore more compressed and heavier, is drawn into this area. This causes a wind from the sea to blow towards the land, that is a sea breeze.

Towards evening and during the night, on the other hand, the wind changes direction and goes from the land to the sea, that is a land breeze. This happens because the land cools more easily and brings about a similar cooling of the air which therefore moves to replace the air above the sea which now remains warm. This is well known to all fishermen who time their departure by it. Nowadays when boats use engines and are no longer dependent on the wind it is no more than a pleasant feature of coastal areas.

Why there are winds

Atmospheric pressure, that is the weight of the air above the Earth, is subject to continual variations. Like all gases the air increases in volume as the temperature rises, which means that a cubic metre of cold air weighs more than a cubic metre of hot air.

The air moves from the cold regions of the Earth where the air is heavier to the warm regions and displaces the lighter air there which tends to rise and cause rarefied zones in the lower levels of the atmosphere. It is this displacement which causes winds.

A wind therefore is a horizontal displacement of air from a high pressure area to a low pressure one and vice-versa. The wind varies in strength according to the difference in pressure between the two areas.

Winds can be classified as periodic, constant, local and cyclonic. Constant winds are those which blow in the same direction all the year round as can be seen over the oceans when there are no disturbing influences. Local winds are those which only affect small areas. Periodic winds are those which blow in one direction at one time and in the opposite direction at another time.

Why cyclones occur

Cyclonic winds are exceptionally violent movements of air masses. They blow mostly from the tropics where areas of hot air are formed. The surrounding colder air flows towards them with a whirling movement which spirals upwards or spreads out horizontally.

The atmospheric disturbance which they cause is called a cyclone. Cyclones blow from west to east and often cause extensive damage in the areas over which they pass. They also change the pattern of atmospheric precipitation all around. For this reason they are carefully studied and tracked in their movements, even with the use of special weather planes. These can penetrate into the eye of the cyclone, that is the centre of the enormous and turbulent vortex of clouds, where the air is very quiet and they are therefore able to study the conditions without being tossed dangerously about by the wind.

Weather maps show that there are relatively permanent cyclonic centres in the northern Atlantic and Pacific oceans.

Why tornados occur

During a hurricane or cyclone it can happen that vortices of air are formed at some points and although they are not very extensive they are very fast.

In certain conditions two whirlwinds of air, one on the ground and the other in the sky, may meet and touch one another with opposite points, like two cones one on top of the other with the points in contact. The two frightful forms then unite and, revolving tumultuously with a speed of rotation of as much as 200 kilometres an hour, move in the dominant direction of the wind.

The speed at which a tornado moves is not very high, about 60 kilometres an hour, and the diameter of the vortex is only a few hundred metres at the most.

Tornados carry away objects, root up trees and houses and often cause the death of people and animals (above right). Waterspouts (bottom right) cause less damage because they can more easily be anticipated.
Enormous damage is, however, caused by sandstorms (below). The fine grains of sand penetrate everywhere and damage machinery and equipment over a wide area through their abrasive action.

Why the sea sometimes rises and floods large areas of land

Because of the complex state of equilibrium of the surface strata of the Earth's crust there is in many places, right beneath our feet, a constant rising or falling of the ground which occurs century after century, but it is so slow as to be imperceptible to our normal senses'.

This phenomenon, which causes slow, vertical movements of the Earth's crust, is evident on the coast. Here it is possible to see whether a rocky coast was once higher or lower in relation to the sea level than it is at the present time because traces of erosion still remain.

If we see a rock with signs of erosion by the waves at a height of 15 or 20 metres, we can deduce that at one time it was 15 or 20 metres lower, otherwise how could we explain this hammering by the waves at that height?

If, then, this phenomenon takes place on low lying coasts the land which sinks is covered by the sea advancing over quite a long distance; or vast areas rise and then it is the sea which retreats little by little leaving behind the uncovered land.

Sometimes these movements alternate: that is to say that for centuries the land continues to rise and then begins to sink once again.

Evidence of this is to be found at Puzzuoli, an ancient seaside town in southern Italy. The volcanic qualities of the area have resulted in hot springs and changes in the level of land. Buildings have been submerged by the sea. An example of this is the temple of Serapis, which was certainly built on firm ground far from the sea. Then the land sank, the sea was able to advance and the temple was submerged up to a certain height. Later the land rose again but the columns still retain traces of erosion and of some small marine animals.

Fifty years ago the temple was entirely on dry land but today it has again begun to sink.

A column from the temple of Serapis at Pozzuoli

Why waves form on the sea

There are many kinds of waves both on the surface and inside the sea. They are caused by the wind blowing over the sea, by underwater earthquakes and by the effects of the Sun and Moon. The last are called astronomical tides.

If we blow across a basin full of water we can see at once the way in which waves are formed by the wind. It blows over the surface of the sea, making the waves large or small according to its force and intensity.

But the wind does not cause any movement of the water from one place to another, or drive it in any one direction; even when it forms very high waves the water remains practically still.

That is to say that the waves are the rise and fall of the individual drops of water on the surface of the sea; they make a closed circular movement in a vertical direction.

The movement spreads and therefore the waves seem to chase one another as far as the eye can see.

Why there is sand on the beach

Beaches are the dumping grounds of the seas. For millions of years the winds and the tides have beaten day and night against the rocky coasts, hammering, shaking and bombarding them with fragments.

Under these blows the rocks very gradually crack, split, crumble and are reduced to minute grains. This is how sand is made as a result of the continuous struggle between the sea and the rocks. The waves then carry off the

very fine particles of rock and the ocean currents take them far away.

In the quieter inlets along low lying coasts the waters of the sea calm down and allow the sand they are carrying to fall onto the bottom. In the course of time this accumulates into large deposits and the waves spread it out gently on the shore to form the beach.

Not all the sand comes from the rocks which the sea wears away along the high coasts; a very large proportion of the sand is brought to the sea by the rivers which carry it down from the mountains.

Why the Great Barrier Reef was formed

The Great Barrier Reef which extends for thousands of kilometres along the north-east coast of Australia from Torres strait to beyond the tropic of Capricorn, is the most famous coral formation in the world. It is like an enormous wall erected between the sea and the land, and is formed of a very high layer of coral composed of the accumulation of coral skeletons. By their unceasing activity over

with no thin ramifications which would be broken.

On the other side where the barrier reef itself creates an area of calm sea, the colonies of polyps make a diversity of shapes, flowers, shrubs and bone-lace which create a dream landscape.

The spaces between one colony and another are filled with coral fragments broken down by the sea and forming a fertile sludge.

On this limestone soil brought down by the waves, numerous algae grow and many marine

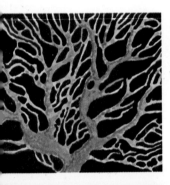

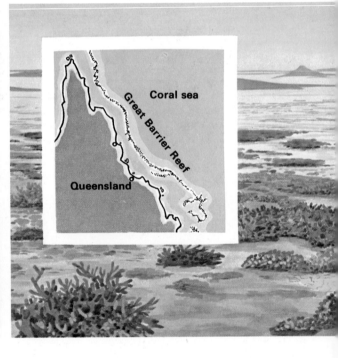
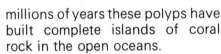

millions of years these polyps have built complete islands of coral rock in the open oceans.

In these warm, tropical seas the water is rich in food, the light of the Sun is strong and the coral colonies prosper and produce brightly coloured, fantastic shapes.

Towards the open sea where the waves beat violently on the reef the layers of coral are compact

animals flourish with their vivid colours and curious shapes. Shoals of fish pass by the brilliant expanses of coral and disappear into the darkness.

Typical inhabitants of the coral reefs are the butterfly fish, small and brightly coloured, which nose among the crevices of coral in search of food.

Why there are tides

Tides are periodical fluctuations of the sea which occur twice a day. When the water is high we call it high tide and when the water is low it is low tide. Naturally the rising level of the sea leads to a horizontal movement on the low-lying coasts and the water covers large areas of sand; at low tide the beach becomes dry once more.

The extent of the tides is not always the same and equal in all parts of the world. It is very strong at the new Moon and the full Moon because tides are caused by the attraction of the Moon, which at those periods is added to that of the Sun. It is also more accentuated in the open seas.

It would not be correct, however, to imagine that the Moon acts like a huge magnet and draws towards it the seas which come under its influence. The nature of this attraction is much more complex because the effect of the Moon interferes with the effects of the Earth's gravity and the centrifugal force due to the speed of rotation of the Earth.

Why some islands are ring-shaped

Ring-shaped islands, called atolls, are very common in the Pacific Ocean. They are formed of millions of coral shells piled on one another and cemented together.

In the warm seas these colonies of tiny animals flourish in huge numbers and build picturesque layers of coral shells in the most varied shapes. When the coral polyps attach themselves to the coasts of a small submerged island, they gradually build all around it a ring of coral which increases in size.

The island continues to sink and is submerged to a considerable depth: all around on the surface of the water is a large ring of coral colonies which go on developing. At a certain point the island may begin to rise again and lift up with it the ring of coral until it is above the water level. The wind and the waves then carry on to it the first seeds and the atoll is covered with vegetation.

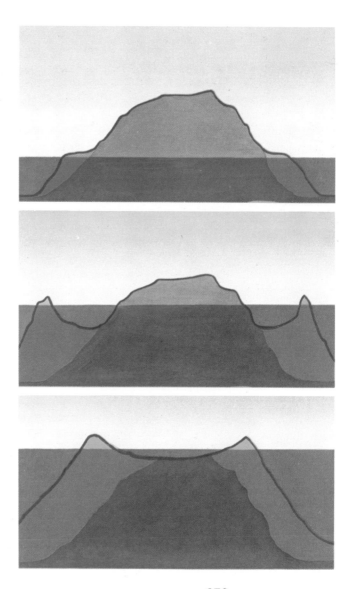

Why the water in artesian wells rises higher than the level of the ground

Why the seas never dry up

The amount of water which evaporates from the sea in the course of a year is enormous: millions of cubic metres. Eventually, therefore, you would expect that the seas would dry up. However the balance of nature is so perfect that, season by season, all the water which was drawn up into the skies returns in various ways to the seas. That is why the level of the seas can remain constantly the same despite evaporation.

The tiniest drops of water vapour condense in the high strata of the atmosphere, form into clouds and return to Earth as rain, snow and sleet. If they fall on the sea the balance is restored at once. On the other hand if they fall on the land they go to feed the springs and streams which carry them back to the sea. This cycle of water continues for ever.

So long as it continues to meet porous material such as gravel, sand and limestone, rain water sinks deeper into the ground, but when it meets a layer of impermeable rock or clay it is forced to stop. The water then spreads out and saturates all the ground above the impermeable layer and at the same time seeks a way out. In this state the subterranean water can be reached by wells from which it can be pumped up to the surface.

But the sheet of water contained in the porous material may find itself imprisoned between two layers of impermeable rocks at an angle or in the form of a basin. The water is then almost as if in a pressure pipe and its pressure is greater than atmospheric pressure. If we bore into the ground, that is open up a way out for it, the water will rise spontaneously to the surface, often gushing to a height. Wells of this type are called artesian wells.

Why even large rivers have several tributaries

At its source even the greatest river is only a small stream or tiny waterfall of little importance. If it were not enriched by other water along its course it would never even manage to reach the sea.

A watercourse can have a definite origin such as a spring or the region of a glacier, but most often it is formed from rain water or the melting of snows, the water of which runs down in rivulets and collects into one bed.

Watercourses are generally divided into streams and rivers, but it would be more correct to say that streams are simply early forms of watercourses which run down and are swollen by the water from tributaries and thus become rivers.

A watercourse can be regarded as a river when it flows slowly over almost level plains and its volume of water is quite regular.

In the plains the watercourses flow towards the sea at a speed which is related to the height of their source: the lower the source, the slower the speed. As the water no longer has the impetuous force which it possessed in the mountain valleys, it cannot scoop out for itself a straight path in the plain and therefore every small obstacle (harder ground, rocky projections and even merely tangles of roots) may force the river to change direction.

As a result the course of the river becomes winding and it sometimes meanders across the plain. At this stage the river gives up finer detritus and deposits it on the river bed and on the banks in the form of a very fine mud.

Why some regions are desert

By desert we mean an area where it rains very little and at long, irregular intervals.

Rainfall is determined by the massing of clouds in a given region, and so what is very largely responsible for deserts is the wind which fails to bring clouds to some areas.

If we look at a map of the world we shall see that almost all the deserts are concentrated in a band about 20° latitude north and south: just those areas known for their stable high pressures where the conditions never arise for the formation of cloud systems.

Another reason for the formation of deserts is the great distance of some areas from the sea. The cloud systems which come from the oceans discharge their rain on the way and have no water left when they reach these regions. For the same reason deserts can occur at the foot of high mountains: the clouds are unable to pass over the mountains and so drop all their rain on one slope, leaving the other side dry.

The zones which now appear desert may not still be so in the distant future, any more than they used to be in the past. The slow rate of change is due precisely to the characteristics of a desert region. If the ground were covered with dense vegetation the moisture in the soil would be protected from the rays of the Sun and evaporation would be much reduced. Modern techniques of dry cultivation may make it an economical proposition to apply this process of a covering of vegetation, which is the only way to ensure the definite recovery of vast areas of the Earth which are at the moment sterile.

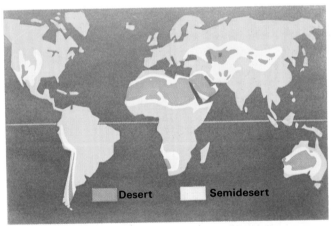

Desert   Semidesert

Why embankments are built along rivers

Floods generally occur when there is a thaw and it is difficult to forecast when this will happen.

For this reason the banks of the large rivers are reinforced by powerful embankments calculated to withstand any increase that may occur during the flood season.

The oldest types of such dykes were made of beaten earth strengthened by stakes or beams: today they are made of cement blocks and metal baskets filled with stones.

But the river water, carrying with it detritus of all kinds, erodes, scrapes, demolishes and the dykes are in serious danger. It is therefore necessary to keep a careful and continuous watch on these protective works.

Why dams are built

Many watercourses do not have a constant flow: periods of flood alternate with periods of low water according to the season and this could bring industry and electric power stations to a complete standstill.

But man found a remedy for this: all he had to do was to close the valley through which the water ran by a dam so that the water could accumulate and form an artificial lake, a valuable reservoir for bad times.

The use of dams and embankments goes back to remote times. The Indians built them 5,000 years ago and in ancient Egypt some very imposing ones were constructed of stone. These lakes provided a convenient reserve of water for the dry season and irrigation could then continue even in summer.

With the discovery of electricity and the turbines for making it, dams multiplied rapidly. Today many stretches of valley in mountainous regions have been transformed by the patient and intelligent work of man into picturesque and useful lakes.

By means of pipes these lakes feed with absolute regularity power stations lower down the valley; many such dams are to be found, real masterpieces of engineering skill.

Sometimes, however, even the strongest dams give way to unusual forces of nature and then the water rushes down carrying destruction and death.

Among the most notable dams are the Aswan Dam across the river Nile, the Boulder Dam on the Colorado, and the Kariba Dam on the Zambesi.

Why lakes vary in size and shape

Lakes are found in nearly every kind of surroundings but are most abundant in high latitudes and in mountainous regions. They are also common along rivers and in the lowlands near to the sea. They vary considerably in size and may be either fresh or salt water; some are even more salty than the sea.

In the course of its long history the Earth has undergone numerous changes. The crust has risen frequently, splitting in many places and causing folds and depressions sometimes of immense size.

These movements of the Earth's crust are the origin of one kind of very deep and vast lake, which is very common, especially in Africa. Some of them, like the Caspian and the Dead Sea, are so big that they deserve the name of seas.

The Kariba dam on the Zambesi

277

Welsh lake

There are other lakes, sometimes quite small, caused by the blocking of valleys or watercourses by various means.

Mounds of lava, glaciers, landslides, many natural obstacles can block a valley and prevent the water from flowing freely away. A lake is then formed above the barrier which may persist for a long time or may disappear as soon as the water succeeds in finding another way out down the valley.

Sometimes such lakes formed among the mountains are very beautiful and become famous tourist attractions.

The various shapes of lakes are therefore due to the nature of the terrain surrounding them and the particular character of the confining walls.

Often in the course of time lakes change their shape to some extent. This can happen, for instance, when part of their basin is filled with detritus carried down by the rivers which transform them into alluvial plains.

Why some lakes are of glacial origin

More than a million years ago, for reasons which we do not yet fully understand, the Earth became cold and glaciers covered a large part of the continents. In the valleys and basins the enormous masses of ice eroded the ground by their slow movement over it and dug out great hollows. They also pushed along in front of them large masses of stones and soil.

These masses of material, called moraine, formed real walls at the foot of the glaciers and as the glaciers retreated they became a barrier in the way of water coming down from the mountains. Lakes were formed in this way and were called glacial lakes because of their origin. They filled the hollows scooped out by the glaciers and were hemmed in by the old moraines.

Why some lakes are called crater lakes

Crater lakes are those which occupy the craters of old extinct volcanoes or lie in hollows where several old volcanic outlets emerge.

Generally, because of their origin, crater lakes are circular in shape and are never very large. Nor are they usually very deep. They can have streams running into and out of them but there are some crater lakes which do not appear to be fed by any running water.

Some crater lakes, especially in America, have unusual features (hot water, sulphur water and so on) which are connected with previous volcanic activity.

Why there are many extinct volcanoes

Originally a volcano was a crack in the Earth's crust through which molten material erupted and accumulated to form a cone surmounted by a funnel-shaped opening called the crater.

In a volcano we can distinguish the following parts: the chimney formed of a number of irregular passages through which the white hot material comes to the surface; the crater or external mouth; the cone formed of ejected volcanic material. Often several secondary craters can open in the sides of the volcano, each with its own cone.

When a volcano ceases both its main eruptive activities (lava and stones) and also its secondary activity (smoke and sulphurous gases) it is said to be extinct but it is by no means unknown for a so-called extinct volcano suddenly to come to life again. The eruption of Vesuvius in A.D. 79 is an example of this, for the volcano had been dormant from the earliest recorded times.

The reason why a volcano ceases to be active is not yet quite clear: it is probably due to the chimney becoming blocked by a subsidence of the Earth's crust.

Volcanoes are distributed on the Earth's surface mostly in long series and these volcanic zones correspond to areas where crevices or areas of lower resistance of the crust are to be found.

The chief line of volcanoes is the Pacific Fire Belt which stretches almost all around the Pacific Ocean. The North-South Atlantic chain is composed of a line of volcanoes extending in the Atlantic Ocean from one Pole to the other. The Mediterranean chain comprises the volcanoes of the Carib-

bean, of the Mediterranean and of some Asiatic regions. Finally the African chain extends along the Great Rift Valley of the African lakes.

Why hot springs are found in some areas

There are two different phenomena where water and gases are ejected from cracks in the Earth: those in which the jet is continuous, called fumaroles, and those where the jet is intermittent, called geysers.

The first are vents from which continuous volcanic vapours issue at a high temperature carrying with them boric acid and other salts.

Industry makes use of fumaroles as a source of both thermal energy and boric acid.

Geysers, on the other hand, are hot springs which spurt jets of water and steam into the air. These jets sometimes exceed 100° of heat and rise as high as 50 metres at intervals ranging from a few minutes to several hours.

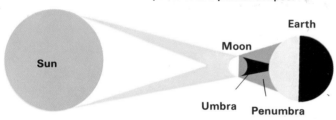

Why eclipses of the Sun and Moon occur

Eclipses of the Moon and of the Sun have been the subject of study from the earliest times. The Sun used to be regarded as a benevolent deity and men were terrified when it suddenly became dark. Even today primitive peoples panic when an eclipse takes place, and animals show signs of extreme agitation. A total eclipse does not last very long, however; seven and half minutes at most.

Nowadays we know the exact mechanism which causes the partial or total darkening of the Sun or Moon. An eclipse occurs when, through their movements of rotation and revolution, the Earth and the Moon are in perfect alignment with the Sun. The illustration shows the position of the three heavenly bodies which causes a total eclipse of the Sun: the Moon is exactly in front of the Earth and prevents the direct rays of the Sun from reaching parts of the Earth's surface. If we are in line with its cone of shadow we have a total eclipse of the Sun, and the Moon appears like a dark disk completely covering the Sun. On the other hand if we are in the area of the penumbra, the eclipse will be partial.

It has been observed that during a total eclipse of the Sun life on our planet undergoes strange changes. One of them which it is easy to check, is that of the slowing down of the clotting time of the blood. This can be repeated experimentally quite easily by having the operating theatre underground. It is easy to see the importance of such a fact in medicine but it is not so easy to explain it.

Eclipse of the Sun (below). In the area of the umbra there is a total eclipse and in the penumbra a partial eclipse.

Sun　　　　Moon　　　Earth

Umbra　Penumbra

Total eclipse of the Sun

Why the study of eclipses is important

To us the Sun appears to be the largest and brightest of the stars visible to the naked eye, but it is really one of the smallest and faintest.

The illusion arises because it is the nearest star to us: the next nearest is nearly 300,000 times as far away.

Modern science has confirmed what the ancients had already observed, that the Sun is of fundamental importance for us. This is not only because it makes life on Earth possible, but also because the phenomena and disturbances which take place inside it affect all the planets of the solar system, and these effects are sometimes very far-reaching.

The mysterious spots which can be seen on its surface and which are thought to increase in size every eleven years and then regress again, for instance, cause serious disturbance of radio transmissions and also seem to have some effect on climate.

The violent explosions which take place in the chromosphere, the most superficial part of the Sun, and throw up gigantic columns of incandescent gases upon the corona of the Sun, also have a great influence on life on Earth.

Whilst many things which occur in the Sun can now be observed directly by means of suitable instruments, those which happen in the Sun's corona and particularly in its rarefied extremities, can only be properly observed during an eclipse of the Sun. The Moon then covers the disc of the Sun, leaving only the corona showing with its protuberances and incandescent plumes.

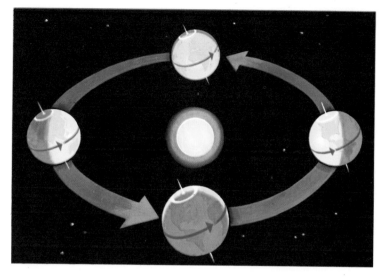

Why we have changes of seasons

The year is divided into four seasons which, in Europe, are associated with the annual pattern of plant life. They do not depend upon the greater or shorter distance of the Earth from the Sun, but on the varied inclination of the axis of the Earth at different times in relation to the Sun's rays.

Passing through the atmosphere the Sun's rays are filtered and cooled. The greater the distance to be travelled, the greater the amount of cooling.

For the same reason it is hotter on the equator than in other regions. Since the Earth is a sphere the Sun's rays are perpendicular at the equator and therefore pass through a shorter stretch of the atmosphere, whereas, when we approach the Poles, the rays become more oblique and cool down more.

The inclination of the axis of the Earth can correct this situation when the surface of one of the hemispheres moves into a more perpendicular position towards the Sun (it is then summer) or more inclined (and then it is winter).

The changing aspect of the Earth and its position relative to the Sun, produces the seasons.

THE WHY OF ART

Why every nation has produced its own form of art

It was believed for a long time that the only valid and acceptable art forms were the classical ones, that is those produced by the western Greco-Latin civilizations. Any other forms of artistic expression were commonly regarded as the work of dabblers of little value. The sole exception was Egyptian art, which attracted universal attention chiefly because of the magnificence and size of its architectural works.

Today, however, many people consider that any form of art has its own intrinsic value and that there can be no question of any preconceived and universally accepted standards for judging the validity of all the varied artistic manifestations. In fact every nation has produced its own special type of art, different from all the others, because the spirit has been different which has animated artists, different also the culture in which they lived and by which they were influenced, and different, in particular, the inspiration which springs from a world always different and irrepeatable.

The truth of this can be seen when we consider that even artists belonging to the same nation, to the same culture and to the same tradition have produced different forms of art during their various periods of history.

Ancient figure of animal god

Why artistic inspiration is often derived from religion

From rock drawings to the most modern forms of art we find throughout human history that religious faith has inspired innumerable artists in every field: from painting to architecture, from sculpture to mosaics.

The reasons for this are quite clear. Man has always had a strong belief in something transcendental, that is in something superior to himself, some power or powers to which he feels himself linked by profound spiritual bonds. To express through art his own interior world signified very often to approach divinity, to glimpse a part, even if only a very small part of it, in some way to share in it.

It was inspiration of a religious nature which moved the architects of all the temples in the world, the sculptors both known and unknown of the innumerable statues of divinity, the painters who adorned the places of worship, the tombs, the dwellings of the religious orders.

Even though today the world of scientific techniques has led men to considerations of a practical nature, artistic inspiration based on a religious faith, whichever it may be, has not lessened, although, as is to be expected, it has taken on new characteristics in tune with the times. Coventry Cathedral is an example of how religion has inspired modern artists.

Why we find the mother figure represented so much among the primitives

One thing above all else dominated the mind of primitive man: the survival of the race. The very hard life he was compelled to lead, the dangers surrounding him, the high rate of infant mortality, all developed in him the instinct of self-preservation, which was translated into a profound respect for fertility.

In the eyes of artists motherhood therefore assumed a magical and propitiatory significance. This can be seen from cave drawings and paintings but above all from the numerous small statuettes of pregnant women which have been found among so many different peoples.

The mother about to give life to another creature, the symbol of fertility, represented the hopes of the tribe and guaranteed its survival.

The famous Willendorf Venus statuette, nearly 30,000 years old

Why the Egyptians built tombs in the form of pyramids

In ancient Egypt the pharaohs were regarded as divine and were accorded the greatest veneration.

In this lies the reason behind the story of the pyramids. Some 3,400 years before Christ the tombs were covered with mounds of earth. In order to distinguish them from the tombs of ordinary mortals the tombs of the pharaohs were covered with a tumulus of bricks visibly larger than on others.

Four hundred years later, that is about the year 3000 B.C., the architect Imhotep was commissioned to build a special tomb for the pharaoh Zoser at Saqqarah. He placed a series of tumuli one on top of the other, each smaller than the previous one so as to form steps on the four sides. This was the first step pyramid of Egypt. The first pointed pyramid was built about 300 years later by the pharaoh Cheops at Giza.

Cave paintings found at Lascaux

Why the colours of rock paintings have lasted until now

The actual nature of the limestone forming the caves which our remote ancestors chose for their paintings has ensured that they

have been preserved and very often improved.

This is how the Stone Age artist produced his work: first of all he cut into the rock face the outline of the figure with flint chisels or knives and then he filled in these incisions and often the whole figure as well with colour. Drawing and painting, therefore, arose as twin arts, each complementing the other.

The commonest colours were red, black, brown and yellow; this was inevitable as these colours are provided by nature in the form of mineral oxides and fossil carbon.

In the course of time the primitive painters began to mix their colours with animal fats and other oily substances and then spread them over the figures like pastels. If the wall was very rough they blew on the colours directly by means of a bone tube. The limestone then slowly absorbed the colours and the moisture kept them fresh and bright.

Why some wall paintings are called frescoes

A fresco is a special technique for painting on walls. The name indicates the nature of this type of painting, for it means fresh, that is to say, painting straight on to a wall on which the plaster is still wet.

The painting of frescoes probably originated and was developed most in Italy, and takes advantage of a special characteristic of lime: this is mixed with water and sand to produce a cement which will absorb the colours spread on its surface while it is still fresh. The colours dry and set with the plaster and become a permanent part of the wall.

The artist who devotes himself to this type of painting must have a perfect knowledge of the technique which requires great speed of execution to prevent the fresco from drying, and a sure hand as it is not possible to make corrections or to do any retouching.

To give the work smoothness and polish special marble rollers are used to smooth down the walls.

Why we use the terms oil paintings, tempera and water colours

To amalgamate the pigments and enable the artist to use them for painting special substances known as binders are needed.

Oil is one of the commonest substances used for this purpose, and may be walnut, hemp or poppy oil. To make the pigments flow better linseed oil is also used together with turpentine and lavender oil. Oil paintings are characterized by mellow and brilliant colours.

The binders used for the pigments known as tempera are gums, glues and even wax dissolved in volatile oils. Sometimes, particularly during the fifteenth century, the pigments were mixed with egg yolk. Today we use animal glues kept fluid in a water bath.

Water colours use pigments diluted in gums. With these it is necessary to know exactly how much water to use to dilute the colours. The uniformity of the shades depends upon this ability.

Years of experience are needed in order to succeed in this apparently commonplace activity. That is why many people think that painting in water colours is the most difficult.

Why clothes chests were sometimes painted or carved

The furnishings of private houses were very modest in olden times. In the Middle Ages wood workers began to make furniture of some artistic style and beauty but it was

not until the Renaissance that the art of making furniture really began.

Among the most typical articles to be found in a house during the Renaissance period was the clothes chest. This was a wooden chest fitted with a lid and short legs. It was used as a bench for sitting on and so was sometimes provided with a back and arms, and it was also a place for storing dresses and linen. It became the habit to give a clothes chest, decorated and painted in oils or carved, to the bride as part of her dowry. These chests were real works of art and quite valuable articles in themselves.

these wooden units by a similar but stronger and more durable material, stone. That is how stone pillars came about.

At first they were no doubt very rough, probably not even round, and without any decoration at all. In the course of time they became more beautiful and elegant and were improved by additions such as bases and capitals.

When stone buildings became fully developed, pillars were used more and more, sometimes alone and sometimes in groups, or merely as decorative elements without any practical function.

Why the column is one of the basic elements of architecture

It is very difficult to establish exactly when man changed from being a simple builder and became an architect; that is to say when he changed from artisan to artist. What is certain is that one of the original architectural concepts, probably the first, was the column.

The idea of arranging two or more supports, the columns, to carry another unit, the architrave, seems to have originated in the dawn of Egyptian civilization, that is about 5,000 years ago.

First of all they were rough columns without much grace surmounted by beams which were just as rudimentary. In the course of time, however, the builders' taste developed more and more perfect forms. This is not strange when we remember the very delicate functions which they have in the complex structure of the whole edifice.

As supporting structures it was inevitable that columns should have a position of pre-eminence both as functional units and as

Why stone pillars replaced wooden ones

The material used for building the first human habitations was wood. In fact, even today the houses of many backward peoples are still built of wood and straw.

In Mesopotamia primitive columns were made of bundled reeds and mud; by 3000 B.C. they were covered with small glazed tiles which were both waterproof and decorative.

In Europe the first columns were crude wooden posts.

The trunks of trees were used for holding up the roofs and supporting the outside walls, and these became gradually bigger and stronger.

However the durability of tree trunks was very limited and they rotted and had to be replaced; also they could easily be burned down. Gradually man replaced

decorative ones. This depended to a large extent on the types, proportions and qualities of the columns if the building, in addition to remaining erect, is to express harmony, power and grace. This is shown by the countless columns which adorn buildings of all ages, from the imposing buildings of ancient Egypt to the grandiose buildings of modern reinforced concrete in which large numbers of columns continue to fulfil their supporting and decorative purposes.

Why columns were often decorated in various ways

In his work every artist gives expression to his inner drive. His feelings and attitudes are inspired by the world in which we live, by the customs of the people, the historical circumstances which characterize a nation in any particular epoch. Therefore works of art are a reflection of the world into which the artist was born.

This is true of all art but perhaps particularly so of architecture. For instance Egyptian columns are rich in decorations which reflected the world of

The Egyptians built their colossal temples by transporting enormous masses of stone by human labour.

nature: lotus flowers, palm leaves and figures of men and animals. It is the expression of a world full of fantasy, vivacity and mystery, which was ancient Egypt.

The columns of the Doric style, austere and powerful, free from decoration and adornment, reflected the way of thinking, sober but still rich in harmony and artistic intuition, of ancient Greece.

The Ionic columns, light and

Why the Romans substituted the arch for the architrave

An indispensible complement of the columns was the architrave, that is the supported part which rested on the columns and upon which was then placed the roof of the building. As a general rule the architrave was composed of a single block of stone which could be decorated or not according to the various styles.

In the course of time architects learned, however, that a system based on columns and architrave did not enable a large enough area of space to be covered over and free from obstacles. Even expanding the space between one column and the next did not solve the problem. First of all it was impossible to find marble architraves long enough and strong enough, and in the second place it would not be an aesthetic advantage.

The Romans resolved the problem by using the arch. This was not an original invention: the Assyrians and the Egyptians knew how to build arches but had never made effective use of them.

The Romans probably learned of the arch from the Etruscans who were masters of architecture and the first exponents of arch construction in Europe. They may well have passed on their knowledge to the Greeks as well as to the Romans.

Roman builders more than any others had the idea, which has proved to be correct, that the arch was the architectural feature of the future. They perfected its structure to such a point that they used it in all their buildings: from temples to amphitheatres, from baths to aqueducts, and, of course, in the triumphal arch.

The baths of Diocletian in Rome (A.D. 305): concrete and bricks faced with marble and stucco

graceful and with volute capitals, express the sentiments of a gentle and elegant people.

The Corinthian style columns, the style preferred by the Romans with the capitals decorated with ornate clusters of leaves at the sides, is the original expression of elegance and wealth.

Why architecture is regarded as an art

Although the art of building houses developed a long time after painting and sculpture, it achieved a high degree of aesthetic value in a short time.

If an artist is one who translates his imagination into visible works, the architect can be regarded as an artist when he is able to enliven architectural forms with his inspiration. The more his work pleases and stimulates those who admire it, the more he can consider his aim as achieved and his inspiration realized.

In architecture as a form of art, one can never dissociate the technical element from the aesthetic. Anyone who wants to build a house, must have very precise scientific knowledge ranging from statics (the science of weight and of balance) to building materials, mathematics and geometry.

It will be true art, however, only if to such knowledge there is added a special flair for arranging the masses, for balancing the solids and the spaces, in adding elegance to shape, in arranging and balancing all the different aspects of decoration.

Why the keystone is the most important element in the arch

It is said that the arch used in building was taken from the shape of the bow used in archery. The curve of the arch is exactly that of the bow when it is bent under the pull of the string.

But what is the principle on which the arch, and the vault also, is based? The very elementary factor of the weight. The blocks or wedge stones of which the arch is made adhere together and support one another because they bear by their weight upon the two columns which support them: the bricks on the right upon the right hand column and those on the left upon the left hand column.

At the top, however, there is a brick or stone which has a special purpose. It thrusts to both right and left, thus forming the decisive point of equilibrium of the arch: without it neither arch nor vault could stay up and that is why it is called the keystone. In Etruscan, Roman and Renaissance arches it often projects slightly and is decorated with scrolls or figures.

Why we talk of semicircular and lancet arches

As soon as the arch had been discovered builders began to intro-

duce variations, some of them quite considerable. It remained a feature of architecture but was adapted to the style of various periods.

The first type to be developed and the commonest in Rome was the so-called semicircular arch, that is one which is a perfect half circle. Numerous examples of this can be seen in buildings of almost every period.

The other very usual type of arch is the pointed arch, also known as the lancet arch. It is made by two curved lines which join at the top to form an acute angle. This type was widely used during the Gothic period when a great variety of arch forms occurred.

In the rebuilt choir of Canterbury Cathedral (after 1174) architects used arcs of different size and radius to produce lopsided arches and even introduced angles into the arc.

Why Romanesque art flourished in the Middle Ages

Christian art, from the humble beginnings of the catacombs to the impressive art of the basilicas, had not given expression to anything new or really original.

It is true that a certain monotony in architecture had to some extent been corrected by the Byzantine influence but this was confined almost exclusively to interiors, rich with gold, enamel and multi-coloured mosaics. Exteriors had remained very modest if not actually rough, with the sole exception of the cupola which, when well placed, could be beautiful and effective.

However in the time of Charlemagne a new style, particularly in architecture, began to spread very quickly, the Romanesque. Its name indicates one definite influence, that of Roman art. Solidity, clarity of line, elegance, a prevalence of solid planes over openings gave an impression of majestic and solemn calm of the classical type.

Why the flying buttress was widely used in Gothic architecture

The Romanesque architects, mostly monks, were very clearly influenced by the spirit of asceticism which yielded little to imagination, nature or inspiration. Their art was certainly sublime but it was also cold.

At the time when the Romanesque was reaching its peak in the twelfth century, a new style came from France, the Gothic. Its aspiration was obvious; a longing for height, vertical lines, delicacy and lightness.

But this explosion of inspiration and imagination had to come to terms with the inexorable laws of statics. Verticality, the prevalence of hollows over solids demanded completely new solutions. Supporting walls to carry the weight of the tall building would have had to be so thick that they would have spoiled the lightness of line which was the dominant feature of this style.

New solutions were therefore studied. First of all the semi-circular arches and vaults were transformed into pointed ones to reduce the proportions of weight bearing on the support structures.

A system of supports was evolved to give stability and security to the vital points of the edifice. These supports took the form of thrusts provided by the so-called flying buttresses. They were arches or half-arches which rested upon strong and high buttresses, soaring upwards to the vital points needing support and reinforcement.

Why some buildings are called Flamboyant

The innumerable fluted columns, the abundance of windows, rosettes, tiny belfries and stone tracery, the presence of imposing but airy flying buttresses, the prevalence of pointed vaults and arches are the features which distinguish the Gothic style.

Such was the architects' zeal for buildings with lightness that more than once the buildings collapsed before they were finished. Nevertheless the new style had found its place and had been accepted. Until the coming of the

Construction of an old cathedral

Renaissance and beyond, the Gothic style produced some immortal works of art throughout Europe.

But, as so often happens, in the course of time the style became more complicated. In the attempt to become too beautiful it became affected and unstable. Gradually, unrestrained fantasy took over, resulting in works where the search for ornamentation, tracery, trimmings and virtuosity led to an over-abundance of decorative elements which often fell into affectation and artificiality.

Hence the name of Flamboyant was given to this method of interpreting the original inspiration.

It may seem strange that just at the moment when it was taking on more refined forms, a style should become decadent when it had originally been called, clearly in a depreciative sense, Gothic, that is barbaric.

Why the style of the eighteenth century was called Neo-Classic

As with all human activities which are subject to recurrent tastes and reversions, in art the fever of the Baroque was succeeded by a period of reaction.

Palladian villa

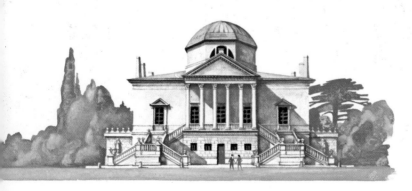

In architecture the tumult of Baroque lines gave way to sobriety and classical simplicity. It was a return to origins, to the inspirations of that classical refinement which Western culture regards as its source. That is why the term Neo-Classic is used, meaning the new classical style which began from about the year 1700 onwards.

The Renaissance was also a period of classical rediscovery, of a return to certain aesthetic criteria, but of much larger scope because enriched by another and different inspiration.

The Neo-Classical style, freed from the robust sense of art which characterized the Renaissance, was reduced to a cold and formal return to the classical. Its buildings were solid, linear and rather severe, tending towards archaeological precision. Often they were merely uninspired copies of ancient monuments.

The movement was towards simplicity and rigidity, and some people wished to abandon all decoration, even classical decoration.

Why the Renaissance is regarded as the richest period of art

Towards the middle of the fifteenth century geographical discoveries, new inventions, the intensification of scientific study instead of philosophy signalled the end of the Middle Ages.

A new age was born in which men rediscovered the values of reason, reality and nature. Free from the preconceptions and fears of the Middle Ages and favoured by a period of relative peace, culture turned again to the beauty of the Greek and Roman classical periods.

People became aware that life was beautiful and should be lived intensely, so that the pleasures of the spirit and the refinement of aesthetic taste dominate this period, the Renaissance.

Architecture, like all the arts, translated this spirit of rebirth into unequalled beauty. A harmonious combination of mediaeval and classical forms, the architecture of the Renaissance acquired a spirit of elegance, solemnity and strength. Its fundamental law was the rational investigation of reality which was the most important contribution of the period. In this reality there was no place for excessive ornamentation; it was dominated by the laws of perspective which created order and proportion, harmonious elegance, grandeur and purity of line.

The Renaissance initiated the modern age by expressing as an aesthetic whole all that was most perfect in human achievement at that time.

Why there are so many Baroque churches in Latin America

The Spanish conquerors and colonizers of America were almost always accompanied by Roman Catholic priests who, in addition to acting as chaplains to the Spaniards, set up new native Christian communities.

In the course of this colonization, South America became enriched with religious buildings. It was natural that the dominant style of these buildings should be the one most in favour in seventeenth-century Spain.

So it came about, as a result of the work of the colonizing priests, many of whom were Jesuits, that the Baroque style which domin-

ated the European artistic scene in the seventeenth century, spread throughout America.

How did this style arise? The rare perfection of Renaissance art, its stupendous balance of forms, had ended by falling into affectation. A new idea in art was born which according to its founder, the Italian poet Giambattista Marino, should arouse wonder and surprise. From such ideas arose an art completely devoted to creating grandiose works, unexpected, even spectacular.

Architecture was also strongly influenced by it: no more classical simplicity but exuberant decoration, no longer clarity and purity of line but grotesqueness and virtuosity. In short it was the triumph of irregularity and caprice. All this is indeed shown in the name of this style, Baroque, which in Spanish means irregular.

**Peruvian church
of the sixteenth century**

THE WHY OF MATHEMATICS

Why we cannot do without mathematics

How many times in a day's work do we have to use mathematics and calculations? It is difficult to say exactly but it is certain that there is no activity, however remote it may seem, that is not in some way connected with numbers.

Let us take a few examples from everyday life. Mother usually begins her day by thinking of what she will have to buy for the family's meals; father goes off to work and whatever means of transport he uses he will sooner or later need money; the children think of the times of their lessons, the time for play and the time to leave school; grandfather looks through the newspaper and cannot avoid getting involved in economic and financial articles. In short, the day has hardly begun and we have all come face to face with figures. By the end of the day the number of calculations done by each one of us will be quite considerable, even though we may not be aware of it. It may be a matter of mental arithmetic or done on paper, it may be easy or it may be difficult but it is all necessary for human existance. If this happens in our normal everyday life, what will happen in large professional or business concerns?

A numerical exercise is bound to be needed sooner or later: everything is indissolubly bound up with mathematics and calculations.

Before crossing the road, we need to calculate the speed of the approaching traffic, and our own speed, in order to decide on the most direct route.

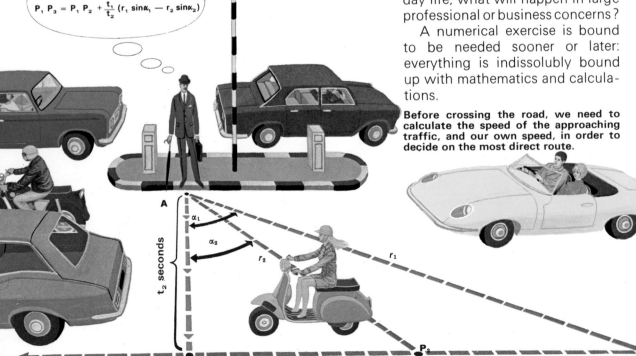

$$P_1 P_3 = P_1 P_2 + \frac{t_1}{t_2}(r_1 \sin\alpha_1 - r_2 \sin\alpha_2)$$

A

α_1

α_2

t_2 seconds

r_2

r_1

P_2

P_3

B

t_1 seconds

Why we use the decimal system

If we wish to discover the origin of some of our old customs which date back to the very early days of our history, it is often very useful to look at habits and customs which still exist.

This is the case with numbers. Ethnologists, men who study man's history and origins, discovered that among primitive people counting is usually done on the fingers and sometimes on the toes as well.

This is probably the origin of the system of numbers and the method of calculation commonly in use among the majority of people today. Decimals began with the number of fingers on our hands. It was therefore a natural and spontaneous development: discovery and invention at the same time.

However, surprising as it may seem, according to the opinions of some experts and despite its natural origins, the decimal system is not as practical and convenient in use as systems of calculation based on the numbers six, twelve or twenty-four.

The decimal system, therefore, may be a natural thing but is not as simple as it might appear to those who have been accustomed to it from infancy.

Did all primitive peoples use the decimal system? Certainly not and there are people today who still use very different methods. The binary system, for instance, which is the basis for modern electronic calculators, was used by the Chinese more than 3,000 years ago and a rather complicated development of it is still in use among the Bengalis, who are regarded as expert calculators.

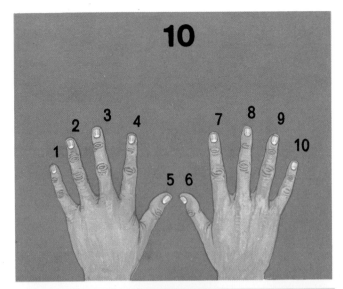

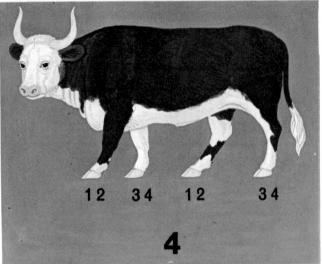

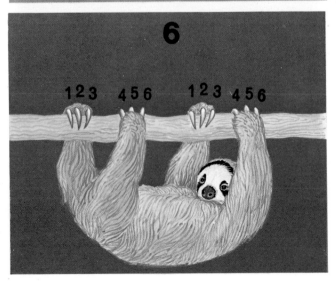

Why many primitive people only count up to twenty

Although a system of numbers based on our fingers and toes is in a certain sense the most convenient because the means of counting are always to hand, it can nevertheless be very limiting: in other words, there is a risk of never exceeding the number twenty.

This has happened among some backward peoples. The Australian aborigines, for example, usually count on the fingers and toes in this way; 1 = one finger, 2 = two fingers, 3 = three fingers, 4 = two fingers and two fingers, 5 = half the fingers or one hand, 6 = one hand and one finger, 10 = two hands, 15 = two hands and one foot, 20 = two hands and two feet. They inevitably stop at this point. To continue to count means to them to begin again from one and arrive once more at twenty.

Why the Babylonians were such good mathematicians

The civilization which developed in the area of the river Tigris and the river Euphrates reached its greatest splendour with the second Babylonian Empire about 2,500 years ago. At that time the Babylonians were distinguished from the other highly civilized nations around them by the intensive trading which they carried on.

Their foreign trade was perhaps the greatest factor which upheld the economy of the state. As they had no raw materials and widely used articles such as metals, timber, silk and spices, the Babylonians were forced to look for these things wherever they could be found. Trade on such a vast scale demanded a considerable knowledge of mathematics, and Babylonian merchants possessed this to a degree.

Early explorers trading with natives in North America

Why the Egyptians must have been good at geometry

Whenever we talk about ancient Egypt our thoughts immediately go to the huge buildings, the colossal monuments erected by the genius of this exceptional people. Pyramids, temples, sphinxes and obelisques could not be built by anyone who did not have an extensive knowledge of the laws of geometry.

The Egyptians were indeed surprisingly skilful in this science despite the fact that they had to rely for the necessary measurements on a system of calculation which was anything but rapid.

In the opinion of the Greek historian Herodotus (about 484 to 424 B.C.) who was well acquainted with Egyptian civilization, the origin of the study of geometry among this people is to be found in a colossal undertaking which was often repeated, that is the measuring of the land, and that is how this science got its name: geometry means measurement of the Earth.

Every Nile flood brought with it the benefit of very fertile mud but at the same time it also washed away all the boundary marks between the various properties and divisions of land. After every flood, therefore, it was necessary to repeat all the observations, measurements and divisions to restore things to their previous state.

From this very practical need to measure and remeasure the ground arose, it seems, the Egyptian interest in geometry. Measurement of the ground was connected with another very important factor, the payment of taxes which were based on the amount of land which a man possessed.

Ancient Egyptian instruments for measuring time. The ancient Egyptians were among the first people to recognize the need for measuring instruments of all kinds. The particular natural conditions in Egypt, where the Nile caused continual flooding, meant that they had constantly to recalculate the divisions of land and property.

Most of our figures were first used in India. The Arabs learnt of them at the end of the eighth century and in about 825 a small book appeared on the subject. This was translated into Latin by Abelard of Bath around 1120, and Arabic figures were introduced into European arithmetic during the Middle Ages.

The new method of counting, based on simple rules, produced not only cultural but also practical benefits because it facilitated trade and commerce.

Why nought is the most important numeral

The figure nought which we use with such ease and assurance was unknown among the ancients and was introduced only with the system of calculation devised by the Indians. It did not become known in Europe until about the twelfth century.

The symbol nought was soon recognized as more important than the other figures. With it, it is possible to indicate various mathematical situations, some of them very complex, for example in connection with decimals. First of all nought is used to indicate that in a whole there are no units. If, for example, there are not any balls in a box, we say that there are no balls. Nought is also the result of subtracting two equal numbers. By taking away three balls from a heap consisting of three balls, the result is no balls. Secondly the use of nought makes it possible to express any number, however large and complex, by means of the other nine numerals. The difference between our system of numbers and other systems which do not have a nought, as

Leonardo da Vinci; a great scientist and artist

Why we use Arabic numerals

The Arabs, Persians, Egyptians and Hindus have all claimed to be the originators of what we call Arabic numerals. But perhaps it was the traders who carried these symbols from one country to another so that our numbers came together from several different sources.

for instance that of the Romans, is clear.

The nought, like the other nine numerals, has more than one meaning. For example in the number 250 its value is quite different from that in the number 205 although exactly the same figures are used in both. In the Indo-Arabic system the value of a figure depends upon its position but only the nought has no numerical value but still has a positional value. The numeral nought has quite rightly been defined as a small number of enormous importance.

Why the human mind cannot understand the exact meaning of some numbers

If, after counting up to twenty, the Australian aborigine wishes to express a large number he merely says 'many'.

Confronted with the number 1,000 million many of us would begin to feel like the aborigine. Purely as a matter of curiosity if we wished to count 1,000 million pounds, pound by pound, it would take us seventy years.

What can be said, then, about a light year? That is, the distance travelled by light in 365 days. In round figures, light travels at a speed of 300,000 kilometres a second; in a year it travels nearly 10 million million kilometres; can anyone comprehend such a distance?

The human mind is very limited when it comes to understanding very high numbers. It is true that we continue to calculate them even when they indicate colossal amounts, but we do so in purely mathematical terms, without being able to understand their full implication.

Why we say that mathematicians are very absent-minded

The traditional belief that studious people in general and mathematicians in particular are very absent-minded is supported by numerous stories.

Perhaps it is because, in the olden days, the science of calculating was closely connected with astronomy, and when one is interested in the stars it is logical to walk along the street with one's face turned towards the sky. The image of a studious person lost in the clouds was given by Plato

The symbol for nought was introduced by the Indians, adopted by the Arabs, and transmitted to Europe

himself. He said that many an astronomer finished by falling into a well because of his habit of looking upwards.

A very famous episode is that about Newton who, wanting to boil an egg when his mind was taken up with calculations, put his watch into the boiling water and timed it with the egg in his hand.

Why among ancient peoples there was a great similarity in the way numbers were written

Man's ability to make calculations is certainly very old. For instance, barter, the primitive form of trading, required some form of calculation, however elementary.

According to some scientists, however, it seems that primitive man made longer calculations to signify the passage of the days and months. He cut notches in a tree trunk or stick, short ones for

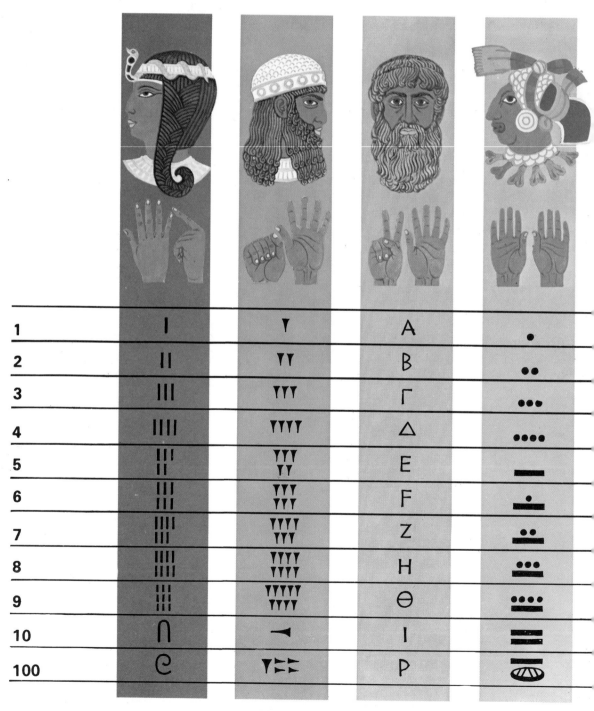

1	I	𒁹	A	•
2	II	𒁹𒁹	B	••
3	III	𒁹𒁹𒁹	Γ	•••
4	IIII	𒁹𒁹𒁹𒁹	Δ	••••
5	IIIII	𒐖	E	▬
6	IIIIII	𒐗	F	▬•
7	IIIIIII	𒐘	Z	▬••
8	IIIIIIII	𒐙	H	▬•••
9	IIIIIIIII	𒐚	Θ	▬••••
10	∩	◄	I	▬▬
100	ℓ	𒐕	P	◑

Egyptian, Babylonian, Greek and Mayan numerical systems

the days and long ones for the months. One notch indicated a day, two notches two days, and so on.

It appears that from these notches originated the strokes which were used for counting. One significant proof of this is that the symbols in use among different nations bear a great resemblance to one another.

The Egyptians, who had papyrus leaves to write on, used a genuine stroke, as also did the Romans, but the Babylonians, who had to write on clay tablets, made wedge-shaped marks. The Mayas, on the other hand, were more expeditious and used dots.

Why the Romans could not do complicated calculations

Roman numerals, which are still in use for certain purposes, were rather rudimentary and perhaps that is why the Romans, who were very advanced in certain respects, were certainly no good at mathematics.

There were two great difficulties which they had to overcome in calculating: the somewhat complicated method of writing the signs and the lack of the figure nought. It is quite incomprehensible to us how they could ever carry out a simple multiplication such as 58 times 234. A task like this, which does not present any great difficulty to a school child, must have been rather complicated for them. For instance, the number 58 was written thus: LVIII, and the number 234: CCXXXIV.

Finally the lack of a nought among their figures complicated matters enormously.

It is a significant fact that although experts in the subject are able to explain quite clearly the Roman system of numerals they are quite unable to explain how calculations were done, particularly complicated ones with high numbers.

Why we can say that animals are able to count

It may seem rather strange to say that animals are able to count, but some interesting experiments have been carried out in this connection.

For instance a hen was fixed in such a way as to be able to peck and grains of corn were arranged in lines on a sheet of cardboard. The odd grains (1, 3, 5, etc.) were free but the even ones (2, 4, 6, etc.) were fixed firmly to the cardboard. In a very short time the hen learned to ignore the even grains and to peck contentedly only at the odd ones, one after the other. The experiment was varied by placing a free grain in every third position and the hen soon learned this lesson also. The same occurred with three and then four grains between the free ones. It was only after this that the bird became uncertain.

The number five may possibly be the limit to which the birds can count.

Crows never return to their nests if there is anyone near them. A hut was built near a crow's nest and a man went into it. The crow did not return until the man had left. Two men went in and the bird would not return until both of them left. This went on up to five, after which the bird became confused.

The Feast of Herod by Israel van Meckenem

Why there are seven musical notes

Music based on the seven notes of the diatonic scale is only about a thousand years old. It was in fact invented by Guido d'Arezzo, a Benedictine monk who was extremely fond of sacred music and who lived from about 990 to 1050.

Until that time there were no real musical notes as such but only signs called neumes which means accents. They were used in singing to indicate the syllables on which the voice had to be raised or lowered.

The suggestion which led to the invention of notes was taken by Brother Guido from a Latin hymn dedicated to St. John. This hymn was composed of verses all of which began with a sound higher than the preceeding one. Guido used the syllables with which these verses commenced to construct the succession of sounds which we now know as the musical scale.

Here are the verses: *UTque laxis, REsonare fibris, MIra gestorum, FAmuli tuorum, SOLve polluti, LAbii reatum.* Later the UT was changed to DO and the seventh note TE was added.

A harpist from an Egyptian wall painting

Why there is a difference between solar time and sidereal time

We all know that the Earth moves in two distinct ways: one of revolution around the Sun and the other of rotation on its own axis. The first movement takes nearly 365 days and 6 hours and the second takes 24 hours.

There is a difference, however, between the solar day and the sidereal day. The solar day is calculated by measuring the time it takes the Earth to make one complete rotation around its axis, using the Sun as the point of reference. This time is exactly 24 hours. As each hour consists of 60 minutes and each minute of 60 seconds we can also say that a day is a period of 1,440 minutes or 86,400 seconds.

However, if instead of using the Sun as our point of reference we used a remote star, we would see that the Earth takes exactly 86,164 seconds for one complete rotation (sidereal time).

How can we explain this difference of 236 seconds? By the fact that while the Earth is completing one full rotation, it has moved a short distance on its journey around the Sun, to be precise 236 seconds.

Why our calendar is called Gregorian

The calendar which we use today is named after Pope Gregory XIII who reformed the Julian calendar then in existence. This reckoned the year at 365 days and 6 hours, which created an extra day every four years (leap year). However, more exact calculations established that the solar year was 365 days, 5 hours, 49 minutes and 46 seconds.

This discrepancy of 11 minutes and 14 seconds meant that ten days had been lost by 1582, and so Gregory directed that October 15th should follow October 4th to make up the time. Portugal, Spain, France and various Italian states adopted the new calendar in 1582. It was not until 1752 that Britain adopted Gregory's calendar, whilst Russia did not alter until 1917.

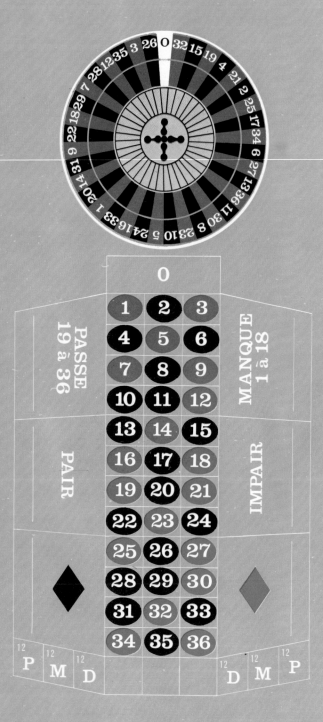

A standard European roulette board employing one zero

Why many houses have meters

Few houses today are without electricity and gas. The user of these services has to pay, in addition to a fixed charge, an amount based on the quantity of electricity or gas actually consumed.

Automatic meters are fitted in the houses to measure the amount used by the consumer. For instance, whenever you turn on the gas the meter is operated by the flow of the gas through the pipes. The flow turns a special counter which progressively adds up the amount of gas used. A similar thing happens with electricity. Special inspectors call at every house and read these meters. The value of the amount which has been consumed is then worked out and a bill sent to the consumer.

The consumption of water can also be measured in this way, and this can be very important in places where there is little rainfall, and the supply of water is limited.

Why it is difficult to win at roulette

Roulette is a gambling game played in the casinos of Europe and North and South America.

Those who organize casinos are well aware of the theory of probabilities whilst the players seldom or never know much about it; also the bank or casino is able to guard against surprises by various devices.

Let us take a look at a roulette table with its numbers up to thirty-six, that is eighteen black numbers and eighteen red ones, plus nought.

Suppose that we exploit only

the pairs of probabilities: evens and odds, red or black, high or low. To begin with these probabilities are not exactly equal because of the figure nought, one of the devices mentioned, because if the nought comes up everything not on nought is lost except for the even numbers which remain valid for the next turn.

What are the chances of a particular number coming up, including nought? Twice in seventy-four turns, equal to thirty-seven losses, thirty-six wins and one returned. This seems quite an advantage to the player but that small margin is enough to guarantee the bank against surprise.

Why graphs are used

Numbers have always been very useful instruments of human progress but sometimes a great deal of ability and analysis is required to interpret them.

To make certain mathematical and geometrical situations comprehensible to ordinary people without the use of numbers, we use graphs. As the world indicates these are drawings which show in diagram form the stages of an operation, the ratios of a quantity, and so on.

Here are two examples.

If the sales of a business are increasing, the situation will be shown graphically by an oblique sloping line on a background of squares (linear graph).

To give a visual idea of the comparative parts which make up a substance, a circle is drawn divided into segments of different sizes in relation to the amounts they represent (circular graph).

Why computers are necessary in modern war

When weapons were very simple man could use them without the need for any special apparatus. This is no longer the case today when their speed and complexity make automation essential.

Let us take the example of an aerial attack. Two radars follow simultaneously the movements of the enemy supersonic bomber and of the ground-to-air missile launched against it. The signals picked up by the two radars are fed into an electronic computer which works them out and communicates the details of the missile's course to a transmitter which is guiding the missile on to the target.

All this takes place simultaneously, within a split second. How could a man calculate at such speed?

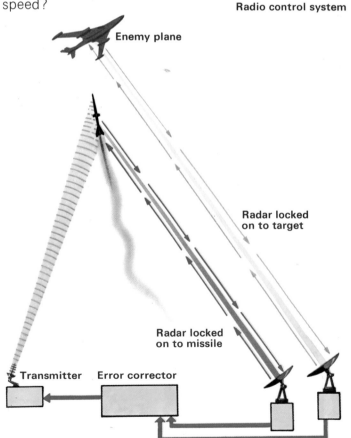

Radio control system

Enemy plane

Radar locked on to target

Radar locked on to missile

Transmitter　　Error corrector

THE WHY OF SCIENCE AND TECHNOLOGY

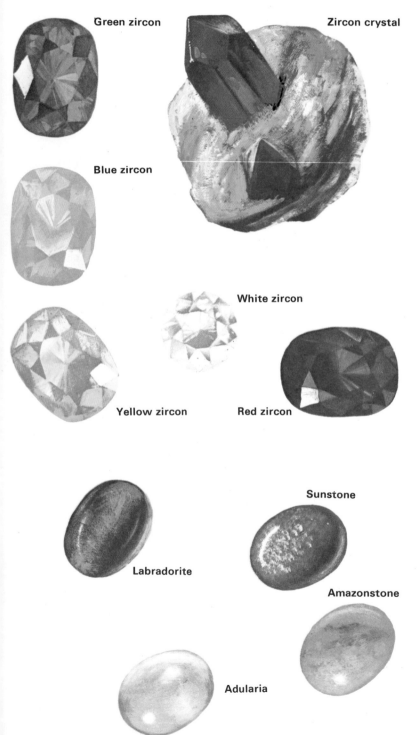

Green zircon

Zircon crystal

Blue zircon

White zircon

Yellow zircon

Red zircon

Sunstone

Labradorite

Amazonstone

Adularia

Why the last two centuries were so important for scientific progress

In the past 150 years the rate of human progress has increased enormously. There is not a single field of science and technology that has not been examined, extended or revised by the large-scale developments which have taken place during the past two centuries.

This phenomenon has caused a psychological reaction among the public in general which in one sense may appear natural but in another sense is quite astonishing; that is the easy acceptance of new things, however unexpected and amazing they may be.

During the past few years and particularly since the conquest of the Moon, people no longer marvel at anything and show scarcely any interest in the ever-increasing flood of inventions. They are convinced that now nothing is impossible to the human mind with its ability to overcome all obstacles and solve all difficulties.

It will depend upon man's capacity for making the best use of the world's natural resources whether we shall have a peaceful life in future, but it will depend even more upon his wisdom whether these resources are to be used for the real progress of man and not for the total destruction of man and his environment.

Why airships are no longer used

As a means of transport airships had their golden age in the early decades of this century, although they originated some fifty years before. It seemed that they might develop to such an extent as to be able to compete with sea transport. But the sudden and tremendous disaster (36 dead) which struck a giant Zeppelin on 6 May 1937 marked the abrupt end of airships, the so-called lighter-than-air machines.

The reason for such a rapid disappearance, which is rare in the world of modern technology, was due to two factors: the lack of safety and the slow speed. Modern aeroplanes offer greater safety and incomparable speed.

Airships built for special purposes appear to have come back again in recent years but it is extremely unlikely that they will ever again be used for passenger transport.

Why in future we shall have to purify sea water

The life of modern man calls for an ever increasing consumption of water. To take one example from industry: to build a single motorcar needs two and a half million litres of water. The situation is just as surprising with regard to food: the maize plant absorbs an average of 200 litres of water for every kilo of seed it produces; for a loaf of bread 3,000 litres of water are required.

Moreover, the world water reserves are continually decreasing: for instance, glaciers are tending to retreat and glaciers are nature's reserves of fresh water.

The comfortable interior of the Graf Zeppelin

In contrast to the shortage of water and the increasing demand for it there is the enormous amount of water to be found in the oceans and seas.

There is, therefore, a pressing need to purify sea water. One actual example is Kuwait, where all the fresh water used is obtained by distillation of sea water.

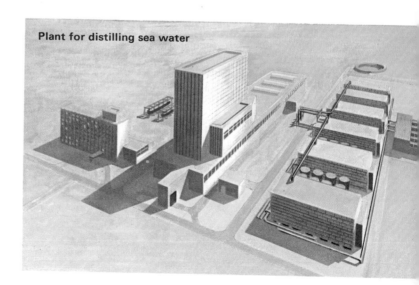

Plant for distilling sea water

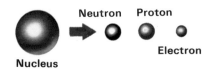

If the nucleus of an atom measured about 1 centimetre in diameter, the whole atom would have a diameter of about 180 metres

All materials whether organic or inorganic are made up of atoms

Why the atom is so important in our everyday lives

Everything which exists in nature, all living creatures and non-living things on the Earth, are composed of atoms.

These tiny particles, infinitely small as they are (their diameter is one hundred millionth part of a centimetre), are of astounding vitality. Each atom is composed of a central nucleus of protons and neutrons around which electrons circle continuously.

Modern science has made a discovery which is destined to have enormous consequences in the life of man. It has been able to split the atom, an action which used to be considered absolutely impossible.

The immediate effect of splitting the atom is the release of the energy it contains. It is therefore possible to obtain energy in colossal quantities by bombarding atoms.

To get some idea, however approximate, of the importance of this phenomenon, let us take just one example: the energy obtained by the breaking down of one kilo of Uranium 235 is equal to that which would be obtained by burning 6 million tons of coal.

The very complex apparatus needed to produce atomic energy is called a nuclear reactor. There are many of these now functioning very well in several countries of the world and more are being built. The electrical energy which they produce is used in a thousand different ways to the benefit of mankind.

Some large naval units are also now driven by atomic energy. Complicated apparatus for distilling sea water also works through nuclear reactors. Many electric power stations convert nuclear energy into electrical energy.

Radio-active isotopes are widely employed in medicine, agriculture and industry. By their help ways are being discovered of fighting disease, substances useful for human nutrition are being discovered and machines are being built of high technical precision and outstanding performance.

Why quasars are studied

Scientists at the Mount Palomar astronomical observatory in the United States recently made an extraordinary discovery: they identified the quasars or quasi-stellar radio sources. These are types of stars which emit radio waves and which can be observed by this means even though they are far beyond the range of optical telescopes. In fact, they are calculated to be many millions of light years from Earth. They produce a vast amount of energy compared to their small size.

(top) *Quasar* 3C 273

Why radio telescopes are better for observing the most distant stars

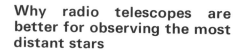

(bottom) The radiotelescope at Jodrell Bank

Technical and scientific progress first made available to man instruments such as the telescope which enabled astronomers to bring the heavenly bodies nearer and study them more closely.

About forty years ago astronomical science discovered that it is possible to observe the distant universe even beyond the range of the most powerful optical telescopes, even as far as several millions of light years from Earth. What they discovered was, in fact, that many stars relatively near to us, such as the Sun, and many very remote ones send out special radio waves.

To collect these waves and analyse them to obtain precise information is the task of the radio telescopes, that is telescopes which observe by radio the remotest forms of stellar activity. This has increased to an enormous extent the scope of astronomical discovery.

Why the first cars had solid tyres

When a technical discovery is made and something new is produced it is based logically upon ideas and materials which already exist.

This is what happened to the motor car. At first it was really a coach in which the engine replaced the horse as the motive power. It had the same shape, the same hood, the same cover, the same steps for getting in and out and, of course, the same wheels and the same solid tyres.

The reason for the solid tyres is simply that pneumatic tyres had not yet been invented. They were invented by John Boyd Dunlop, a Belfast veterinary surgeon, in the year 1887. It was a rubber tube containing compressed air for the purpose of mitigating the shocks the vehicle received on the roads which in those days were particularly rough. Pneumatic tyres were first invented for bicycles but were very soon fitted to every type of vehicle, except, of course, trains.

Why balloons must have means of rising and descending quickly

The force of ascension of balloons is given, in accordance with the principle of Archimedes, by the difference between the weight of the mass of air displaced by the envelope and the weight of the gas contained in the balloon. Balloons are in fact lighter-than-air machines. Whilst it is relatively easy to make these machines rise, it is very difficult to control them when they are in flight. To make them rise or descend at the wish of the pilot is sometimes a rather tricky undertaking. During navigation balloons are subjected to uncontrollable forces. For instance condensation of water vapour or ice may form on the envelope, there may be escapes of gas or gusts of wind. In these circumstances, to ascend or descend may mean the difference between safety and mortal danger for the crew. Methods have therefore been studied to allow quick changes of height. Two devices are of particular importance: a rip cord on the balloon to provide quick release of gas in case of emergency, and a load of ballast, usually sand, which can be jettisoned to lighten the machine and cause it to rise.

Why James Watt was a pioneer of the industrial age

The steam engine originated in England early in the eighteenth century.

At that time two patents were taken out for atmospheric pressure steam engines but their use was confined to pumping water and they had a number of working faults.

It was left to James Watt, a Scottish instrument maker, to perfect the steam engine by a device which was both simple and decisive: the condenser ensured that the steam engine could continue to run without loss of pressure. After much experiment Watt patented his improvements in 1769.

From that moment the most varied applications of steam engines to industrial machines became possible.

In 1781 Watt built the first large scale steam engine which he later improved still further.

Why the first trains were drawn by steam engines

The first types of true motor cars were steam engines applied to vehicles. This fact alone would not have guaranteed them against competition by other kinds of motors if, as far as the railways are concerned, locomotives had not immediately proved to be such powerful and practical engines able to meet any demand. Even the most sceptical individuals were soon convinced. In forty years England had passed from the few kilometres of the Liverpool-Manchester railway of 1830 to almost 22,000 kilometres in 1870.

No other engine could compete with the steam engine although as early as 1879 the first electric locomotive had appeared but it was very small. The first English electric railway was opened on 3 August 1883. However steam engines dominated the scene for many years and are still in use on some railways.

Why electrical charges form in the sky

The clouds which mass in the sky before a storm become charged with electricity through passing over strata of air at different temperatures. As a general rule positive charges prevail at high cloud levels and negative charges at low levels.

When the heavily charged

clouds descend towards the Earth, the latter, through the phenomenon of induction, becomes charged with electricity of opposite sign. Two electromagnetic fields, often of very great extent, are thus formed. At this point the negative charges are strongly impelled to discharge towards the positive charges, because opposite charges attract one another. However the air offers a strong obstacle to the passage of electrical charges as

it is not a good conductor of electricity. It undergoes a rapid process of ionization which creates conditions which permit the passage of electricity. An infinity of minute electrical charges erupt through the ionized zones in perfect and rapid succession but we see them as one long, forked and twisted discharge. We call it lightning.

Lightning passes not only from the clouds to the Earth, but also in the opposite direction, and goes, too, from cloud to cloud, although this is rare. It is often followed by that other phenomenon, thunder.

Why electricity is transmitted at high tension

The use of electricity has reached enormous proportions. Consequently there arose a need to transport electricity to ever greater distances. This raised a serious problem. Direct current had to be transmitted at the output voltage of the dynamo which produced it, but because of the electrical resistance of the wires along which it passed there was a considerable drop in the voltage after a short distance. This meant that some of the power was lost along the way. It was not possible to reduce the resistance by increasing the thickness of the wire as this would have made the wires impossibly large and heavy.

To overcome these losses, the use of alternating current was introduced, as alternating current can be transported at the desired high voltages.

As the loss of power of electrical energy during its passage along wires is caused by the amount of current and as the carrying potential is equal to the current multiplied by the tension, we are

312

able by increasing the tension to transport large amounts of current using relatively thin wires.

At the points where the electricity is to be used suitable transformers are connected to reduce the voltage to a less dangerous level, such as 240 volts which is normal for domestic use in Britain.

Why electric current does not pass from the wires to the metal pylons

The huge pylons which carry the electric cables are a normal sight today. These pylons are made of steel and are able to carry high tension electric cables without themselves being affected by the current.

This is due to special insulators. One of these for use with high tension is the bell-shaped insulator. It is made of tempered glass or porcelain and is used in series of ten or more. The various insulators are fitted with metal connecting bolts and hooks for fastening at the top to the pylon brackets and at the bottom to the conducting cable.

Because of the way it is built the series of bell insulators is able to yield to the force of the wind without any risk of damage to the cables. The insulators are fitted with special arresters which absorb the effects of any lightning that may strike the line. As the dust which settles on the insulators could, if covered with rain water, become a conductor of electricity, each insulator has special collars fitted in such a way as to increase the distance for any possible short circuits.

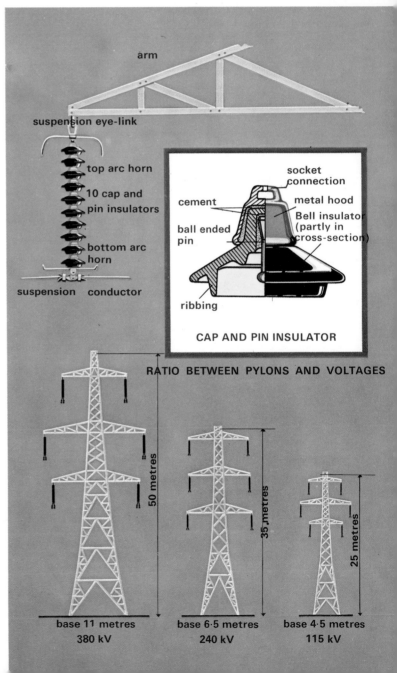

arm

suspension eye-link

top arc horn

10 cap and pin insulators

bottom arc horn

suspension   conductor

socket connection

cement

metal hood

ball ended pin

Bell insulator (partly in cross-section)

ribbing

CAP AND PIN INSULATOR

RATIO BETWEEN PYLONS AND VOLTAGES

50 metres

35 metres

25 metres

base 11 metres
380 kV

base 6·5 metres
240 kV

base 4·5 metres
115 kV

Why trains need rails

Trains were born on rails and still continue to run on them. This association of trains and rails is due to the way in which trains evolved.

In both the days of horse-drawn vehicles and steam engines the great need was to eliminate friction as much as possible. The growth of the railways and the increased traffic on them increased the importance of the rails which made the railways a safe, fast and comfortable means of travel.

There has been steady and constant progress from cast-iron rails, which wore out very quickly, to iron rails and finally to steel rails.

Today the rails are manufactured in long lengths and are connected together in such a way that the rumbling which used to be a feature of the old rails has been removed.

Why automatic signals are used on the railways

With the ever increasing speeds of the trains and the continued development of the tracks it became necessary to have a system of distant signals, both day and night, which could give a guarantee of safety. That is why the light and sound signals which we know today were installed.

But to make railway travel safer, it was soon realized that it was necessary to provide the railways with an automatic signalling system, both in the stations and on the trains. Indeed, when you think of the number of trains which are dealt with by the large stations, the complexity of the instruments on modern railways and natural difficulties such as fog, landslides and avalanches, you can see how essential an automatic signalling system must be.

Why it is possible to break the sound barrier

You have probably all heard the characteristic noise like an explosion which a jet plane makes when it crosses the sound barrier.

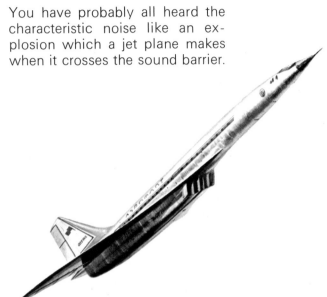

Why aircraft are able to fly

Man has always dreamed of being able to fly but it was not until quite recent times that this dream was fulfilled, first by lighter-than-air machines such as balloons and airships, and then by heavier-than-air machines or aeroplanes driven by airscrews or jet engines. Aeroplanes are able to leave the ground because they can overcome the force of the Earth's gravity. It does not matter whether they are propeller driven or jet machines; what does matter is that the thrust must be great enough to overcome the force of gravity. If, for instance, during flight the engine of an aeroplane stalls and the propulsion ceases, the plane will then fall to the ground.

Flight is therefore movement; immobility is not permitted for heavier-than-air machines.

Before the invention of jet propelled planes no aeroplane had the power to do this.

The sound barrier is a natural obstacle which consists of a sudden marked increase in the resistance of the air to the passage of an aeroplane when it reaches the speed of sound, that is 332 metres a second.

Such resistance increases with increased speed. When the speed approaches that of sound the resistance becomes very great. The indication that the resistance has been overcome is the explosive sound mentioned above.

After this phase the air resistance falls suddenly even when the speed of the plane continues to increase.

It has only been possible to break the sound barrier as a result of technological and scientific progress which have provided stronger materials and improved instrumentation.

THE WHERE OF EUROPE

Where you can find the most densely populated state

There are thirty-four states which together make up the whole of Europe; and one of these alone, the U.S.S.R., is so big that, even without its Asiatic part, it covers one half of Europe. Of the others, seven are minute: in descending order they are Luxembourg, Andorra, Malta, Lichtenstein, San Marino, Monaco and the Vatican City.

Of these seven, Monaco holds an extraordinary record; it is one of the most densely populated states in the world. Its territory occupies an area of approximately one and a half square kilometres and its population of about 25,000 averages 17,000 people to every square kilometre. No other state in Europe is as thickly populated as this piece of land set on the Côte d'Azur which with its beauty and temperate climate has become an ideal holiday resort.

In addition to its natural beauty, the Principality of Monaco also boasts cultural attractions. The Museum of Oceanography is renowned for its unique collection: very rare, stuffed marine animals; ancient boats; fishing nets of extraordinary size and shape; and every other object which can be related to sea life. The Museum also possesses a beautiful aquarium which houses a splendid selection of marine fauna.

Where shrews live

Shrews are tiny animals which live in moist places in the woods, burrowing into leaf mould in search of their food.

These creatures are often mistaken for mice and yet there are many differences between the two: shrews have a longer snout which juts out beyond the lower lip, and an extremely sharp set of teeth, whereas mice have chisel-like teeth. Furthermore, a shrew has a long, supple tail almost as long as its body, and on its side it has a gland which emits a strong, rather repellant, musky smell which is a means of defence against its enemies.

In spite of their small physique, shrews are ferocious, carnivorous animals, capable of attacking prey larger than themselves. They feed mainly on insects, snails, worms and small mammals and are very active, eating almost continuously.

Where you can find the cork-oak tree

Cork, a material used mainly for bottle-stoppers, insulation and floor coverings, is produced from a special type of evergreen oak

tree which grows, sometimes wild, in the coastal regions of the Mediterranean.

The cork-oak has a thick, dark foliage, formed from noded branches, covered with tough, oval leaves which are small and slightly jagged.

Its thick, tall trunk is completely wrapped in an outer bark of cork which is covered with fine brown grooves. The tree is first stripped of its cork, which will be rather hard and knobbly, when it is about sixteen years old. It is then stripped again every nine to ten years, depending on its location, and each time it will produce a good, light cork just over three centimetres thick.

After about 150 years, these trees cease to produce good quality cork and they are then felled.

Where you can find the land of fiords

Inlets, gulfs, indented coastlines can all be found along every coast of Europe and the other continents. The most characteristic, however, are the fiords of the Norwegian coasts and the Polar, Arctic and Antarctic regions.

These are long, narrow arms of the sea, usually extending far inland. They reach depths of more than 100 metres, and some far exceed this; Sognefjord in Norway, for example, is about 1,320 metres deep. Sometimes they have been called 'marine rivers'.

During the Quaternary Era, in the north-western part of the Scandinavian mountains, glaciers thrust down into the sea, and as time went on they carved deep U-shaped valleys in the rocks. The waters of the sea invaded these valleys, forming inlets known as fiords.

Today it is estimated that there are about 1,700 glaciers in Norway and some are still forcing their way ahead until they touch the sea.

The megalithic monument, Stonehenge, near Salisbury. It was built around 1800–1400 B.C.

Where you can find Megalithic monuments

Of all the monuments that the ancient inhabitants of the Earth have left behind as proof of their civilization, the stark magnificence of such constructions as the Egyptian pyramids are often the most striking.

In Great Britain we have typical examples of unadorned monuments, which can be traced back to the Neolithic Age, in the so-called 'henges'. These are circular in form and consist of vast stone blocks arranged in groups. They are surrounded by a bank and beyond this a circular ditch broken by entrance gaps. They can be found in the north of England and in Scotland, but the place most famous for its prehistoric monuments is Stonehenge.

Where you can find the land of the tulips

The tulip is undoubtedly one of the best known and most popular flowers in the world. Its vivid colours and the simple lines make it a small masterpiece, much prized in both gardens and homes.

The ancient origin of the tulip is unknown, but we have much information on its introduction into Europe. It was the Turks who brought this flower to the West some 400 years ago. The name tulip means 'turban' which the flower is thought to resemble.

There is probably no other flower which has been given such an enthusiastic welcome or spread so quickly throughout Europe. Within the space of a few years, the craze for tulips grew into 'Tulipomania', reaching its height in Holland.

Certain rare varieties fetched astronomical prices: by 1610 some tulip bulbs were worth as much as an ale-house or a mill. One bulb was paid for with a new carriage, complete with two horses, another was exchanged for 12 acres of land. Materials and lace were decorated with designs of tulips. This craze lasted for almost half a century.

Although indigenous to hot countries, the tulip also adapts well to colder climates. Today, Holland is universally renowned as the homeland of the tulip. The Dutch became the prime cultivators of this flower which through four centuries of acclimatization in Europe has undergone certain transformations which have given it the structure and colour we know today.

Where the lynx was seen again in Europe

The lynx is a large, wild, feline animal found in many parts of central Europe. It has unusually large paws, a mottled tawny to cream coat and a black-tipped tail.

The lynx lived in the Alps until half a century ago: the last time this creature is known to have been captured was at the beginning of this century, near Chieri in Piedmont. The animal has not been heard of since.

It is more likely to be the clearance of all trees from the mountains which has caused its disappearance than the fact that it has been hunted down. A deer which had been completely ravaged as if by a lynx, was recently found in a Swiss forest, where there were also impressions in the fresh snow which scientists have identified as tracks typical of this feline creature.

It is thought that, in a few years time, the lynx may reappear on the slopes of the Italian Alps. It usually lives in dense forests where it can find its favourite prey, the roe-buck and the stag.

Where you can find the valley of the temples

Beside the town of Agrigento in Sicily is the valley of the temples where, in the days of the Magna Graecia, the people erected sanctuaries in honour of their gods.

'Fairest of mortal cities' as the Greek poet, Pindar, described it, Agrigento was one of the richest and most beautiful towns of ancient times. It was founded in 582 B.C. by settlers from Rhodes and Crete and by others who came from nearby Gela. The region was rich in grain, oil, wine and cattle; as the years went by the town added to its wealth by constructing a spacious boundary wall and magnificent buildings, including some splendid temples.

Very soon, however, its power clashed with that of the Carthaginians. Strongly fortified and allied with the people of Syracuse, Agrigento defeated the Carthaginians in the famous battle of Himera (480 B.C.).

Most of Agrigento's art treasures were destroyed when it was sacked in 406 B.C. during the wars between the Romans and the Carthaginians.

Where you can find the smallest state in the world

Covering an area of less than half a square kilometre the Vatican City is the smallest state in the world.

Approximately half of its territory is occupied by famous constructions: the Basilica of St Peter standing at the head of a large square which is encompassed by Bernini's magnificent colonnade; the Vatican palaces, the residence of the Pope; the Vatican museums, rich in works of art; and the Sistine Chapel. In the remaining area are gardens, shops, squares, a railway station and an astronomical observatory.

St Peter's, with its famous dome by Michelangelo

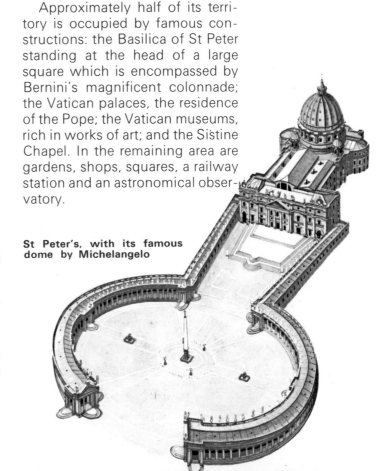

Where the brown bear lives

A bad-tempered, unsociable type of person is often said to be 'grizzly' like a bear. The bear is, in fact, a solitary, irascible animal which shuns not only the presence of human beings but even avoids close proximity with his own fellow-creatures. It is difficult to find two bears together, except of course for a couple with their offspring.

There was a time when bears were inhabitants of all Eurasian countries as they adapted well to all climates, although they preferred rigorous weather conditions.

Today, the areas of Europe in which the bear has survived are greatly reduced in both number and size. In particular the brown bear now lives in some of the valleys of the Alps (the Genoa valley and the Tovel valley) in the Pyrenees and the Carpathians.

This bear is of a considerable size, although it is not as large as the polar bear or the grizzly bear of Alaska. It can reach a length of nearly 2 metres and a weight of 150 kilogrammes, although the race from eastern Siberia is almost as large as the grizzly bear.

Where you can find crocodiles in Europe

Outside the tropical and sub-tropical regions crocodiles can only be found today in museums and zoological gardens, but in distant times the crocodile also lived in Europe, mostly in the Mediterranean basin.

In the days of the great dinosaurs some land masses such as the Italian peninsula had not yet emerged from the seas, but large islands, surrounded by cliffs which were forming vast lagoons, were surging up around the Alps and the Pre-Alps. The climate was very much hotter than it is today, as a result of which the vegetation was similar to that which is now found in the islands of the South.

There were extensive forests of palm trees and other tropical plants, and a great variety of reptiles crawled through the undergrowth which was teeming with insects. Gigantic turtles periodically crossed the narrow straits of the sea; large serpents, similar to the boa which is today an inhabitant of America, climbed lazily along the branches of the trees; numerous crocodiles were waiting to pounce on any prey which rashly approached the banks of the sea.

As evidence that these crocodiles once lived in Europe, there still exist fossils which can be seen in Bolca in the province of Verona in Italy. In those far off times, Bolca was a lagoon island. Fortunately, the plants and animals populating this island were preserved in a very fine slush which turned to stone; they became fossilized and have reached us today in excellent condition. Amongst these fossils there are some of ancient crocodiles.

Where the ancient town of Spina once stood

In the delta of the river Po, about 7 kilometres west of modern Comacchio, the remains of an imposing cemetery have been found. These have been attributed to the town of Spina which was once situated in that area.

Excavations began in 1922 when drainage of the land unearthed the remains of nearly 2,000 tombs dating back to the sixth century B.C. Many bronzes and a large collection of Greek pottery were discovered.

The town of Spina was the meeting point of two great pre-Roman civilizations, the Grecian and the Etruscan. It was founded as a result of the Etruscan advance into northern Italy at the end of the sixth century B.C. and became a commercial centre for the market of products which had been brought across the Adriatic from Greece. Considered by Hellenic writers as a true Greek town, it was also an important Etruscan centre and, together with nearby Adria and Ravenna, it gave the Etruscans of northern Italy access to the sea.

Spina was a frontier town, born on the spot where there had once been an indigenous village. Its position gave it great importance, from both a commercial and a cultural point of view. A large colony of Greek merchants resided in the town and they were undoubtedly responsible for mingling Greek with Etruscan culture. This brought Italy spiritually closer to the Greek world. This town was, therefore, more than a large market market place: it was a crossroads of civilizations. Soon after 400 B.C. it was sacked by the Gauls and its importance rapidly declined.

Where you can find the home of the bagpipes

Every land is justly proud of its own customs, traditions and products which reveal its individual character.

This is the case with Scotland, which for centuries has been famous for its kilts, bagpipes and whisky as well as for the beauty of its scenery and the history of its people.

Pipers were always part of the regular retinue of the Highland chieftains, and frequently handed on their office from one generation to another. The clan piper still takes an important part in Highland festivities, funerals and other formal occasions. There is a piper at the royal castle of Balmoral and pipers are attached to all the Highland regiments.

It is because of the Scots' love of tradition that processions of pipers are so popular today. Their distinctive dress with the tartan kilts showing the clan to which they belong, are familiar sights on ceremonial occasions.

To play the bagpipes, the piper blows into a tube so that his breath inflates an airtight leather bag. From this bag the air proceeds through three wooden pipes which contain reeds of fixed tone, called drones. It then goes through another reeded pipe, the chanter, which produces the melody.

When playing the piper has the drones over his left shoulder, the bag tucked under his left arm and he holds the chanter with his fingers.

A variety of music, especially marches and dances, have been composed for the bagpipes. Until recently it was written down in a notation of its own, but now ordinary musical notation is used.

Where you can find the fish which produce caviar

The sturgeon, a shark-like, bony fish, is caught mainly for its flesh, which is sold fresh, pickled or smoked, and its eggs, more commonly known as caviar.

It prefers the waters of temperate or cold areas and can be found only in the Northern Hemisphere.

During the breeding season in early summer, large shoals of sturgeon swim into the rivers or towards the shores of freshwater lakes. In Europe sturgeon occur from Scandinavia to the Mediterranean and, in particular, several species are found in the Caspian Sea and the Black Sea.

Where you can find forests full of beech trees

In parts of western Asia and all Europe as far as southern England, beech trees can be found growing in gardens and large avenues.

There are many different kinds of beech, including the dark-leaved copper beech and the weeping beech, often to be seen in parks.

The best beeches are found in chalky soil, some of them reaching from about 30 to 45 metres high. Many were first planted in the eighteenth century on huge estates.

The timber of the beech is heavy and hard and is extremely useful as firewood. It also has many other uses and is especially noted for making fine furniture and all sorts of different wooden articles.

Where the edelweiss grows

Is it true that these splendid flowers only grow on the face of a steep, rocky mountain, facing an abyss, in a virtually inaccessible place?

So many mishaps have befallen the inexperienced mountaineers whose desire to pick an edelweiss has driven them up to the top, that many imagine that this flower only grows on impossible mountain peaks.

In actual fact, the edelweiss grows wherever the soil is calcareous, at an altitude of more than 1,500 metres, and it can also be found at a lower altitude, in the valleys. In certain areas, at more than 2,000 metres, which are rarely visited by man, it is possible to find these flowers growing in open spaces, among the grass.

In easily reached places, however, this flower has been almost completely destroyed by excessive gathering. This is why the edelweiss now only inhabits the almost inaccessible and dangerous parts of the mountain.

This plant can be cultivated in rock gardens and, given ideal conditions, it will produce a very large corolla. It also grows in open country but here its petals tend to lose their hairy protection and assume a greenish colour.

Where you can find a land full of windmills

Since ancient times man has exploited the forces of nature in an effort to obtain from them the greatest possible aid for his work. One of these forces is the wind: caught in the sails of a boat or used for turning the sails of a windmill, it is the workman's oldest tool and a help to human labours.

Today, the country famous throughout the world for its windmills is Holland, a flat, windy country whose people have the reputation of being among the most industrious and enterprising in the world.

For many centuries the characteristic towers of the windmills have made the countryside of the Low Countries quite unmistakable. These windmills have varying forms: rounded and slightly conical, prismatic, pretty, decorative or unadorned. All of them, however, are positioned so as to receive the greatest force of the wind: the sails, which a breath of air will put in motion, rise over them all.

In Holland, windmills are used more for lifting water than for milling grain. In order to drain the land, they are used to pass water from one canal to another and it is in this way that a country which has always been at war with water manages to maintain hydraulic balance.

The commercial centre at Rotterdam

Where you can find the remains of ancient human settlements in northern Europe

The most ancient settlers came to northern Europe between 5000 and 4000 B.C. in the Neolithic Age and established themselves in the regions which today correspond to Poland and Germany.

The Danubian culture reached Germany and the Netherlands and was widespread at about 4000

Neolithic shelter, Norway

B.C. The people lived in fairly large villages of rectangular timber houses. Remains have been found of their pottery, decorated with incised spiral patterns.

The Ellerbek culture, as it became known, flourished at a later date and there exist many interesting items belonging to this period: wooden hoes, vases with a conical base and ceramic oil lamps.

Another Neolithic culture in Europe is the one characterized by its beakers with funnel necks which, in 3500 B.C., spread from Holland as far as Poland.

Where you can find the most famous natural grottoes in Europe

The celebrated grottoes of Postojna are situated in a karst field in West Slovenia, Yugoslavia. Tortuous galleries, caves, magnificent rooms richly decorated with stalagtites and stalagmites stretch for nearly 30 kilometres. It is here that the river Pivka flows along in one of the most fantastic sub-

The remains of a cremation from the Iron Age, found in Finland

terranean beds in the world.

The grottoes of Postojna have been famous since 1213: engraved in one wall you can read the signatures of people who visited the grottoes as long ago as 1250. But the caves were unknown in modern times until 1818.

Today, tourists can visit the caves in a small electrified railway. Among the most celebrated are the Concert Hall, the Ballroom and the Paradise Grotto.

324

Where Palladio's art is supreme

The most famous architect of the Renaissance is Andrea di Pietro, named Palladio by his patron, Trissino.

Born in Padua in 1508, he spent most of his working life in Vicenza. After lengthy preparation in Rome, he planned and built his first great monumental work: the town hall in Vicenza, known as the Basilica. Here Palladio erected a two-storey arcade of white stone around three sides of the mediaeval Hall of Reason (Sala della Ragione).

Also in Vicenza, he designed the Loggia del Capitano which remained incomplete and the Teatro Olimpico which was constructed after his death.

His work on private buildings was of even greater renown; his villas and palaces are famous and although he built so many they were all original: Chiericati, Thiene, Valmarena, Barbarano and Capra palaces are amongst his most famous: the villas of Bagnolo and of the Foscari family called La Malcontenta and the Rotonda built on the Monte Berico are noteworthy.

The works of Andrea Palladio can also be seen outside the town and province of Vicenza, but he always built within the region of Veneto.

The churches of S. Giorgio Maggiore and Il Redentore at Venice are the most well-known of his more important constructions.

The Public Buildings of Udine, the Fratta Villa in the delta of the river Po and the Maser Villa in the province of Treviso are further examples of the works which Palladio has left to us.

Where sleighs are still being used as taxis

It seems impossible that in the age of the motor vehicle there are still places where animal traction is used for public transport.

This is the case in some parts of Switzerland, for example between Zermatt and Taesch, where transport during the winter months is by horse-drawn sleighs. It is like taking a leap into the past, when noise and pollution were almost unknown words.

During the summer, transportation of passengers and goods is carried out by battery-operated locomotives which are completely silent and so do not disturb the calm of the valley.

The Chiericati Palace

Finnish draught horse

Where you can find the land of lakes

Looking at a map, Finland seems like a piece of lace, a tunnel riddled with an infinite number of very characteristic lakes.

Finland has, quite rightly, been called the land of lakes: in fact, from the smallest, which is virtually a puddle, to the largest, the Saimaa situated in the south, it has tens of thousands of lakes which cover 9·4 per cent of the country. This lake district with its inland archipelagos has been less effected by outside influences than the coastal regions.

Someone once said that there are two dominant colours in Finland, blue and green; the blue of the lakes and the green of the forests. If we add to these colours the white of the snow that for a good part of the year covers Finnish territory, we have named the three national colours of Finland. The snow feeds innumerable rivers which often link the lakes.

One feature which may seem strange in country as flat as that in southern Finland is the way the lakes are on different levels. Sometimes characteristic waterfalls, which the Finns have used for the production of electric energy, are formed by a river flowing rapidly from one lake to another.

Where you can find the famous valley of the roses

'The valley of the roses' could be the title of a novel or a romantic film, one of many fantasies; instead it actually exists in Bulgaria.

It is a narrow valley (enclosed by two mountain chains and crossed by the Tundza, the principal tributary of the river Maritza) which at harvest time becomes a sea of roses, a unique spectacle. Until the height of summer every morning at the first signs of dawn the petal pickers fill their large sacks and hurry to deliver their product to be processed before the petals lose their fragrance.

Rose essence, known and appreciated in all parts of the world, is extracted from the petals.

Where there exist many relics of ancient Roman life

Some Roman buildings have come down to us in good condition but these are usually the grand and monumental. We would have little idea of the appearance of a Roman town and its populated districts if Vesuvius had not erupted in A.D. 79. It buried under its ashes two flourishing cities situated in the region of Campania, Pompeii and Herculaneum, which excavation has restored to us almost intact.

Both of these towns were overwhelmed in the middle of their busy lives and it is this daily life that we can see around us as we tour the ancient streets. We admire the Forum with its public buildings, the theatres, the amphitheatre, the gymnasium, the baths and especially the houses with their elegant arcades, painted walls and mosaic floors. There are shops too, such as a type of coffee house where money to pay the last bill had been left on the counter by a customer, or the clothes shop where the owner had painted on his window-sill the emblem of his trade and of his goddess protectress.

Wandering around the dead town, along the streets marked with deep tracks cut by the carts, we can read the electoral notices with which a candidate nearly 2,000 years ago exhorted electors to vote for him.

Where you can find the island of fire

One of the most active volcanic areas in the world is Iceland: in addition to craters which have been dormant since time immemorial, the island has some thirty active volcanoes.

Iceland possesses other volcanic features, such as thermal springs and solfatara (which emit sulphur and water vapour gases); the most notable are the geysers which are jets of water at a high temperature.

The Icelanders have taken advantage of these hot springs: they have directed them into a system of pipes which heat homes, swimming pools and greenhouses. Since 1943 the whole city of Reykjavik has thus been able to solve its heating problems.

Reconstruction of a typical house in Pompeii

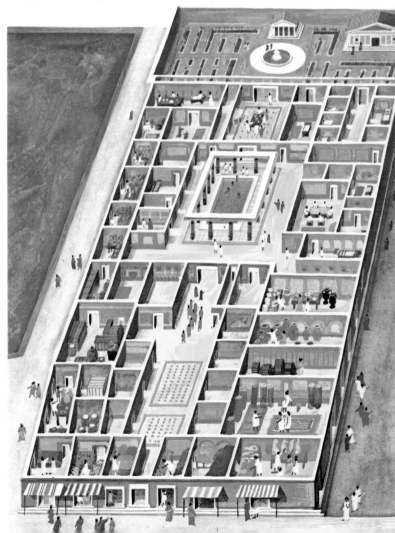

THE WHERE OF AFRICA

Where the water in oases of the Sahara desert comes from

Desert oases occur at points where a spring of water rises to the surface. But where does this water come from, since it hardly ever rains in the desert? To find out we must understand something known as ground water which lies under the soil to form a layer called an aquifer.

In rainy places three things happen to rainfall once it has reached the ground: the rain is carried away in rivers or stored in lakes, it is turned into clouds through evaporation by the heat of the sun, or it seeps through into the soil.

Water seeps through the soil and passes through permeable or porous rocks. When the rainwater meets an impermeable or non-porous rock such as clay or shale, it can go no farther. The rainwater then spreads out to form the aquifer. It lies there like an underground reservoir until it finds an outlet. This occurs when the clay or shale formations break through to the surface. The rainwater then emerges as a spring.

Sometimes these springs are situated far from where the rain first seeped into the soil. This explains why water can be found in arid zones such as deserts.

In the Sahara the spring waters which form the oases have come many hundreds of miles from mountain regions in the north where the rain first fell.

Where the desert rat lives

Desert rats can be seen during moonlit nights scampering and hopping about the desert sands. These animals, also known as jerboas, come out of their hiding places only after dark in search of food.

But they do not seem to be looking for food as they jump about. Their bodies are about 20 centimetres long and the tail, which ends in a tuft, is some 25 centimetres. The front limbs are extremely short while the hind pair are about six times as long. They are very funny to watch as they hop about on their long hind legs that look like those of kangaroos.

Desert rats live in burrows which they dig with their nails and teeth. They are shy animals and this, together with their agility, makes them difficult to catch. They live quite well in captivity, however, and are extremely clean in their habits. They have a sand-coloured coat, as most desert-dwelling animals have.

Where the cheetah hunts its prey

The cheetah is a member of the cat family which lives in the vast stretches of the African savanna where it reigns supreme among animals.

The cheetah is about the same size as a leopard, but its body is much more slender. It has long legs with powerful bared claws, for, unlike other cats, it has no sheaths for retracting its claws. Its coat is of crisp, coarse, sandy-yellow fur with black spots. It is a fierce animal but it will never attack people. In fact, if it is captured while still a cub, it can be domesticated and even kept as a pet. It is not bred in captivity.

The cheetah is one of the swiftest land animals and can reach speeds of between 104 and 112 kilometres an hour. It hunts alone or in small groups, stalking its prey, usually antelopes, and then running it down. Speedy as it is, the antelope cannot escape.

Antelopes are a large group of grass-eating animals who live in the savanna where they can find plenty of food. They vary in size, in the shape of their horns and in the colour of their coats. One of the smallest of the antelope family is the dik-dik which stands only about 30 centimetres high at the shoulders. Like other members of the antelope family the dik-dik lives in large herds.

When antelopes are not feeding they trot along in single file following the oldest male who acts as leader. Their ears and nostrils are always straining for the slightest sound of danger because they know that their chances of escape will be much greater the sooner they find out there is an enemy near.

Where savanna plant life grows

The African savanna is a grassy plain scattered with trees and occurs in places that have warm, dry weather for long periods interrupted by brief spells of heavy rainfall.

During the rainy season the savanna is a brilliant green with tall grass and flowers, but it becomes parched and brown during the dry season. There are few large trees although some of them, like the baobab, have enormous, barrel-like trunks. Much of the savanna's tree life forms part of scrubland which also includes bushes and thorny shrubs.

Where to find dome-shaped huts

There is no other part of the world that has such a wide variety of dwellings as Africa. These homes range from the most primitive huts to modern skyscrapers of advanced design. This is one of the features of Africa today, that it is a land of rich contrasts.

The primitive dwellings of Africa are mainly huts. The word 'hut' to a European has a simple meaning. But in Africa a hut can be a single wall providing shelter from the wind or it can be quite a complicated structure with several floors and built partly with hard materials such as dried clay.

The dome-shaped hut is a typical African home. Sometimes the dome is rather pointed and the hut has an oval shape, resembling a beehive. Dome-shaped huts look like the igloos in which Eskimos live.

Most African huts are simple to build. The men of the village make a framework of intertwined branches which the women then cover with straw, leaves or grass. The roof framework is sometimes built on the ground and then lifted into place, so that it can be easily moved to other walls when the first ones rot. One African tribe called the Benné covers the framework of branches with clay. In Cameroon huts are also covered in clay but the huts have a pointed top. These dome-shaped huts can be quite small, like those built by the pygmies, or they can be as large as a king's palace, as in Uganda. These large huts are more than 8 metres high and 10 metres wide.

The cattle-raising Hottentots who move from one water hole to another, make an easily transported hut of reed mats sewn over a frame of light poles.

Other African peoples who live in huts include the Bushmen of southern Africa, certain Nilotic peoples in north-eastern Africa, the Bantu of southern Africa and some of the Zulu tribes in south-eastern Africa.

Where great herds of zebu are reared

There is an open plain between Kenya and Tanzania where almost the only form of wealth is cattle. This is the land where the Pastoral Masai people live. They have more than a million cattle and cattle-breeding is their main occupation.

Pastoral Masai men and women worry only about their animals. These people still recall a terrible disease that killed many beasts in 1883.

The most commonly raised animal is the zebu, a hump-backed ox. The Pastoral Masai also breed many donkeys, sheep and goats but they have no chickens or other domestic fowl and they do not hunt or grow crops.

Cattle provide the Pastoral Masai with their main foods: milk, meat and blood. Only the women are allowed to milk the cattle. The men take blood from the animals every month by extracting it from the zebu's jugular vein.

The animals are considered so precious that the Pastoral Masai eat meat only on certain feast days. On such days they will not drink milk with their meat. Honey-beer is drunk and most adults chew tobacco or use snuff.

As well as obtaining milk from the zebu, the people like to shape the animals' horns by bending them into various shapes as soon as they start growing.

The Pastoral Masai live in a kraal camp. This consists of a large circular thornbush fence inside which the women build igloo-like mud huts. At night the cattle are taken into the camp as protection against wild animals.

Where to find wild peacocks

Wild peacocks live together in large flocks in the forests of central Africa. They scratch about in the ground during the day for seeds to eat and at nightfall they fly up to the trees where they perch and sleep.

Every peacock has several wives known as peahens. The female birds build their nests on the ground and lay from four to six whitish, sometimes spotted eggs. During the mating season the male utters a harsh raucous cry.

Peacocks were first brought to Europe in the days of Alexander the Great. At one time they used to be kept on many farms, but today they are usually found in zoos or public parks.

Peacocks are extremely beauti-ful birds with their brightly coloured plumage. The male bird makes a magnificent display when it opens up its huge fan-like tail to preen itself. The female is more dully coloured and does not have the large ornamental feathers.

(above) Peacock
(below) Malay Argus Pheasant

331

Where to find Africa's largest national parks

The animals of Africa, many of them belonging to species which are now rare, today live under special protection from the danger of being hunted into extinction.

These animals live in national parks, huge areas reserved for them in central and eastern Africa. By 1970 there were about thirty-five countries with national parks or reserves which have become great tourist attractions. Every year thousands of people come from all over the world to see the giraffes, elephants, lions, gazelles, rhinoceroses, hippopotamuses and countless species of birds and reptiles living in freedom in these reserves.

There are good tracks and smooth roads and visitors can drive for hundreds of kilometres through these national parks. Some of Africa's most important reserves are in Kenya and Tanzania. The Serengeti National Park in northern Tanzania covers an area of 15,000 square kilometres and extends from Lake Victoria to Mount Kilimanjaro. It has the finest collection of plains animals in Africa and is especially famous for its lions.

There is a park with rich animal life and many birds, especially flamingoes, near Lake Manyara. Visitors can drive close up to the animals in their cars and take photographs.

Hunting is totally forbidden in these parks and game wardens and zoologists are constantly trying to increase the number of animals that live there.

Where to find the Victoria Falls

The Zambesi is one of Africa's longest rivers and gives rise to the world-famous Victoria Falls. These falls were named by the British missionary and explorer David Livingstone who became the first European to see them in 1855.

Livingstone was then exploring the upper reaches of the Zambesi, a river which was almost unknown. The Africans knew where to find this mighty course of water which they called 'the smoke that thunders' because of the noise the falls make as they drop over the cliff. But the Africans were afraid of taking Livingstone to the place: they were superstitious and feared they would be punished by

the gods whom, they believed, lived inside the falls.

Livingstone succeeded in persuading the Africans to help him and at last he was able to see one of the most impressive sights in the world as the Zambesi plunged 108 metres down a narrow gorge.

Livingstone was able to produce an almost perfect map of the Zambesi's course, showing the exact location of the Victoria Falls. They are situated at the far eastern end of the border that separates Zambia from Zimbabwe Rhodesia. It was not until the railway from Bulawayo was opened in 1905, however, that many people were able to visit the falls.

Where the cola used in making soft drinks comes from

During the nineteenth century the Africans who acted as porters and carried heavy loads for European explorers had a simple cure for the exhaustion of travelling through the forest: they would gather a few cola seeds and chew them during rest halts.

The Africans knew that cola seeds contain a substance that acts as a stimulant on the body. By chewing cola seeds, these Africans were able to walk for hours without feeling tired. Later, scientists discovered that cola seeds contain the drug caffeine.

The tree on which the cola grows is common throughout western Africa. It became the basis of an important industry when cola began to be used as an ingredient in soft drinks. The trees vary in height, from 10 to 15 metres. The fruit of the tree is star-shaped, each point of the star containing a few seeds, known as cola nuts.

The secretary bird

Where to find the bird that snakes fear

Throughout many regions of Africa from the Tropic of Cancer south to the Cape, there lives a large bird that seems to have declared war on all snakes. This is called the secretary bird, a long-legged relation of the hawk family. The bird gets its name from the long feathers that grow from the back of its head. These feathers resemble quills, or old-fashioned pens, and they make the bird look like a clerk with pens stuck behind his ears.

The secretary bird is over a metre tall. It is one of the most powerful birds of prey and has a fierce curved beak. Its favourite food is snakes, including poisonous ones.

There is no bird that can rival the secretary bird for agility. This bird relies on its swiftness to catch and kill snakes while at the same time leaping back to avoid their poisonous bite.

When the secretary bird attacks it holds its short wings forward like a shield. The wings have bony knobs on them which help to protect the bird from bites and are also useful weapons for attacking its prey.

Where the crowned crane lives

Cranes are elegant birds that strut about on their stilt-like legs, stretching out their long necks and holding their heads slightly to one side. Whenever they stop to rest in a field or by the side of the river, they tuck one leg underneath their bodies and stand on the other, sometimes remaining like this for many hours.

The crowned crane has a beautiful crest of yellow feathers on its head and its dark plumage is broken here and there by a few patches of colour. It lives in most tropical regions of Africa in large flocks near lakes or rivers, feeding on seeds and insects which it finds on the ground. The crane

flies up to the trees after dark to spend the night safely perched on a branch.

Where the nomads of northern Africa roam

In parts of the Spanish Sahara, there are many people who live a nomadic, or wandering, life. These nomads are shepherds and live in black goat-hair tents, where they shelter from the burning rays of the sun as their flocks graze and search for food which is none too plentiful.

The Berbers of Algeria who used to be farmers, became nomads to avoid the unending invasions of their fertile but unsafe valleys. To escape from their enemies, they took to the mountains of the Atlas range and to the high plateau of the Sahara desert where they became nomads and raised livestock. What they did was unusual because more often nomads become settled farmers and few tribes change to a wandering life.

In Libya, many nomad tribes live near places where engineers drill for oil. The nomad's life is very hard: there is the great heat of the burning desert sands and winds that can sometimes blow at more than 100 kilometres an hour.

The nomads of Libya are also known as the Tuareg. When they move from place to place they travel on camels, without which it would be impossible to make long journeys across the desert.

Nomad tribes also live in the Sudan where they form about 14 per cent of the population. They breed livestock and are always looking for supplies of water and grazing grounds for their animals.

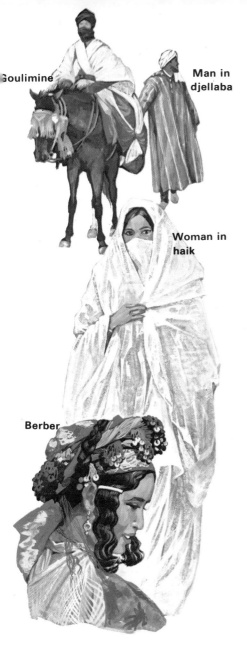

Goulimine

Man in djellaba

Woman in haik

Berber

For weeks the workers in every encampment have filled up sacks with salt. When the time comes to set out only those people who cannot face the rigours of the desert stay behind: women, children and old people. The most experienced of the Tuareg is the camel leader and behind him all the camels are linked together in a long line. The Tuareg stop along the way at oases where they leave supplies of food to eat on the return journey. When the rainy season starts, the Tuareg caravan stops at the edge of the desert so that the rain will not spoil their goods. By the end of October the Tuareg reach their destination which is Niger or Chad. The return journey takes three months and the caravan, consisting of between 100 and 150 camels, is laden with goods obtained through barter: millet, rugs, sugar and various cloths.

The rocks that line the caravan trail are marked with scratches, some a few days old and others thousands of years. This is *tifinagh*, the mysterious hand-writing which the Tuareg have used since they began their wanderings 4,000 years ago.

Where the salt road passes through the Sahara

In addition to water, camels and mutton, salt is a valuable commodity for barter among the Tuareg desert nomads who find plentiful supplies of it in the Hoggar, a mountain range in the central Sahara.

When the rainy season is over at the end of June, the 'salt caravan' sets out from the Hoggar. For the Tuareg people this is a very important event.

Where the Kei apple grows

The *Aberia* or Kei apple tree derives its name from Mount Aber in Ethiopia where the first tree of this species was found in that county. The Kei apple, however, grows in its natural state only in southern Africa, in the Cape of Good Hope and Natal, where it grows wild in the Kei Valley.

The trees of the *Aberia* family are shrubby and thorny and can grow to a height of 10 metres. The leaves alternate with rather small flowers. The Kei apple tree is very thorny and in southern Africa it is used as a hedge or a fence.

The common name of the velvety, bright yellow fruit is due to its resemblance to an apple although it is only between 2 and 4 centimetres in diameter and is more the size of a plum. The fruit is very popular in the regions where it grows and is eaten fresh. It has a sugary flesh with a slightly sour tang. The fruit has a pleasant smell and its flavour improves when it is cooked. Kei apples are good for making jam and jelly and attempts are being made to grow the plant in other tropical regions for industrial purposes.

Where the world's largest tree grows

The baobab is a fairly common tree in the dry regions of central Africa and especially in the savanna. It is a very strange tree and typical of these regions. It is not very tall, growing only to a height of some 20 metres, but its trunk is enormous and in some cases reaches 9 metres in diameter.

The baobab rises out of the ground like some huge gasometer. A few short branches grow out from the trunk and the tree has such a strange appearance that an old Arabian legend declares that 'the devil plucked up the baobab, thrust its branches into the earth, and left its roots in the air'.

The inside of the trunk is designed to withstand conditions of long drought: the wood is soft and spongy, full of small holes filled with water obtained during the rainy season and stored there for use during the dry season.

For this reason the wood of the baobab tree is not very good for building or making furniture, although sometimes the trunks of living trees are hollowed out to form houses. The tree's bark is made of a very tough fibre used in making rope and coarse woven materials.

Where the okapi lives

The okapi is an animal that remained completely unknown until 1900. It lives only in the dense jungles of the Zaire River and is very difficult to find.

The okapi's hindquarters and legs are covered in black and white stripes, in strong contrast to the rest of the animal's body which is reddish-brown in colour. These black and white stripes immediately identify the okapi. On closer examination this grass-eating animal reveals several other individual characteristics.

The okapi resembles but is smaller than the giraffe, with shorter legs and neck. It has large ears and, like the giraffe, the male okapi has a pair of short horns covered in fur except at the tips. The okapi feeds on leaves and shoots which it bites away from the branches of trees.

Unlike the giraffe which lives in the savanna, the okapi prefers the dense forest where this timid animal can hide itself easily. It is a shy, nocturnal animal that lives singly or in pairs.

Where the Masai live

The Masai are a people who live in the steppes of eastern Africa, broad, open plains. Some 50,000 live in Tanzania and 154,000 in Kenya.

The Masai are divided into five districts: Kaputi, Enaiposa, Laikipia, Uasin-gisa and Kisongo. There are four tribes: Aizer, Mengana, Mokezen and Molelyan. The Aizer provide the political and religious leader of all the Masai, known as *doiboni*. This man must be able to see into the future and have magical powers.

The Kwavi, a settled people, are also part of the Masai. Other members are the N'dorobo, who live by hunting and gathering wild food, and the Datoga.

337

THE WHERE OF ASIA

Where the evil-smelling *Rafflesia* flourishes

The *Rafflesia* grows in the mountain forests of Malaysia. It is a parasite and grows on large woody vines, the seeds germinating in the rough bark of the stems of the vine which lie on the ground. The *Rafflesia* has no green, for it does not contain chlorophyll, which gives plants their green colour.

The leaves of the *Rafflesia* are like small fish-scales and the only unusual feature of the plant is its flower. This has a fetid smell resembling that of rotting meat, which attracts several kinds of insects.

Rafflesia flowers are usually large. They have five limp, fleshy petal-like segments of a reddish- or purplish-brown colour which grow out of a very short stalk.

The largest *Rafflesia* known is the *Rafflesia arnoldi* which has flowers more than a metre across of a very bright red dotted with white. It is found in the equatorial forests of Sumatra and Java.

Where the raw material for strychnine is produced

Dense forests containing trees and and plant life of many kinds cover much of south-east Asia near the equator, where the climate is hot and moist. In regions where there is less rain, the soil is dry and scorched for most of the year. It is in these places that the *nux vomica* tree grows from which the poison strychnine is obtained.

The *nux vomica* flourishes in India and Indo-China. It is a majestic tree with thick foliage and the trunk can measure 3 to 4 metres in circumference. Its fruits resemble oranges. Buried inside the extremely bitter pulp are from five to eight seeds from which strychnine is extracted.

Where the armies of Alexander the Great marched

Alexander III of Macedonia was a mighty soldier whose ambition was to conquer the entire world and rule it. In the summer of 327 B.C. he led his army on a campaign towards Asia, entering lands that no one had previously dared to visit. He crossed the river Indus, entering the vast territory of India.

Alexander and his soldiers conquered every army that tried to stop them. He finally reached the Thar desert, a huge, unexplored and mysterious place that lay along what is now the border between India and Pakistan. Alexander was only twenty-nine years old and he wanted to march on eastwards on his great road to conquest. But his soldiers were tired and refused to go further in the tropical rain. Alexander agreed to go back and returned to his homeland. Because of his magnificent exploits he became known as Alexander the Great.

Where the 'Roof of the World' is located

The highest mountain in the world is in the Himalayas: it is Mount Everest. For hundreds of years nobody succeeded in reaching the summit. The people of Tibet called it Chomolungma, meaning 'father of mountains', and believed that strange wild creatures wandered about the mountain's perpetual snows.

Many people thought it would be impossible to measure or climb Mount Everest. The British, who ruled India until after the Second World War, established an office in the 1800s to survey the mountain and measure it. The man who had the idea to start the office was George Everest and he also wanted to measure all the other mountains in the Himalayas. After much work the task was completed in 1852. The height was finally calculated as 8,840 metres (later established more precisely as 8,882 metres). The mountain was named after Everest in 1863.

Another century passed before the peak of Everest was finally reached. In 1953 Edmund Hillary, a New Zealander, and Sherpa Tenzing, a skilled mountaineer of Nepal, climbed to the summit. Hillary and Tenzing had to wear

oxygen masks to help them breathe in the thin air. The two climbers planted the flags of Britain, Nepal, India and the United Nations on the peak on which man had never before set foot.

Where the elephants of Asia live

The elephants of Asia roam freely in parts of India, Thailand and Sumatra. Some elephants still live in Indo-China but many were destroyed during the fighting and bombing of the Vietnam war.

The elephants we see at circus performances trained to do many tricks come from Asia. Asian elephants are tamer and quieter than the elephants of Africa. The Asian elephant is smaller than the African one: an Asian bull, or male, elephant is about 3 metres tall and weighs between 3 and 6 tons. It also has smaller ears and a hollow forehead.

In Asia many elephants are trained to do heavy work in the forests. The elephants use their long, powerful trunks to lift huge logs of timber or roll them along the ground.

Elephants are fairly long-lived animals. The normal life-span for an Asian elephant living in its natural surroundings is about fifty years, but one captive elephant in India is recorded to have lived to an age of 130 years.

White elephants, also known as albinos, are rare. They occasionally appear in Thailand and Burma where they are regarded as sacred and never allowed to work.

Where camphor comes from

Camphor comes from the camphor laurel which grows in Formosa, China and Japan. It is a vegetable oil with an aromatic smell and is found in all parts of the tree. Usually the camphor is obtained from the leaves which are gathered twice a year and chopped up. The camphor oil is then extracted from the leaves and distilled.

In 1909 scientists invented a way to make artificial camphor and about half the camphor used commercially is now produced synthetically.

Where to find the most beautiful city in Japan

The cities of Japan have grown extremely rapidly since the Second World War mainly because of the spread of new industries which provided work for people but made the cities rather ugly. One city escaped this fate: Kyoto, the ancient capital of Japan founded by the Emperor Kwammu in A.D. 794. For a thousand years Kyoto was the capital of the Japanese empire. During this time it became rich in monuments and the architecture of its buildings resembled that of Chinese cities. Kyoto had stout walls built all round it as a defence against attackers and the city was approached through eighteen gates in the walls. Inside were many gardens and temples

of the Buddhist and Shinto religions.

Kyoto is also famous for its works of art and craftsmanship, especially porcelain and silks, and is today visited by many tourists.

Where the city of Troy stood

Until the 1850s many historians thought that the great adventures described by Homer in the *Iliad* and *Odyssey* were all fables which had existed only in the poet's imagination. But between 1870 and 1890 excavations carried out by a German businessman, Heinrich Schliemann, established not only that the great city had actually existed but that nine different Troys had stood on the spot. Each city had been destroyed and a new one rebuilt during a period of 3,000 years.

Later excavations by other archaeologists confirmed Schliemann's belief that these ruins were really the remains of Troy. The archaeologists also found that the seventh stratum, or layer, of the

Fifth century vase painting showing Achilles killing Penthesilea

ruins dated back to the great battles and siege in which this city, ruled by King Priam, was destroyed. Today we are certain that Troy did exist and that its towers rose from the summit of a hill called Hisarlik that now stands in Turkey by the waters of the Hellespont.

Detail from an early sixth century Corinthian vase, showing the wooden horse of Troy

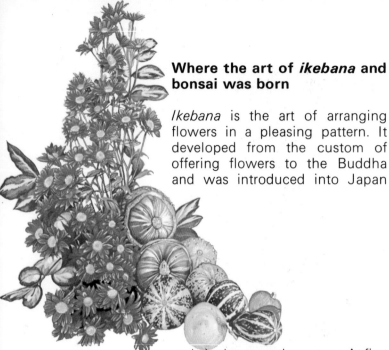

Where the art of *ikebana* and bonsai was born

Ikebana is the art of arranging flowers in a pleasing pattern. It developed from the custom of offering flowers to the Buddha and was introduced into Japan early in the seventh century. At first *ikebana* was used only as a form of worship of the Buddha. Priests decorated Buddhist temples with flower arrangements which were not only beautiful but also symbolized various religious ideas. Later, towards the thirteenth century, *ikebana* was also used to adorn the royal palaces and the houses of the nobility. Later still *ikebana* spread to the homes of

A Chinese juniper which is 200 years old and about 90 cm. high

ordinary people and today it is one of the most graceful traditions of Japanese life.

Bonsai is the art of arranging plants into certain shapes and is the Japanese word literally meaning 'tray-planted'. It is an older art than *ikebana* and first began in China. *Ikebana* uses fresh flowers and other decorative material such as twigs, mosses and leaves. Bonsai is the art of growing fully developed trees in miniature. This is done by keeping them to a small size while still making them look like real trees. It is a very difficult art and requires a great deal of patience and time. To produce a dwarf tree between 30 and 40 centimetres high can take up to 100 years of careful work. The art of bonsai is passed on from father to son and one tree can be handed down from one generation to the next as a valued possession.

Where ginger is produced

The ginger plant was used in India and China in very ancient times. By the first century A.D. it had travelled to the Mediterranean region and it was well-known in England by the eleventh century. Today it is grown in all the tropical regions of the world.

The essential oils and gums found in the ginger plant are used as stimulants in certain drugs. Ginger is used by doctors, in the manufacture of beverages and as a spice in cooking.

The ginger plant is propagated by cuttings of the rhizome, or root. Nine or ten months after planting, the stems turn yellow and wither and the ginger is then ready to be gathered. Green ginger, used in cooking, is the fresh rhizome. Pieces of rhizome can be washed

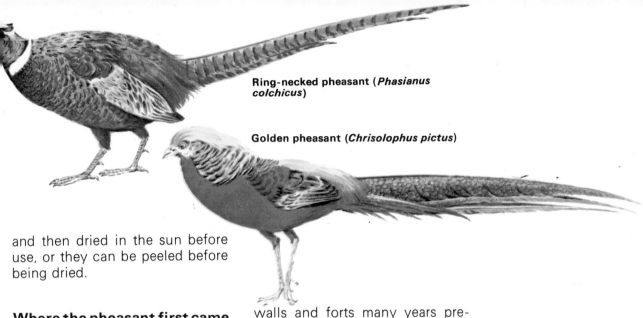

Ring-necked pheasant (*Phasianus colchicus*)

Golden pheasant (*Chrisolophus pictus*)

and then dried in the sun before use, or they can be peeled before being dried.

Where the pheasant first came from

The pheasant, a beautiful bird often sought by hunters, first lived in the mountainous region cf the Caucasus. The ancient Romans brought it to Europe.

In its natural state the pheasant likes to make its home in moist woodlands, especially on hillsides. The cock, or male, has brightly coloured feathers which have a metallic sheen. The hen, or female, is plainer, and is of a brownish colour. Both male and female have very long tails.

Many varieties occur in different parts of Asia, the Japanese green pheasant being particularly notable. In Europe, pheasants are often bred as game birds for sport.

Where the Great Wall of China was built

This gigantic fortification was designed as a defensive barrier to protect the Chinese empire against attacks from invading hordes of barbarians. The Great Wall was built along the northern border of China from about 200 B.C. Local feudal lords had already built some

walls and forts many years previously in places such as gaps in the mountains where enemy soldiers could easily slip through into China. It was not until the great emperor Shih Huang Ti who reigned from 221 to 210 B.C. that all these walls and forts were linked up and extended as one barrier.

The Great Wall reached a length of about 2,400 kilometres, the longest wall ever built, winding its way up mountains and down into valleys. The height of the wall ranges from 6 to 16 metres and along its top there used to be a road more than 4 metres wide. Every so often there was a huge tower where soldiers lived and kept guard.

Chinese costumes

343

The Great Wall of China was repaired and improved in later years. Today it is mostly in ruins. The government of the People's Republic of China has rebuilt sections and many tourists go to admire these great structures.

Where the Ainu live

In the Japanese islands of Hokkaido, Sakhalin and Kuril lives a group of people who are unlike the vast majority of people in Japan. These are the Ainu. They do not have slanting eyes, a yellow skin or wiry, black hair, but they look more like Europeans, with a light-coloured skin and thick hair. The men usually have heavy beards which are not very common in Japan.

The Ainu may be descendants of early Caucasoid peoples, that is the group to which most Europeans belong. They are known as aborigines because anthropologists believe they were the first inhabitants of Japan before the Koreans and other yellow-skinned people came to the country during the Stone Age. The Ainu may have reached Japan from the West in prehistoric times.

The original Ainu speech had no known connection with any

Gentiana sind-ornata

other language, but today it has been largely replaced by Japanese. The Ainu live in small villages, leading a very simple life, hunting, fishing and gardening. Their numbers are greatly reduced and they seem to be dying out except where they have intermarried with Japanese.

Where the most beautiful gentian in the world grows

There are about 400 varieties of the gentian plant. Some grow quite tall, with yellow or purple flowers, and some have pale blue flowers. There are also acaulescent types which have little or no stems and are the best-known with their deep or brilliant blue flowers, and gentians with branches that have small bunches of flowers.

Oddly enough gentians do not grow in Africa, but they are common in other parts of the world, especially in the highlands of the Himalayas. In these regions are found some of the most beautiful and rare types of gentians.

In Europe, gentians grow on the Alps. Ten species of gentian are found in Britain.

Ainu costumes

Where rice is more important than wheat

There are hundreds of millions of people in the world who have never tasted a piece of bread. This is because their main food is rice. They live chiefly in eastern Asia, in such countries as India, China, Japan and the islands of Indonesia.

In the warm, humid regions of the tropics, farmers harvest the rice twice a year to help feed the many millions for whom this grain is their staple food. Farmers have grown rice in China and India for over 4,000 years. Gradually the cultivation of rice spread and it was introduced to Europe in mediaeval times by the Arabs.

Rice grows as small grains from the flower of the rice plant. Each grain has special layers of protective covering which are removed when the rice is polished and turned into a white grain. Rice is rich in starch, a vital substance in feeding the human body, and also contains other important substance such as vitamins. These vitamins are found inside the protective layers of rice grains, so when the grains are polished the vitamins are lost. In some places in Asia where many people eat a lot of polished rice, they do not receive these vitamins and so suffer from diseases which make them weak through vitamin deficiency.

In China people eat rice with pork, chicken, beef or fish, the meat being cut into small pieces and flavoured with soya sauce or spicy gravy; in India rice is eaten in a curry made with powdered spices, meat and vegetables; in Japan the people eat rice with fried or raw fish and chopped, raw vegetables.

A farmer in his rice field

The picturesque Irawadi rice-boat

Elephants carrying
logs of teak in a
Burmese forest

Teak trees grow to an average height of 20 metres, although mature trees of 100 years old or more can reach 30 to 40 metres. The bark of the tree is about a centimetre thick and is brownish-grey in colour. The sapwood is white and beneath this is the heartwood which has a strong aromatic fragrance and is a golden brown colour, which on seasoning darkens to brown marked with darker streaks.

In warm countries teak is chiefly valued for its durability. Well-preserved teak beams have been found in buildings several centuries old and there are even instances of teak beams having lasted for more than 1,000 years.

Teak is used in building ships and houses and also for fine furniture and wood carvings. A great deal of teak is shaved into very thin slices, called veneers, which are stuck to furniture made from other, cheaper woods. It was once used to make the decks of sailing ships because it did not rot as easily as other woods. Today it has become very popular in furniture-making but most of the woods sold as teak are really imitations that look like the original.

Where to find teak

Teak is wood obtained from a type of tree known as *Tectona*. It is one of the most valuable woods because it is extremely hard and durable and can withstand the attacks of insects which bore holes into other kinds of wood and spoil them. The strength of teak comes from an essential oil present in the wood.

Tectona trees grow only in the dense forests of equatorial regions. It is difficult to transport the trees from these forests and for this reason teak is very expensive.

Burma produces most of the world's supply of teak, with India, Thailand, Java and Sri Lanka (formerly Ceylon) coming next.

Where the persimmon came from

Until the nineteenth century the persimmon was almost unknown in Europe. Today this yellowish-red fruit which looks rather like a tomato, is often seen in homes in Mediterranean countries such as France and Italy. It is also grown on a small scale in the United States.

The persimmon is a native of China and Japan where it has grown since ancient times. Persimmon trees soon became accustomed to the Mediterranean weather when they were first brought to Europe during the nineteenth century. The trees have dark-green leaves and are often planted in gardens where they give shade against the hot summer sun.

Persimmon fruit is no longer as popular as it was, but the wood from the tree is used in making furniture and looks like ebony.

Where the tiger likes to make its home

The jungles and the forests of Asia which have rivers flowing through them are the favourite haunts of the tiger, one of the fiercest and most dangerous animals in the world.

Unlike the lion, this beautiful big cat with the striped yellow coat is not satisfied to kill just one animal for its food. It will attack whole flocks of animals as they drink at waterholes in the jungle, slaughtering them for the sheer pleasure of killing and spilling blood.

As the tiger grows older it becomes weaker and more dangerous and will then attack human beings and become a man-eater. Once a tiger has tasted human flesh it will always want more, attacking any person who strays too far into the jungle from the villages. Man-eating tigers will even break into houses to seize their human victims.

Where jute, kapok and ramie are found

Jute is a substance obtained from various plants that grow in warm and moist regions of Asia. It is cheap and used in making rope, twine and material for sacks.

Kapok is a fluffy substance from the outer covering of certain tropical plants. The most common of these is the *Ceiba pentandra*, a tree that is grown mainly in Indonesia and produces hundreds of football-shaped pods. Kapok is very light and soft and is used as stuffing for sleeping-bags, cushions and mattresses.

Ramie is a very strong material obtained from the stalks of plants belonging to the nettle family. It was grown in ancient Egypt where it was used to wrap mummies, and is native to China and Taiwan. Today it is used in fire hose, fishing nets and upholstery.

Where to find the pangolin

This very strange mammal lives in the dense equatorial jungles of Asia and is common in the islands of Malaysia. Another type of pangolin makes its home in the forests of Africa.

The pangolin is a shy, harmless, nocturnal animal with a long body up to a metre in length which resembles the anteater. It has a small head, short legs and a thick tail which is always curled up like a question mark. The skin of its throat and the underparts of the body is soft, but the rest of the pangolin's body is covered in hard, horny, yellowish-brown scales which are so made that the pangolin can roll itself up into a ball when it is frightened or in danger.

The name 'pangolin' comes from a Javanese word meaning 'the animal that rolls up into a ball'. The pangolin, which has no teeth, uses its long, sticky, snake-like tongue to scoop up ants and termites, insects that provide its only food. The pangolin also has very strong claws on its forefeet, but it uses these only for tearing down anthills to force the insects out into the open ground.

Pangolin

Where the dugong lives

This strange, seal-like mammal lives along the coast of the Red Sea, the Indian Ocean and in the China seas. A long time ago fishermen who saw the dugong thought that this animal looked rather like a woman and behaved strangely like a human being, shedding real tears and whimpering and sobbing when caught. The fishermen's tales about the dugong were soon spread round the world and people kept adding more details until the myth was born that the dugong had the head and body of a woman and a long fish-tail. Perhaps this was how all the old beliefs about mermaids and sirens began. In olden days sailors believed that mermaids sang sweetly to seamen on passing ships and tried to lure the ships on to dangerous rocks.

In actual fact the dugong belongs to the order of animals known as *Sirenia*. It is from 2 to 3 metres in length and browses in small groups in the shallow waters of bays and inlets. When feeding underwater it surfaces every five to ten minutes for a supply of air. People on the coast often hunt the dugong with spears or harpoons for its flesh is considered a delicacy. Oil is obtained from its blubber.

Where opium is grown

Opium is one of the most frequently used drugs in the world, especially in the East where it is smoked or chewed. It is obtained from the milky juice of a poppy known as *Papaver somniferum*, the 'sleep-bringing poppy'. When the milky juice is extracted from the poppy it turns dark when

Dugong

An old legend says Fujiyama was born in a single night about 300 years before the birth of Christ. As the volcano rose from the ground the earth a few hundred kilometres away collapsed to form Lake Biwa.

Every year many thousands of pilgrims climb to the top of Fujiyama. They throw gifts into the vast crater to please the gods of the underworld who are believed to be responsible for the many earthquakes so feared in Japan.

Where to find the Chinese alligator

Many alligators live in the great rivers that flow across China and are especially common in the lower reaches of the Yangtze Kiang. These alligators look different from the crocodile because they have shorter jaws. The fourth tooth of the Chinese alligator's upper jaw is also large and sticks out when the animal has its mouth closed.

The American alligator which lives in the Mississippi River grows to about 6 metres in length, but the Chinese alligator is rarely longer than one and a half metres. It is too timid to attack large animals and presents no danger to human beings. It prefers, instead, to catch fish, water-birds and small mammals.

A woman from Anatolia

exposed to the light and becomes hard. The hardened juice is then rolled into balls and sent to refineries where it is prepared for medical uses.

Opium is a narcotic drug, easing pain and helping people to sleep, but it is also a dangerous drug because people who take it can soon become addicted.

Where to find the sacred volcano

The people of Japan regard the extinct volcano of Fujiyama as a holy mountain. Fujiyama stands on the island of Honshu and rises to a height of 3,776 metres, its snow-covered peak dominating the surrounding countryside.

THE WHERE OF NORTH AND CENTRAL AMERICA

Where the fur hunters of America tracked their prey

The fur hunters and trappers of America explored the vast areas of the northern part of the continent. These hunters were rough and ready and during the 1600s they hunted fur animals in places where no other white man had ever set foot, defying wild Indians who lived there and showing no fear of the many dangers that surrounded them.

The greatest hunting ground was Canada. It was so rich in fur animals that the British fought the French to win possession of this huge country. In 1670 the British had set up the Hudson's Bay Company and in 1821 this company incorporated its rival, so gaining a monopoly of all the fur trade.

From about 1820 the valley of the river Missouri in the United States and the region of the Rocky Mountains became important hunting areas. These places were explored by the 'mountain men' led by General Ashley who was the first to establish the American fur trade on a permanent basis in the Rockies. These men helped to open up the Wild West for settlers to go and farm there.

Where to find the world's most famous waterfalls

The most famous waterfalls in the world are at Niagara. Some 500,000 tons of water rush over

English and Indian trappers

the Niagara precipice into a gorge below every minute and make this one of the best sources of hydroelectric power in America. The dull roar of the waters can be heard from a great distance. The people who live near the falls are used to the sound and would be quite nervous if it should suddenly stop. This almost happened one night in March 1848 when the waters of the river Niagara were blocked by huge masses of ice and the great falls were reduced to a trickle for a few hours.

There are two falls at Niagara and they are separated by a huge rock, called Goat Island. The larger of the falls is in Canada and the other is in the United States. Engineers have bored a tunnel in the rock through which people can go to see the marvellous spectacle. The falls are very beautiful in winter because of the ice round them. They are visited by over 4 million sightseers a year.

Where the winged lizards lived

In the days of the dinosaurs the sky was crowded with huge winged reptiles such as the pterodactyl. These flying reptiles had a wing span of more than 7 metres and would constantly glide above the waters, catching fish and crab-like animals. They were excellent fliers and could travel over 100 kilometres away from the land in search of their food.

Pterodactyl

Pterodactyls were probably the most skilful fliers of the winged reptiles, but their huge wings were a hindrance to them whenever they landed to rest. At such times the pterodactyl would have to drag itself painfully along the ground in contrast to its agility and grace in the air.

The fossil remains of the pterodactyl have been found in several parts of North America. This means that these flying lizards must have lived in that part of the world.

Where to find the most majestic valley in the world

There is a region in the United States where erosion by water and wind has produced a majestic effect. This area forms part of three states: Arizona, Utah and Nevada. The river which has carved out such beauty is called the Colorado. The waters of the Colorado empty into the Pacific Ocean but before they finish their journey they pass through a valley that has steep sides. This valley was cut out of the earth by the Colorado River over a period of millions of years.

The valleys consist of a series of canyons which all lead to the magnificent Grand Canyon. In some places the valley is more than 1,600 metres deep and 25 kilometres wide. The canyon presents a breathtaking sight with its red walls rising sheer out of the ground. Where the various valleys meet, isolated peaks rise out of deep depressions. During the wet season torrential rains flood the Colorado River when its waters rise by more than 40 metres, and the mass of soil it contains is constantly reshaping the walls of the Grand Canyon.

Where to find poisonous snakes that are helpful to man

It seems incredible that there are snakes so poisonous that their bite is greatly feared and that at the same time these snakes should behave in such a way that they help man.

These are the coral snakes which live throughout America. They allow themselves to be picked up by people for they are very shy and tame and it is rare for anyone to be bitten by one. But it is not safe to play around with the coral snake: their poison is very powerful and can cause a swift death.

Coral snakes are shy only with people; with other snakes they are extremely aggressive. They eat many other reptiles, most of them poisonous, and in doing this, the coral snake destroys many poisonous creatures and clears large areas of reptiles which are dangerous to man.

Coral snakes have a brightly coloured skin marked with red, yellow and black rings. They live in sandy places where they bury themselves. When their victims come along the coral snake darts out from its hiding place and kills them.

Laughing falcon with coral snake

Where some of the earliest reptiles appeared

One of the groups of animals from which the dinosaurs were descended was probably the *Seymouria*. The first fossilized remains of this animal were found in the lower Permian, a layer of rocks that dates back about 270 million years, in the red earth of Texas, near old pools of water.

The *Seymouria* was a small reptile whose remains have almost always been found in little hollows or crevices. For this reason some scientists believe the *Seymouria* lived in holes which it dug out by the sides of lakes and rivers. It is also possible that the bodies of these animals could have been dragged after their death into a crack that was already there. We know that the *Seymouria* moved very slowly along the ground, but in water it was an excellent swimmer.

An examination of their fossilized skeletons does not make it easy to see how the *Seymouria* breathed: they obviously had a very primitive respiratory system, consisting of swallowing air which

Two coral snakes

was then pushed into the lungs through the movement of the ribs that covered the thorax, or chest.

Seymouria must have been very common because their fossilized remains have been found also in Bohemia, Czechoslovakia, and in Kazakhstan in the Soviet Union. It was a species of animal that soon died out.

Where the big cattle trails crossed the American prairies

At the end of the American Civil War in 1865 it has been estimated that there were 5 million head of cattle in the rich grasslands of Texas. There were so many cattle that they were worth only five dollars each as compared with forty dollars in the northern states. Because they wanted better prices for their animals, the Texan cattle-men decided to send their live-stock to the growing industrial centres like Chicago and other cities in the north. But to reach the Kansas-Pacific Railway which transported the animals to their destination, the cattle had to be taken for hundreds of kilometres on exhausting journeys across territory that lurked with danger from hostile Indians, bandits and bad weather.

Huge herds of up to 4,000

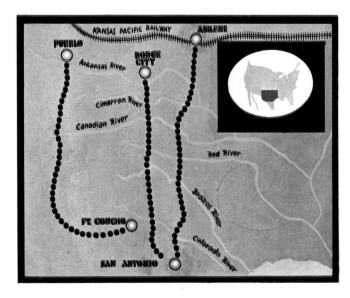

cattle would be driven along the prairie trails amid great clouds of dust by tough cowboys. The main cattle centres were in Abilene on the Chisholm trail, Dodge City on the Western trail and Denver on the Goodnight-Loving trail.

Sometimes the herds would be taken to the distant grasslands of the state of Dakota, the cowboys and cattle travelling for months at a time. When they arrived in the towns and received their wages the cowboys would have a wild time, drink vast quantities of whisky and get into fights and all sorts of trouble. When they had spent all their money the cowboys would go back to the ranch and their normal working life.

Where bison live

The bison are typical ruminants of the great prairies of North America where they are commonly called buffalo. When the first settlers went to the west there were an estimated 60 million of these animals who provided the Indians with their major source of food and skins; but the Indians only killed when necessary.

Then the white man came and the massacre began. During the years across the continent, these animals were wantonly slaughtered by the hundreds of thousands. The white settlers only used the tongue of the bison and the animal's bones were sold by the ton for a few dollars to be made into fertilizer.

Finally all but a few bison were killed. Today they are carefully protected and are breeding again in great numbers.

Where the main battles between the Indians and the whites took place

The massacre of the bison by the whites was one of the causes of Indian anger that led these nomads of the prairie to declare a merciless war.

Those responsible for the extermination of the Indians knew very well that the only way to crush Indian resistance was to deprive them of their bison, their main source of food. These white men, led by Phil Sheridan, went hunting the bison: even the American army encouraged this activity. For several years bands of hunters went through the prairie, leaving behind them a land strewn with the carcases of thousands of dead animals. The famous Buffalo Bill alone killed 4,280 bison in seventeen months.

At the end of this mad hunt

Skirmish between soldiers and the Sioux

more than 50 million bison had been killed. In the meantime the hatred of the Indians had been roused. Indian attacks on the whites which had previously been sporadic, now increased. From east to west ran the word: 'Death to the white man'.

The first of the cruel massacres of this unequal war between the two peoples took place in 1862 in Minnesota when Little Crow led his Sioux warriors in a massacre of 644 settlers. Many other massacres followed in various parts of the west. One well known one was the killing of eighty men led by Captain Fetterman who had come from Fort Kearny in Wyoming some time earlier at Christmas 1866. Perhaps the most famous was the massacre on 25 June 1876 of 300 cavalrymen under the command of General Custer at Little Bighorn in Montana by 4,000 Indians led by Chief Sitting Bull.

But these episodes which enraged the whites and stirred them to revenge, were only a reply, often a weak reply, to the very cruel massacres which the settlers and soldiers carried out in Indian villages. These villages were almost always defenceless and populated by old men, women and and children. The stories of the time often failed to mention the damage that was being done against the Indians in order to stress the cruelty that was suffered by the whites.

Apart from the individual episodes the words of Chief Red Cloud uttered to the white leaders remain true: 'When you first came to this land you were few and we were many. Now we are few. . . . In other days our people possessed vast areas of land, today we have no more than an island.'

The last conflict between the Sioux and the American army took place at Pine Ridge on 29 December 1890 when soldiers of the U.S. Seventh Cavalry massacred by gunfire more than 200 Indians in a village, most of them women and children. A few days earlier Chief Sitting Bull, who had been taken prisoner by the army, had been killed.

Where the pioneer trails to the west were made

The date of the start of the conquest of the west by the American pioneers can be fixed at 1843. It was in this year that thousands of families set out for the territory of Oregon, urged on by the preaching of the missionary Marcus Whitman who told them about all the wonders of the new promised lands.

The move to the west attracted growing numbers of people in the years that followed. In 1850 alone at Fort Laramie, which was one of the stopping points on the journey, there were 37,750 men, 825 women and 1,126 children. The journey west was full of all kinds of danger. The pioneers travelled in covered wagons, pulled by oxen, inside which were their household goods, farm tools, seeds and all their worldly belongings.

The Oregon trail passed through the prairies and climbed up the mountains for more than 3,200 kilometres until it reached the river Columbia. At that point the pioneers continued their journey on rafts. There were three main trails that began at Missouri River and led to the lands of the west: the Oregon trail, the California trail and the Santa Fe trail. Many thousands of pioneers died and were buried along these trails, the victims of storms, mud, disease and the attacks by wild Indians. Those who lived through these dangers were sustained by their courage until they reached their promised land in the west that was to reward all their hopes. During those years the pioneers laid the foundations of new and important cities in America.

Where the trail of the legendary Pony Express ran

By 1860 there were many large cities and towns established by the settlers in the American west. These towns needed a form of rapid communication with the rich cities of the east where practically all of America's industry and trade had its headquarters. In 1858 the stage-coaches of John Butterfield operated a week-

ly service between the civilized east and the wild west. The stagecoach services were quite regular in spite of attacks by Indians and bandits.

But a quicker form of communication was needed and in 1860 the Pony Express service came into being, making it possible to deliver mail quickly between the east and California. The riders who carried out this service were picked from the finest and bravest men of the west. A Pony Express rider had to cover a distance of 125 kilometres a day, changing horses in a few seconds and carrying a satchel containing 10 kilogrammes of mail.

From St Joseph in Missouri the trail of the Pony Express went across savage territories for 2,944 kilometres as far as Sacramento in California. It passed through Fort Kearney, Fort Laramie, Fort Bridger, Salt Lake City and Carson City. The entire journey took nine days but the record was seven days seven hours. When the first teiegraph service was opened the Pony Express came to an end.

Where the Pacific Railroad began

With the arrival of hundreds of thousands of settlers in the American west, many cities and towns had sprung up. It became necessary to have some means of carrying the large amounts of farm produce as quickly as possible from the lands of the west to the rich cities on the Atlantic coast, and return with the goods manufactured by the growing industries of the United States.

On 10 June 1861, President Abraham Lincoln signed a decree for the construction of the Pacific

A rider of the Pony Express

Railroad. Two large companies, the Union Pacific and the Central Pacific, started work at the same time from opposite ends of the planned route. On 10 May 1869, after many difficulties, the two lines were joined together at Promontory Point in Utah.

The Union Pacific and the Central Pacific met in Utah in 1869

Objects dating from before Columbus' arrival in America

In Central and South America from about 2000 B.C. there are traces of several villages and places of worship. The oldest of these are situated in the mountains of Peru, but there are others in Mexico too. This region appears to have been the cradle of America's major civilizations. It was here that the civilization and culture of the Toltecs, among others, was born. The Toltec civilization was probably the most important in ancient America and influenced the later civilizations of the Aztecs and the Mayas. The Toltecs' main centre was at Tula, a city-state that was the seat of a great dynasty of kings.

Where to find the legendary Fort Alamo

Fort Alamo, the scene of a terrible massacre in which the famous Davy Crockett was killed, is in Texas where the city of San Antonio now stands. Texas was a Mexican colony which Americans began to infiltrate from 1820. In 1836 there were so many of these Americans and they had become so powerful that they demanded independence from Mexico. They defied the troops of the Mexican army but at the Alamo, behind the stockade of an old Spanish mission, about 187 of them were trapped and besieged by the army of General de Santa Anna. The bravery of the fort's defenders could only stand up to the enemy for two weeks and on 6 March 1836 Santa Anna led his troops in a final attack, killing everyone in the fort. Some weeks later, however, the Mexicans were defeated by the colonists at San Jacinto and the Texans won their independence.

Where to find America's most ancient human settlements

We know that the first inhabitants of the Americas were of Asian origin. These people crossed the Bering Strait about 20,000 years ago and followed the frozen trails of Alaska, moving gradually southwards. It would therefore seem reasonable to believe that America's longest-inhabited places were in the north. In this region the ancient Americans would have established their settlements before sending advance parties farther south.

Archaeological excavations, however, prove that the oldest inhabited centres first arose in Central and South America. There must have been some early settlements in the north but little trace of these has been found.

Where Columbus landed

When Columbus finally sighted land on 12 October 1492, after a voyage of more than two months, he was convinced that he had reached India. He was so sure that the first savages he met after going on land he called Indians.

We now know that on his first voyage Columbus did not even touch the American continent but merely explored some of the islands of the Bahamas. One of these was San Salvador which Columbus named in Spanish after the Holy Saviour, Jesus Christ, in gratitude for the success of his journey.

Before returning to Europe, Columbus reached the shores of Cuba. He was still sure he was in India but he was disappointed that he found no gold or spices. At last, on 5 December 1492, Columbus landed at Hispaniola, which today is divided into the two countries of Haiti and the Dominican Republic. On this is-land he left a garrison of Spanish volunteers to take charge of the new lands.

Columbus landing at Hispaniola in 1492

patches over the eyes. It has long ears and a pointed snout and its voice is a bark. This animal is the American equivalent of the Euro-pean pole-cats and martens.

The ring-tail cat is an excellent climber and often lives in trees where it catches birds, small mammals and other little creatures on which it feeds. Sometimes it lives in deserts. It spends the day in well-sheltered lairs and comes out at night.

Where the ring-tail cat lives

In the regions of Central America, in certain parts of the United States and especially in Mexico, the ring-tail cat is a very common animal. In Mexico City it is kept as a household pet like an ordinary domestic cat, although the ring-tail cat is not easily domesticated.

The most striking feature of this small mammal is its long, bushy tail marked with black and white rings which give this cat a very individual appearance. The ring-tail cat's body fur is greyish-brown, thick and soft, with white

still live in scattered, poor villages known as pueblos. Today these places have none of their past splendour.

In parts of Colorado there are the remains of ancient pueblos which reached their greatest development about 1300. Perhaps the most beautiful of these is Pueblo Bonito in the valley of the Rio San Juan. This village is shaped like an amphitheatre in which the houses rise like steps one above the other.

Pueblo houses were built of bricks made from compressed and dried mud and sometimes consisted of up to four storeys. They were often built in stepped-back style, so that the strongly built flat roofs of the lower rooms formed terraces for the rooms above and provided the only means of access.

Where the civilization of the ancient American Pueblo Indians flourished

The Pueblo were a people who lived in villages in North America. Before the Spanish conquest they were spread over a vast territory which included southern California, northern Mexico and the land to the east as far as Texas. The descendants of these people

Where the cashew grows

The *acaju*, or cashew, is a native plant of tropical America but today it is cultivated in most warm countries for its excellent nuts. The tree grows on ground that is lower than 800 metres and needs a warm, moist climate. The fruit, which is particularly popular in

Brazil where it ripens between November and January, is quite odd-looking. It resembles a large pear as big as a man's fist, at the bottom of which is a woody growth shaped like a kidney.

In actual fact the real fruit is this curved nut at the bottom of the fruit. The most striking part of the fruit is the pear-shaped part which is really the greatly swollen stalk of the tree's blossom. This stalk becomes fleshy and rich in sugar substances.

Where to find Death Valley

The American pioneers gave this grim name of Death Valley to a very deep depression in Inyo, California, which at its bottom lies 85 metres below sea level. The entire valley had to be crossed by the prospectors in search of the famous gold deposits of California and many of these men lost their lives in Death Valley, dying of exhaustion and thirst. The pools of water that form in certain parts of the valley's floor are extremely salty, the climate is torrid and not one blade of grass grows there. It is a real hell-on-earth and the gold prospectors struggled to get through it, but often it was the end of their hopes.

In the 1870s when gold was discovered in the nearby mountains, thousands of skeletons of dead animals left behind by the pioneers marked the Death Valley trail. Hundreds of carcases littered the route and the ground was covered with wooden crosses on the graves of those people who had paid with their lives for the attempt to pass through its desolate wastes.

Guatemalan costumes

Where the Mayas lived

The region where the Maya civilization developed forms part of what is now Yucatan, Guatemala and Honduras. It is a broad area that lies between the Atlantic and Pacific Oceans, with a tropical climate and where abundant rainfall has created large and flourishing forests. The territory is crossed by a chain of mountains which are volcanic in origin.

The Mayas first came to this land before the birth of Christ. For a long time they lived a primitive form of life but towards A.D. 300 their civilization began to develop. The Mayas had a different appearance from other inhabitants of the region: they were round-headed and usually not very tall. They lived in city-states and kept alive their awareness of being one race.

The largest Maya city, founded in 416 and named Tikal, included five groups of great buildings which were joined by elevated roadways. This city had eight gigantic pyramids more than 70 metres high, the ruins of which still give us an idea of their ancient splendour.

THE WHERE OF SOUTH AMERICA

Where to find the world's largest forest

The world's largest forest covers the vast river basins of the Amazon and the Orinoco. The enormous growth of vegetation in this zone is due to its proximity to the equator. It is extremely warm and the air is very humid because of the heavy rainfall that can last from six to eight months.

The sub-equatorial forest is dense and impenetrable with many layers of vegetation, each growing to a different height. Flying over such a forest in an aeroplane one can only see the tops of the highest trees which, massed together, give the impression of an immense sea of green from which only those trees with very tall trunks emerge to heights of more than 40 metres.

Underneath this top layer grow tree ferns and beneath them are shrubs, grasses and climbing plants known as *lianas*. Human beings or large animals can only go through such forests by following the almost invisible tracks made by animals going to their water-holes.

South American fuschia

FALKLAND ISLANDS

Where the first fuchsia plants were found

The dense forests of South America are the native places of the fuchsia, those beautiful flowering plants that can be kept in a pot or grown in gardens. There are many species of fuchsia which vary considerably in size and other characteristics.

The fuchsia were used to the dark atmosphere of dense forests and when the first plants were brought to Europe they did not stand up well to strong sunlight. Later, as hybrid forms of the plant were produced, stronger specimens began to grow and flourish in almost every kind of climate. The many varieties of fuchsia are quite easy to grow and are very resistant to many plant diseases. In winter, however, they should be kept in a greenhouse.

Usually the brightly coloured flowers in shades of red, blue, purple and white, droop down from the branches, but there are also fuchsias which have flowers that stand up straight and the plant is as big as a small tree.

Where to find the world's highest railways

In Peru the trains climb up the Andes mountains to a height of 4,816 metres. This is the railway line that starts at Callao on the Pacific coast and goes to La Oroya: it is the highest railway line in the world.

The railway line from Rio Mulato to Potosi reaches a height of just over 4,787 metres, almost as high as Mont Blanc, Europe's tallest mountain. The highest railway line in Europe is at the Jungfrau in Switzerland and reaches a height

of just over 3,454 metres.

On these South American lines the trains set out at sea level and reach great heights so rapidly that nurses travel on them to help the passengers with oxygen masks if they feel ill as a result of the rapid change in air pressure and the thinness of the air. The railways across the Andes provide vital links between the lowland regions, but the cost of construction and maintenance is very great.

Trains climb the mountains to a height of 4,816 metres

Bolivian girl

ing too much. For thousands of years they have been used to living at great altitudes and their bodies have become adapted to the severe climate of the Andes. As a result of breathing in the thin air they have developed large chests to extract as much oxygen as possible from the air.

Bolivia has no sea coast and its territory is almost completely covered by mountains. These include high mountain chains in the west and a number of high plateaux, most of them arid and all of them about 4,000 metres above sea level. In the east the land slopes gently away downwards to the immense river basin of the Amazon.

Where to find the world's highest capital city

At the foot of the soaring peaks of Mount Illampu (6,550 metres) and Mount Illimani (6,459 metres) on the Andes mountain range, stands the city of La Paz, the capital of Bolivia, founded by the Spaniards in 1548.

Situated on a high plateau a little south of Lake Titicaca, this city of almost 400,000 inhabitants rises to a height of 3,658 metres, the highest capital city in the world. But it is not the world's highest city. Oruro, for example, which has almost 100,000 inhabitants is 3,715 metres above sea level. There are even higher inhabited places: the village of Chacaltaya, lost in the mountains of the Andes, is 5,130 metres above sea level which is higher than the summit of Mont Blanc.

At such altitudes the air is very thin and contains less oxygen, but the Indians can live and work in these conditions without suffer-

Where the world's most famous carnival takes place

Washed by three waters of Guanabara Bay and dominated by the Pâo de Açucar (Sugarloaf Mountain), Rio de Janeiro is one of the most fascinating cities in the world. Discovered by the Portuguese in 1502, it was the capital of Brazil until 1960 when Brazilia became the new capital. Rio is a busy trading port, has flourishing industries and more than 4 million inhabitants. But what has made this city famous throughout the world is the carnival that takes place there every year.

In February of each year Rio turns into a huge and colourful stage for dancing and for decorated floats that parade past huge crowds from all over the world. For a whole month music and laughter reign supreme, but it is during the last three days that the festival reaches its climax, and there is non-stop dancing in the streets of Copacabana.

Where the monkey puzzle tree comes from

These strange trees are ever-green and their branches are covered in thousands of dark-green, scale-like leaves. They resemble the fossilized remains of very ancient trees that grew many millions of years ago. These are trees of the *Araucaria* family, conifers that first grew in Brazil and in the Andes mountains, and later became popular in Europe.

The best-known is the *Araucaria araucana*, the Chile pine or monkey puzzle tree which was introduced into Britain in 1796. In South America this tree grows as high as 50 metres. It has a blackish, wrinkled bark and the branches grow straight out from the trunk, separated into tiers. The leaves have no stems and are small and stiff with a spiky end. From a distance the tree looks as if it has green branches with no leaves and has a stiff, rigid appearance.

Where alpacas are reared

Recent archaeological excavations in the Andes where the oldest Indian civilizations once flourished, have discovered valuable remains of old woven cloth that dates back to about 4,000 years ago. These woven materials were made from the wool of the alpaca, an animal greatly valued by the ancient peoples of South America for its long, soft fur.

The alpaca is a typical animal of the Andes mountains. It is a close relative of the llama and, like the llama, is descended from the wild guanaco, which is still hunted in the mountains of Peru and Bolivia. The alpaca rather resembles a sheep, with a neck and face similar to a camel, but it is not a gentle animal like the sheep and is quite bad-tempered. Its wool grows to a length of more than 20 centimetres and is shorn every year.

Alpacas live in a semi-wild state on the slopes of the Andes

Marmoset

Where American monkeys live

Almost all the monkeys of the American continent live in the dense forests around the Amazon River. These monkeys spend most of their time in trees and are extremely agile acrobats, using their long tails to hang on to the branches. The best-known of these animals are the capuchin monkeys which were once the inseparable companions of travelling musicians and organ-grinders.

The capuchin monkeys are easily domesticated for they are gentle and good-natured and live well in captivity. For this reason there are always many of them in zoos and they are often sold in pet shops. They are not much bigger than a cat and are greyish-brown in colour with a long, hairy tail which is not so good at gripping things. They live mainly on fruit but also eat tender shoots and buds, insects and eggs which they steal from birds' nests.

Where to find the highest peak in the Andes mountains

When the first Spanish explorers reached the Andes mountains and began to clamber up these gigantic rocks towards Cuzco and other cities of the Incas, they were amazed by the dizzy heights of this huge range. The descriptions they wrote of what they saw are full of wonder, and yet these Spanish explorers did not even see the highest peaks of this chain of mountains, some of which rise to more than 6,000 metres.

Today we know that the tallest mountain in the Andes is Mount Aconcagua (7,035 metres). This mountain stands in the Mendoza province of north-west Argentina on the border with Chile and a little to the north of Rio de las Cuevas. From about 5,000 metres upwards this mountain is covered in eternal snows and glaciers. The glaciers are more numerous on the southern slopes where the river Aconcagua rises to flow into the Pacific Ocean. As well as being the name of a mountain and a river, Aconcagua is also the name of a province in Chile at the foot of the Andes.

Mount Aconcagua is an extinct volcano. It was climbed for the first time in 1897 by Stuart Vines and Mattias Zurbriggen who reached the summit from their base camp at Puente de Inca. Later expeditions used the same base camp because it is the best

Squirrel Monkey

place for delivering supplies.

As well as being the highest mountain in the Western Hemisphere Aconcagua is much easier to climb than other peaks in the Andes which, although lower, still resist the attempts by mountaineers from many countries to climb them.

Where sweet potatoes come from

The sweet potato is a large tuberous plant that is a native of America's central regions. Today the plant can be grown in temperate zones including parts of southern Europe.

The roots of the sweet potato are rich in sugar and have a floury texture. Root colours range from white to orange and sometimes purple inside, and from fawn to brown or red outside. The upper part of the plant consists of a stem that climbs or trails along the ground and which is from 3 to 6 metres long.

The sweet potato plant has beautiful heart-shaped leaves with long stems which are very decorative and for this reason it is sometimes grown indoors.

Where to find the world's highest lake

Of all the great lakes that lie within the various continents the highest above sea level is Lake Titicaca which is situated in a vast, high plateau on the Andes between Peru and Bolivia. The lake is 3,809 metres above sea level which is about 1,000 metres lower than the summit of Mont Blanc. It has an area of 8,135 square kilometres and is divided into two by the Strait of Tiquina. The whole lake is 178 kilometres long and is very deep (370 metres).

A number of narrow strips of land jut out into the lake from the shore and form broad stretches of sheltered water where very tall reed forests grow. The local Indians use these reeds to make boats. They also use the reeds to make big rafts which they load with soil and convert into floating gardens that produce beans, peppers, marrows, potatoes and other vegetables.

The entire region round Lake Titicaca is fairly well populated because the climate is mild and good for farming. The clear waters of the lake contain many kinds of fish.

Reed boat on Lake Titicaca

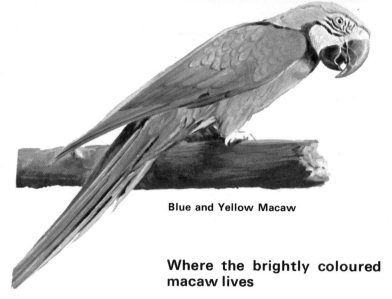

Blue and Yellow Macaw

Hyacinthine Macaw

Red and Yellow Macaw

Where the brightly coloured macaw lives

The world's largest parrots live in the forests round the Amazon River. They are the macaws, birds with splendidly coloured plumage that can be seen in any zoo, making a terrible din with their harsh, squawking cries.

The macaw, which lives in a region that stretches from Mexico to Bolivia, can grow to more than a metre in length from its beak to the tip of its tail. Two varieties noted for their size are the blue and yellow macaw (*Ara ararauna*) and the green macaw (*Ara militaris*). Macaws have an amazing display of colours, all of them very bright and contrasting with one another.

Parrots are common in the forests and open spaces of tropical zones in the southern hemisphere, except in southern Africa. There are more than 300 species, including bantam and giant varieties. Parrots all have the same kind of large, strong, curved beak which they use to crack open the hard shell of fruits that they live on. All parrots also have identical claws with the first and fourth toes turned backwards, enabling them to keep a tight hold when they perch on trees. They are tree-dwelling birds but they are also very good fliers.

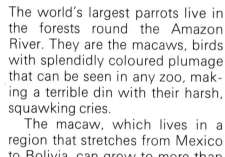

Where the first potatoes were discovered

The potato is a native of Chile and Peru where the local inhabitants had grown it for a long time before the first Europeans arrived. The Spaniards first came across the potato plant during their conquest of America and they brought it to Europe. It was many years before this new vegetable became commonly known. It was only towards the end of the eighteenth century that potatoes began to be cultivated on a large scale in Europe.

The potato plant has a herbaceous stalk about 60 centimetres long and oval leaves that are whitish underneath. The part of the plant that is eaten is not the fruit, but merely the underground part of the stalk. This is known as the tuber and acts as a storage place for the substances needed to feed the plant.

The ancient Incas knew of some sixty different varieties of potato, all of them adapted to growing in differing weather conditions. In this way the Incas could grow potatoes near desert land or at altitudes of more than 4,000 metres near Lake Titicaca.

The potato is eaten as a vegetable and is also used to produce a type of flour, dextrin and alcohol.

Where the Brazil nut grows

The Brazil nut is a large woody nut which, with its three sides, rather resembles the slice of a mandarin orange. Inside the dark, rough shell lies a hard, white kernel which has a sweetish taste.

The tree on which the Brazil nut grows is the *Bertholletia excelsa*, also called the Pará nut tree, which grows in the forests around the Amazon River in Brazil. The tree must have a hot, humid climate and it cannot be grown in Europe even under hot-house conditions. It has evergreen leaves and is tall and majestic, growing to a height of more than 40 metres.

The Brazil nut is not really a fruit but a seed. From fifteen to twenty of these seeds are contained inside the real fruit which acts as a capsule or covering. This capsule is large, round and woody with a soft husk.

The Brazil nut is a very important food for the Indians who live in Brazil. It also provides a valuable oil which can be used as a foodstuff or for lubricating delicate machinery. Because of their high oil content Brazil nuts tend to turn sour quickly.

Where the jaguar lurks

The jaguar is one of the best-known members of the cat family in America, living at the edge of the forests in marshy regions of tropical zones. The ground colour of its coat varies from white to black but most jaguars are orange-brown in colour, the black spots arranged in rosettes with a black spot in the centre.

The jaguar resembles the leopard but is more heavily built. It hunts its prey by night and can catch its food by fishing in rivers or pouncing on monkeys or birds in trees, for this animal is a skilful climber and a good swimmer. Cattle or horses are its favourite victims and for this reason the jaguar is a threat to remote farms where livestock grazes in the open.

The jaguar will also attack

Jaguars can swim with ease and often do so whenever it is necessary to catch their prey

people and tear them apart as a tiger does. It is a very fierce animal and difficult to tame, even if captured while still very young. In its attacks on other animals the jaguar displays a strength and ferocity much greater than that of the big cats of Africa and Asia.

Armadillo and (right) rolled into a ball

Where armadillos live

The armadillo is a strange mammal that is common throughout South America. It is covered in a kind of armour composed of solid plates and movable bands which go round its body so that the animal can roll up into a ball. The number of these bands varies from species to species: the best-known armadillo, the peba, which can also be found in North America, has nine bands. The head of the armadillo is protected by a horny helmet and its tail resembles a knight's sword and is kept inside a sheath which is jointed so that the animal can move the tail.

There is one variety of armadillo that lives in the pampas of South America whose tail is so short that it can scarcely be seen. This is the *Chlamyphorus truncatus*, also

Giant Armadillo

known as the *pichiciego*, a small armadillo about 15 centimetres long with pink scales which cover only part of its body.

Where the shells of the glyptodons were found

Armadillos are usually little creatures which live in almost every part of South America. They are the direct descendants of the glyptodon, a giant animal that lived many millions of years ago.

The glyptodon was a peaceful animal. It was able to protect itself against the terrible monsters of those days because of its stout shell which covered its entire body. It defended itself rather as the armadillos do today, or even the tortoises. Whilst it was under attack the glyptodon would withdraw into its shell and stay there until its enemy grew tired of waiting. If the enemy refused to go away, the glyptodon would then use its strong tail like a club. This tail was covered in sharp spikes that could do much damage.

Many fossilized shells of glyptodons have been found in the plains of South America. These animals first appeared about 40 million years ago but we do not know exactly when they became extinct to make way for more advanced forms of animal life. They still wandered the Earth when the first human beings appeared.

It is quite possible that the shells of glyptodons were used as homes by primitive peoples. These shells were more than 4 metres long and a human skeleton was once found lying underneath one. Beneath other glyptodon shells have been found ashes and the remains of fires that men must have lit, with flints and other man-made objects beside them.

Where the *buriti* race takes place

In the heart of Brazil, where the forests end and the grassy plains begin, live the Kraho Indians who were robbed of their hunting grounds by the white people. From the air a Kraho village looks like a big wheel: the white sandy road round the houses is the rim of the wheel and the village roads form the spokes, each road running from a house to the square at the centre of the village. The Kraho Indians have an old legend which says that they are the descendants of the Sun and Moon who were hunters and quarrelled about taking a wife. For this reason the Kraho tribe today is divided into two parties.

During the hunting season the Kraho leave their village and camp out in the plains. They share whatever they catch and they also keep something for members of the tribe who cannot hunt. But whoever in the tribe fails to come back with a dead animal from the hunt becomes the laughing stock. When the hunt is over the Kraho give thanks to their gods in a picturesque sporting competition: the *buriti* race. The *buriti* is the trunk of a palm tree weighing about 90 kilogrammes. The competitors form two teams and race against each other to carry the trunk to the village. The winner is the man who is first to throw the palm trunk in front of the patron lady of the festival.

Where to find the longest road in the world

America is a continent of records, huge construction schemes and the continent which has the longest road in the world. This is part

Glyptodon

of the Pan American Highway System and links the distant northern regions of the American continent with Tierra del Fuego in the southernmost tip of South America with an extremely long ribbon of road.

Work on the Pan American Highway System began in 1923. The longest road runs for almost 22,300 kilometres, from Anchorage in Alaska to southern Chile, following the Pacific coast for most of its extent.

Highway in Caracas

THE WHERE OF OCEANIA

Where to find pigeons that 'suckle' their young

The blue-crowned pigeon, or Queen Victoria crowned pigeon as it is also called, is a close relative of our pigeons and is the largest member of this family of birds. It is about the size of a small turkey, with long, very strong legs and beautifully coloured feathers. On its head is a lace-like crest that is always upright and looks just like a crown.

The blue-crowned pigeon lives in the forests and swamps of New Guinea, feeding on worms, grubs and seeds which it pecks up from the ground. Whenever danger arises it flies up to the highest branches in the trees and utters sad, gloomy cries.

Like all pigeons this bird 'suckles' its young. Just before the young pigeons are hatched from their eggs their mother begins to produce a thick fluid known as 'milk'. This fluid is produced from two pouches inside the bird's throat and is the only form of food that the baby birds receive during the first three weeks of their life. The young birds instinctively poke their beaks into their mother's wide-open beak and gather up the nourishing milk fluid produced from the pouches.

Where to find the main religious centre of Polynesia

At one time Raiatea, the largest of the Iles Sous le Vent in the Society Islands, was the religious and political centre of all Polynesia. The big canoes with their outriggers carrying huge sails made of pandanus leaves travelled for thousands of kilometres across the open Pacific to reach the lagoon of Raiatea.

Many religious relics have been found in Raiatea: one of them, which lies abandoned in thick forest, is the *mare*, a grim altar made of black stone. It lies along a line running east to west that follows the path of the Sun god

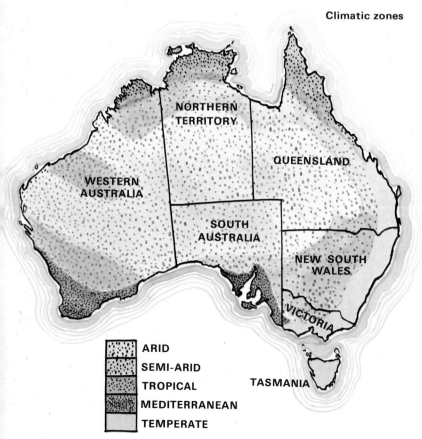

Climatic zones

NORTHERN TERRITORY

QUEENSLAND

WESTERN AUSTRALIA

SOUTH AUSTRALIA

NEW SOUTH WALES

VICTORIA

TASMANIA

- ARID
- SEMI-ARID
- TROPICAL
- MEDITERRANEAN
- TEMPERATE

in the heavens. It was on this altar that the priests sacrificed their victims. Raiatea still has the Stone of the Chiefs, a stone pillar more than 2 metres high. The Polynesian chiefs used to stand against the pillar when they held their meetings on the island and whoever was taller than the pillar was elected King of Kings and High Priest.

The existence of these extremely tall men has been proved by the large bones found in the burial places of ancient warriors. Raiatea is also famous for its *tiki*, colossal images made of wood or stone which watched over the people and ensured the fertility of the soil. The most sacred *tiki* were in the centre of the island and kept under the waters of the lagoon. The ancient Polynesians regarded this as the most sacred point of the universe where the land and the oceans began.

Budgerigars, native birds of Australia

live quite happily in a cage. These birds do not require any special care and are easy to breed. Once they become a family pet, budgerigars rarely want to leave their home. They are often allowed to come out of their cages but care must be taken that there are no cats around to attack them.

Where budgerigars come from

Budgerigars are brightly coloured miniature parrots which are a very popular cagebird and are kept as pets in many homes. These birds are specially bred but their natural home is Australia where many can be seen flying free in forests. In the wild this little parrot has pale green feathers on its back and bright green plumage on its chest, but selective breeding has developed yellow, grey, violet, blue and green varieties. Like all members of the parrot family it has a long tapering tail and a slender and graceful body.

In Australia budgerigars live together in large groups in forests and plains, fluttering from tree to tree. They are very tame and can be easily domesticated and

Budgerigars in flight

Where to find black swans

The beautiful black swan is so common round the coasts of Australia that it has become the emblem on the government coat-of-arms of Western Australia. In this region there are many black swans which live in lakes along the coast. They have also been introduced into New Zealand.

Like the white swans of the northern hemisphere, black swans are splendid swimmers. They prefer to stay in one place close to where they were born and are the only swans which do not migrate.

During the nesting season black swans build a large nest among the reeds on an island lake. The nest is simply a heap of twigs with a hollow in it. The eggs are laid and hatched between August and December which are the spring months in the southern hemisphere. The baby swans are covered in grey, downy feathers and are very lively, learning to swim within a few hours. They eat grubs, insects and molluscs scooped up by their mother's beak and ride on her back, nestling down in the soft feathers between her wings.

Where to find mammals that lay eggs

Oceania is a place full of surprises in the animal kingdom. In this region there still live the last examples of prehistoric creatures, odd-looking animals with strange habits who, because of the isolation of this part of the world, have retained the features of their weird ancestors of millions of years ago.

One of the strangest and most mysterious of these animals is the spiny anteater which lives in the sandy and rocky regions of south-eastern Australia and in Tasmania. The spiny anteater is an odd mixture: it has sharp quills like a porcupine, an elongated beak-like snout and feet shaped like those of an elephant. The feet have powerful claws and the animal has a long, thin, sticky tongue like other anteaters. When the spiny anteater is in danger it rolls up into a ball or rapidly digs itself a hole where it hides so that it is difficult to take the animal by surprise and watch it.

The spiny anteater lives on insects. Its favourite food is ants and termites which it scoops up with its long, sticky tongue. The animal uses its strong claws to tear ant-hills apart or to break down the hard clay dwellings of termites.

Like the duck-billed platypus,

Spiny Anteater, showing the egg pouch

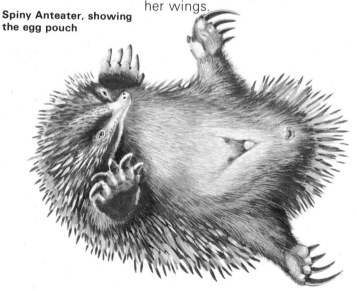

this strange mammal lays eggs. But the spiny anteater carries its eggs in a special pouch in its skin until they are hatched. The babies stay inside their mother's pouch where they suck her milk through special hairs on her body. As soon as the babies grow quills of their own which prick the mother, she makes them leave the pouch and become independent.

Where to find the great deserts of Australia

The eastern coast of Australia is a fertile region with plenty of rain and a mild climate. These good conditions are caused by the Great Dividing Range, or Eastern Highlands as it is also called, a chain of mountains that runs all the way from north to south forming a narrow coastal plain. These mountains act as a barrier to the trade winds from the Pacific Ocean, so that when the clouds reach them they let fall their rain on the coastal region.

But just as the Great Dividing Range makes the coastal plain fertile it also makes the land to the west into a desolate, arid desert. Once the clouds have crossed the mountains they have no more rain left for Australia's central regions so that this land is all desert with only a few thorny acacia trees dotted around.

About two-thirds of the total land area of Australia is desert in which human life is impossible. The biggest deserts are the Great Sandy Desert in the north-west, and the Great Victoria Desert in the south, both of which are almost completely flat and present an ugly and monotonous landscape.

The supply and conservation of water are among Australia's greatest problems. The aridity of the interior is relieved by the presence of artesian wells, including the Great Australian or Artesian basin which is the largest artesian area in the world.

About two-thirds of the land in Australia is desert

Tree Kangaroo

pouch, but they have to find it by themselves. To help the baby, the mother kangaroo uses her tongue to leave a long wet trail of saliva along her stomach which leads to her pouch. The baby kangaroo, pink and hairless, begins to climb up his mother's stomach by holding on to the fur, instinctively following the wet trail until it reaches the opening of its mother's pouch and creeps inside.

Where to find kangaroos that climb trees

Of the many kinds of kangaroo that live in Australia one of the strangest is the kangaroo that climbs trees to eat the fruit and tender shoots. Unlike ordinary kangaroos, this animal has much bigger front legs which are almost as well developed as its hind ones. The tree kangaroo also has sharp claws to help it clamber among the trees with all the acrobatic skill of a monkey.

Like all marsupials, kangaroos give birth to tiny, helpless babies which must be placed immediately into the warmth of the mother's

Where rabbits are a public menace

Until the 1850s there were no rabbits at all in Australia. Then it was decided to import some of these animals and breed them as food. After several attempts at introduction three pairs of breeding rabbits were let loose in New South Wales. This turned out to be the greatest disaster for Australian farmers for the rabbits settled down so happily in their new surroundings and produced so many litters of young rabbits, that soon the entire continent was invaded by them. Farmers' crops faced the danger of being completely eaten up and it was estimated that between 1876 and 1885 rabbits caused millions of pounds worth of damage.

Rabbits breed extremely rapidly. A female can produce up to twelve baby rabbits every forty days. In this way, under perfect conditions, a pair of rabbits can in three years produce 13 million rabbits. In order to fight this terrible threat tall wire fences were built to keep the rabbits away from cultivated fields, but the rabbits burrowed underneath them. Today rabbits are hunted mercilessly in Australia and every year many millions are killed.

Where to find Australia's richest mines

Almost every month in recent years news comes of the discovery of new major mineral deposits in Australia which will be exploited in the future. The Australian government has launched a broad research programme to survey the land and draw up a complete list of its natural resources. The plan is revealing that this immense territory is one of the richest in the world for the many kinds of natural wealth that lie underneath its soil.

It was already discovered during the second half of the nineteenth century that some zones, especially Queensland and Western Australia, were rich in valuable minerals. Australia, too, had its 'gold fever' which attracted many people in search of this precious metal. Gold was certainly abundant in Australia but it was not the only form of natural wealth. Australia is also rich in such minerals as tungsten, manganese, cobalt, and uranium. It is the world's greatest producer of lead and possesses vast quantities of zinc, gold, silver, tungsten and lignite. Iron ore is widely distributed throughout the country.

Australia's most important mineral deposits today are at Mount Isa in Queensland and at Broken Hill in New South Wales. New deposits are being found in other zones, however, especially on the eastern coastal strip where large deposits of coal also occur.

Australia is rich in minerals because many of this country's rocks are among the oldest in the world. The minerals have been produced in these rocks through the geological processes that have taken place over thousands of millions of years.

Kalgoorlie Gold Mine

Emu with its young

Where kava is the national drink

Kava is the national drink of Polynesia. It is made by the *taupo*, the Polynesian word for the most respected girl in the village. This girl is chosen as mistress of ceremonies: she chews the roots of the pepper plant from which the drink is made and prepares the beverage.

First of all a young man fills a large wooden bowl with the chewed kava powder. Then he

Costumes of the Fijian Islands

Where the male bird hatches the eggs

The emu, the second largest living bird, inhabits the great, semi-arid plains of Australia where it wanders about in small groups through the flat grasslands.

During the mating season the male emu chooses a wife and starts a family with her. The male not only makes the nest, a shallow pit in the ground, but he chases his mate away and sits on the eggs himself.

An emu nest can contain up to fifteen large, blue-green eggs, each weighing about 600 grammes. The hatching period lasts two months and when the baby emus, covered in striped down, are born they are ready to walk about and look for their own food.

The emu has been greatly reduced in numbers and is in danger of dying out. Attempts are being made to breed it domestically for its meat.

pours the milk of a coconut over the *taupo*'s fingers and some more of the milk into the kava powder. The *taupo* then moves her hands in accordance with a ritual pattern, stirs the mixture into a paste and strains it through hibiscus. More milk is added; the *taupo* opens her hands and rests them on the edge of the bowl and the drink is ready. Those taking part in the ceremony then clap their hands rhythmically while a cup-bearer fills a cup and raises it to his head. He pours out the yellowish-green contents and the kava is then passed round according to the rank of those present.

Where Australia is richest in water

Australia's only great river is the Murray which flows into the ocean near Adelaide. The valley of the river Murray runs south-west from the Great Dividing Range the southern slopes of which are rich in forests of eucalyptus trees and the home of most of Australia's characteristic animals. Farther to the west the forests give way to broad grassy plains with scattered thickets of acacia trees.

The Murray is 2,550 kilometres long and its main tributary is the river Darling. Along its twisting course the Murray receives the waters of many small rivers and streams. Because of the varying rainfall the Murray does not have a steady rate of flow: it can be reduced to a trickle or suddenly become swollen. Imposing dams have been built to make the river flow in a more regular manner and to exploit its waters. As a result the wastelands around Adelaide and Victoria are giving way to cultivated fields and orchards.

The explorer George Grey, threatened by natives

Where cockatoos live

The cockatoo differs from the parrot in the shape of its beak and the feathers on top of its head. Its beak is smaller than that of a parrot and is also more compressed. On top of its head, the cockatoo has a handsome tuft of feathers which can open out like a fan when the bird is excited or alarmed.

The white cockatoo is easily recognized because of its white plumage, unknown in any other species of parrot. The feathers on the cockatoo's head are a beautiful sulphur-yellow, the only splash of colour on an otherwise completely white body.

This bird lives in large groups on the edges of dense forests in Australia. It prefers open spaces near forests, with light and room to fly, and the forests provide its food which consists of green shoots and tuberous roots. Its nest is usually in a high tree hole where the baby birds, naked and blind when hatched, are fed by the parents for about three months.

These parrots seem to love the sound of their own voices. They also imitate other sounds, including the human voice, and are very clever at repeating phrases which are spoken to them.

Other varieties are the rose-crested and the bare-eyed cocka-toos and the galah. The giant black cockatoo with its naked cheeks which go red with excite-ment, lives in the forests of New Guinea.

Where fish are caught with lassos

The Polynesians regard the shark, especially the man-eating shark, as a kind of god. For this reason shark-hunting in Polynesia is a very ancient ceremony with some-thing sacred about it.

The fishermen put out to sea at dawn, using large canoes with outriggers to keep the vessel stable during the hunt. On the orders of the *tavana*, the leader of the fishermen, the men rattle bells loaded with bait close to the water. This is a very dangerous moment for many fishermen have lost fingers or even a whole hand to the shark.

As everybody keeps a sharp look-out a shadow suddenly ap-pears underneath the water: it is the shark. Some bait is lowered into the sea to draw the fish to-wards the trap. The fisherman with the lasso waits for the right moment and when it comes he throws the rope round the shark's neck, tightens the noose and then pulls the fish in. The other fisher-men then join in and beat the shark to death with heavy clubs as the water turns red with its blood.

The fishermen keep speaking to the shark until it is dead as if the animal understands them. The dead fish is then tied to the out-rigger and the islanders spend the rest of the day fishing, followed by huge flocks of gulls.

When the fishermen go back ashore they are so laden that as they reach the shallows of the rocks they have to jump out of their canoes and push them in front of them.

The whole village gathers to-gether to celebrate their return as a triumph of man over the hostile forces of nature.

Rose-crested cockatoo

Galah cockatoo

Giant black cockatoo

Where the cassowary lives

The cassowary is a large, flightless bird, over one and a half metres in height, which resembles the emu. It has long, thick, black plumage; its bare neck is knobbly and its head is also bare and crowned with a peculiar swelling that resembles a helmet.

The cassowary lives in the forests of New Guinea and the nearby islands and the north-eastern tip of Australia. It feeds mainly on fallen fruit and on small animals such as snails, lizards and the chicks of other birds.

These birds live in groups. They are rather timid and wary but are easily detected by the sound of their deep, windy sighs. They run away from any danger and can reach speeds of up to 50 kilometres an hour.

Where to find mammals which have beaks

The duck-billed platypus is the most archaic, or outdated, of all the mammals, more like a reptile or a bird. It lays eggs but when the babies are hatched they live on their mother's milk. Instead of teeth, the platypus has a beak. It lives only in Australia where it has survived to our own day because of that continent's isolation from the rest of the world.

The platypus is an aquatic animal, with webbed feet, rather like a beaver in its habits. It is an excellent swimmer and builds its home in the bank of the river. The entrance, which is under the surface of the water, is a long tunnel that leads to a roomy chamber lined with dry grass. This is where the baby platypuses are born and the mother keeps them in her pouch where they feed on her milk.

The platypus feeds by dredging the muddy bottoms of rivers with its flat beak. It lets the water run out of the sides of the beak and the little animals that live in the river mud are trapped inside its mouth. The platypus immediately stores these animals in roomy pouches in its cheeks and eats them later in the quiet of the riverbank. From time to time the platypus leaves the river and rests on the shore when it eats what it has caught slowly and with great enjoyment.

Platypuses
(*Ornithorincus anatinus*)

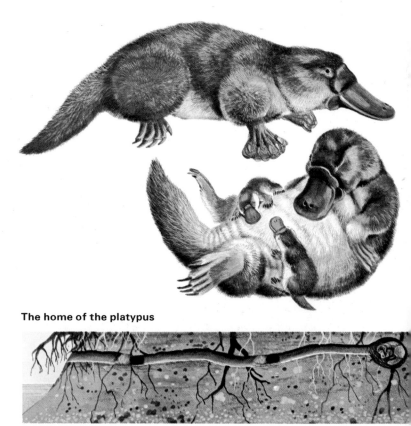

The home of the platypus

Hei-tiki,
a Maori charm

civilization but they were never able to form themselves into one state. When the Europeans came to New Zealand the Maoris withdrew farther into the interior of the country. According to the 1971 census their number has been reduced to 227,414 scattered throught the northern zones of the island. Intermarriage between Maoris and European New Zealanders is increasing steadily and a growing number of Maoris are moving into the towns.

Maori society was based on an aristocratic structure and ruled by chiefs and priests. The people were divided into three classes: the nobles, the warriors and the slaves. In many tribes cannibalism was practised and human heads were preserved by being smoked.

The traditional dress of the Maori consists of heavy robes made of woven fibres and decorated with kiwi feathers. Their houses are rectangular in shape and the villages are protected by strong palisades. The Maoris are skilful artists and are especially known for their sculptures and wood carvings.

Where the last of the Maori tribes live

The Maoris are a people of Polynesian origin who moved to New Zealand between about the eleventh and the thirteenth centuries. They brought to South Island agriculture and the arts of weaving and pottery. The Maoris achieved quite a high degree of

Where the wild breadfruit tree grows

The first navigators to explore the South Seas and their remote islands found that the natives ate bread although they had never seen wheat. The flour for this bread was obtained from the fruit of a large tree which grows to a height of 12 to 20 metres. The wood of the tree is excellent for making canoes and furniture; the bark provides a fibre that can be woven into material; and glue is obtained from the milky juice that oozes from cuts in the trunk. But the

Maori costumes

most valuable part of this tree is its fruit which can be harvested three times during the year.

The greenish-brown breadfruit is roundish and from 10 to 20 centimetres in diameter. It has a white, pulpy flesh that can be eaten raw, boiled in water, or even fried or roasted. When the pulp is dried it can be ground into a flour which the islanders use to make small loaves.

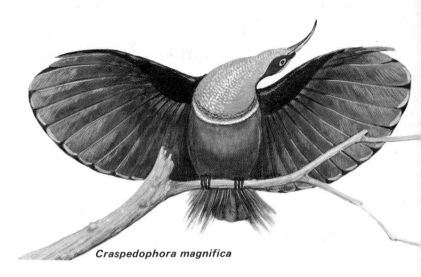

Craspedophora magnifica

Where the wombat lives

The wombat is a largely nocturnal animal that lives in Australia. Like the kangaroo, the wombat is a marsupial, but unlike the kangaroo it does not have a long tail and cannot jump. Wombats look rather like koala bears but they have a pair of sharp, continuously growing incisor teeth on their upper jaw and another pair on the lower jaw so that, like any rabbit or other rodent animal, they have to keep gnawing at hard foods to prevent these teeth from growing too long.

Wombats are vegetarians and eat grasses, the inner bark of shrub and tree roots and occasionally fungi. They use their very strong forefeet to dig tunnels, pushing the soil back with their hindfeet. These tunnels can be up to 3 metres long and a few have been found more than 30 metres long.

The flesh of the wombat is prized locally and these harmless animals have been almost completely wiped out by hunters.

There are two species of wombat: the naked-nosed wombat makes his home in Tasmania and the hilly or mountainous regions of south-eastern Australia; the hairy-nosed group lives only in southern Australia.

Where the wonderful dancing birds live

The male bird of paradise is among the most beautiful birds in the world. During the mating season it dances for the female, hopping and hovering on a leafless branch, beating its wings majestically, stretching out its neck and ruffling up its feathers to display plumage of vivid orange, yellow, blue, green, brown and red.

Birds of paradise are quite common in Australia and New Guinea. One of the most beautiful species is the royal bird of paradise, a quick, mischievous creature forever greedy and hungry like a crow.

(Vombatus hirsutus) Common wombat

THE WHERE OF THE SEAS AND THE OCEANS

Where divers reach their greatest depths

Underwater exploration is almost as old as man himself. There is evidence that primitive man went swimming under the sea although he did not go down as far as divers do today in the search for whatever gifts the depths of the seas have to offer. However, diving under the sea with no breathing equipment and relying simply on holding the breath, was not done to any great extent until the present century. This type of underwater swimming has proved valuable in helping to understand how the human body behaves in such conditions.

One of the most famous divers of this type is Raimond Bucher who in 1952 reached a depth of 39 metres. This was a great feat because this depth is considered the limit of human endurance under water.

In recent years men and women have been able to dive to even greater depths. These have not been as impressive as Bucher's achievement because these divers used special breathing equipment including masks, rubber diving suits, and cylinders containing compressed air which the diver carries on his back and from which he breathes through a mouth-tube. These skin-divers also have flippers on their feet to help them swim faster under the water.

Bucher is also one of the world's greatest skin-divers and has discovered a way of avoiding the painful and dangerous condition which attacks the body if a person comes back to the surface too quickly from deep water. He has carried out over 1,000 dives to a depth of more than 80 metres and even reached depths of about 100 metres.

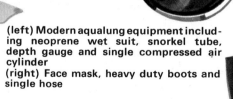

(left) Modern aqualung equipment including neoprene wet suit, snorkel tube, depth gauge and single compressed air cylinder
(right) Face mask, heavy duty boots and single hose

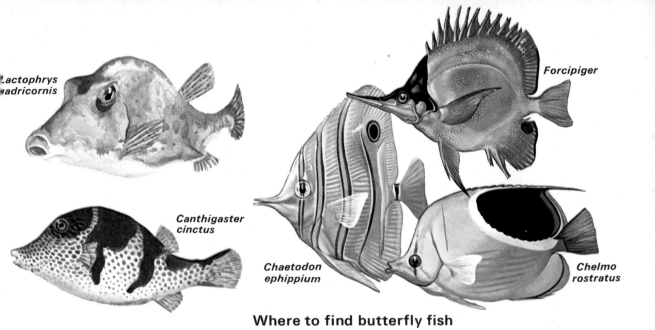

Lactophrys
quadricornis

Canthigaster
cinctus

Forcipiger

Chaetodon
ephippium

Chelmo
rostratus

Where the world's largest fish lives

The world's largest known fish is the whale shark which can grow to a length of more than 18 metres and weighs several tons. The whale itself cannot be regarded as fish because it is a mammal that lives in the sea.

The jaws of the whale shark are big enough to swallow a man, but this huge fish is harmless to human beings and lives on plankton, the tiny animal and plant life that floats near the surface of the oceans. The whale shark scoops up the plankton as it swims along and strains it through its rows of small teeth. This shark lives in tropical seas and swims near the surface for most of the time.

To catch a whale shark is a real stroke of luck for fishermen because this is a valuable fish. Every part of its body is used, the flesh as meat and the skin for leather. The liver of the whale shark provides an excellent oil; the Chinese use the dried fins to make a delicious soup; the bones and the entrails produce fertilizer; and the teeth are sold as curios or good-luck charms.

Where to find butterfly fish

Butterfly fish live in tropical seas. They dart swiftly among the coral reefs in shallow waters in large numbers, always ready to hide away in dark rocky corners should danger arise.

It is very difficult to catch a butterfly fish and most fishermen do not bother to try because it is not very good for eating.

The fish's name makes it clear that this is a beautiful creature and the vivid colours make one think of a light-winged butterfly fluttering from flower to flower. These fish are boldly marked with black bands and frequently have eye marks, although no two fish have identical patterns. Their markings together with their brilliant colours, mostly yellows, make them very conspicuous.

The butterfly fish is small, rarely exceeding 20 centimetres, and narrow, like a flounder, but it has enormous fins, often unusual in shape. The mouth is small with bristle-like teeth and the body is covered with rough scales. Baby butterfly fish do not resemble the adults at all: they have no colour on their scales and they have a collar or sheath round the neck, which they lose as they mature.

Where coral grows

Coral needs clear, running water and light, the two indispensable elements of life for the polyps, the small creatures who live in coral. The light stimulates these tiny animals and the running water brings them their food, consisting of bits of plant and animal matter. The sea must also be clean because mud would kill the polyp colony. For this reason, coral is scarcely ever found at the mouths of rivers where mud usually gathers.

When the polyps feed they push out little branch-like tentacles, each containing a tiny bag of stinging liquid which has the same effect as a nettle. When the polyp pushes out all its tentacles it makes a beautiful sight, but as soon as any danger comes along the tentacles are quickly withdrawn.

The colour of corals varies from a bright vermilion red, through

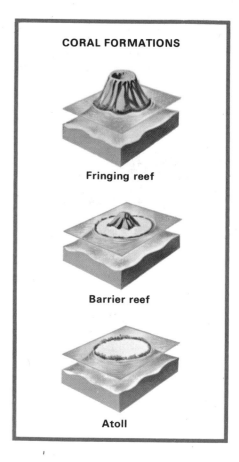

CORAL FORMATIONS

Fringing reef

Barrier reef

Atoll

pink, to white, due to the presence of iron salts which the calcium of the polyps soaks up.

Many coral banks are destroyed by primitive methods of fishing that are sometimes used to bring these beautiful things to the surface. It is difficult for any man to swim down to the depths where fine corals grow so many fishermen use a heavy piece of wood shaped like a cross to which nets are attached. The fishermen drag this piece of wood along the bottom and as the wood strikes against the corals it breaks off pieces which are then caught inside the net. This method of fishing makes it difficult to bring up large pieces of undamaged coral and also does great harm to parts of the coral colony which are still in the process of growing.

The *Gertruyd* of the
Dutch East India
Company

Where the road to India lay

The East India Companies that operated during the seventeenth and eighteenth centuries were extremely powerful commercial and political organizations. The most important were the East India Company of Britain and that of Holland, but the French and some other European nations also operated several of these organizations.

These companies did not restrict themselves merely to the exploitation of the rich trade in spices and other eastern products, but formed empires of their own in various parts of Asia.

The swift sailing ships were amongst the most beautiful and the best-armed in the world. Their route to India went by the west coast of Africa and round the Cape of Good Hope, for the Suez Canal was not yet open. After the Cape the ships followed various sea routes to India and Malaysia.

Where to find the great depths of the oceans

The depths of the ocean are much greater than the height of even the tallest mountains. Mount Everest, for instance, is 8,882 metres above sea level while the bottom of the Pacific Trench lies 11,022 metres below the surface of the water. This huge abyss is also known as the Mariana Trench. Another abyss, in the Atlantic Ocean, the Puerto Rico Trench, also known as the Milwaukee Trench, is 9,219 metres deep.

One of the great pioneers in exploring the lower depths of the oceans was Auguste Piccard who in 1953, in his specially built bathyscaph, *Trieste*, went down to a depth of 3,150 metres and to 3,700 metres in 1956. Piccard's son Jacques carried on his father's work and in 1960 he went down into the Mariana Trench to a depth of 10,916 metres.

Piccard's *Trieste*

Where the cod islands lie

The cod is a cold-water fish which lives mainly in the north Atlantic, the North Sea and the Baltic Sea, swimming in the open seas at depths of about 300 metres.

The best place for cod fishing is round the Lofoten Islands off the north-west coast of Norway, where at one time more than 5,000 fishing vessels used to trawl during the fishing season.

Where sea-monsters have been seen

There are many sailors' tales, some highly improbable. about encounters with huge monsters at sea. Recent reports, however, are more exact in their details and reliable witnesses maintain they have seen gigantic sea-monsters

Diagram of a trawler positioned over a shoal of fish with sound waves being reflected

emerge from the depths of the sea.

Some scientists believe these creatures could be the last descendants of the enormous sea-dinosaurs which were thought to have died out 70 million years ago.

One of the most sensational encounters with a sea-monster was reported to have taken place in the Pacific Ocean on 13 January 1852. On that day a ship called *Mononghaela* was sailing through calm seas when suddenly, a few hundred metres away, there appeared an enormous beast like a snake. The monster was brownish-green with a huge head and a great fin on its back like that of an eel. The tail was crested and covered in bony knobs.

The sailors could not believe their eyes. Yet the monster was there before them, threshing about in the waves as if it were fighting some other huge animal. Then the master of the ship, Captain Seabury, lowered the boats and the sailors surrounded the animal to riddle it with harpoons. The monster shattered two of the boats into matchwood with powerful blows of its tail before it sank mortally wounded. The next day, with the help of a ship called the *Rebecca Sims*, the sailors recovered the animal and towed it to the shore. The eyewitnesses said it was a huge serpent more than 35 metres long, with a head almost 3 metres long and a body more than 10 metres wide at its thickest point. The huge mouth contained about 100 extremely sharp teeth and the skin was so tough that the sailors could not chop it up with their axes.

The sailors' description of this monster is surprisingly like that which scientists have pieced together from the fossilized remains of sea-dinosaurs.

Where oil is extracted from the sea

The demand for oil is growing rapidly. World reserves are gradually becoming less and there is a risk that they will be completely used up. For this reason, scientists are studying other possible sources of power such as atomic power or solar energy.

Until these two sources can be harnessed the search for oil has been extended to the sea. The first oil wells at sea were placed in shallow waters near the coast but gradually these oil wells were built farther away from land and out in the open sea. This has been made possible by special floating platforms which can be anchored even in the ocean in order to drill for oil deposits on the sea-bed. These oil wells have been drilled in such places as the Persian Gulf, the Caribbean Sea, the Adriatic, the Caspian Sea and the North Sea.

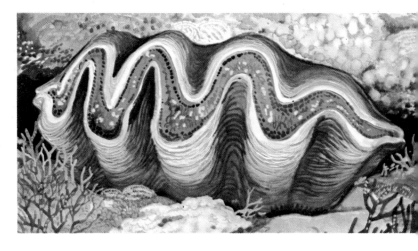

Where to find giant clams

Giant clams with shells more than a metre long, live along the coral reefs of the South Seas.

The best-known of the giant clams has the scientific name *Tridacna*. It is composed of two shells, or valves, which are covered in a beautiful glistening substance called mother-of-pearl. The shells are corrugated with wavy edges.

The giant clams anchor them-

Oilfield rigs at Abu Dhabi in the Persian Gulf

selves to coral banks and are fully exposed when the tide goes out. Then the clam keeps its valves tightly closed, but at high tide, when the clam is completely submerged in the water, it opens its valves slightly to filter scraps of food from the water.

Where sponges are gathered

The bath sponges that we use are fished in the Mediterranean Sea and the Atlantic Ocean. They are sea animals that live on rocks in shallow waters near the shore. The part of the sponge that we use is the skeleton of the animal from which the soft body has been removed. Sponges are among the most simple of animals that can feed and reproduce themselves.

There are about 5,000 different kinds of sponges. Their bodies consist of a fleshy mass full of cavities or small holes which are connected with the outside world by means of pores. Through these pores the sponge filters seawater to obtain plankton, the minute animals that float near the surface of the sea and which are the sponge's food.

Where to find some of the world's strangest and ugliest fish

The order of fish known scientifically as Lophiiformes contains some of the strangest creatures in nature, often with such monstrous and bizarre shapes that they seem to have come out of a nightmare. Many of them live in tropical seas or in the farthest depths of the ocean which are the deepest part of the Earth. There are also some in the Mediterranean.

The angler fish is included in this order. It is a delicious fish to eat but so ugly that fishermen have to cut off its head and skin

Porcupinefish

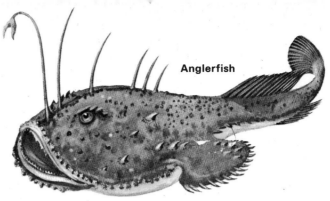

Anglerfish

it before they can sell it. Not many people would like to eat such a monster with a large head and its body covered in prickles, warts and all kinds of knobs. Another ugly feature are the fins which look like legs.

The angler fish grows up to 2 metres long and its head takes up half of the whole body. Because of its enormous head the angler fish is a slow swimmer and prefers to drag itself along the sea-bottom.

Where to find the world's biggest crab

There are many varieties of crab, all interesting creatures because of their habits and instincts which make them the most intelligent members of the crustacean family.

Many crabs are caught as food and one of the most valuable of these is the crab which lives around the British and European coasts. It has a flattened body and a smooth shell which is roughly triangular in shape. From this shell there grow five pairs of legs, the first pair being much larger than the others and ending in pincers.

The biggest member of the crab family lives in the seas around Japan. The legs of this giant are sometimes more than 4 metres long and give it an awkward appearance as it moves along the sea-bed.

Where to find crowds of seagulls

Seagulls are proud and wild birds who spend most of their time in the air, wheeling and turning as they utter their harsh, unmistakable cries. For sailors, the presence of seagulls is a sure sign that land is near.

These birds are beachcombers who rid the shoreline of all sorts of refuse. They are always hungry and very daring in their constant search for food, snatching fish from boats and fishing baskets and going close to houses when bad weather drives them inland.

391

Where the great ocean currents are formed

Ocean currents are caused by differences in temperature of the water. In the region of the equator the water is warm as it receives the full force of the Sun's heat which comes in rays that run straight down to the surface of the Earth. The rays of the Sun at the equator travel a shorter distance through the Earth's atmosphere than at any other part of the globe and so lose less of their heat.

As the waters of the ocean become warm they expand. The waters around the equator are therefore less dense than those around the polar regions which are much colder. This difference in water temperatures leads to a movement in which the warm water flows out to colder regions and the cold water is pushed towards the warm areas. The speed and direction of these currents is determined by winds and the rotation of the Earth.

Where eels go to lay their eggs

Eels are quite common in the rivers of Europe where they are often caught for their meat. Every year they migrate in large numbers on mysterious journeys to distant waters.

The eel spends most of its life in rivers, although there are also sea-dwelling eels such as the conger and the moray eel. But

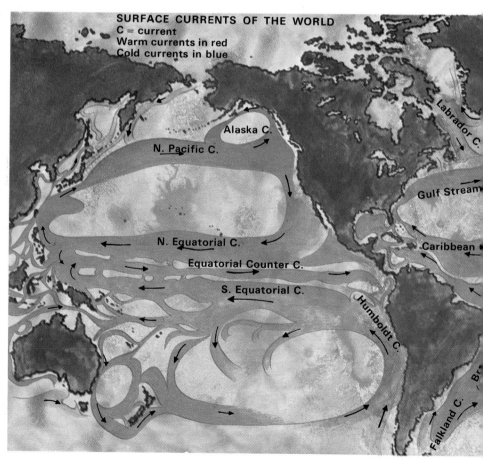

SURFACE CURRENTS OF THE WORLD
C = current
Warm currents in red
Cold currents in blue

Alaska C.

N. Pacific C.

Labrador C.

Gulf Stream

N. Equatorial C.

Equatorial Counter C.

Caribbean

S. Equatorial C.

Humboldt C.

Falkland C.

when the time comes for these snake-like fish to lay their eggs they leave their streams and rivers and head for the open sea. For thousands of kilometres they swim along until they reach their destination which is the Sargasso Sea in the western Atlantic.

The baby eels are born in the Sargasso Sea. About two and a half years later these young eels, known as elvers, are back in the rivers and streams of Europe. They stay there for about fifteen years until they are adults. Then they feel the call of the sea and set out on their long journey.

Scientists have put forward many possible answers to why the eels swim all the way to the Sargasso Sea to lay their eggs but so far it still remains a mystery.

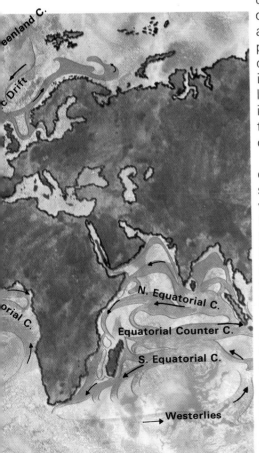

Where man-eating and harmless species of sharks are found

The word 'shark' always conjures up the picture of a very fierce, dangerous, man-eating fish. In actual fact, sharks which attack people are few and many species of shark live near coasts presenting no threat or danger to human life. Some sharks are quite small including varieties in the Mediterranean which are caught because they are very good to eat.

The sharks which are most dangerous to man live in warm seas. These include the terrible white shark which is 12 metres long and attacks seals, sea turtles, large fish and occasionally man. Other sharks involved in attacks on humans are the tiger, the blue, the grey nurse and the hammerhead.

Along certain stretches of the Australian coast the danger from sharks is so great that beach-guards keep a look-out for them and shout warnings through loudspeakers to bathers. A shark's presence in the sea is announced by its tall, sail-like fin sticking up through the water.

THE WHERE OF THE POLAR REGIONS

Where the Eskimos live

Modern anthropologists believe the Eskimos first came from central Asia during the last great Ice Age. In their appearance, Eskimos resemble Mongoloid peoples who live in eastern Asia: their skin is a pale yellow, their hair is straight and black, they have dark, slanted eyes and high cheekbones. Eskimos are stocky in build and have broad chests although their hands and feet are small. One feature in the Eskimo which is different from the Mongoloid face is the nose which is quite long and narrow.

The Eskimos are probably all descended from the same group of people because their way of life throughout the regions they inhabit is the same. They are divided into tribes scattered over vast areas of the northern polar regions and this makes it impossible for there to be complete contacts among all the various tribes. But the Eskimos all share a similar way of life. Their customs, clothes, the tools they use to hunt and fish, their methods of catching animals and their social organization are all the same whether in Siberia or northern America.

Most Eskimos live around the shores of the Arctic Ocean and on the eastern and western coasts of Greenland. Eskimos also live on the Labrador coast, round Baffin Bay and in the far north of Canada.

In all there are about 5,000 Eskimos and it is thought that they never numbered more than that. Their language is very complex and few foreigners have learned to speak it fluently; in Alaska even the Eskimos are beginning to simplify it. The people are very hardy and are able to endure the rigours of the ice and snow which last from six to nine months of the year.

Where to find elks

The elk, which is called the moose in America, is the largest animal member of the deer family and lives in marshy regions and forests of the far north. The male, or bull, elk is a majestic-looking animal both in its size and the shape of its enormous antlers. A fully grown elk is more than 2 metres tall at its shoulders and can weigh up to 700 kilogrammes.

The male elk sheds its antlers every year in autumn. They grow again in the spring and in a fully-grown animal the antlers have about twelve points. The female elk, or cow, is smaller than the bull and has no antlers. The elk likes to live in open marshy areas where it wanders in search of grazing grounds. It also eats leaves, the bark of trees and water-plants.

Because of their antlers and large size, elks are sought as trophies by hunters. They are also killed for their meat, which is rather like beef. Their numbers have been greatly reduced by hunting and they are now usually protected by law.

Where the caribou lives

In the far north of the American continent, above the sixtieth parallel, lives the caribou, a grass-eating animal that is a close relation to the reindeer. The caribou is also known as the woodland reindeer and is quite common in northern forests.

During the summer it roams north, feeding on moss, lichens and the other few forms of plant life that grow in those regions. In winter, caribou gather together in large herds and migrate south to search for their food. In former

days this was the time when the animal was hunted and many of them were slaughtered. In the first half of this century over-hunting reduced their numbers from nearly 2 million to 200,000.

There are two main kinds of caribou: the barren-ground caribou that lives in wastelands, and the larger woodland species that makes its home in woods. Caribou that live in the Arctic belong to the first group. These animals are not easily domesticated but for the Eskimos they are a vital source of meat, wool and skins for making clothes. The reduction in their numbers caused serious problems for some inland Eskimos who had to be moved to different areas to avoid starvation.

Eskimo costumes

Where the polar bear lives

The polar bear is a large beast of prey which lives amid the ice-floes inside the Arctic Circle. Nature has been generous with this large animal: it has given it a thick, white fur which enables the bear to stand up to extreme cold; a very fine sense of smell which helps it know where its prey is, even at a very great distance; and such enormous strength that it can knock down a strong man with a single blow of its paw.

The polar bear has great cunning and has completely mastered the art of moving across the ice, approaching its victim silently from behind. It seldom goes without food, therefore, even though it lives in cold and barren places. The bear's favourite victims are seals, but it will also snatch salmon and other fish out of rivers with its paws. This animal swims very well and is often found many kilometres from land or ice packs. It has been known to follow migrating seals as far south as the Gulf of the St. Lawrence in America.

Where the polar pack ice forms

The vast stretches of ice around the polar regions present one of the most impressive spectacles in the world. After the very short polar summer season the wind begins to blow and snow covers the ground as far as the eye can see. Great packs of ice form which spread out over the ocean, joining together the mainland and islands into one solid white mass. As the pack ice rests on the sea it cracks in places and moves about in the current.

This inhospitable world which has remained largely unexplored for thousands of years, is the home of the Eskimos, a people who can stand up amazingly to biting cold, hunger and exhaustion. It is difficult to understand how the ancestors of these people chose such an icy and cold place to live in and such hostile surroundings.

There is one theory that the Eskimos are descended from Stone Age peoples who became used to living and hunting in the ice during the great Ice Age. When the ice

melted and retreated to the north, the animals that lived on it also went northwards. The hunting tribes therefore decided to follow what had become their only source of livelihood and they moved to the north too.

Where igloos are built

The Eskimo home that is best-known is the igloo although it is not the most commonly used dwelling place of these people. The igloo is built only in the far north of the Canadian Arctic and is always a temporary home. About three-quarters of the Eskimos have never built an igloo.

Home for an Eskimo is a snug chamber dug out of the ground and covered with pieces of wood. The cracks in the wood are sealed with dried moss and lichens.

The igloo is only a shelter for anyone travelling or hunting. It can be built in half an hour or even less by cutting blocks of snow with a large knife and placing them on top of each other to form a dome-shaped house. The entrance is through a long tunnel, dug in the snow, and this helps to keep the warmth inside the igloo. Animal skins are placed on the floor and light comes from a lamp which burns oil extracted from seals' meat. It is warm in the igloo even when the temperature outside is 50° below zero.

Where the huge prehistoric mammoths lived

The remains of mammoths, which lived about 100,000 years ago and were related to present-day elephants, have been found in quite large numbers in Siberia where the vast plains between the glaciers in the north and the forests in the south provided ideal surroundings for them.

Mammoths were well protected against the cold for their bodies were covered in thick, woolly fur. They were big, powerful animals and few other creatures dared to attack them, so they lived quite peacefully grazing on the plains or feeding on leaves. Some of these huge animals were still living when man first appeared on the planet.

Wolves

in the polar regions are caused by magnetic storms. These storms send out charged particles which travel to the Earth's poles. When they collide with the Earth's atmosphere the particles glow. The lights are often green though they are occasionally pink and yellow. The auroras take place about twenty-four hours after the passage of a sunspot across the Sun.

Where to see the aurora polaris

One of the most unusual natural happenings to be seen in the skies are the aurora polaris which light up the heavens above the North or the South Poles. These auroras are called the northern lights or aurora borealis ('northern dawn') when they take place in the northern hemisphere and the aurora australis when they occur in the southern hemisphere.

The northern lights are the better-known of the two. They can sometimes be seen as far south as the Mediterranean, but they display their full majesty inside the Arctic Circle.

It is difficult to describe this great wonder of nature. Some auroras simply bathe the night sky with a serene milky light just above the horizon. Others consist of rather sinister colours like flickering flames, haloes of light, bright, hanging curtains or arcs or mysterious shapes that ripple and wave in the air.

For hundreds of years all sorts of fables and legends grew around these lights. As with most great natural phenomena, many people thought they were some sort of warnings from another world.

Today astronomers know that these strange and beautiful lights

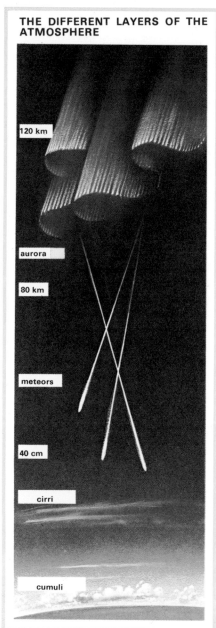

THE DIFFERENT LAYERS OF THE ATMOSPHERE

120 km

aurora

80 km

meteors

40 cm

cirri

cumuli

Where wolves are plentiful

Wolves have disappeared from most regions inhabited by man but they still live in packs in the tundra, the barren plains of the Arctic, where they present a constant threat to other animals.

They are powerful creatures, often measuring over 2 metres long, including the bushy tail, and the only animals who can stand up to them are the musk oxen which always live together in big herds. When wolves attack them the oxen stand shoulder-to-shoulder in a huge ring with their horns pointed outwards.

The musk ox is a stubborn fighter and the wolf knows it and prefers to attack something less dangerous such as foxes, hares, lemmings and other mammals, only rarely hunting large animals such as reindeer or caribou.

Where to admire the midnight Sun

The North Cape is a rocky promontory north of the Scandinavian peninsula. The water round it does not freeze in winter because it is near the warm current of the Gulf Stream. Every year thousands of tourists flock here to see one of the most impressive and extraordinary sights: the midnight Sun.

Night and day at the North Pole coincide with the seasons. Day, for example, lasts about sixty-five days and coincides with the summer. The Sun never rises high in the sky, it is never too bright and it seems to move very slowly. Towards the evening it begins to set until it reaches the horizon when it appears to hesitate. This happens at midnight.

Then, very slowly, the Sun begins to climb again in the opposite direction. This phenomena depends on the angle of the axis of the Earth. When the Earth is at its summer solstice, the Sun shines on the North Pole. The Earth is tilted in such a way that the Sun never sets even though the Earth is going round and night and day take place in other parts of the globe.

Aurora polaris

The different shapes and colours of the aurora polaris

Liverwort
(Pellia epiphylla)

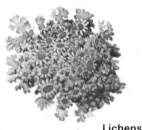

Lichens
(Leptogium)

Where plants still grow in the far north

It seems impossible but even amid the icy wastes of the Arctic there are plants that grow, flower and reproduce themselves. They grow wherever the land thaws, even if it is only for a few days in the year.

These plants are small and stand up to the cold. Their life cycle is very short but they still represent a triumph of life over the great difficulties presented by the Arctic.

In some Arctic zones the only plant life known are the lichens. Lichens are really pioneer plants, even tougher than mosses, and can take root on rocks. As they hook themselves on to the bare rocks these plants produce an acid which gradually corrodes the rock so that small pieces of it constantly fall away. These minute particles, together with the remains of dead lichens, provide a fertile base on which higher forms of plant life can grow.

Lichens are unique in being a combination of plants from entirely different groups, a fungus and a type of seaweed. These two forms of plant life combine their qualities into one plant that can survive in difficult conditions.

Mosses are also common in the tundra. These mosses grow in large expanses which are enlivened here and there by splashes of colour from heather which become green during the summer. When winter comes the heather grows dry and tough, but grass-eating animals still look for them because when food is scarce these plants can provide a meal.

Also fairly common in the Arctic are plants of the *Carex* family which form yellowish clumps that turn green in the spring thaw. These plants include the saxifrages and a few snow-poppies.

Where to find puffins

The puffin, also known as the sea parrot or bottlenose, is a sea-bird that is very common along the northern coasts of Canada and Alaska, in Iceland and in northern Scandinavia.

A puffin can be recognized by its very odd beak which is high and flattened at the sides and is covered in yellow, blue, orange and red stripes. Puffins live in large colonies on island cliffs or on rocks where they build a strange nest which is more like a burrow because puffins dig out long tunnels in the ground. They also use burrows that have been abandoned by rabbits. They lay their eggs in a little cave about 2 metres under the ground.

Puffins feed mainly on fish and can catch as many as ten small fish in succession, carrying them dangling across their beaks to their young.

Puffin
(Fratercula artica)

Where dogs still pull sledges

Today civilization has reached the polar regions and explorers travel on powerful vehicles fitted with caterpillar tracks to move over the snow and ice. But sledges pulled by dogs are still the most sure form of transport through the icy wastes and, for the Eskimos, these sledges are a necessary means of survival. Without them contacts between the scattered villages would be impossible and it would also be very difficult to go hunting for food.

Eskimos use almost any material for making sledges. When wood is scarce, bits of old plank or any other flotsam washed up by the sea is used; sometimes the antlers of a reindeer are turned into a sledge; the frozen skin of a seal is often used or simply a piece of deep-frozen meat.

The sledge is pulled by a team of dogs known as huskies, incredibly tough animals able to stand up to the terrible cold, hunger and exhaustion. They are faithful and valuable friends to man when he is out hunting and have an excellent sense of smell which can detect the presence of game birds at great distances.

Huskies can pull a sledge along at more than 30 kilometres an hour for up to eighteen hours at a stretch. When the Eskimos feed their dogs they are always careful to serve the leader of the sledge team first so that it retains the respect of the other dogs.

The sledge is mostly used for carrying goods such as fish for the dogs, provisions and clothes for the Eskimo and hunting weapons. The Eskimo goes on foot steering the sledge from behind, and wearing skis or snow-shoes when the snow underfoot allows it.

Where seals take their ease

Several varieties of seal live in the Arctic and although they differ in shape and size, they all share a similar way of life. These animals are all superb swimmers, able to lie still for hours in the water and then rush off at incredible speed.

Seals often sleep in the water, letting the waves gently rock them to and fro. They can dive down to great depths but have to come up to the surface often in order to breathe. Their main food is fish, but they will also accept any other small sea-creature.

On land and on the ice they

alarm signal. Magellan called the region 'Tierra del Fuego' which is Spanish for 'the land of fire'.

Having discovered the strait that was later named after him, the great navigator sailed through it. After enduring terrible storms and overcoming the most severe hardships he came to a huge expanse of ocean. To the sailors who had come through such an ordeal this ocean seemed very calm so they called it the Pacific, which means 'peaceful'.

Magellan continued his journey to the north, sailing along the coast of Chile, and then westward and eventually reached the Philippine islands. On 27 April 1521, he went ashore on one of these islands and was killed in a fight with natives. Of the five ships that set out only one returned, and of the original crews only eighteen men saw their homeland again; but these men were able to claim they were the first to have sailed round the world.

Where penguins live

Penguins are flightless birds that live only in the southern hemisphere. They have become so well adapted to their life in the sea that they are among the best swimmers in the southern oceans. The first explorers and travellers to visit the Antarctic regions were amazed when they first saw penguins which look as if they are wearing male evening dress of white tie and tails and walk along in a funny, stiff manner that makes them seem quite pompous.

These birds live in large colonies along beaches and the early travellers thought them to be extremely intelligent creatures by the way they laid and hatched their eggs

move very clumsily dragging themselves along with their flippers. They never stray too far from the water and are ready to dive into the sea at the slightest sign of danger. Their hearing and sight are very sharp but this does not prevent them from being frequently caught and killed by polar bears.

Where to find the Strait of Magellan

The Portuguese navigator Ferdinand Magellan left from Spain on 20 September 1519, with five ships and sailed all round the coast of South America including its southernmost tip.

Magellan also explored the stretches of water that separate Patagonia from the mainland. He found there a bleak and desolate land which seemed uninhabited by day, but when night fell the sky was lit up by scores of fires which the natives had lit as an

and found food for their chicks in a strictly organized manner. But what the penguin shows is not so much intelligence as a perfect adaptation to sea life. Their bodies are streamlined; their feathers are like small scales and their wings have become like flippers.

Penguins only come ashore during the breeding season when as many as 40,000 of them will crowd together on the same island, although they are not really social animals and are individuals by nature.

Some species of penguins migrate and others stay in the same place. When there is no danger about they are lively and happy creatures: they love to hop about, dive in the sea and spin round on their toes, barking and making lowing sounds and filling deserted bays with their noise.

Where the walrus lives

The walrus was known several hundreds of years ago but accounts of this animal were few and vague. The first accurate descriptions came with the early polar expeditions. The explorers who came across herds of these animals found them a good source of food for themselves and their dogs which pulled the sledges. Walruses are massive animals: the males are much larger than the females, reaching a length of up to 4 metres long and weighing more than a ton.

Though big, the walrus is a peaceful and lazy animal. It lives in large herds on rocky banks and on ice sheets along the shores. When walruses are not sleeping they go for a swim in the icy cold sea, usually keeping to comparatively shallow water

Ringed Penguin and Gentoo Penguin looking for fish

and digging out clams from the seabed. They are often hunted for the excellent ivory in their tusks, for their very tough skin, and for the oil which can be extracted from their blubber.

Adelie Penguin

403

Where blue whales were hunted

The blue whale is the largest animal in the world. The enormous size of this sea-dwelling mammal made it an extremely valuable catch for a whaling ship. The blue whale, which weighs 150 tons and measures up to 30 metres in length, provided a large range of valuable products which were extracted on the factory ship that processed these animals on the seas of the polar regions.

A very strange thing about the blue whale is how such a huge animal manages to live on tiny, shrimp-like creatures which are no more than 5 centimetres long. The whale eats about 3 tons of the small creatures every twenty-four hours, catching them by swimming through the sea with its jaws open. It uses a bony sieve hanging from the roof of its mouth, known as the baleen, to strain its food from the water.

Today there are very few blue whales left for over-fishing has brought this animal close to extinction. Since 1966 the hunting of blue whales in the southern hemisphere has been prohibited by international agreements.

Where the limit to human habitation lies in the southern hemisphere

The fifty-fifth parallel in the southern hemisphere crosses the southern tip of the island of Tierra del Fuego. This line marks the last regions to be inhabited by people living in the desolate regions of the south.

The islands of Tierra del Fuego were discovered in 1520 by Ferdinand Magellan who gave them their name. The islands lie at the southernmost tip of South America and consist of one large island, known as Isla Grande, a few smaller ones and many tiny islets.

The climate in this region is unfriendly. Often the mountain glaciers send long fingers of ice down to as far as the sea. In the northern islands of the group some plant life manages to grow; there are also forests and broad grassy pastures where cattle and sheep are reared. Some 10,000 people live in this region. The forests, livestock-breeding and deposits of coal and oil provide them with work. Most of these people are of European, Argentinian and Chilean origin: they went there during the last century, attracted by the sheep farming and the discovery of gold and other minerals.

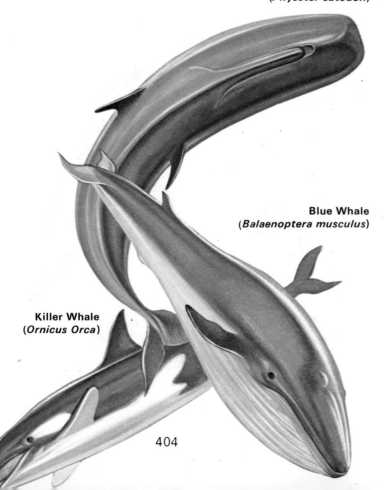

Sperm Whale
(*Physeter catodon*)

Blue Whale
(*Balaenoptera musculus*)

Killer Whale
(*Ornicus Orca*)

404

Where the killer whale lives

The killer whale is the biggest member of the dolphin family, growing to a length of up to 10 metres and weighing several tons. It is black with white underparts and white splashes over the eye and on the back, and has a very high, triangular back fin. This whale lives in practically every sea throughout the world but is most common in the cold sea of the polar regions.

The killer whale is one of the most dangerous animals of the Antarctic. It is always hungry and very daring, attacking any other animal it meets. Its targets include fish, porpoises, molluscs, penguins and seals. Sometimes it even attacks whales, tiring them out by frequent and sudden attacks. This aggression has given rise to many legends about the killer whale. Sailors in olden times feared it and believed that this animal was strong enough to capsize their ships or upset ice floes on which men were standing.

exploring the region have always had to seek another, less difficult route to unload men and materials. The ice comes from the heart of the continent which lies under incredibly thick glaciers. Streams of ice move slowly down the slopes from these glaciers and merge slowly into one another to form one huge mass which is pushed on into the sea by the pressure of the great ice caps at the centre of Antarctica.

Where to find the Ross Ice Shelf

The Ross Ice Shelf is an enormous wall of ice whose sides rise sheer out of the sea to more than 80 metres off the coast of Antarctica. It is a huge floating peninsula which covers about 400,000 square kilometres of the Ross Sea which was discovered by the British polar explorer, Sir James Clark Ross in 1841. It presents a most impressive sight: huge icebergs detach themselves from the wall of ice and are carried away by the current.

This barrier is an insurmountable obstacle to any vessel and ships

Charles Darwin at Tierra del Fuego

INDEX